Christmas 1979

To Albert

May the peace, joy and hope of
Christmas be yours.
With love
Mother and Dad.

The Ministers Manual for 1980

By the same editor

Holy Holy Land
The Treasure Chest
Words of Life
Our American Heritage
1010 Sermon Illustrations from the Bible
Worship Resources for the Christian Year
Stories on Stone: A Book of American Epitaphs
American Epitaphs: Grave and Humorous
The Funeral Encyclopedia
A Treasury of Story-Sermons for Children
Treasury of Sermon Illustrations
Selected Poems of John Oxenham
Poems of Edwin Markham
Notable Sermons from Protestant Pulpits
Treasury of Poems for Worship and Devotion
88 Evangelistic Sermons
Speaker's Resources from Contemporary Literature
Christmas in Our Hearts (with Charles L. Allen)
Candle, Star, and Christmas Tree (with Charles L. Allen)
When Christmas Came to Bethlehem (with Charles L. Allen)
The Charles L. Allen Treasury
Lenten-Easter Sourcebook
365 Table Graces for the Christian Home
Speaker's Illustrations for Special Days
Table of the Lord
The Eternal Light
Twentieth Century Bible Commentary (co-editor)
Prayers for Public Worship (co-editor)
Christmas (with Charles L. Allen)
A Complete Sourcebook for the Lord's Supper

FIFTY-FIFTH ANNUAL ISSUE

The
MINISTERS
MANUAL
(Doran's)

1980 EDITION

Edited by
CHARLES L. WALLIS

Published in San Francisco by
HARPER & ROW, PUBLISHERS
New York, Hagerstown, San Francisco, London

Editors of THE MINISTERS MANUAL

G.B.F. Hallock, D.D., 1926–1958
M.K.W. Heicher, Ph.D., 1943–1968
Charles L. Wallis, M.A., M.Div., 1969–

THE MINISTERS MANUAL FOR 1980.
Copyright © 1979 by Charles L. Wallis. All rights reserved.
Printed in the United States of America. For information
address Harper & Row, Publishers, Inc., 10 East 53rd Street,
New York, N.Y. 10022. Published simultaneously in Canada
by Fitzhenry & Whiteside Limited, Toronto.

FIRST EDITION

Library of Congress Cataloging in Publication Data

The ministers manual; a study and pulpit guide.

1. Sermons—Outlines. 2. Homiletical illustrations.
I. Hallock, Gerard Benjamin Fleet, 1856– ed.
BV4223.M5   251.058   25–21658 rev*
ISBN 0–06–069025–9

79 10 9 8 7 7 6 5 4 3 2 1

PREFACE

This edition of *The Ministers Manual* marks my twenty-fifth year as an editorial associate with this publication.

In 1955 the Rev. Dr. Merlo K. W. Heicher, who had been editor since the mid-1940s, invited me to his home in Claremont, California, where he discussed his concern that there be some assurance of editorial continuity for *The Ministers Manual.*

Subsequently I did numerous editorial chores according to his gracious and patient guidance and then more than a decade ago assumed the responsibilities of editor.

This has been a rewarding experience in which doors have opened and friendships encouraged with contributors and readers throughout Christendom.

The format and content of *The Ministers Manual* since its initial publication fifty-five years ago show the changes one would expect to find in the preaching of a dynamic church in a dynamic society. Yet this edition and the first one have family characteristics, and the various editors have resisted the temptation to set aside the old in favor of the new.

A deliberate effort has been made to avoid the inclusion in a new edition of homiletic and resource materials previously published in *The Ministers Manual.*

Whatever values readers may find in *The Ministers Manual* come from the rich variety of ideas and the creative homiletic interpretations of the contributors. To these men and women—ministers, educators, biblical and social commentators, and laity —I express my sincere appreciation.

The Ministers Manual represents a commitment to glorify God and especially as we know and experience him through the redemptive life, teaching, death, and resurrection of the Lord Jesus. This seems best achieved in a resource book of this kind by those emphases of the faith which are commonly held by all Christians.

My correspondence indicates that *The Ministers Manual* is a tool in the work not only of pastors but also of church school teachers, evangelists, missionaries, and chaplains and has been circulated among Catholic priests and Jewish rabbis.

Section X of this edition, titled "Ideas and Suggestions for Pulpit and Parish," represents a considerable expansion of "The Idea Box," which was formerly included in Section I.

Rev. Charles L. Wallis

Keuka College
Keuka Park, New York 14478

CONTENTS

SECTION I. *General Aids and Resources*

Civil Year Calendars

1980

JANUARY
S	M	T	W	T	F	S
		1	2	3	4	5
6	7	8	9	10	11	12
13	14	15	16	17	18	19
20	21	22	23	24	25	26
27	28	29	30	31		

FEBRUARY
S	M	T	W	T	F	S
					1	2
3	4	5	6	7	8	9
10	11	12	13	14	15	16
17	18	19	20	21	22	23
24	25	26	27	28	29	

MARCH
S	M	T	W	T	F	S
						1
2	3	4	5	6	7	8
9	10	11	12	13	14	15
16	17	18	19	20	21	22
23	24	25	26	27	28	29
30	31					

APRIL
S	M	T	W	T	F	S
		1	2	3	4	5
6	7	8	9	10	11	12
13	14	15	16	17	18	19
20	21	22	23	24	25	26
27	28	29	30			

MAY
S	M	T	W	T	F	S
				1	2	3
4	5	6	7	8	9	10
11	12	13	14	15	16	17
18	19	20	21	22	23	24
25	26	27	28	29	30	31

JUNE
S	M	T	W	T	F	S
1	2	3	4	5	6	7
8	9	10	11	12	13	14
15	16	17	18	19	20	21
22	23	24	25	26	27	28
29	30					

JULY
S	M	T	W	T	F	S
		1	2	3	4	5
6	7	8	9	10	11	12
13	14	15	16	17	18	19
20	21	22	23	24	25	26
27	28	29	30	31		

AUGUST
S	M	T	W	T	F	S
					1	2
3	4	5	6	7	8	9
10	11	12	13	14	15	16
17	18	19	20	21	22	23
24	25	26	27	28	29	30
31						

SEPTEMBER
S	M	T	W	T	F	S
	1	2	3	4	5	6
7	8	9	10	11	12	13
14	15	16	17	18	19	20
21	22	23	24	25	26	27
28	29	30				

OCTOBER
S	M	T	W	T	F	S
			1	2	3	4
5	6	7	8	9	10	11
12	13	14	15	16	17	18
19	20	21	22	23	24	25
26	27	28	29	30	31	

NOVEMBER
S	M	T	W	T	F	S
						1
2	3	4	5	6	7	8
9	10	11	12	13	14	15
16	17	18	19	20	21	22
23	24	25	26	27	28	29
30						

DECEMBER
S	M	T	W	T	F	S
	1	2	3	4	5	6
7	8	9	10	11	12	13
14	15	16	17	18	19	20
21	22	23	24	25	26	27
28	29	30	31			

1981

JANUARY
S	M	T	W	T	F	S
				1	2	3
4	5	6	7	8	9	10
11	12	13	14	15	16	17
18	19	20	21	22	23	24
25	26	27	28	29	30	31

FEBRUARY
S	M	T	W	T	F	S
1	2	3	4	5	6	7
8	9	10	11	12	13	14
15	16	17	18	19	20	21
22	23	24	25	26	27	28

MARCH
S	M	T	W	T	F	S
1	2	3	4	5	6	7
8	9	10	11	12	13	14
15	16	17	18	19	20	21
22	23	24	25	26	27	28
29	30	31				

APRIL
S	M	T	W	T	F	S
			1	2	3	4
5	6	7	8	9	10	11
12	13	14	15	16	17	18
19	20	21	22	23	24	25
26	27	28	29	30		

MAY
S	M	T	W	T	F	S
					1	2
3	4	5	6	7	8	9
10	11	12	13	14	15	16
17	18	19	20	21	22	23
24	25	26	27	28	29	30
31						

JUNE
S	M	T	W	T	F	S
	1	2	3	4	5	6
7	8	9	10	11	12	13
14	15	16	17	18	19	20
21	22	23	24	25	26	27
28	29	30				

JULY
S	M	T	W	T	F	S
			1	2	3	4
5	6	7	8	9	10	11
12	13	14	15	16	17	18
19	20	21	22	23	24	25
26	27	28	29	30	31	

AUGUST
S	M	T	W	T	F	S
						1
2	3	4	5	6	7	8
9	10	11	12	13	14	15
16	17	18	19	20	21	22
23	24	25	26	27	28	29
30	31					

SEPTEMBER
S	M	T	W	T	F	S
		1	2	3	4	5
6	7	8	9	10	11	12
13	14	15	16	17	18	19
20	21	22	23	24	25	26
27	28	29	30			

OCTOBER
S	M	T	W	T	F	S
				1	2	3
4	5	6	7	8	9	10
11	12	13	14	15	16	17
18	19	20	21	22	23	24
25	26	27	28	29	30	31

NOVEMBER
S	M	T	W	T	F	S
1	2	3	4	5	6	7
8	9	10	11	12	13	14
15	16	17	18	19	20	21
22	23	24	25	26	27	28
29	30					

DECEMBER
S	M	T	W	T	F	S
		1	2	3	4	5
6	7	8	9	10	11	12
13	14	15	16	17	18	19
20	21	22	23	24	25	26
27	28	29	30	31		

Church and Civic Calendar for 1980

JANUARY

1 New Year's Day
  The Name of Jesus
5 Twelfth Night
6 Epiphany
13 Baptism of Jesus
15 Martin Luther King, Jr., Birthday
18 Conversion of St. Peter
18-25 Week of Prayer for Christian
  Unity
19 Robert E. Lee Birthday
20 Missionary Day
25 Conversion of St. Paul

FEBRUARY

1 National Freedom Day
2 Presentation of Jesus in the Temple
  Groundhog Day
10 Race Relations Sunday
12 Lincoln's Birthday
14 St. Valentine's Day
15 Susan B. Anthony Day
17 The Transfiguration
17-24 Brotherhood Week
18 Presidents' Day
  Washington's Birthday
19 Shrove Tuesday
20 Ash Wednesday
22 Washington's Birthday (alternate)
24 First Sunday in Lent

MARCH

2 Second Sunday in Lent
7 World Day of Prayer
9 Third Sunday in Lent
16 Fourth Sunday in Lent
17 St. Patrick's Day
23 Fifth Sunday in Lent
  Passion Sunday
30 Sixth Sunday in Lent
  Palm Sunday
  Passion Sunday (alternate)
30-5 Holy Week

APRIL

3 Maundy Thursday
4 Good Friday
5 Easter Eve

6 Easter (Orthodox and Western)
13 Low Sunday
25 St. Mark, Evangelist
  Arbor Day

MAY

1 May Day
  Law Day
  Loyalty Day
  St. Philip and St. James, Apostles
4 May Fellowship Day
4-11 National Family Week
11 Mother's Day
  Festival of the Christian Home
15 Ascension Day
17 Armed Forces Day
19 Sovereign's Birthday (Canada)
25 Pentecost (Whitsunday)
26 Memorial Day
30 Memorial Day (alternate)

JUNE

1 Trinity Sunday
5 Corpus Christi Day
8 Children's Day
11 St. Barnabas, Apostle
14 Flag Day
15 Father's Day
24 Nativity of St. John the Baptist
29 Independence Sunday
  St. Peter and St. Paul, Apostles

JULY

1 Dominion Day (Canada)
4 Independence Day
22 St. Mary Magdalene
25 St. James the Elder, Apostle

AUGUST

6 World Hunger Day
6 The Transfiguration (alternate)
15 Mary, Mother of Jesus
25 St. Bartholomew, Apostle
26 Women's Equality Day
31 Labor Sunday

SEPTEMBER

1 Labor Day
14 Holy Cross Day

17 Citizenship Day
21 St. Matthew, Apostle and Evangelist
26 American Indian Day
29 St. Michael and All Angels

OCTOBER

5 World Communion Sunday
6 Child Health Day
12 Laity Sunday
Columbus Day
13 Columbus Day (alternate)
Thanksgiving Day (Canada)
18 St. Luke, Evangelist
24 United Nations Day
26 Reformation Sunday
29 St. Simon and St. Jude, Apostles
31 Reformation Day
National UNICEF Day

NOVEMBER

1 All Saints' Day
2 World Temperance Day
All Soul's Day

4 Election Day
7 World Community Day
9 Stewardship Day
11 Veterans Day
23 Bible Sunday
Christ the King
Thanksgiving Sunday
27 Thanksgiving Day
30 First Sunday in Advent
St. Andrew, Apostle

DECEMBER

7 Second Sunday in Advent
10 Human Rights Day
14 Third Sunday in Advent
15 Bill of Rights Day
21 Fourth Sunday in Advent
St. Thomas, Apostle
25 Christmas
26 St. Stephen, Deacon and Martyr
27 St. John, Apostle and Evangelist
28 The Holy Innocents, Martyrs
31 New Year's Eve
Watch Night

Lectionary for 1980

The following scripture lessons, with oc-
casional alterations according to denominational preferences, are commended for
use in public worship by various Protestant churches and the Roman Catholic
Church and includes first, second, and
gospel readings according to Cycle C from
January 1 to November 23 and according
to Cycle A from November 30 to December 28.

CHRISTMASTIDE

January 1 (New Year's Day): Isa. 49:1–10;
Eph. 3:1–10; Luke 14:16–24.

EPIPHANY

January 6 (Epiphany): Isa. 60:1–6; Eph. 3:
1–6; Matt. 2:1–12.
January 13: Gen. 1:1–5; Eph. 2:11–18;
Luke 3:15–17, 21–22.
January 18–25: Isa. 55:1–5; Rev. 5:11–14;
John 17:1–11.
January 20: Isa. 62:2–5; I Cor. 12:4–11;
John 2:1–12.

January 27: Neh. 8:1–3, 5–6, 8–10; I Cor.
12:12–30; Luke 4:14–21.
February 3: Jer. 1:4–10; I Cor. 13:1–13;
Luke 4:22–30.
February 10: Isa. 6:1–8; I Cor. 15:1–11;
Luke 5:1–11.
February 17: Jer. 17:5–8; I Cor. 15:12–20;
Luke 6:17–26.

LENT

February 20 (Ash Wednesday): Zech.
7:4–10; I Cor. 9:19–27; Luke 5:29–
35.
February 24: Deut. 26:5–11; Rom. 10:8–
13; Luke 4:1–13.
March 2: Gen. 15:5–12, 17–18; Phil. 3:17
to 4:1; Luke 9:28–36.
March 9: Ex. 3:1–8, 13–15; I Cor. 10:1–12;
Luke 13:1–9.
March 16: Josh. 5:9–12; II Cor. 5:16–21;
Luke 15:11–32.
March 23: Isa. 43:16–21; Phil. 3:8–14;
Luke 22:14–30.
March 30 (Palm Sunday): Isa. 59:14–20; I
Tim. 1:12–17; Luke 19:28–40.

HOLY WEEK

March 31 (Monday): Isa. 50:4–10; Heb. 9: 11–15; Luke 19:41–48.

April 1 (Tuesday): Isa. 42:1–9; I Tim. 6: 11–16; John 12:37–50.

April 2 (Wednesday): Isa. 52:13 to 53:12; Rom. 5:6–11; Luke 22:1–16.

April 3 (Maundy Thursday): Num. 9: 1–3, 11–12; I Cor. 5:6–8; Mark 14:12–26.

April 4 (Good Friday): Hos. 6:1–6; Rev. 5:6–14; Matt. 27:31–50.

EASTERTIDE

April 6: Ex. 15:1–11; I Cor. 15:20–26; Luke 24:13–35.

April 13: Acts 5:12–16; Rev. 1:9–13, 17–19; John 21:1–14.

April 20: Acts 5:27–32; Rev. 5:11–14; John 21:15–19.

April 27: Acts 13:44–52; Rev. 7:9–17; John 10:22–30.

May 4: Acts 14:19–28; Rev. 21:1–5; John 13:31–35.

May 11: Acts 15:1–2, 22–29; Rev. 21:10–14, 22–23; John 14:23–29.

May 15 (Ascension Day): Acts 1:1–11; Eph. 1:16–23; Luke 24:44–53.

May 18: Acts 7:55–60; Rev. 22:12–14, 16–17, 20; John 17:20–26.

PENTECOST

May 25: Isa. 65:17–25; Acts 2:1–13; John 14:25–31.

June 1: Prov. 8:22–31; I Peter 1:1–9; John 20:19–23.

June 8: I Kings 8:41–43; Gal. 1:1–10; Luke 7:1–10.

June 15: I Kings 17:17–24; Gal 1:11–19; Luke 7:11–17.

June 22: II Sam. 12:1–7; Gal. 2:15–21; Luke 7:36–50.

June 29: Zech. 12:7–10; Gal 3:23–29; Luke 9:18–24.

July 4 (Independence Day): Dan. 9:3–10; I Peter 2:11–17; Luke 20:21–26.

July 6: I Kings 19:15–21; Gal. 5:1, 13–18; Luke 9:51–62.

July 13: Isa. 66:10–14; Gal. 6:11–18; Luke 10:1–9.

July 20: Deut. 30:9–14; Col. 1:15–20; Luke 10:25–37.

July 27: Gen. 18:1–11; Col. 1:24–28; Luke 10:38–42.

August 3: Gen. 18:20–33; Col. 2:8–15; Luke 11:1–13.

August 10: Eccl. 2:18–23; Col. 3:1–11; Luke 12:13–21.

August 17: II Kings 17:33–40; Heb. 11:-1–3, 8–12; Luke 12:35–40.

August 24: Jer. 38:1–13; Heb. 12:1–6; Luke 12:49–53.

August 31: Isa. 66:18–23; Heb. 12:7–13; Luke 13:22–30.

September 7: Prov. 22:1–9; Heb. 12:18–24; Luke 14:1, 7–14.

September 14: Prov. 9:8–12; Philemon 8–17; Luke 14:25–33.

September 21: Ex. 32:7–14; I Tim. 1:12–17; Luke 15:1–32.

September 28: Amos 8:4–8; I Tim. 2:1–8; Luke 16:1–13.

October 5: Amos 6:1, 4–7; I Tim. 6:11–16; Luke 16:19–31; (World Communion Sunday) I Chron. 16:23–34; Acts 2:42–47; Matt. 8:5–13.

October 12: Hab. 1:1–3, 2:1–4; II Tim. 1:3–12; Luke 17:5–10.

October 19: II Kings 5:9–17; II Tim. 2: 8–13; Luke 17:11–19.

October 26: Ex. 17:8–13; II Tim. 3:14 to 4:2; Luke 18:1–8; (Reformation Sunday) Ex. 33:12–17; Heb. 11:1–10; Luke 18: 9–14.

November 2: Deut. 10:16–22; II Tim. 4: 6–8, 16–18; Luke 18:9–14.

November 9: Ex. 34:5–9; II Thess. 1:11 to 2:2; Luke 19:1–10.

November 16: I Chron. 29:10–13; II Thess. 2:16 to 3:5; Luke 20:27–38.

November 23: Mal. 3:16 to 4:2; II Thess. 3:6–13; Luke 21:5–19.

November 27 (Thanksgiving Day): Deut. 8:6–17; II Cor. 9:6–15; John 6:24–35.

ADVENT

November 30: Isa. 2:1–5; Rom. 13:11–14; Matt. 24:36–44.

December 7: Isa. 11:1–10; Rom. 15:4–9; Matt. 3:1–12.

December 14: Isa. 35:1–6, 10; James 5: 7–10; Matt. 11:2–11.

December 21: Isa. 7:10–15; Rom. 1:1–7; Matt. 1:18–25.

December 24 (Christmas Eve): Isa. 62: 1–4: Col. 1:15–20; Luke 2:1–14.

CHRISTMASTIDE

December 25: Isa. 9:2, 6–7; Titus 2:11–15; Luke 2:1–14.

December 28: Eccl. 3:1–9, 14–17; Col. 3: 12–17; Matt. 2:13–15, 19–23.

Four-Year Church Calendar

	1980	1981	1982	1983
Ash Wednesday	February 20	March 4	February 24	February 16
Palm Sunday	March 30	April 12	April 4	March 27
Good Friday	April 4	April 17	April 9	April 3
Easter	April 6	April 19	April 11	May 12
Ascension Day	May 15	May 28	May 20	May 22
Pentecost	May 25	June 7	May 30	May 29
Trinity Sunday	June 1	June 14	June 6	May 29
Thanksgiving	November 28	November 26	November 25	November 24
Advent Sunday	November 30	November 29	November 28	November 27

Forty-Year Easter Calendar

1980 April 6	1990 April 15	2000 April 23	2010 April 4
1981 April 19	1991 March 31	2001 April 14	2011 April 24
1982 April 11	1992 April 19	2002 March 31	2012 April 8
1983 April 3	1993 April 11	2003 April 20	2013 March 31
1984 April 22	1994 April 3	2004 April 11	2014 April 20
1985 April 7	1995 April 16	2005 March 27	2015 April 5
1986 March 30	1996 April 7	2006 April 16	2016 March 27
1987 April 19	1997 March 30	2007 April 8	2017 April 16
1988 April 3	1998 April 12	2008 March 23	2018 April 1
1989 March 26	1999 April 4	2009 April 12	2019 April 21

Four-Year Jewish Calendar

	1980	1981	1982	1983
Purim	March 2	March 20	March 9	February 27
Passover	April 1	April 19	April 8	March 29
Shabuoth (Revelation of the Law),	May 21	June 8	May 28	May 18
Rosh Hashanah (New Year),	September 11	September 29	September 18	September 8
Yom Kippur (Day of Atonement),	September 20	October 8	September 27	September 17
Sukkoth (Thanksgiving),	September 25	October 13	October 2	September 22
Simhath Torah (Rejoicing in the Law),	October 3	October 21	October 10	September 30
Hanukkah	December 3	December 21	December 11	December 1

Holidays begin at sunset on the evening before the date given.

Traditional Wedding Anniversary Identifications

1 Paper	7 Wool	13 Lace	35 Coral
2 Cotton	8 Bronze	14 Ivory	40 Ruby
3 Leather	9 Pottery	15 Crystal	45 Sapphire
4 Linen	10 Tin	20 China	50 Gold
5 Wood	11 Steel	25 Silver	55 Emerald
6 Iron	12 Silk	30 Pearl	60 Diamond

Colors Appropriate for Days and Seasons

White. Symbolizes purity, perfection, and joy and identifies festivals marking events, except Good Friday, in the life of Jesus: Christmas, Easter, Eastertide, Ascension Day, Trinity Sunday, All Saints' Day, weddings, funerals.

Red. Symbolizes the Holy Spirit, martyrdom, and the love of God: Pentecost and Sundays following.

Violet. Symbolizes penitence: Advent, Lent.

Green. Symbolizes mission to the world, hope, regeneration, nurture, and growth: Epiphany season, Kingdomtide, Rural Life Sunday, Labor Sunday, Thanksgiving Sunday.

Black. Symbolizes mourning: Good Friday.

Flowers in Season Appropriate for Church Use

January. Carnation or snowdrop.
February. Violet or primrose.
March. Jonquil or daffodil.
April. Lily, sweet pea, or daisy.
May. Lily of the valley or hawthorn.
June. Rose or honeysuckle.
July. Larkspur or water lily.

August. Gladiolus or poppy.
September. Aster or morning glory.
October. Calendula or cosmos.
November. Chrysanthemum.
December. Narcissus, holly, or poinsettia.

Historical, Cultural, and Religious Anniversaries in 1980

10 years (1970). *April 22:* first Earth Day. *May 4:* four Kent State students killed by National Guard during protest over U.S. action in Cambodia. *June 22:* voting age in national elections lowered from 21 to 18. August 12: independent U.S. Postal Service created.

25 years (1955). *February 12:* U.S. provides military aid in Vietnam War. *March 25:* Soviet Union grants sovereignty to East Germany. *April 6:* Churchill resigns as prime minister. *May 5:* West Germany becomes independent. *May 14:* Warsaw Pact signed. *July 27:* Austria regains independence. *December 1:* bus boycott under leadership of Martin Luther King, Jr., began in Montgomery, Alabama. *December 5:* merger of AFL and CIO.

50 years (1930). Worldwide economic depression develops. *March 12:* Gandhi opens civil disobedience campaign in India.

75 years (1905). Einstein publishes account of special theory of relativity. Richard Strauss composes *Salome. June 7:* Norway declares independence from Sweden. *September 5:* signing of peace treaty concludes Russo-Japanese War.

100 years (1880). Dostoevsky writes *The Brothers Karamazov.* Lew Wallace writes *Ben Hur.* Congo made a French protectorate.

150 years (1830). First major woman's magazine, *Godey's Lady's Book,* published in Philadelphia. States' rights debates between Senators Hayne and Webster held. Tennyson publishes *Poems, Chiefly Lyrical. April 6:* Mormon Church founded by Joseph Smith. *April 27:* Bolivar resigns as supreme chief of Columbia and dies on December 17. *May 28:* Indian Removal Act results in forced resettlement of 70,000 west of the Mississippi. *July 28:* revolution in France results in abdication of Charles X who was succeeded by Louis Philippe I.

200 years (1780). *May 12:* British capture Charleston, S.C. *August 16:* British defeat Americans in Battle of Camden, S.C. *September 25:* Major General Benedict Arnold defects to British. *October 2:* British spy, Major John Andre, hanged.

300 years (1680). New Hampshire becomes separate province.

350 years (1630). Settlement established at Boston, Mass. *November 15:* Johannes Kepler, German astronomer, dies.

400 years (1580). Last miracle play performed at Coventry. Montaigne publishes first volumes of *Essays*.

450 years (1530). Correggio paints "Adoration of the Shepherds."

550 years (1430). Joan of Arc captured by Burgundians at Compiegne.

600 years (1380). Wycliffe begins translation of the New Testament.

1300 years (680). Caedmon, first English Christian poet, dies.

1350 years (630). Moslems conquer Mecca, spiritual center of Islam.

1600 years (380). Christianity made official religion of Roman Empire.

1800 years (180). Emperor Marcus Aurelius, author of *Meditations*, dies.

1850 years (130). Pantheon built in Rome and becomes Christian church in 609.

1900 years (80). Colosseum built in Rome.

Anniversaries of Hymns, Hymn Writers, and Composers in 1980

20 years (1960). Death of Thomas O. Chisholm (b. 1866), author of "Great is thy faithfulness"; Cecil Armstrong Gibbs (b. 1899), composer of hymn-tune LINGWOOD ("Judge eternal, throned in splendor").

25 years (1955). Death of Cyril A. Alington (b. 1872), author of "Good Christian men, rejoice and sing."

50 years (1930). Publication of "God of grace and God of glory" and "The prince of peace his banner spreads" by Harry Emerson Fosdick; "Men and children everywhere" by John J. Moment. Birth of Ronald Arnatt, composer of hymn-tunes LADUE CHAPEL ("Thou whose purpose is to kindle") and SOUTH GORE ("Christ is the king"); James H. Hargett, author of "From the shores of many nations"; W. F. Jabusch, author of "The king of glory." Death of Louis F. Benson (b. 1855), author of "For the bread, which thou hast broken," "The light of God is falling," "O sing a song of Bethlehem," "O thou whose gracious presence blest," etc.; Henry Burton (b. 1840), author of "Break, day of God"; E. Taylor Cassel (b. 1849), author of "Loyalty to Christ"; Vachel Lindsay (b. 1879), author of "An endless line of splendor"; Carrie E. Rounsefell (b. 1861), composer of hymn-tune for "I'll go where you want me to go"; Franklin L. Sheppard (b. 1852), composer of hymn-tune TERRA PATRIS ("This is my father's world").

75 years (1905). Writing of hymn-tune VOX CELESTIS ("Where is your God? they say") by Myles B. Foster; "To thee, eternal Soul, be praise" by Richard Watson Gilder; hymn-tune LANIER ("Into the woods my Master went") by Peter C. Lutkin; "Thy kingdom, Lord, thy kingdom" by Vida Scudder. Birth of A. Gregory Murray, author of hymn-tunes ANGLORUM APOSTOLUS ("Father of heaven, whose love profound") and REX SUMMAE ("Thy hand, O God, has guided thy flock"). Death of Jean Baptiste Calkin (b. 1827), composer of hymn-tune WALTHAM ("Fling out the banner, let it float" and "I heard the bells of Christmas day"); Mary Mapes Dodge (b. 1831), author of "Can a little child like me"; Lewis Hensley (b. 1824), author of "Thy kingdom come, O Lord"; James R. Murray (b. 1841), composer of hymn-tune MUELLER ("Away in the manger").

100 years (1880). Publication of hymn-tune PENITENTIA ("Here, O my Lord, I see thee") by Edward Dearle; "At all times praise the Lord" by John S. Howson; "From ocean unto ocean" by Robert Murray; "O Master, let me walk with thee" by Washington Gladden; "Break thou the bread of life" by Mary A. Lathbury; "These things shall be—a loftier race" by John A. Symonds. Birth of Grace Wilbur Conant (d. 1948), composer of hymn-tune FEALTY ("I bind my heart this tide"); Harry Webb Farrington (d. 1931), author of "I know not how that Bethlehem's babe"; William M. Vories (d. 1964), author of "Let there be light"; Healey Willan (d. 1968), composer of hymn-tunes ST. BASIL ("Eternal, unchanging, we sing to thy praise") and STELLA ORIENTIS ("Brightest and best of the sons of the morning"); Ira B. Wilson (d. 1950), author of "Make me a blessing." Death of Anton P. Berggreen

(b. 1801), composer of hymn-tune AMEN, JESUS HAN SKAL RAADE ("Master, speak! thy servant heareth"); John Goss (d. 1880), composer of hymn-tunes ARTHUR'S SEAT ("March on, O soul, with strength") and BENEDIC ANIMA MEA or LAUDA ANIMA ("Praise, my soul, the king of heaven" and "Thanks to God whose word was spoken"); Jeannette Threlfall (b. 1821), author of "Hosanna, loud hosanna."

150 years (1830). Publication of "My faith looks up to thee" by Ray Palmer; hymn-tune ST. PETER ("Father, whose will is life and good," "From thee all skill and science flow," "How sweet the name of Jesus sounds," and "In Christ there is no east or west") by Alexander R. Reinagle; hymn-tune TOPLADY ("Rock of ages, cleft for me") by Thomas Hastings; hymn-tunes HEBRON ("So let our lips and lives express"), LABAN ("My soul, be on thy guard"), UXBRIDGE ("The heavens declare thy glory"), and WESLEY ("Hail to the brightness of Zion's glad morning") by Lowell Mason. Birth of Charlotte A. Barnard (d. 1869), composer of hymn-tunes BROCKLESBURY ("Savior, who thy flock art feeding") and for "Give of your best to the master"; Arthur H. Brown (d. 1926), composer of hymn-tunes SAFFRON WALDEN ("Just as I am, thine own to be") and ST. ANATOLIUS ("The day is past and over"); Elizabeth C. Clephane (d. 1869), author of "Beneath the cross of Jesus"; Henry Collins (d. 1919), author of "Jesus, my Lord, my God, my all"; Alexander Ewing (d. 1895), composer of hymn-tune EWING ("Jerusalem the golden"); John S. B. Hodges (d. 1915), composer of hymn-tune EUCHARISTIC HYMN ("Bread of the world in mercy broken"); Phoebe P. Knapp (d. 1908), composer of hymn-tune ASSURANCE ("Blessed assurance, Jesus is mine"); Herbert S. Oakeley (d. 1903), composer of hymn-tune ABENDS ("At even, ere the sun was set" and "Again, as evening's shadow falls"); Lewis H. Redner (d. 1908), composer of hymn-tune ST. LOUIS ("O little town of Bethlehem");

Christina G. Rossetti (d. 1894), author of "In the bleak midwinter," "Love came down at Christmas," "None other lamb," and "O Christ, my God"; Christopher E. Willing (d. 1904), composer of hymn-tune ALSTONE ("On Jordan's bank the Baptist's cry").

200 years (1780). Publication of "All hail the power of Jesus' name" by Edward Perronet. Birth of George Croly (d. 1860), author of "Spirit of God, descend upon my heart"; Freedom Lewis (d. 1859), composer of hymn-tune MEDITATION ("O thou, in whose presence"); John Marriott (d. 1825), author of "Thou whose almighty word."

300 years (1680). Birth of Simon Browne (d. 1732), author of "Come, gracious Spirit, heav'nly dove"; Johann Ludwig Steiner (d. 1761), composer of hymn-tune GOTT WILL'S MACHEN ("There's a wideness in God's mercy"). Death of Joachim Neander (b. 1650), author of "Praise to the Lord, the almighty" and "Heaven and earth, and sea and air" and hymn-tunes ARNSBERG ("God himself is with us") and UNSER HERRSCHER ("God of love and God of power," "Open now thy gates of beauty," and "See the morning sun ascending").

350 years (1630). Birth of Jean Baptiste de Santeuil (d. 1697), author of "All honor and praise, dominion and might." Death of Johann Hermann Schein (b. 1586), composer of hymn-tunes CAROL ("Come, ye faithful, raise the strain") and EISENACH ("Captain of Israel's host," "O love of God, how strong and true," and "O thou who camest from above").

450 years (1530). Writing of "Away in the manger" by Martin Luther.

1450 years (530). Birth of Venantius Fortunatus (d. 609), author of "Hail thee, festival day," "Sing, my tongue, the glorious battle," and "Welcome, happy morning."

1550 years (430). Death of Synesius of Cyrene (b. 375), author of "Lord Jesus, think on me."

Quotable Quotations

1. Christian hope is not wishing; it is assurance.—Harold G. Bender.

2. Open a window on the Godward side. —Rufus M. Jones.

3. Our real journey in life is interior.—Thomas Merton.

4. Joy is the most infallible sign of the presence of God.—Teilhard de Chardin.

5. Every day we live is a priceless gift of God, loaded with possibilities to learn something new and to gain fresh insights into his great truths.—Dale Evans.

6. A lack of goals removes all meaning from living.—Viktor Frankl.

7. The chiefest sanctity of a temple is that it is a place to which men go to weep in common.—Miguel de Unamuno.

8. Love is the medicine for the sickness of the world.—Karl Menninger.

9. The true work of art is but a shadow of the divine perfection.—Michelangelo.

10. He who wants to see the living God face to face should not seek him in the empty firmament of thought but in the love for his fellowman.—Fyodor Dostoevsky.

11. The perception of good and evil—whatever choice we may make—is the first requisite of spiritual life.—T. S. Eliot.

12. A child is a person who is going to carry on what you have started. The fate of humanity is in his hands.—Abraham Lincoln.

13. It is impossible for a man to be saved in ignorance.—Richard L. Evans.

14. If God had meant for us to live in a world of moral uncertainty, he would have given us ten suggestions rather than ten commandments.—Daniel E. Weiss.

15. Prayer is not so much God doing things for us as it is we and God doing things together.—William Barclay.

16. The cross was a comma and the resurrection an exclamation point in God's plan.—Joe L. Marine.

17. God's grace enables us to face the music even when we don't like the tune.—*Christian Herald.*

18. The sun is shining somewhere all the time.—John M. Drescher.

19. God is articulate in his universe.—A. W. Tozer.

20. Create a ganglion chain of redeemed personalities in a commonwealth, and all things become possible.—Walter Rauschenbusch.

21. Christ always took time for individuals.—Judson J. Swihart.

22. Kindness has converted more sinners than zeal, eloquence, or learning.—Frederick W. Faber.

23. The soft answer that turneth away wrath also makes it easier if you have to eat your words.—Dorthea Kent.

24. Most of our comforts grow up between our crosses.—Edward Young.

25. There is no worse suffering than a guilty conscience and certainly none more painful.—Paul Tournier.

26. Flowers are the sweetest thing that God ever made and forgot to put a soul into.

27. Easter is not an event in time; it is a timeless event.

28. Recollection is the only paradise from which we cannot be turned out.—Jean Paul Richter.

29. Through prayer man has the challenging opportunity to visit personally with God.—Edward J. Thye.

30. Paul never could think of God without seeing the face of Jesus, and he could never commune with Jesus without feeling the presence of God.—James S. Stewart.

31. When you see a brother stumble and fall, your first thought should be, I am most likely to fall in that same way.—Thomas a Kempis.

32. Each moment of the year has its own beauty, a picture which was never seen before and which shall never be seen again.—Ralph Waldo Emerson.

33. Hopelessness means living on the wrong side of Easter.—Harold E. Kohn.

34. Earn the heritage of your fathers in order to possess it.—Goethe.

35. The Christian community is the Easter community. Our faith is an Easter faith.—Karl Barth.

36. A generous person is always sorry he cannot give more.

37. Death and love are two wings which bear men from earth to heaven.

38. Everything is waiting to be hallowed by you.—Martin Buber.

39. Every step toward Christ kills a doubt.—Theodore L. Cuyler.

40. There are no limitations in life except those we impose upon ourselves.

41. It is a good and safe rule to sojourn in every place as if you meant to spend your life there, never omitting an opportu-

nity of doing a kindness or speaking a true word or making a friend.—John Ruskin.

42. Stewardship is what a man does after he says, "I believe."—W. H. Greever.

43. How else, except through a broken heart, may Lord Christ enter in?—Oscar Wilde.

44. The woods would be very silent if no birds sang there except those who sang best.—John James Audubon.

45. We like someone because. We love someone although.—Henri de Montherlaut.

46. A Christian is nothing but a sinful man who has put himself to school to Christ for the honest purpose of becoming better.—Henry Ward Beecher.

47. Without dependence on God our efforts turn to ashes and our sunrises into darkest night.—Martin Luther King, Jr.

48. Maturity is the art of living in peace with that which we cannot change.

49. Your life is without a foundation if, in any matter, you choose on your own behalf.—Dag Hammarskjold.

50. We are marching along the endless pathway of unrealized possibilities in human growth.—Francis W. Parker.

51. To try too hard to make people good is one way to make them worse; the only way to make them good is to be good.—George Macdonald.

52. When a person leaves God, things start happening to him or her, and when a person comes to God, things start happening for him or her.—John M. Drescher.

53. Jesus lived in vain if he did not teach us to regulate the whole of life by the eternal law of love.—Gandhi.

54. Anyone can carry his burden, however hard, until nightfall. Anyone can do his work, however hard, for one day.—Robert Louis Stevenson.

55. To know someone here or there with whom you can feel there is understanding in spite of distances or thoughts unexpressed—that can make of this earth a garden.—Goethe.

56. No man can give himself heart and soul to one thing while in the back of his mind he cherishes a desire, a secret hope

for something very different.—Willa Cather.

57. A saint is never consciously a saint; a saint is consciously dependent on God. —Oswald Chambers.

58. The human body is an instrument for the production of art in the life of the human soul.—Alfred North Whitehead.

59. To meet a good man is like finding an oasis in the desert.—Gerald Kennedy.

60. It is almost impossible to smile on the outside without feeling better on the inside.

61. It is not merely the trivial which clutters our lives but the important as well.— Anne Morrow Lindbergh.

62. Social concern without Christian conviction runs out into the desert of despair.—Joseph McCabe.

63. The nobler the soul, the more objects of compassion it hath.—W. Bramwell Booth.

64. Most humans want to escape the pain of being alive and, most of all, of love. —John Osborne.

65. Let us devote our life to worthwhile actions and feelings, to great thoughts, real affections, and enduring undertakings.—Benjamin Disraeli.

66. Your capacity to say "no" determines your capacity to say "yes" to greater things.—E. Stanley Jones.

67. It is a joy to accept forgiveness, but it is almost a greater joy to give forgiveness.—Corrie ten Boom.

68. There are two things you cannot do alone: marry and be a Christian.—Paul Tournier.

69. You can live if you can love.—Karl Menninger.

70. The trouble with man is two-fold: he cannot learn truths which are too complicated; he forgets truths which are too simple.

71. If we will not give up evil for good, we will give up good for evil.—Harry Emerson Fosdick.

72. The times are evil, but live nobly and you will change the times.—St. Augustine.

73. The unsurrendered self works out from its own motives and resources; the

surrendered self works out from the motives and resources of Christ.—E. Stanley Jones.

74. We must not only believe in God but believe God.

75. Suffer with Christ and for Christ if thou desire to reign with Christ.—Thomas a Kempis.

76. People cannot change truth, but truth can change people.

77. To be content with what we possess is the greatest and most secure of riches.—Cicero.

78. When God pardons, he consigns the offense to everlasting forgetfulness.—Merv Rosell.

79. If forgiveness is real, each life can make a new redemptive start each day.—Elton Trueblood.

80. What do we live for if it is not to make life less difficult for each other?—George Eliot.

81. All people smile in the same language.

82. Tomorrow may be the day of judgment. If it is we shall gladly give up working for a better future but not before.—Dietrich Bonhoeffer.

83. It is not in life's chances but in its choices that happiness comes to the heart of the individual.

84. The head seeks God, but it is the heart that finds him.

85. If you are planning for a year, plant grain. If you are planning for a decade, plant trees. If you are planning for a century, plant men.—Chinese proverb.

86. The vocation of every man and woman is to serve other people.—Leo Tolstoy.

87. God's promises are like the stars: the darker the night, the brighter they shine.—David Nicholas.

88. Every man must do two things alone: he must do his own believing and his own dying.—Martin Luther.

89. Blessed is the life that does not collect resentments.—Harry Emerson Fosdick.

90. The greatest and noblest pleasure which people can have in the world is to discover new truths, and the next is to shake off old prejudices.—Frederick the Great.

91. The social order cannot be saved without regenerate men.—Walter Rauschenbusch.

92. The better part of one's life consists of his friendships.—Abraham Lincoln.

93. God can forgive us, not because of what we do, but because of what Christ did.—Erwin W. Lutzer.

94. Most successes are built on failures.—Charles Gow.

95. To pray is to expose the shores of the mind to the incoming tide of the Holy Spirit.—Ralph W. Sockman.

96. No duty is more urgent than that of returning thanks.—St. Ambrose.

97. It is impossible mentally or socially to enslave a Bible-reading people.—Horace Greeley.

98. It is well for us to think that no grace or blessing is truly ours until God has blessed someone else with it through us.—Phillips Brooks.

99. Man is bound in stewardship to take care of this earth until he gets a better one.—Sherwood E. Wirt.

100. We cannot speak with any truth or realism about our faith in the future unless we understand the past.—Peter Marshall.

Questions of Religion and Life

These questions may be useful to prime homiletic pumps, as discussion starters, or for study groups.

1. What particular message does the church have for the world today?

2. In what ways are traditional Christian values being threatened?

3. Is ecology a proper Christian concern?

4. Is Christ present at the Lord's Supper?

5. Are all books of the Bible of equal value for Christian teaching?

6. How may churches develop a sense of fellowship?

7. Is the church gaining or losing ground throughout the world?

8. Is the Apostles' Creed outmoded in language and content?

9. How might the church make a stronger appeal to young people?

10. Are most public servants actually motivated by self-serving?

11. Is there nowadays less emphasis on sex and violence in television programing?

12. Why did the apostle Paul consider love to be greater than faith and hope?

13. What is the significant role of theologians in Christian history?

14. How does music contribute to communal worship?

15. Are the benefits of prayer mostly subjective?

16. Explain the second birth?

17. How does the belief in Christ's return influence Christian behavior?

18. Is Christ superior to all other religious leaders? Why or why not?

19. What civic responsibilities do Christians as Christians have?

20. Are Christian homes in peril?

21. Do we underestimate goodness and exaggerate evil in the world?

22. Why are so many churches silent about the increasing use of alcohol?

23. What are the pros and cons regarding abortion?

24. Should labor be permitted to endanger the national welfare by strikes even if the reasons for striking are valid?

25. How did Moses affect human history?

26. How committed are the mainline churches to world missions?

27. What permanent contributions do Sunday schools make to Christian life?

28. What must I do to be saved?

29. Have churches changed their teachings concerning divorce?

30. Is world hunger so widespread throughout the world as to make our efforts inconsequential?

31. What is biblical preaching?

32. How should the ascension of Christ be interpreted?

33. Is the church full of hypocrites?

34. Does our need for oil determine the direction of our foreign policy?

35. Why do people join monastic orders?

36. What value should Christians attach to money?

37. Whatever happened to the Lord's Day?

38. In what ways may Christ be said to have died for our sins?

39. How important is the cross in Christian teaching?

40. Do we neglect important portions of the New Testament?

41. Do religion and politics ever mix?

42. Can I be saved apart from the church?

43. Can you explain why Christmas so noticeably influences our lives?

44. Why do we say amen at the conclusion of our prayers?

45. Are our attitudes and values too greatly influenced by advertising?

46. Are there any genuine prophets in the contemporary church?

47. Can prayer become a substitute for action?

48. Is it realistic to believe that mankind can ever achieve international peace?

49. To what extent should ethical considerations determine scientific manipulations of the processes of birth and death?

50. How do the four gospels differ in their interpretations of Christ?

51. Why was the sinless Christ baptized by John?

52. Is there anything that the church can do to raise the moral quality of popular entertainment?

53. Has gambling become a national obsession?

54. If Jesus were to be born today would his life and ministry differ greatly from what we find in the gospels?

55. Do miracles similar to those recorded in the New Testament occur today?

56. What, according to biblical guidelines, constitutes the good life?

57. Does the church have a responsibility for caring for the poor or is this now primarily a responsibility of government?

58. How can the meek be said to have inherited the earth?

59. In what ways are the ten commandments still revelant?

60. Does God always answer prayer?

61. What difference does the church make in the life of the community?

62. Are most people honest?

63. What determines Christian character?

64. Have our ideas of the afterlife changed?

65. Why do many ministers wear robes or other clerical garments in church?

66. What can Protestants learn from Catholics and vice versa?

67. Can you explain the incarnation in everyday language?

68. Do people become more religious as they become older?

69. Is there a Christian interpretation of sex?

70. Which Old Testament characters seem closest to the spirit of Christ?

71. Where in Christian activity is the need for full-time Christian workers greatest?

72. How important is hope to the achievement of Christian serenity?

73. In what ways can our homes become Christ-centered?

74. Has organized Christianity become less racially oriented?

75. How do Christian and Jewish teachings differ and in what ways are they similar?

76. In relation to Christ do the words "son of God" and "son of man" mean the same thing?

77. Can Christ be the personal savior of millions of individual Christians?

78. How can God become more real to me?

79. Should partisan politics be taken into the pulpit?

80. What methods of evangelism are winning most people to Christ?

81. Should confessing Christians marry only confessing Christians?

82. Is it unchristian to grieve over the loss of a loved one who has gone home to God?

83. How important is symbolism in Christian education?

84. How can moral man survive in an immoral society?

85. How does the contemplation of the beautiful influence our lives?

86. Can lying ever be justified as an immoral means to a worthy end?

87. Did Christ require his followers to be baptized?

88. In what ways have human beings changed and in what ways have they not changed since the time of Abraham?

89. Should persons seeking public office make a big deal of their religious activities and beliefs?

90. Where in the world today are Christian missionaries most welcomed and most needed?

91. What benefits should I expect from a habitual reading of the Bible?

92. What is heaven like?

93. What does the Bible say concerning the final judgment and eternal punishment?

94. Why do so many people go to church?

95. What is meant by Christian freedom?

96. When can a person be said to have achieved integrity?

97. What can the black and the white churches teach one another?

98. Why did Jesus call upon his followers to remember him in their observances of the Lord's Supper?

99. In what ways does Christian education differ from secular education?

100. Why do so many questions seem to have no conclusive answers?

Biblical Benedictions and Blessings

The Lord watch between me and thee, when we are absent one from another.—Gen. 31:49.

The Lord bless thee, and keep thee; the Lord make his face shine upon thee, and be gracious unto thee; the Lord lift up his countenance upon thee, and give thee peace.—Num. 6:24–26.

The Lord our God be with us, as he was with our fathers: let him not leave us, nor forsake us: that he may incline our hearts unto him, to walk in all his ways, and to keep his commandments, and his statutes, and his judgments, which he commanded our fathers.—I Kings 8:57–58.

Let the words of my mouth, and the meditation of my heart, be acceptable in thy sight, O Lord, my strength, and my redeemer.—Ps. 19:14.

Now the God of patience and consolation grant you to be likeminded one toward another according to Christ Jesus: that ye may with one mind and one mouth glorify God, even the Father of our Lord Jesus Christ. Now the God of hope fill you with all joy and peace in believing, that ye may abound in hope, through the power of the Holy Ghost. Now the God of peace be with you all.—Rom. 15:5–6, 13, 33.

Now to him that is of power to establish you according to my gospel, and the preaching of Jesus Christ, according to the revelation of the mystery, which was kept secret since the world began, but now is manifest, and by the scriptures of the prophets, according to the commandment of the everlasting God, made known to all nations for the obedience of faith: to God only wise, be glory through Jesus Christ for ever.—Rom. 16:25–27.

Grace be unto you, and peace, from God our Father, and from the Lord Jesus Christ.—I Cor. 1:3.

The grace of the Lord Jesus Christ and the love of God, and the communion of the Holy Ghost, be with you all.—II Cor. 13:14.

Peace be to the brethren, and love with faith, from God the Father and the Lord Jesus Christ. Grace be with all them that love our Lord Jesus Christ in sincerity.—Eph. 6:23–24.

And the peace of God, which passeth all understanding, shall keep your hearts and minds through Christ Jesus. Finally, brethren, whatsoever things are true, whatsoever things are honest, whatsoever things are just, whatsoever things are pure, whatsoever things are lovely, whatsoever things are of good report; if there be any virtue, and if there be any praise, think on these things. Those things, which ye have both learned, and received, and heard, and seen in me, do: and the God of peace shall be with you.—Phil. 4:7–9.

Wherefore also we pray always for you, that our God would count you worthy of this calling, and fulfill all the good pleasure of his goodness, and the work of faith with power: that the name of our Lord Jesus Christ may be glorified in you, and ye in him, according to the grace of our God and the Lord Jesus Christ.—II Thess. 1:11–12.

Now the Lord of peace himself give you peace always by all means. The Lord be with you all. The grace of our Lord Jesus Christ be with you all.—II Thess. 3:16, 18.

Grace, mercy, and peace, from God our Father and Jesus Christ our Lord.—I Tim. 1:2.

Now the God of peace, that brought again from the dead our Lord Jesus, that great shepherd of the sheep, through the blood of the everlasting covenant, make you perfect in every good work to do his will, working in you that which is well-pleasing in his sight, through Jesus Christ, to whom be glory for ever and ever.— Heb. 13:20-21.

The God of all grace, who hath called us unto his eternal glory by Christ Jesus, after that ye have suffered a while, make you perfect, stablish, strengthen, settle you. To him be glory and dominion for ever and ever. Greet ye one another with a kiss of charity. Peace be with you all that are in Christ Jesus.—I Pet. 5:10-11, 14.

Grace be with you, mercy, and peace, from God the Father, and from the Lord Jesus Christ, the Son of the Father, in truth and love.—II John 3.

Now unto him that is able to keep you from falling, and to present you faultless before the presence of his glory with exceeding joy, to the only wise God our Savior, be glory and majesty, dominion and power, both now and ever.—Jude 2:24-25.

Grace be unto you, and peace, from him which was, and which is to come; and from the seven Spirits which are before his throne; and from Jesus Christ, who is the faithful witness, and the first begotten of the dead, and the prince of the kings of the earth. Unto him that loved us, and washed us from our sins in his own blood, and hath made us kings and priests unto God and his Father; to him be glory and dominion for ever and ever.—Rev. 1:4-6.

SECTION II. Vital Themes
for Vital Preaching

January 6. Faith for the New Year
TEXT: Isa. 40:31.
I. Life is a journey: live it trustingly. (See Ps. 23:4.)
II. Life is a task: live it obediently. (See I John 3:22.)
III. Life is a mission: live it helpfully. (See Eph. 4:32.)
IV. Life is a contest: live it earnestly. (See I Cor. 16:13.)—Carl J. Sanders.

January 13. Three-Fold Mission of the Church
TEXT: Acts 14:27.
I. The church of Jesus Christ has a mission to proclaim the good news of God's love and Christ's redemptive ministry to the end that people comprehend the work that God has done for them in Jesus Christ and believe in Jesus as their savior, becoming children of God.
II. The Christian community is to care for people who are in need by providing food, clothing, shelter, guidance, and comfort with its own material resources and by facilitating the help and resources of other sympathetic people. The church should bring comfort and protection to many people by those avenues that are most appropriate to each situation.
III. The church of Jesus Christ is to be the salt of the earth. It is to have a penetrating and preserving influence in society. It is to bear witness to the truths of God in such a way that secular errors are corrected or at least amended. It is to bear

testimony to God-given principles of righteousness and justice so that the world is never comfortable operating by other standards. Those who believe in Jesus Christ are so to live and work in the world that government, private agencies, and business are conducted more humanely and more fairly. This penetrating influence will ordinarily be accomplished more effectively by individual Christians than through the direct action of denominations.—Foster H. Shannon.

January 20. Go Back Home (Missionary Day)
SCRIPTURE: Mark 5:1-20.
I. The man said, "My name is legion, for we are many." A Roman legion consisted of six thousand fighting men. This poor fellow felt like he had six thousand fighting men inside of him all pulling in different directions. No wonder he lived in the local cemetery.
(a) We are legion in the things we must do. We are legion in the things we can do. Our standard of living and our mobility provide us with so many choices that we sometimes get frustrated.
(b) We are legion in our loyalties. Our work requires much time and energy. We all want to spend time with our families, a feat which means determined planning well in advance. At the same time good friendships cannot be cultivated in isolation. We want and need to spend time in fellowship with friends. Our desire is to be

loyal to God and to work through the church. But unfortunately the organization of some churches has become so complex that it contributes to the disunity of our lives. When will we learn that there is no salvation in meetings?

II. Jesus had the power to exorcise the demons and to heal the poor man.

(a) The paragraph preceding this account in Mark's gospel tells of Jesus being awakened by his terrified disciples caught in the midst of a violent storm at sea. His power over nature was amply demonstrated as "he awoke and rebuked the wind and said to the sea, 'Peace! Be still!' " The account concludes with the wide-eyed disciples saying to one another, "Who then is this, that even wind and sea obey him?"

(b) He was lord of nature, but Mark wanted to show that Jesus was even lord over demonic forces, even when present in legions. Such power was staggering to those who first read this. But even here the progression was not complete. Later in this same chapter Mark included the account of Jesus' raising a little girl from the dead. Thus the progression is complete: he is lord over nature, lord over demonic forces, and even lord over death.

(c) We live in another era. For most of us the terminology has changed. Our demons are abstract nouns like bureaucracy, heredity, environment, habits, and nature. These are the demons to which we sometimes feel totally subjected, as though six thousand pressures are pulling at us from the inside.

(d) The message is still the same. Jesus is even lord over abstract nouns. Through the power of God he gives the power to find a peace which no one else can understand.

III. As Jesus was getting into the boat to leave, the healed man, who was then "clothed and in his right mind," begged Jesus to let him go with him. He was really committed. He was prepared to leave home and in effect become a foreign missionary. But Jesus refused. He said to the man, "Go back home to your friends, and tell them how much the Lord has done for you."

(a) That's quite a command. "Go back home." But, lord, I'll go anywhere in the world! "Go back home." I'll live for you in a straw hut in darkest Africa! "Go back home." Ever hear of a more difficult assignment? Go back home to those who know your faults, your failures, and your adolescent stunts.

(b) There's not much glamor in it. You take out the garbage, you wash the dishes, you go to work, you grill hamburgers, and you mow the grass. You try to show up at the meetings you're supposed to attend. You do battle with that legion of everyday pressures.

(c) Those people at home see you when you are fresh in the morning and when you are about to fall out at night. And there you are, trying to give witness to someone who has changed your life.

(d) So the healed man turned back to his own home, while Jesus and his disciples sailed off without him. What he didn't know was that Jesus was really still with him as he stumbled back into his old hometown to face those people.—Thomas R. McKibbens, Jr.

January 27. Be Angry But Do Not Sin

TEXT: Eph. 4:26.

Responsible psychology has demonstrated the stupidity of thoroughly repressing anger just as irresponsible popular psychology has exhibited the stupidity of advocating uninhibited expressions of anger in the name of honesty and group therapy. Between these two extremes we might do better to look again at Paul's words and remember Jesus.

I. Paul wrote to the Ephesians, "Be angry but do not sin." (a) Today we might say recognize and accept the feelings stirred up in your daily life and take them seriously. Look at yourself and the feelings you possess, but do not let aggressive or destructive feelings take possession of you. It may be all right to be angry, but it is not all right to avoid the work of doing anything about it or to surrender to angry impulses.

(b) Such avoidance or surrender is harmful to yourself and to others—yes, even a sin in God's sight when it leads to broken relationships and missed opportunities because we are too wrapped up in ourselves to reach beyond ourselves to touch and help and heal another, too divided within to sense the spirit that unites us, the common bond drawing all God's children together, what Paul called the unity of the spirit in the bond of peace.

II. Remember what Jesus did with his anger. He faced it squarely, changing it from the peril of hurting to the possibility of healing. When the Pharisees gathered around him in the synagogue on the sabbath to see if he would break the law by healing a man with a withered hand, Jesus posed a question: "Is it lawful to do good or do harm on the sabbath, to save life or to kill?" The Pharisees were silent. They were angry because Jesus threatened their authority. They came not to teach but to trap. In the words of Mark's gospel, Jesus "looked around at them with anger, grieved at their hardness of heart." Then he took the man's withered hand and healed it.

III. Jesus was angry, and he knew it. But he did not use the occasion to lash out at the Pharisees. Nor did he shrink from his duty, avoiding a face-to-face confrontation with the Pharisees, running away, and then complaining amidst more sympathetic company. Neither did he put on a stiff upper lip and smolder quietly by himself. Rather he used the occasion to transform a conflict into a healing possibility.

IV. If anger has taken deep root in your life, no one can promise you an immediate rose garden in its place. But there is in our anger the possibility of healing as well as the peril of hurting. If you discover that anger has locked up your life, remember the words Paul wrote from another kind of prison: "Be angry but do not sin." Let the day of your anger be the day of your reconciliation. That is one certain step toward making the new life he spoke of in Eph. 4:22–23 more clear and real in your life.—G. Stewart Barns.

February 3. Appreciation Is Life-Giving

TEXT: Phil. 2:3.

I. Appreciation is the chief source of happiness. William Lyon Phelps put it like this: "Appreciation begets grati-

tude and gratitude begets happiness."

(a) Appreciation does not take life for granted but is grateful for it. Ingratitude makes for misery and unhappiness. A woman said to her physician, "Doctor, why am I seized with these restless longings for the glamorous and far-away?" The doctor replied, "My dear lady, they are the usual symptoms of too much comfort in the home and too much ingratitude in the heart."

(b) It is a delusion to believe that only those who have a lot in life are the most thankful or the happiest. Satisfaction in life is not dependent upon substance. Some of the most radiant people you and I know have little substance. Yet they are happy.

(c) A person's real wealth consists in the condition of his mind and heart which makes for happiness. That condition depends upon how thankful he is for what he has. There is no greater virtue than that of gratitude. It is the basis of real satisfaction in life and real happiness.

II. Appreciation is the magic word which sets tired and discouraged men upon their feet again. It has a way of awakening sleeping powers within and helps restore self-confidence.

(a) Appreciation is the opposite from depreciation. Depreciation is sterile; appreciation is life-giving. "Appreciation stimulates and depreciation discourages."

(b) William Lyon Phelps wrote: "As a professional teacher I have had abundant opportunity to observe the developing power of encouragement and the sterilizing effect of scorn. People endeavor to live up to praise and to justify it, whereas cynicism and indifference will often extinguish a spark of talent."—W. Wallace Fridy.

February 10. Everybody Is a Somebody (Race Relations Sunday)

TEXT: Luke 8:45.

I. Everybody is a somebody. One life counts. Jesus said, "Who touched me?"

(a) The story of Jesus is a saga of human values. Always he was reaching out to individuals, giving meaning and worth to their lives. Never is his personal concern for individuals more obvious than with the woman in the crowd near Capernaum.

(b) There is a vital link between the rejection of God and of Jesus and today's ruthless inhumanity. Abraham Lincoln claimed the dignity of men and women is derivative. It is the belief that all people are valuable in God's sight which alone makes human life safe and free. The belief that everybody is a precious somebody derives from God.

II. Personal needs matter. (a) Jesus was stopped by compassion for a woman in need. He sensed her helplessness and hopelessness. Human need took precedence over everything else. He came to set a woman here, a man there, free truly to live.

(b) Let us imagine a crowd today. Anonymous people reach out hands of need. There amid the crowd are the desperately lonely, the unemployed, the sick of body and sick of heart, the sinful, and the guilty, people fearful of living and frightened of dying. The hands reach out, as of long ago, but so few see them or respond to them.

III. Every life can find fulfillment. (a) The historian Eusebius, writing about 300 A.D., says the nameless woman whom Jesus healed lived in Caesarea Philippi. He says he visited the house where she had lived and tells of a statue he saw in the garden. On an elevated stone was a brass statue of a kneeling woman with hands reaching out in supplication toward a standing figure of Jesus.

(b) A woman remembered who had made her whole. She had heard reports of Jesus. Those reports stimulated enough faith to act. She could not do much, but she could go where Jesus was and she could reach out and touch him. That faith was enough for Jesus. He was able to do so much with so little.

(c) We are not helpless. At least we can reach out a hand in faith and touch Jesus. He stands near to us in his risen power. His compassionate heart cannot pass human need by.—Alan Walker.

February 17. Caring (Brotherhood Week)

TEXT: Gal. 6:2.

I. Caring involves an affirmation of the other. I care when I feel deeply and am able to communicate that I believe the other is as capable of living his or her life as I am of living mine. I respect the other and his or her capacity to struggle with problems, find solutions, grow, and develop.

II. Caring requires me to distinguish carefully between what I can do and what I cannot do.

III. Caring is involved in the whole life of the other. I experience caring when my friends rejoice with me in my joy and acknowledge my success. You will care in times of tragedy, in times of trouble, and in times of puzzlement. You will also care in times of jubilation, in times of joy, and in times of daily routine.—Leo Rippy, Jr.

February 24. The Challenge of a Personal Faith (Lent)

TEXT: Rom. 10:8.

I. An inner radiant faith of our own that is worth having must always be adventurous.

II. We develop a creative, glorious faith as vicariously we make the truth of yesterday come alive in our own experience and thought.

III. An inner personal faith worth having must square with our word of truth, with reality, and with that which is intellectually acceptable.

IV. An inner personal faith makes a great difference in what we say, think, and do.

V. A faith worth having gives us power in the face of situations we wish to change. —Frank A. Court.

March 2. The Bible Speaks of Salvation (Lent)

TEXT: John 3:3.

As Jesus led Nicodemus to an understanding of God's plan of salvation, so the Bible clearly shows us the way to be saved.

I. The Bible teaches that every person needs to be saved. (See Isa. 53:6; 64:6; Jer. 17:9; Rom. 3:23.)

II. The Bible teaches that no one can save himself. We cannot save ourselves even though we do all kinds of good deeds including visiting the sick and feeding the poor. We must still go to Jesus by way of the cross. (See Prov. 14:12; John 14:1–6; Tit. 3:5.)

III. The Bible teaches that Jesus has already provided for the salvation of every individual. (See John 3:16–18; II Cor. 5: 21; I Pet. 3:18.)—C. R. Tedder.

March 9. What Christ Says (Lent)
TEXT: Heb. 5:9.

What are we to make of Christ? There is no question of what we can make of him. It is entirely a question of what he intends to make of us. You must accept or reject the story.

The things he says are very different from what any other teacher has said. Others say: "This is the truth about the universe. This is the way you ought to go." But he says, "I am the truth, and the way, and the life."

He says: "No man can reach absolute reality, except through me. Try to retain your own life and you will be inevitably ruined. Give yourself away and you will be saved."

He says: "If you are ashamed of me, if, when you hear this call, you turn the other way, I also will look the other way when I come again as God without disguise. If anything whatever is keeping you from God and from me, whatever it is, throw it away. If it is your eye, pull it out. If it is your hand, cut it off. If you put yourself first you will be last. Come to me everyone who is carrying a heavy load, I will set that right. Your sins, all of them, are wiped out, I can do that. I am rebirth, I am life. Eat me, drink me, I am your food. And finally do not be afraid, I have overcome the whole universe." That is the issue.—C. S. Lewis.

March 16. The Christian's Accent (Lent)
SCRIPTURE: Matt. 26:69–75.

I. *The Christian accent of certainty.* Peter's initial accent of confusion started his downfall: "I don't know what you are talking about," he said. Similarly some nominal Christians betray their ignorance and confusion. But Jesus' words had a note of authentic truth: "The crowd was astonished at the power behind his teaching. For his words had the ring of authority." (Matt. 7:29, PHILLIPS.)

II. *The Christian accent of confession.* Peter's next step was to disclaim any personal knowledge of Christ. "And Peter said with an oath, 'I do not know the man!' " Three years of blessed friendship were thrown to the winds. The master's matchless teachings; the lord's patient treatment of his very impetuous nature; Christ's trusting friendship—all denied in the accent of ignorance. There was a time at Caesarea Philippi when Jesus asked, "Who do you say I am?" Peter had replied with the positive confession, "You are the Christ, the son of the living God!" (Matt. 16:16).

III. *The Christian accent of commitment.* Peter's final downward step was the disavowal of his personal ties to the Christian fellowship. "I do not belong to them!" he insisted. Sadly enough it was at least temporarily true. He was with the wrong crowd; he was influenced by their hostile thinking. Unfortunately, even though they may not disclaim the Christian church, many believers surely act as though they did not really belong to it. The Christian church certainly deserves a high priority in all our relationships. And that requires the Christian accent of personal commitment in belonging to Jesus and to his cause.— Emil Kontz.

March 23. The Way of the Cross (Passion Sunday)
TEXT: Gal. 6:14.

I. The cross is the chief symbol of Christianity. We place it at the center of our altars, erect it at the top of our church steeples, even use it as an emblem hung around our necks.

II. The cross is the evidence of God's love. It is a constant reminder of the greatest gift ever given to humankind and is a way in which the creator has said to the human race, "I love you."

III. The cross is the unveiling of the heart of God. It tells us that our heavenly Father is not a stern judge but a creator of love and mercy. He is the kind of God that will suffer for humankind, forgive the worst of sins, and even stop making worlds to attend the funeral of a little sparrow. He sees the widow's mite and searches for the lost sheep.

IV. The cross is a philosophy of life. It tells us that we only gain our lives by losing them. It says in the language of Arthur J. Moore: "You cannot bless unless you bleed. You cannot save unless you serve. You cannot lift unless you stoop. No great reform has ever come to pass, no great advancement in any field of life has come until somebody forgot himself, until somebody rid himself of selfishness and thought in terms of stewardship and cross bearing."

V. It is the way of the cross that shall achieve life abundant upon this earth and heaven beyond it. It is the greatest possession that we have.—William M. Holt in *Wesleyan Christian Advocate.*

March 30. The Majesty of Jesus (Palm Sunday)

TEXT: Mark 15:2.

I. We see the majesty of Jesus in the way he speaks with directness about the kingdom of God. He makes no effort to negotiate with Pilate or the crowd. He declares his purpose is to reveal God and his kingdom to all persons.

II. We see the majesty of Jesus in his heroic physical courage. Here is one place where our belief in the incarnation must be clear. It was the human Jesus who confronted the cross. God did not somehow immunize Jesus against the physical torture and mental anguish of these hours. Nothing less than heroic physical courage could have enabled him to bear all this with the dignity and concern for others that were apparent in so many instances.

III. We see the regal majesty of Jesus in the poised silence of the master in the face of the events that now were transpiring. He spoke "not a mumblin' word" in the face of this injustice, threat to his own life, apparent failure of his mission, outrageous lies of those who accused him, and complete failure of Pilate to see the dynamics in which he found himself with Jesus.

IV. The secret of that majesty is found in the fact that the source of Jesus' power is in God. He was not "on his own" as was Pilate. He was linked to a divine source of strength which gave him power beyond his own in that and any situation. If it was his power that gave him the regal majesty we see in these fateful hours, then you can be certain that it was a divine power which God makes available to every person in his own form of the human predicament.— Hoover Rupert.

April 6. Stones that Are Rolled Away (Easter)

TEXT: John 20:1.

I. G. Ashton Oldham said that "the stone was moved not to let Jesus out but to let the disciples in." The open tomb let the disciples enter into the glory of a new faith. They came expecting to find a dead Jesus; they were met with the revelation of a risen Lord. They came in the depth of despair; they left radiant with joy. They came in fear; they left with courage.

II. What happened to Jesus is our hope. What happened to his followers is our great assurance.

(a) It is good to know that truth cannot be entombed; it is encouraging to realize that believers cannot be excluded from what lies beyond the stone. Evil may seal the hopes of mankind in some grave, but God never stands for that too long. When God enters life, stones are rolled away.

(b) "The guards trembled." Of course they did. Man cannot defeat God. The moral order of the universe can be a frightening thing. But to all who believe, it is the ground for hope.—Roy L. Minich.

April 13. Why We Come to Worship

TEXT: Mic. 6:6.

I. Not because it is a duty but because it is a delight.

II. Not because a preacher called on us but because God hath called to us.

III. Not to display to the world our faith in God but to witness to the world our faith in God.

IV. Not to smirk at others for our goodness but to search together for God's righteousness.

V. Not to listen as others are condemned but to be told how we have sinned.

VI. Not to be satisfied with knowing religion's rules but to surrender all to the kingdom's rule.

VII. Not to take away what God will give

us but to go away fitted for service.—
Thomas Russell.

April 20. Call to Discipleship

TEXT: Luke 9:23.

I. Discipleship demands self-denial: "let him deny himself." (a) The disciple has said no to self-sufficiency for the central issues of life.

(b) The disciple says no to self-service as central motive for living.

II. Discipleship centers in the cross: "let him . . . take up his cross daily." (a) The disciple has said yes to the cross of Christ as the foundation of his entire Christian life.

(b) The disciple says yes to the cross of Christ as the mode of his daily Christian living.

III. Discipleship focuses in Jesus: "let him . . . follow me." (a) The disciple simply follows Jesus as the enabler for life.

(b) The disciple continually follows Jesus as the model for living.—Frank G. Carver.

April 27. Keeping Your Balance

TEXT: Heb. 12:2.

I. Realize that everything that is happening to you has probably happened to thousands of others before you, perhaps in slightly different settings, but they're basically the same trials, temptations, and pressures.

II. Cultivate a sense of God's place in human history. The Bible is full of prayers which are in effect a reminder to him that he has delivered his people before, so they are expecting him to do it again.

III. Realize that God will never ask you to do anything for which he will not also give you his all-sufficient grace.

IV. Cultivate a healthy sense of humor. There is a time to weep, but there is also a time to laugh. It is a wise person who knows how and when to laugh at life.

V. Cultivate a wholesome humility. To know that God does not need you to run the universe is a healthy realization; and to know that you need him—need him every split second of your life—and that he will not turn you away is like opening a window in a darkened room on a sunny day.

VI. Become involved in a cause greater than yourself—something big enough for God to get into.

VII. Learn the value of prayer when under pressure.

VIII. Learn that one deliberate step of obedience to God banishes fear and opens the door to his miracle power in your life. —Robert A. Cook.

May 4. Creating a Christian Climate in the Home (National Family Week)

TEXT: II Cor. 3:18 (PHILLIPS).

I. A Christian family believes in God as revealed in Jesus Christ and the word of God.

II. A Christian family accepts Jesus Christ as lord and savior of each individual life, as master of collective life, and as manager of household life.

III. A Christian family takes the biblical purpose of family living seriously and strives to teach (Deut. 6:7), to train (Prov. 2:6), to nurture (Eph. 6:4), to provide (II Cor. 12:14), to respect (I Tim. 3:4), and to love (Tit. 2:4).

IV. A Christian family shares together in worship experiences, in Bible reading time, and in loving relationships in the spirit of the living God.

V. A Christian family lives in a climate of the fruit of the Spirit and sets the family thermostat at "love, joy, peace, patience, kindness, goodness, faithfulness, gentleness, and self-control" (Gal. 5:22–23; NIV). —Paul L. Walker.

May 11. Guidance for Christian Parents (Mother's Day)

TEXT: Luke 18:16.

Faith is caught, not taught. It is a spirit which comes from God through other people. It does not come from right living; right living comes from it. We act according to what we believe; we do not believe according to how we act. If a parent is going to transmit faith to his child, he must practice that faith by teaching, by prayer, and by example. Here are a few basics:

I. Teach the child to pray by praying with him at night.

II. Ask a blessing before every meal.

III. Do not send your children to church school. They know when they are being sent. Lead them by going to church yourself. They will take it just as seriously as you but not more seriously.

IV. Read them the Bible or a book of Bible stories.

V. Live, talk, think, act, and pray as though Christ is a member of your family. Then he will be. And your child will be his child in this life and in the world to come. —Jack Van Ens.

May 18. The Christian's Company

TEXT: Matt. 18:20.

Most of us know what it is to wait for a friend to meet us. Even though a time and a place have been agreed on, some are habitually late. Not so with Jesus, for his presence goes with us. There is no waiting for him.

I. *The promise of his presence.* Jesus, the Christian's company, assured his followers that he would be with them. His presence provides the needed company for one on all occasions. There is much talk about loneliness in the world today, especially among the elderly. It will be well to claim the promise of Jesus: where two or three are gathered, I will be with you.

II. *The purpose of his company with believers.* To give a sense of security, a sense of unity, a mission to perform, and a message to proclaim. Jesus wants to go into the world through the life of his followers, to love the sinner through his people, and to teach his people how to live in the world.

III. *The power of his company.* The church needs power to carry on the work which the lord intends. For the power the church does not depend on the presence of a large number of people, but the church does depend on the presence of Christ. By such power the faith of each believer is increased and those in sin come to know Christ.—Gowan Ellis.

May 25. The Early Church Prevails (Pentecost)

TEXT: Acts 4:32.

The church was able to make it through those early trials because the group had four things in common besides their money.

I. A common fear, not fear of opposition but fear that they might fail.

II. A common need, for they needed each other's encouragement and companionship.

III. A common memory, for they shared the story of the life and work of Jesus.

IV. A common expectation, for they believed that the reign of God, already manifested in Jesus, would become fully triumphant.—Irwin Edman.

June 1. Young People Looking Ahead (Baccalaureate)

TEXT: Jer. 1:7 (RSV).

I. Present yourself wholly unto God. That seems rather obvious, and you can well reply that you did that a long time ago, perhaps when you first joined the church. But there is a very practical benefit in reviewing this act of commitment periodically. You may come up with some area of your life that you have never really committed. Nor is this just you alone searching yourself, but it is allowing God to search you.

II. Practice a spiritual discipline in your life. This is an absolute necessity to maintain a growing edge to our faith. Failure at this point contributes largely to the spiritual anemia of our present Christian experience. "God does not reveal his will for your life by air mail, special delivery." He works it out in our consciousness, day by day, year by year, as we walk closely in step with him.

III. Seek your place in the church. The New Testament nowhere considers the idea that a Christian can exist apart from the church. But what is your role in it? We all have different gifts. Discover your gift, your talent, and then value it as highly as the God who gave it to you. It won't be the same as your neighbor's, else the world wouldn't need both of you. Do your thing.

IV. Make love the cardinal principle of your life. Jesus went to the synagogue on the sabbath day. The rest of the week he was out on the streets, in the marketplace, down by the seashore, wherever the people were. And he carried his ministry of love wherever he went.—J. Sherrard Rice.

June 8. Who Has the Right to Judge?
SCRIPTURE: John 8:3–11.

I. Who has the right to judge? Jesus' answer would be, "No one, for only those without fault have any right to judge the faults of others." Since all of us have faults, only God has the right to judge. A pastor told me: "I've discovered that judging is God's business, and he can do a much better job than I can. Since I've left that to him, I am much happier."

II. What should our attitude be to someone who has sinned? The old golden rule which is ever new would apply here: "Do unto others as you would have them do unto you." Instead of seeking to punish the sinner, we should ask, "What can I do to help?"

III. Is Jesus too free in his forgiving and does he overlook sin? (a) He said to the woman: "I do not condemn you either. Go, but do not sin again." He was not saying: "Don't worry. It's all right now. You've got it made." He was giving her a second chance. A judge in our modern courts may give a person a second chance. The person found guilty may be given a suspended sentence; if he behaves himself and follows certain requirements, he will not have to serve that sentence.

(b) Along with the second chance, Jesus challenged her to live a better life—"do not sin again." Here is a woman who one moment is confronted with the possibility of dying and the next moment with the challenge to take life and live it on a much higher level than she had ever imagined. Jesus confronts the bad life and gives the challenge to live a good life.—Walter A. Whitehurst.

June 15. What God Is Doing in Your Life
TEXT: Phil. 2:12–13 (TEV).

I. "God is always at work" in our lives through his activity in the universe which is our home.

II. God is the author of the beauty we perceive.

III. God is at work in Jesus Christ.

IV. God is showing that his purpose in

history is to support the good, the true, all that the Bible means by its great word righteousness.

V. When we pass into any valley of shadow—serious illness, personal heartbreak, the loss of someone very dear—God comes as the presence to heal, to comfort, to reassure us that "there never shall be one lost good."—David A. MacLennan.

June 22. Freedom in Three Dimensions
SCRIPTURE: Luke 15:11–32.

I. The father had *freedom unequaled.* If the father in the story represents Jesus—as many of us would think—and if real freedom is freedom to do as we ought, then the prayer of our Lord in the garden, "Not as I will, but as you will" (Matt. 26:39, NIV), is an example of freedom unequaled.

II. The prodigal son had *freedom unbalanced.* There was an overload of self, and it kept the real freedom—love—from getting through.

III. The elder son had *freedom unused.* In v. 31 the father says to the elder son, "My son . . . you are always with me, and everything I have is yours." Paul reminds us in Ephesians of the "unsearchable riches" we have in Christ. And how many of those riches—spiritual freedoms—are unused in our spiritual pilgrimage.—C. Neil Strait.

June 29. Assured of God's Aid
TEXT: Rom. 8:28.

Note the certainty with which Paul writes, "We know," not claiming that everything is good or that things automatically work out for good but that in any and every situation we can rely on God's help. No misfortune can separate us from his love.

I. A condition is attached to this assurance of aid. It is for "those who love him," who respond to God's call. This is a reasonable condition. God can give his powerful aid more effectively to those who love him than to those who ignore him.

II. This assurance, really accepted, enables us to feel a divine companionship as we come up against the troubles of life. We need support beyond our own slender powers and resources.

III. To be assured of God's powerful aid in everything sharpens our insight. We become better able to discover possibilities in limited situations.

IV. Assured of God's powerful aid, we can keep going patiently and persistently, believing there will be a way out although it is not yet apparent. Sometimes we go about as if we had everything to do, yet we discover that in strange and unexpected ways doors are opened, solutions appear to problems, and unrealized strength arises within us. This is much more likely to happen if our faith remains active, if we believe God has ways of working beyond our own, if we do everything we now know to do, and if we wait patiently for new guidance from God.

V. An assurance of God's powerful aid in everything enables us to handle tragic experiences with greater calmness and courage. It is too much to hope life will not involve us each one, sooner or later, in trouble, hardship, and suffering. Perhaps even now some of us feel ourselves to be so involved. Nothing will help us so much in any such experience as quiet acceptance of God's aid and interest.—J. Francis F. Peak.

July 6. Doing What You Can

TEXT: Mark 14:8.

Our Lord praised the woman who anointed him with expensive spikenard. He commended her not merely for what she did but also for doing what she could.

I. All of us need to learn to do what we can. Very little is accomplished by talkers and dreamers who say, "If only I had more money, more time, more ability, or better health." Such individuals sit on the sidelines and do almost nothing for God, others, or themselves. God knows what we can do, and what we can do becomes our responsibility.

II. We need to do what we can while we can. This woman seized the time and opportunity at hand. She couldn't have done what she did a week later. Opportunities must be taken before they slip away, never to return again.

III. We need to do what we can for Jesus. Jesus was the object of her devotion; love for him was her motive. She was not thinking of herself. She was not seeking attention or approval of others.

IV. We need to do what we can even when it calls for sacrifice. Spikenard was a highly prized perfume, worth a year's wages.

V. We need to do what we can regardless of criticism. There is so much that people could do and would do if they forgot about what others might think or say.

VI. If we do what we can, the Lord will praise us. Jesus defended the woman's action, commended her service, and praised her devotion to him. Imagine her joy as he said that her generous act would be proclaimed throughout the world. He saw in her spirit and her service an example of the love of God at work.—Carl R. Nelson.

July 13. How to Change the World

SCRIPTURE: Acts 1:1–14.

I. They had the excitement of personal knowledge. (See Acts 1:1–3.)

II. They had the excitement of fellowship with Jesus. (See Acts 1:4.)

III. They had the excitement of anticipation. (See Acts 1:9.)

IV. They had the excitement of obedience. (See Acts 1:12.)

V. They had the excitement of communication with God. (See Acts 1:14.)—Billy Weber.

July 20. God's Glory Revealed in His Word

SCRIPTURE: Ps. 19:7–10.

I. God's word is perfect. (See v. 7.) The law of God reveals to us our duty both to God and to our fellowman.

II. God's word is sure. (See v. 7.) We can always depend on what the Bible reveals.

III. God's word is right. (See v. 8.) In the Bible man has a perfect standard of righteousness.

IV. God's word is pure. (See v. 8.) God has never commanded man to do anything that is degrading or wrong.

V. God's word is true and righteous. (See v. 9.) It depicts the true course of right conduct.

VI. God's word is desirable. (See v. 10.) It is worth more than money. The spiritual nourishment and enjoyment gained by a study of the Bible far exceeds the satisfaction gained from eating the finest honey. —H. C. Chiles.

July 27. Worldly and Spiritual Success

Text: II Tim. 4:7.

I. God's standards of success differ from the world's. In Luke 16:15 Jesus affirms, "What is highly esteemed among men is an abomination with God."

II. The Bible turns values topsy-turvy, puts first what men put last and last what men put first. It praises the failure that is success and denounces the success that is failure. Paul warns us in I Corinthians that the achievements prized by the world—gold, silver, and precious stones—may be written off by God as wood, hay, and stubble. And when the writer of Heb. 11 lists successful people, the overwhelming majority turn out to be worldly failures—people in conflict with their societies, people like Jesus and Stephen and Paul and Peter who died as criminals, not the sort of ecclesiastical big-wigs who get invited to a presidential prayer breakfast.

III. God has established certain standards of success. His criteria are not pulpit eloquence, communication skill, penetrating insight, remarkable gifts, encyclopedic knowledge, or mountain-moving faith. His criterion is Christlike love (I Cor. 13:1–3). Matt. 20:25–27 tells us that service inspired by a Christlike love is a mark of success. And in Matt. 25:21 a third criterion of spiritual success is the faithful use of the talents God has given us. Whether we have five talents, two or one, we are to use and multiply them in God's service.— Vernon C. Grounds.

August 3. Why?

Text: Ps. 22:1.

I. "Why" goes beyond all considerations of "who," "what," "when," and "where" because of all these "why" is the most inexhaustible. In speaking of various chemicals, physiological structures, behavioral patterns, historical certitudes, advanced dating methods, geographical identifications, or galactic locations we can begin to get a handle on the "who," "what," "when," and "where"

aspects of existence. Not so with "why."

II. "Why" goes far beyond the mere boundaries of description. "Why" implies that there are answers to the deep questions of mankind, questions of purpose, design, and significance. "Why" when posed in continual sincerity addresses God who alone has sufficient perspective to answer the ultimate questions.

III. It is at the feet of God that significance, purpose, and meaning can begin to make sense before the all penetrating "why" of man's insatiable curiosity. Though coming to God does not immediately answer all the "whys" in the universe, it is the foundation from which they begin to unfold. Why "why"? Why else if not the intuition of a grand scheme of which we are part?—Randal Lee Cummings.

August 10. My Church

Text: Rev. 2:19.

I. My church is an inheritance, the result of struggle and sorrow through which multitudes passed in other days.

II. My church is an entrustment, and I must pass on a richer, more spiritual organization to the next generation.

III. My church is the church of my brother, and I must live in helpful relationship to him.

IV. My church is the church of a group, and I must relate myself to their opinions and decisions.

V. My church worships, and I must join others in prayer and praise.

VI. My church is an evangelist, and I must take part in its program in winning others.

VII. My church can only be held together by love, and I must seek to practice and inspire others to live this "excellent way."

August 17. Christians and Animals

Can we define the human attitude to animals taught by the Bible?

I. We should study them. God's works are "studied by all who have pleasure in them" (Ps. 111:2). All Christians should take an interest in natural history, especially town dwellers who have to take greater initiatives to do so. As we study

God's creatures and so "think his thoughts after him," we marvel at them.

II. We may use them. God has given us permission to domesticate the animal creation, so that we may use their strength to carry our burdens (cf. Num. 7:1–11), their skins to clothe us (cf. Gen 3:21), and their flesh to feed us (cf. Gen 9:1–3; Mark 7:19).

III. We are to be kind to them. Kindness to animals is enjoined in scripture. For God himself created and sustains them, as he created and sustains us: "Men and animals are in your care" (Ps. 36:6, GNB). So in the Old Testament animals were to be given their day's rest on the sabbath as well as humans (Exod. 20:10; 23:12), bird's nesting was restricted (Deut. 22:6, 7), and oxen were not to be muzzled while threshing corn (Deut. 25:4). In brief, "a good man takes care of his animals" (Prov. 12:10, GNB).—John R. W. Stott.

August 24. Christian Worship

SCRIPTURE: I Cor. 13–15 (NIV).

Floyd Filson says: "True worship, Paul implies, is never the unaided action of man, even the devout man. It is rather the attitude and expression which the Holy Spirit prompts and guides. The Spirit is the key person in true Christian worship."

I. The true Christian in every worship service ought to pray. (See I Cor. 14:15.)

II. The true Christian in every worship service ought to sing. (See I Cor. 14:15.)

III. The true Christian in every worship service ought to praise God. (See I Cor. 14:16.)

IV. The true Christian in every worship service ought to speak, that is, take his part in participation in the service. (See I Cor. 12:4–6; 14:3.)

V. The true Christian in every worship service ought to be united with fellow believers. (See I Cor. 12:12, 27.)

VI. The true Christian in every worship service ought to worship in love. (See I Cor. 13:1; 14:1.)—Derl G. Keefer.

August 31. Guidelines for the Christian Worker (Labor Sunday)

TEXT: Gen. 2:15.

I. Believe in Jesus Christ. When we walk with the master it becomes possible for us to think properly about our work. Those who have been captured by the grace of Jesus can begin to live without selfishness and fear. They can begin to pattern their lives after the pattern found in the Bible. Following Jesus they find themselves in the company of a person who was known to his contemporaries as a carpenter. And when he described his mission as the son of God, he described it in terms of work: "My father works . . . and I work."

II. Train yourself to seek work that has to be done. There's a job to be done, and it is probably close at hand. If you don't work, the quality of your life will deteriorate.

III. Develop imagination and innovation. One of the reasons many people do not work enough is that they think of work and a job only in terms of some employer coming to them and asking them to work for such and such pay at such and such a job.

IV. Train yourself to do unpleasant work. Someone has said that each of us should do at least one thing that he dislikes doing each day. Don't think that certain kinds of work are beneath your dignity. Some of us have pretty fancy jobs, and we wouldn't be caught doing certain menial jobs around our company. What's the matter? Are you too good to get your hands dirty and take hold of something and lift your part of the load? If you have found that there are certain kinds of work that are too dirty, too strenuous, and too demanding, ask yourself what has happened to you. Get in there and pitch and you'll be the better person for it.—Joel H. Nederhood.

September 7. The Church Needs Teachers (Rally Day)

TEXT: Matt. 28:20.

I. *I should* teach because I must share the faith which others have shared with me, and I realize that I must seek truth if I am to impart wisdom.

II. *I should* teach because I love the smile that lights up the expectant and trusting faces of little children when they are told that Jesus is their friend.

III. *I should* teach because I am moved with joy when young people come to the realization that Christ has an answer for their problems when they follow him as their guide.

IV. *I should* teach because the church needs my voice, my heart, and my hands to point out to all men the eternal way of life.

V. *I should* teach because in this chaotic and confusing world the voice of God must ring clearer and stronger than the turbulent noises of the world.

VI. *I should* teach because it was all settled for me on a hillside outside of Jerusalem when the master teacher commissioned his disciples, "Go . . . teach."—William D. Webber.

September 14. Walking with God

Text: Mic. 6:8.

I. God yearns for us to walk with him because we are the children of his love. He is eager to have fellowship with us. God is so eager for our companionship that he is willing to bear any cross in order to win it. Christ did not die for a mass of people, but he died for the individual. Every person is important to God, and he longs to have fellowship with everyone of us.

II. God longs for our fellowship not only because he cannot be satisfied without us but also because he knows that we can never be satisfied without him. Every man is possessed of a hunger for God that nothing else can satisfy. It is true that we often do not know what it is for which we hunger and thirst, but it remains forever true that there is no true satisfaction for the human soul apart from God.

III. God longs for our fellowship because he knows that it is only as we walk with him that we shall really be just and kind. Justice and kindness at their best flow out of a close relationship with God. When the fellowship is broken, justice and kindness will dry up.—A. Ray Adams.

September 21. Four Steps to Salvation

Text: Rom. 13:11.

I. The first step to salvation is to bring yourself to Christ. (See Matt. 11:28.) Many people delay their coming to Christ with the excuse that they are not able to live a Christian life, and they are right to a point.

They cannot live for Christ in their own strength, but this is where man's extremity becomes God's opportunity. (See Phil. 4:13.)

II. After you come to Christ, the next step is to repent. God commands that you repent. (See Acts 17:30.) Webster's dictionary defines the word "repent" as "a change of mind with regard to the past or intended action; to feel regret, contrition for what one has done or omitted to do." The word of God states that "godly sorrow worketh repentance" (II Cor. 7:10). So when you repent with godly sorrow, you experience a change of mind and heart, your attitude changes, and you become a new person. When this transformation through Christ takes place, you become a new creature in Christ Jesus.

III. The third step to salvation is to believe. To believe is essential to your relationship with God. (See Mark 1:15.) Believing is simply accepting by faith that Jesus Christ has forgiven your sins and that his spirit abides in your heart. (See Acts 16:31.) The act of believing is your weapon against you to make you doubt your new birth.

IV. The fourth step to salvation is to confess. Make known or acknowledge before men that this marvelous transition has taken place in your life. (See Matt. 10:32-33.) To confess or to share Jesus Christ with others is a must to a born-again Christian. If we expect God to acknowledge us, then we must acknowledge him before others.—Owen McManus.

September 28. Empowered to Become

Text: Rom. 12:15.

Empowered by God's love, we can become a church in which people can share diversity without divisiveness and can disagree without being disagreeable, still maintaining the deep friendship and fellowship of continuing dialogue. We can share the hopes and feelings of the apostle Paul as he yearned for a fellowship in Christ that says, "If one hurts, all hurt; if one rejoices, all rejoice." We can receive the power from God to become a dynamic community of faith that will accomplish the following:

I. Bring people together when they are alienated.

II. Restore them to hope when they are discouraged.

III. Lift up their hearts when they are in despair.

IV. Hold before the confused multitudes a vision of a new heaven and a new earth.—James A. Moak.

October 5. In the Fullness of Time (World Communion Sunday)

TEXT: John 17:21.

Today in churches all over the world Christians are united in a common observance of World Communion Sunday. If we may assume that Holy Communion is, has been, or will be observed at the conventional church hour of 11 a.m. in each of the world's time belts, then we here at 11 a.m. are one link in a chain that encircles this globe.

This is a thrilling picture. Granted, Christians around the world have not yet overcome their individual differences of racial intolerance, theological bickering, and denominational pride. Yet a bit of light shines forth for, even though we partake separately and in different modes, Christians around the world have been more closely united by the mutual observance of Holy Communion on this special Sunday.

Is this not the greatest visible evidence of the past few decades that proves a dawning consciousness of the community of oneness of the church of Christ in a severely divided world?

One hundred and fifty years ago there were no Christians in two-thirds of the world's areas. Today there is no land where there are not at least some Christians and only one with no Christian church. In every world capital but two there is a Christian church.

The most commonly used name for the sacrament of the Lord's Supper is eucharist, a term derived from the Greek word for thanksgiving. So Holy Communion is a time of thanksgiving. It is a time of giving thanks for our own knowledge of Jesus Christ and of his saving power and presence in our lives, of giving thanks for the good news of God's love which is covering the world, and of giving thanks for the visible evidence of the unity that is growing between the many groups of people known as his church.

"Thy kingdom come" sounds possible on a Sunday like this one as Christians of every age, race, and creed put aside their self-seeking, prides, and prejudices and worship the Christ.—Harrison R. Thompson.

October 12. Some Things I Have Learned About People (Laity Sunday)

TEXT: Gal. 5:6 (RSV).

Every pastor or counselor has learned many things from the people with whom he or she has worked. These are some of my observations.

I. Everyone has problems. Life is difficult, and no one escapes its difficulty completely.

II. Our problems are a means of growth and strength. An old professor of mine used to say, "It is out of our greatest difficulties that our greatest insights come."

III. People have amazing capacities for courage and inner resources of strength.

IV. Most people are doing about as well as they know how. I do not say as well as they could but as well as they know how.

V. Most people have a potential for growth and development far beyond what they have attained as yet.—Charles F. Kemp.

October 19. Grace According to Paul

TEXT: II Cor. 15:10.

Paul uses the word "grace" 101 times, giving grace an enriched meaning.

I. God's graciousness has been uniquely revealed in his incredible generosity in giving his son to the world. Jesus Christ has been and continues to be God's supreme act of grace, imparting to man new significance and meaning.

II. This grace through Christ can accomplish for man what he cannot do for himself. Through Christ he really becomes alive and "turned on." This is a free gift of God. No matter how hard he tries man cannot earn this gift.

III. Grace not only brings man into a

new standing with God but also releases individual potentialities which enrich the community and glorify God.

IV. Paul's experience of God's grace adds to his humility and his awareness that he owes everything to God.

V. When we must endure suffering such as Paul's "thorn in the flesh," the grace of God sustains us. Grace is love radiating under pressure.

October 26. The New Protestants (Reformation Sunday)

Text: I Pet. 2:9.

I. The Protestant Reformation was an endeavor to simplify the gospel.

(a) Someone described the Christian church in the medieval days as "a ship that had collected a mass of barnacles and needed scraping." We can adorn Christ, worship him, sentimentalize about him, distort him, and miss what he really meant to say to us.

(b) The new Protestants are saying the church seems at times so preoccupied with self and preservation that it has little time or interest in promoting human life. So the new Protestants are asking, "Can the church be freed from the sickness of its self-concern?"

(c) To simplify means that the church's task is to pour out into the world a new quality of human life. It is not just to enhance its own life, but to enhance the life of the world through the spirit of Jesus Christ. Jesus came to save the world, not just the church.

II. The reformers then and now are seeking a new understanding of God. The medieval church believed that God was in the sacred order, and the highest calling was to the holy orders. God was identified primarily with the church. It was interpreted to many to mean that you could not encounter God anywhere else. The secular world was outside the holy, and this division was very sharp.

(a) The new Protestants are asking, "What do we mean by God?" God is not some distant figure to be implored to come and visit us in special moments. He is not one who resides above the world of mankind. We often invoke God's presence as though he were far away and we are asking him to come.

(b) These new Protestants are saying if all of life is one, the secular and the sacred all wrapped up together, then God is here and now in our daily living. And if we quit thinking that God is residing in heaven or in cathedrals, we may start seeing him in our needy neighbors whom we so easily ignore.

(c) What the new Protestants are proclaiming has its roots in the Reformation. One's job in dealing with people and issues and problems is just as important as a priest at the altar. God is wherever there are human struggles and human issues and human sorrows.

III. The third thing is what the early Reformers and the new Protestants mean by witnessing.

(a) Some think of witnessing as trying to sell their religion. The apostle Paul in one translation said we are not peddlers of God's word. Peter Marshall said: "That which we call salvation is a free gift. You can't buy it nor can you earn it. No idea hurts me more than suggesting that I am a salesman endeavoring to sell people on the idea of religion."

(b) The new Protestants feel that the faith is a living testimony, not just a talking one. This kind of communication means one is willing to identify and to listen and to respond when there is interest or need. Then people will begin to ask why Christians do the things they do, and the church will earn its right to be heard.

(c) The new Protestants say the authentic way to witness for our Lord is by the values we live by, by the decisions we make every day, by the priority of our time, by simple honesty, and by the attitudes that we emit. Even the work of my hands and of my mind can be of such quality as to give eloquence to my devotion.

(d) An essential truth that both the new and the old reformers have is that the renewal of the church is ultimately God's doing and not man's. Man often becomes anxious and panicky about the state of the church and our hopes for renewal without recognizing that we are powerless to renew the life of the church. As agents we must open ourselves to the inflow of God's grace. If we receive the gift, we can be the agents of renewal.—C. A. McClain, Jr.

November 2. Changed by Looking
TEXT: II Cor. 3:18.

I. *By looking at his teachings.* Jesus was preeminently a teacher and his favorite name for those who came to him was disciple meaning learner or student. In his parable of the two houses (Matt. 7:24–27) Jesus illustrates the crucial importance of his teaching as the only way to an enduring life. (See Jas. 1:21–25.)

II. *By looking at his character.* Jesus was a real human being. The Bible goes to great lengths to insist on his humanity. (See John 1:14; 14:8–9; Col. 1:15.) The essential feature about the Christian religion is not its teachings, important as they are. Its central reality is the person of Christ. He was the living incarnation of his teachings. So we need to focus our attention upon the wonderful divine character of Christ. (See II Cor. 4:6.) People who make a habit of fixing their gaze on the person of Christ will begin to conform to the pattern of his life and likeness.

III. *By following his example.* Jesus enjoyed having people become his students, and he appreciated having people as his admirers. But most of all he wanted people to become his followers. His constant summons was "Follow me!" He wanted the personal commitment which led to loyal obedience to his divine will. He said repeatedly, "I have given you an example to follow" (John 13:15, LB). And it was a demanding challenge. (See Mark 8:34.) He also added this further injunction: "This I command you, love one another" (John 15:17).—Emil Kontz.

November 9. The Prodigal's Conversion
SCRIPTURE: Luke 15:17–20.

The steps of the prodigal's conversion follow a pattern.

I. There was the failure to find fulfillment and meaning in the path he had chosen for his life. This was followed by a certain kind of disgust or disenchantment. Then he experienced some heavy loss which demonstrated for him the transcience of life. We don't have anything forever—our loved ones, our vitality, or our health. After that came a yearning, a reaching of his soul for peace and comfort.

II. He was now ready for an intellectual thought. He thought about his father's house, his father's food, and of his father's forgiving love. He will make me something, if not his son again, then at least his servant. Humility had come to the lad. Humility is a necessary ingredient for anyone who seeks truly to find God. The man in Jesus' parable, who humbled himself in the temple, prayed, "Father, be merciful to me a sinner." Jesus said, "That man went away forgiven."

III. It is one thing to say, "I will arise and go to my father and say to him, 'I have sinned.' " It is another thing to do it. All of his guilt, disgust, hunger, yearning, and humility would have been to no avail had he stayed where he was. He took a look at the hogs. He took a look at the sky overhead. He took a long look at the hills rising up before him in the distance. He stood nervously to his feet, swallowed some tears that were choking him, and headed for home. It was a difficult decision, but it was the greatest decision of his life.—Jerry Hayner.

November 16. How We Silence the Bible
TEXT: Isa. 29:24.

I. The Bible is silenced when it is used to confirm values we already hold.

II. The Bible is silenced when the historical distance between its world and the world of today is ignored.

III. The Bible is silenced when it is left in its own world and not allowed to illumine the present.—*United Church Observer.*

November 23. Thanksgiving in Times of Crisis (Thanksgiving Sunday)
SCRIPTURE: I Cor. 1:4–9.

Anyone can be thankful when things are going well, when health is good, money is in the bank, and life's problems are all solved. But it is a different kind of person who gives thanks to God when things are not going well. Perhaps health is gone, material needs are not being met, loneliness has replaced companionship, and life's problems are multiplying. Anyone can give thanks in times of prosperity. God can help us to be thankful in times of crisis.

I. There is thanksgiving for the promise of God. (See v. 6.) His testimony is now confirmed. What Christ said is true, and what he promised is fulfilled. Like the church at Corinth we tend to forget this. Let us be thankful for God's promise and its fulfillment.

II. There is thanksgiving for the gift of God. (See v. 7.) Here the word *charisma* is used, and it means a gift freely given, a gift not deserved, a gift which cannot be earned. The gift is God's only begotten son, the price of our redemption. Salvation is God's gift to us, and for that we should be thankful.

III. There is thanksgiving for the hope of God. (See v. 8.) We have hope for the future. Judgment day causes no panic in the heart of the Christian whose hope is in Christ. Even in times of crisis we can be thankful for our hope.—James McGraw.

November 30. Interpreting the Second Coming (Advent)

TEXT: II Pet. 3:4.

I. The return did not occur in Paul's day in the form he expected it.

II. Such a return has not yet occurred.

III. The failure of Jesus to return as expected created much difficulty for the early Christian church.

IV. Entire books or portions of books in the New Testament were written for the purpose of clearing up the thinking of Christians on this subject.

V. Paul gave it less and less attention as his ministry progressed.

VI. Many dates have been set for the return, but none has ever proved to be correct.

VII. All efforts to figure out the time have thus far proved altogether fruitless, there being no better evidence in the case now than in the beginning.

VIII. Jesus disclaimed all knowledge of any date that had been fixed.

IX. Controversy over the subject has divided the church and embittered Christians toward one another.

X. Such a subject should be dealt with very cautiously, lest greater harm than good result.—Roy L. Smith.

December 7. The Inconvenience of Christmas (Advent)

TEXTS: Mal. 3:2; Luke 2:6–7.

I. The first Christmas did not come at a very convenient time. The emperor, Caesar Augustus, had issued an order that the inhabitants of his empire return to the city of their family origin to be enrolled in a census and to pay their taxes. That necessitated the carpenter of Nazareth known as Joseph going south to Bethlehem, the city of his ancestors. Much as he probably disliked having to take the journey at that time or having to accommodate the oppressive government of Rome, he set off to do what was commanded.

II. When Christ came into the world on that first Christmas, he came at a very inconvenient time and place. Even poor Joseph and Mary were not ready for him. Had they suspected that he would come on the journey, no doubt Mary would have stayed home. But when the time comes for a woman to give birth to a child, there is not a whole lot that can be done.

III. I wonder if some of us are ever really ready for the coming of Christ. "Some day I am going to stop what I am doing, accept Christ as my lord and savior, join the church, and start living a Christian life. But not right now. I'm not ready yet." Such persons certainly do find the coming of Christ inconvenient. They don't want anything to do with him until they are ready for him. But they never are ready for him.

IV. Christ has come and he keeps coming whenever he chooses, whether we are ready for him or not. He wants to make some changes in us. He has some important business to take care of with us. He wishes to help us get our lives straightened out. He wishes to show us "the way, the truth, and the life." He wants to help us, he says, so that we "may have life and have it abundantly." He wants to stir up within us love and good works which we have never known or shown before.—Charles E. Ferrell.

December 14. A Christmas Sunrise (Advent)

TEXTS: Mal. 3:1–2; 4:2.

I. The Lord will come only if we prepare. E. P. Ellyson said: "The reason we do not see more manifestations of the divine presence is because the way is not prepared. We cry for God to come into our hearts and into our churches, but we expect him to come over the rubbish. We are always disappointed. Can we never learn the lesson?" How much we need to apply the words: "Let every heart prepare him room."

II. The Lord will heal if only we permit. Mal. 3:1–2 is sung in the early part of Handel's *Messiah*. The summer of 1741 was a time of extreme depression for Handel. London had ill received his music, and he felt rejection and failure. Charles Jennens gave Handel a compilation of Bible verses that became the scriptural inspiration of the *Messiah*. Early in his oratorio, Handel knew Mal. 3:1–2 was fulfilled in his life. The Lord had suddenly come. Many can testify that after a time of darkness and despair there came that glorious moment when the sun broke through! Charles Wesley wrote: "Hail, the sun of righteousness! Light and life to all he brings, ris'n with healing in his wings."

III. He will love if only we perceive. Malachi begins (1:2) with a testimony of God's love and his disappointment that men cannot perceive it. John 3:16–17 is a testimony of God's love and vv. 18–19 of his disappointment that men cannot perceive it. What a tragedy that we who live this side of Christmas should not perceive the love of God in Christ! Joseph Mohr magnifies our text and God's love. "Silent night! Holy night! Son of God, love's pure light."—Mark E. Moore.

December 21. Someday a Real Christmas (Advent)

TEXT: Luke 2:15.

I. Someday there will be peace on earth. Someday there will be goodwill toward men. Someday we will believe that faith is more significant than missiles, that Bethlehem's star outshines man's satellites, that Joseph's dreams still outwit Herod's hate, and that our journey to the manger is more important than a trip to the moon.

II. But when? (a) Can it be while men hate each other, deceive one another, envy one another, rob one another?

(b) Can it be while men malign one another and distort truth just to win an election to public office?

(c) Can it be while those who boast of freedom and democracy are intolerant of the views of others in their own communities and really do not believe in freedom of speech for their fellow men?

(d) Can it be while men in foreign lands conspire to enslave their fellow men?

(e) Can it be while men surrender principle and morality and excuse their conduct as necessary to meet "political expediency" in international relations?

(f) Can it be while we prate of morals and idealism and then sell our souls amid the hypocrisies of the hour?

III. Each year the world is reminded of Christmas in an outburst of generosity toward family and friends. But the gifts are mostly of material things. The voice of the spiritual is rarely heard above the din of the crowd. The prophets of old have been silenced. The new prophets urge the advantages of compromise with evil. They regard sacrifice as obsolete. Jesus, they argue in effect, should have appeased the enemy.

IV. Someday there will be a real Christmas that does not vanish in a day but whose principle of justice and tolerance and helpfulness and mutual respect will last all year long and find expression in the affairs of every day. That real Christmas will come when we recognize in Jesus Christ a love that can spread from man to man until it encompasses and unites the whole world. That real Christmas could begin for you and me today.—Myron J. Taylor.

December 28. The Really Good Life (Watch Night)

TEXT: Luke 6:20.

I. Jesus is not recommending poverty,

starvation, and suffering. He is suggesting that those who spend their energies gaining the good life will be disappointed if that is their primary goal. By contrast, people who invest themselves in the kingdom of God—the truly happy persons—experience the really good life. They are happy not because they are poor or hungry or suffering. They are happy because they focus primarily upon the intangibles of the kingdom of God.

II. Seeking the really good life is not an assurance that we will avoid suffering or tragedy. The cross is the best evidence of this fact. Jesus sought the really good life and was killed. His executioners thought that they had the last word. God however raised Christ from death. God's mighty act is an assurance of his power to lift us to the really good life.

III. The earliest Christians were convinced that God raised Christ from death. Following Christ's resurrection, his followers became zealous witnesses to their experiences. With limited opportunities to experience the good life—the followers were fishermen, tax collectors, prostitutes, and not many of the wise or wealthy—they were freed to live the really good life. They traveled throughout the Roman Empire as evangelists of their faith in Christ.

IV. Our world is torn by tragedies—poverty, illness, war, injustice, and racism. We who identify with the Christian church are called to witness to the love and power of God at work in society. A primary responsibility of the church amid life's ambiguities is to help men and women to learn how to discriminate and choose between the good life and the really good life. Recognizing that one day everyone will die, the church has an opportunity to help persons trust themselves to the love and power of a God who resurrected Christ from death.—William H. Likins.

SECTION III. Resources for Communion Services

SERMON SUGGESTIONS

Topic: Table for Sinners
Text: Mark 14:22–25.

I. Although we are unworthy, Jesus Christ invites us to come. He was no naive idealist; he knew what was in men's hearts. In the ritual we pray: "We do not presume to come to this thy table, O Lord, trusting in our own righteousness, but in thy manifold and great mercies. We are not worthy so much as to gather up the crumbs under thy table. But thou art the same Lord whose property is always to have mercy." We come to communion not as the perfected but as the penitent. We come because Jesus Christ loves us, wants us, and invites us.

II. Who gathered for the first communion service? Men who were the disciples of Jesus, who had followed him throughout Palestine, heard his words, and seen his signs. He called them friends, yet what an unfaithful company they were. During the passover meal, Jesus said, "Truly, I say to you, one of you will betray me." And down to the last one they asked, "Is it I, Lord?" Each knew that he was capable of betrayal. Even Peter, who boasted that he would never betray his Lord, was probably not as sure as his statement suggests. And in their own way they all betrayed their Lord. Judas sold him out; Peter denied that he had ever known him; and the rest scattered to the four winds after Jesus had been arrested.

III. His whole ministry might be summoned up succinctly: "He ate with sinners." He went to those who were outcast by the polite society of his day and demonstrated God's love. He said that his mission was not to the righteous but to the sinners. Some of the most beautiful stories in literature are found in Jesus' meeting with sinners and how he forgave them and set them on a new course.

IV. The gospel truth, which so many find hard to accept, is that God in Jesus Christ loves sinners with an unqualified love. He loves them just as they are in their misery, their dirtiness, and their rebellion. Because of this, and only because of this, can the sinner ever repent. Our repentance doesn't earn us God's love; God's love earns us our repentance. Or to put it in traditional language, grace precedes faith. We don't merit God's love; he gives it to us freely.—Michael Daves.

Topic: In Remembrance
Text: Luke 22:19

I. "Do this in remembrance of me." Jesus said that to his disciples that dark night in the upper room in Jerusalem. And for nearly twenty centuries in all parts of the world, Christians have been doing this in remembrance of him. No other command ever given has been obeyed as this one has been. There is nothing in human history to parallel this. There is an indisputable uniqueness in the extent of the response to that command.

35

II. We are gathered here because our Lord said, "Do this in remembrance of me." But this sacrament is no mere memorial. The remembering of Jesus Christ at the holy table is not simply the commemoration of an event long past. It is a creative remembering in which the past is brought into the present. It is a remembering in which Jesus Christ becomes for us a living presence and in which he becomes contemporary for us.

III. The Lord's Supper, the Holy Communion, or the Eucharist is the primary act of worship for Christians. It establishes the norm for all our corporate worship. We must never look upon it as a mere option or as a peculiar little extra which sometimes is tacked on the end of a service of worship. The sacrament is central, not peripheral, in Christian worship.

IV. We have assembled ourselves here because the Lord Jesus Christ commanded his followers, "Do this in remembrance of me." In doing this we go right to the center and source of our faith. In doing this we acknowledge that we are called to share in his servanthood of witness and compassion to all mankind. In doing this we are made aware of the present reality of him who is our hope and our redemption.—J. A. Davidson.

Topic: The Common Table
TEXT: I Cor. 10:17.
Paul would stress that at the Lord's table we are at the point of Christian solidarity.

I. We who come to the Lord's Supper have a common condition. (a) This condition is sin, and we face a common condemnation, for the wages of sin is death. It is like the point made by the repentant thief on the cross when he upbraided his fellow thief: "Do you not fear God, since you are under the same sentence of condemnation?"

(b) This common condition calls for a common Christ. This is another reason for Christian solidarity at the time of communion. We are lost sinners. But to whom do we go for help? There is really none other than Jesus. This is the way the disciples felt when they asked: "Lord, to whom shall

we go? Thou alone hast the words of eternal life."

(c) At communion we realize how badly we need Christ to save us. This is one conviction that every Christian can have, regardless of denominational connection. One thing we do agree on: Christ is our divine savior who alone can reconcile us to God. All other ideas or doctrines are relatively unimportant and superfluous. They do not mean a thing. Salvation is the important issue. True Christians are convinced with the early disciples that there is no other name under heaven by which we are saved except the name of Christ.

(d) As we come to Christ for forgiveness, we all meet at the focal point: the loaf of bread in communion, Christ the bread of life. The closer we come to Christ, the closer we come to each other. It is at communion that we reach the point of solidarity in Christ.

II. If we have a common Christ, it follows that we Christians have a common characteristic. What might it be? Christians have many and varied traits and virtues. Is there really one that is most important and one that is common to all Christians? There is. It is love.

(a) Love is absolutely indispensable and essential if one is to be a Christian. Jesus said, "You are my disciples if you love one another." He taught that the greatest commandments were love of God and of neighbor. You and I cannot be Christians unless we love. This is particularly true in the Lord's Supper. This is a feast of love. At this feast Christ gives us his body and blood out of love that we might have reconciliation. Because of love, we are forgiven, accepted, redeemed, and saved.

(b) Love binds, draws, unites, and solidifies. Because of love Christians are bound together in a tight and close fellowship that is intimate and warm. The early Christians expressed their love with a holy kiss at the end of the communion service. Thus, because of love, we sense a oneness with each other as we come for communion.—John R. Brokhoff.

Topic: The Passover and the Supper
TEXT: Luke 22:15.
How tremendously symbolical was the

ritual of that ancient Jewish festival of the passover!

I. There was the piece of parsley or lettuce that was dipped in the bowl of salt water and eaten. Parsley represented the hyssop with which the lintel had been smeared in Egypt. The salt water stood for the tears of Egypt and for the waters of the Red Sea.

II. There was a collection of bitter herbs to remind them of the bitterness of slavery in Egypt.

III. There was the paste called *charosheth* to remind them of the clay from which bricks had been made in Egypt and sticks of cinnamon to remind them of the straw with which bricks had been made.

IV. There was the passover lamb, which provided the blood by which sign they had been saved from the angel of death.

V. There was bread. (a) On the table were three circles of unleavened bread. At one point in the feast the bread was broken and a little of it was eaten. The bread reminded the Jews of the bread of affliction which they had eaten in Egypt. It was broken to remind them that slaves never had a whole loaf but only broken crusts to eat. As it was broken, the head of the family would say: "This is the bread of affliction which our forefathers ate in the land of Egypt. Whoever is hungry, let him come and eat. Whoever is in need, let him come and keep the passover with us."

(b) Jesus took the bread of affliction, and when he had given thanks, he broke it and gave it to them, saying, "This is my body, broken for you." The bread of affliction became the bread of redemption; the bread of oppression became the bread of salvation.

(c) "Whoever is hungry, let him come and eat." As we eat we become *douloi*— bond slaves—not of Egypt but of Christ.

VI. There was wine—four cups of it. (a) At different stages of the passover feast these cups were drunk. They were to remind the Jews of the four promises in Exod. 6:6–7: "I will bring you out from under the burdens of the Egyptians, and I will rid you of their bondage, and I will redeem you with an outstretched arm, and I will take you to me for a people, and I will be your God."

(b) Jesus took the cup and said, "This cup is the new covenant in my blood which is poured out for you." The promises had been fulfilled; they had come true. The blood of lambs had become the blood of the lamb of God; the life of the vine had become the life of the true vine.—David Irvine.

Topic: The Cup He Took (Maundy Thursday)

TEXT: Matt. 26:27.

I. The cup seemed the symbol of necessary sorrow. Surely the wine was blood red in the cup of suffering which our Lord drank. Yet he drank it without flinching, saying in Gethsemane, "Father, if thou be willing, remove this cup from me; nevertheless not my will but thine be done." He drank it with the brave smile of a winning sportsman, saying to his comrades, "Be of good cheer, I have overcome the world." He drank it without bitterness toward those who inflicted it, praying from the cross, "Father, forgive them for they know not what they do."

II. Because he drank it as he did, that cup of suffering was transformed in our Lord's hands into the cup of grace. Christ could have escaped the cross. He said: "No man taketh my life from me. I lay it down of myself." He went to the cross only through the compulsion of love. He had come into the world to save sinners. He had come to reveal the love of his heavenly Father. And to fulfill that mission he loved even to the end. He gave the last full measure of devotion. He surrendered his life not merely as a patriot dies for his own country and not merely as a martyr dies for a cause but also as a savior dying to redeem all men out of every tongue and race and nation. Thus Christ revealed the grace of God.

III. In Christ's hand the cup becomes the cup of hope. Jesus turned the thoughts of his disciples from the foggy darkness of that fateful last night to the dawn of a new day. When hope shines through a night like that, there must be a powerful light behind it. To stand on the eve of one's own death and talk calmly and confidently about the future is a test of faith and hope which only the strongest can stand. Here is vivid demonstration that "suffering produces endurance and endurance produces character and character produces hope." —Ralph W. Sockman.

Topic: The Last Frontier
TEXT: Mark 14:25.

I. Here is acceptance. (a) "No more." This was the Last Supper. There is no trace of self-pity in these words and no sign of a desperate revolt.

(b) "No more." No more parties with the disciples in city rooms or country inns or out on the hills of Galilee. It was the last time he would look into the eyes of Peter and James and John and the others as they gathered round the table.

II. Acceptance, yes, but this is not all he says. With the same calm certainty with which he accepted the "no more" he speaks of the life to come. This is not the "no more" of the pagan world, the sad echo of mortality. It is "no more until."

(a) How much more impressive is this single sentence spoken in the face of certain death than whole volumes about the immortality of the soul. Do you know of anyone in the whole company of mankind whom you would rather trust when you face the great mysteries of life and death? Can you imagine for a moment that he could deceive either himself or his followers at such a point?

(b) Here is his word of confidence— "until." There is to be another chapter. Of that he has not the faintest doubt. Just as absolutely as he accepts the last frontier, he defies its final power. There is life beyond—"new in the kingdom." The God who has set a limit to this earthly feast is the God who awaits us with a banquet of resurrection life.

III. To teach this triumphant calm in which acceptance and defiance are gloriously fused, we must company with Christ.

(a) We must learn to carry that cross which is the pain and bafflement and frustration of our darkest hours, knowing that he has carried it already.

(b) We drink the wine of our earthly life as those who know that God has better for us "new in the kingdom."

(c) We must so strengthen our ties here

and now with the unseen and eternal that we become familiar with the language of heaven—the language of joy and peace and love.

IV. The supper was not the last supper. It has continued—right across the world in little rooms, in parish churches, in great cathedrals, in every language, and in countless forms—linking heaven to earth and earth to heaven.

(a) Here the bread is broken and the wine is poured as "on the night in which he was betrayed."

(b) Here we know that his body was broken and his blood was shed.

(c) Here we know that beyond the cross he has come back to share his supper with his friends. "I will come again," he said, and he has come.—David H. C. Read.

Topic: Between Already and Not Yet
TEXT: I Cor. 12:11–12.

I. Jesus' message does separate out persons from the crowd because it calls us to a commitment to the Christian life which includes involvement in the community which one finds with other Christians. This community of the faith, this body of Christ, this household of God, this royal priesthood, this temple of the Spirit, or this colony of heaven is the church whose foundations have already been laid by Jesus.

II. Jesus' preaching speaks of the future coming of the reign of God. We see Jesus ushering in the beginning of the reign to be consummated at some later date. Throughout the New Testament we feel the nearness of the "end time," yet that time has not arrived. While we might say it is "arriving," it has not "arrived." We are told that we will not know the day or hour when the Lord will come again, but we are encouraged to be faithful. We understand then that the reign of God has not yet become complete.

III. We as Christians are *between the already* of Jesus' presence and ministry on earth and the time which is *not yet* when the Lord will return. It is precisely between these two points in which the church has been called into being so that those of us who are seeking to follow the will of God might gather and be a part of the body of Christ.

IV. It is the feeling of betweenness that we feel when we observe the Lord's Supper. We are involved in an act of remembrance and an act of anticipation. The elements of communion remind us of the life and ministry of Jesus, and they help us to renew our commitment to living as Christians in the present until he comes again.

V. We are *between* as members of the Christian community, and that is precisely where our ministry is—NOW. Three interconnected words we sometimes use to describe the fellowship of believers are congregation, community, and church. "The three words are not in competition, but compliment one another. 'Congregation' expresses the fact that the *ekklesia* is never merely a static institution but one that exists through the repeated events of a concrete coming together. 'Community' emphasizes that the *ekklesia* is never merely an abstract and distant super-organization of functionaries set above the concretely congregated community but is a fellowship of people who meet regularly at a given place for a given time for a given purpose. 'Church' makes it plain that the *ekklesia* is never merely a disconnected jumble of isolated and self-sufficient religious groups but the members, united through their individual service, of an all embracing fellowship." (Hans Kung.)

VI. Our coming together is important. We do not stand alone as Christians. We stand together committed to making Jesus Christ our lord, and we gain strength as we stand together. As we stand together we develop a deep relationship with one another, and this makes us a part of the larger church universal. We are standing together as a *here and now* evidence of the power of the good news.—Arlo R. Reichter.

ILLUSTRATIONS

LOYAL OBEDIENCE.   When Elizabeth was crowned queen of England, she invited the English nobility to the coronation service in these words: "Whereas we have appointed the second day of June,

1953, for the solemnity of our coronation, these are therefore to will and command. You, all excuses set apart, that you make your personal attendance upon us, at the time above mentioned, furnished and appointed as to your rank and quality appertaineth, there to do and perform such services as shall be required." The invitation of Elizabeth left no alternative to her subjects if they were to be her loyal servants. The lordship of Christ leaves Christians no alternative but to acknowledge his majesty and to serve him in whatever way he may desire. This service is one of loving obedience to the king of kings and lord of lords. Loyalty to the royalty of Christ is a mark of a genuine Christian faith.—Vernon O. Elmore.

PRISON COMMUNION.   Bishop Johannes Lilje tells of the Christmas he spent in a Nazi prison in Berlin when as a special favor he was allowed to hear the confession and give absolution to a condemned prisoner and also to give him communion. The preacher read Isaiah's promise and said: "Tonight we are a congregation, part of the church of Christ, and this great word of divine promise is as true for us today as it was for those years ago. Our chief concern is to believe that God through Jesus Christ has allowed the eternal light to arise and shine upon this world which is plunged in the darkness of death and that he will also make this light to shine for us." Then while quiet tears ran down the prisoner's cheek he made his confession and received the sacrament. "We were prisoners of the Gestapo," wrote Lilje, "but the peace of God enfolded us. It was real and present, like a hand laid gently upon us."—John W. Rilling.

LOVE STORY.   Calvary is the story of love. The thorns and the nails are the pens with which it is written, and the shed blood is the guarantee of God to a race of sinners that his love to them broke over the bounds of his love to his only begotten Son and offered his all that the wandering children of time might have an eternal salvation. As you partake of his broken body and shed blood, do not have a formal, unloving, unemotional attitude toward him as you say, "Lord, what wilt thou have me to do?"—Maitland Alexander.

RELATIONSHIP. When I take my common meal and relate it to the glory of God, the common meal becomes a sacramental feast. When my labor is joined unto the Lord, the sacred wedding turns my workshop into a church. When I link the country lane to the savior, I am walking in the garden of Eden, and paradise is restored. We never see anything truly until we see it in the light of the glory of God.—John Henry Jowett.

ACCEPTED. Grace strikes us when we walk through the dark valley of a meaningless and empty life. It strikes us when our disgust for our own being, our indifference, our weakness, our hostility, and our lack of direction and composure have become intolerable to us. It strikes us when, year after year, the longed-for perfection of life does not appear. Sometimes at that moment a wave of light breaks into our darkness, and it is as though a voice were saying: "You are accepted by that which is greater than you. Do not seek for anything. Simply accept the fact that you are accepted." If that happens to us, we experience grace. In that moment grace conquers sin, and reconciliation bridges the gulf of estrangement.—Paul Tillich.

THE SIMPLE GOSPEL. As a young student of theology John Wesley wanted to be a good Christian. With his brother Charles he gathered about him at Oxford a group of young men who were soon dubbed "the Holy Club." With a strenuous effort of the will John Wesley sought to impose on himself and his companions a Christian standard of conduct, only to discover that there was no peace and little joy in the endeavor. Seeking help, John and Charles Wesley traveled across England to William Law who told them that they were trying to make something complicated and burdensome out of Christianity. "Religion," said Law, "is the plainest and simplest thing in the world. It is just this: 'We love because he first loved us.' " —S. Robert Weaver.

INASMUCH. The bread you do not use is the bread of the hungry; the garment hanging in your wardrobe is the garment of him who is naked; the shoes that you do not wear are the shoes of one who is barefoot; the money that you keep locked away is the money of the poor; the acts of charity that you do not perform are so many injustices that you commit.—St. Basil the Great.

SECTION IV. Resources for Funeral Services

SERMON SUGGESTIONS

Topic: When Sorrow Comes
TEXT: Isa. 61:1–3.

How can we best stand up to whatever sorrow may come in our lives?

I. When the heart has been broken and the spirit of a person is desolated by grief, we cannot demand of ourselves more than nature itself is able to give. Be willing to see this and to have it so. "The only way to meet sorrow is to pass through it solemnly, slowly, with humility and faith, as the Israelites passed through the sea" (Dinah Maria Mulock).

II. We can express our sorrows. (a) Why do you suppose God gave us the gift of language if he did not intend for us to use that gift to share our deepest thoughts and feelings with others? We clothe our concerns in words, we profess our love in language, and we share our sorrows with speech. If we do not do this, we are depriving ourselves of a God-given way by which we can stand up to our sorrows.

(b) There are those who pride themselves in being private persons, but the pride can be explosively dangerous. We were meant to share life and especially to share it where it counts most. We were not intended to go it alone. It is a strangely false reading of life to suggest that we are supposed to keep all things to ourselves. It is much more satisfying to share, and in sorrow it is sharing that hastens healing.

(c) Sad beyond words is the plight of a person who has no one with whom the deepest experiences of life can be shared, for in the sharing the load is lightened and in the sharing the way ahead becomes more clear.

III. We can get up, get out, and get going! (a) Samuel Johnson wrote in his letter to Mrs. Thrale, "Grief is a species of idleness." Idleness is an unwholesome seedbed for sorrow, and there is hardly anything worse that a person can do than to sit in a rocking chair with his grief.

(b) Grief is a chilling experience, and even as those who suffer from the intense effects of cold become sleepy and want nothing more than to lie down and rest for a time, so those enduring sorrow often seek solitude and inactivity. It is hard for them to push themselves back into life's mainstreams. They simply do not want to face up to getting out again.

IV. A person has to get busy for a purpose. It isn't enough to get up, get out, and get going unless you have a reason for getting up, a place to go when you get out, and a purpose to be served when you get going.

V. Give your sorrow to God and let him bless it. "Blessed are those who mourn, for they shall be comforted." That's God's promise.

(a) In no other experience have I witnessed so clearly the difference between a Christian who believes in the God of our Lord, Jesus Christ, and the unbeliever. Christians sin, alas, just as other people do. Christians are weak, alas, just as other people are weak. But when sorrow comes there is a difference.

(b) God stands with them, and they are not without faith in him. God has not revealed all mysteries to them, but they have come to trust him. They come to God carrying their sorrow, and God shares the sorrow with them and they are not alone.

(c) They do not escape sorrow, but their sorrow moves steadily through the stages of grief until a strange and wonderful serenity embraces them. There is something altogether beautiful about this and by the grace of God, altogether wonderful.—Charles L. Copenhaver.

Meditation: Thinking About Death

What you think about life after death will partly depend on what you think about life before death.

If you think that life is a mean and meaningless affair, filled with horror, unjust, unfair, and absurd, you are not likely to think that there is anything after death. Life here is bad enough, and the thought of its prolongation is intolerable.

If you think that life is a grand and glorious experience, full of opportunities to do and to grow, to enlarge, to accept, to expand, to suffer, to bear with other people burdens that they have to bear, and to take your own aches and pains as ways and means to make life richer for other people, it will be natural for you to think of death leading on to something else.

If you think only of the petty, miserable, and heartless people that you have known, you will think it is just as well to bring their story to an end.

If you think of the people you have known who are alive, alert, responsive, weak perhaps in many ways but willing to admit their weakness and do what they can to strengthen it, outrageous at times but at other times magnificently courageous, lovable in spite of their shortcomings, and rising high above all limitations that life often puts upon them, you will find it almost impossible to think of them as extinguishable. And with people like these are the others—the unfinished lives, the lives spoiled in the making, and the ones who

had never had a chance to do anything but suffer.

In the last analysis it depends on what you think about God. I know that he brought me into this world. I knew nothing about it before I got here. It hasn't always been easy by any means. I haven't always had what I wanted or done what I'd like to do. But I have had many a glimpse of glory and goodness, and there have been times when I could almost smell the sea air, no matter how far inland I was.

There have been times when I was aware of something other than this world of time and space, something breaking in upon me. And when the next step was one that I was either afraid or unable to take, I have always been able to take it. God has always given me the strength to take it in one way or another. If God brought me into this world when I was born and kept me in it as long as I lived, I trust him to take me into another when I die. If it is half as good as the world he brought me into here, I will be satisfied. I leave it in his hands.—Theodore P. Ferris.

Topic: On Accepting Death

Text: II Sam. 12:20.

Let us turn to the experience of King David at the time that his infant son passed away. Though he did not know the assurance of Christian faith which we can call upon, he did have certain insights that might prove helpful to us as we meet the heartaches of separation and death.

I. He recognized death for what it was. He did not attempt to hide the fact of death as if it were a mere illusion. David did not say that the child was merely sleeping, for then he might have expected to awaken him again within his own household.

(a) The Christian hope is found not in denying death but in the hope of resurrection. Jesus Christ tasted death; he was crucified, dead, and buried, but this was not the final chapter. He rose from the dead.

(b) Our first step in meeting the heartaches of this hour is the acceptance of death as a fact of life but not as the final chapter to life. Death is defeated by a changed life, by a new dimension. Just as a seed must first die in the ground in order to produce new growth, so must our bodies die in order to find a new life of immortality in God's very presence.

II. When David learned of the death of his child, he entered into the house of the Lord and worshiped. In the year 125 A.D., a Greek by the name of Aristides wrote to one of his friends about the new religion that had sprung up in his country. He was trying to explain the reasons for the extraordinary growth of Christianity. Listen to a sentence from one of his letters: "If any righteous man among the Christians passes from the world, they rejoice and offer thanks to God, and they escort his body with songs and thanksgiving as if he were setting out from one place to another nearby." If we believe in God, it is a part of our faith that all those who dwell in God belong to his eternal kingdom.

III. David returned to his house, had food prepared, and ate. There is no greater denial of a faith in Christian immortality than to neglect the living for the dead. A sorrow, which saps life from the living on behalf of those who have gone through the portals of death into the very presence of God, shows a lack of trust and faith in the promises and assurances of God.—Don A. Sanford.

Topic: Why Me?
SCRIPTURE: John 9:1–12.

All of us face problems of personal suffering, and there are times when our grief goes so deep that we really don't know what to do. We wonder what is going to happen next or where do we go from here? We often feel sad, depressed, and alone. We may pity ourselves and feel we are being persecuted. The only questions we can ask are "Why did this have to happen to me?" and "What did I do to deserve this?" and "Why me?"

I. Underneath these questions may be a feeling of guilt and a belief that if things had gone differently or if we had done something in a different way, this tragic suffering may not have happened. All of us have a tendency to believe that an illness, death, or other tragedy which brings pain and suffering is produced by something we did or did not do. We feel guilty and look for the sin we have committed. We

feel the burden of a wrongdoing and look for a right we did not do.

(a) Jesus and his disciples came upon a blind man and his disciples asked, "Why?" They were looking for the guilty party because surely someone must have done something terribly wrong for this man to have been burdened with the great tragedy of blindness. But Jesus bypassed their question, saying, "It was not that this man sinned, or his parents, but that the words of God might be manifest in him."

(b) It was not a question of who had sinned or of who was guilty. Instead Jesus said this man was a child of God. The question was "How is God to be made manifest in him?" The question was "How is the redemptive spirit of God and his goodness going to find purpose and meaning in this man's suffering?"

II. We all experience suffering. We go through experiences of losing loved ones and feeling the grief of the loss. We all participate in emotional conflicts which strike so deep that there seems to be no bottom to our pain. Throughout these experiences of suffering and pain we often ask "Why me?"

(a) Jesus did not dismiss his disciples for asking "Why?" but he did direct them to go beyond that question. He is telling us that there is more to suffering than just the why. He is saying that the important question is not in the realm of the past but in the realm of the present and the future. Now that we have felt pain, what have we learned about ourselves and others? Now that we have suffered, what are we going to do with our experience of pain?

(b) What are you going to be, not in spite of what you have suffered, but because of what you have suffered? We have felt the pain, the suffering, and the grief, but what are we now going to be in life and what are we going to do with our lives? How is the redemptive power of God's spirit going to work through you?—David L. Van Arsdale.

Topic: God and Human Suffering
TEXT: Rom. 5:3 (MOFFATT).

I. God is God and he will not be defeated.

II. God was in Christ and knows the

depths of human suffering through the cross.

III. God can help us make creative and redemptive use of suffering.

IV. God helps us use all of life's experiences—including suffering, sorrow, and tragedy—for personal growth.

V. God helps us turn such growth to helping others in their distress.

VI. God helps us creatively to use sorrow and suffering by making the most of it. —Hoover Rupert.

Topic: Through the Valley of Death
TEXT: Ps. 23:4.

I. Comfort is not found in the words "the valley of the shadow of death." Death is something we know we all must face, and yet when it comes we are never fully prepared for it. Death is something that is feared because it holds something of the uncertain before us.

(a) Yet our Christian faith sustains us. Without faith in God we would dwell upon the words "the valley of the shadow of death." But as Christians our faith teaches us to place the real emphasis upon the word "through." "Yea, though I walk through the valley of the shadow of death."

(b) The psalmist leaves no doubt in his psalm. Death is not a thing to be feared. He pictures himself and all others who follow and obey God as walking through the valley of the shadow of death. Death is not the end; it is not the final resting place of the faithful. It is simply a dark valley through which we must walk before we come to the wonderful light of life.

II. To find comfort in these words we must remember to emphasize the words "for thou art with me."

(a) The valley would have been a fearful one if the Lord had not been with the psalmist. It is a fearful one today if the Lord is not with us. But if the Lord is with us, we will have no fear. To know that he will lead us not into but through the valley gives us "peace that passeth all understanding."

(b) If we can boldly say, "Thou art with me!" we will not fear death, for we know that the Lord is our shepherd, we know

that the Lord is with us, and we know that he will never fail or forsake us.—Larry K. May.

Topic: The Father's Home
SCRIPTURE: John 14:1–6.

I. The passage begins with ultimate faith based on God. The KJV translates, "In my father's house are many mansions." Mansions no longer have the appeal they once did. Most of us would settle for a good ranch or split-level. The word "rooms" of the RSV is preferred to "mansions," yet the meaning for us is best found in this translation, "In my Father's abode are many homes." Heaven is a place of security and also one where your identity is not lost. You have a mansion, a room, or a home where your personality can express itself.

II. Jesus continues, "If it were not so, would I have told you that I go to prepare a place for you?" The RSV renders this correctly as a question. The writer of John's gospel makes an appeal to the basic integrity of Jesus in the realm of the spiritual. In the phrase "a place for you" we find again the emphasis on the preservation of individual personality.

III. The close of v. 3 reads, "that where I am, you may be also." Association with God's messiah is on the most intimate of terms. We can put it this way without being misunderstood: God's people are taken into the very heart of the family of God.—Hillyer H. Straton.

Topic: Family Traits
TEXT: John 14:2–4.

We must be careful that, when our ship drops its mooring lines and turns its prow to the open sea, we are booked as passengers and do not travel in the hold or in the brig. We all leave on the same vessel, but a vastly different reception awaits the stowaways and the brigands. Our problem is to avoid the two latter categories and identify ourselves as members of the family. Fortunately our family has certain prominent features that make its members easy to identify in any crowd.

I. First of all comes faith in God. Faith is the consecration of the imagination. It is more than belief that; it is belief in. It is a whole way of life.

II. We have hope. Members of God's family are never hopeless.

III. Another identifying mark is humility. The Christian knows that he has no vested right to heaven more than he has to earth. He is God's guest on earth, but he knows that his brother Jesus has already paid the penalty for his transgressions. He thus has a lively hope despite all his own inadequacies.

IV. Finally comes love of Father and love of brother. Every man and every woman is his brother in a kinship closer than any so-called blood relationship. Even though some may deny the family ties and some we might like to deny, we need each other's love. The Christian will give that love, whether he receives it or not, for to withhold it would be to lose one of the most characteristic family traits.—Moss W. Armistead.

Topic: Eternal Life

TEXT: I Cor. 15:49.

The story of the kingdom of life that lasts forever, that tells us that we believe in the resurrection of the body in the ongoing of personal life and in the life everlasting, and that challenges and inspires us, is it relevant to our daily life? Does it make a difference in how we live? In what manner of person we are?

I. As Jesus stood at the graveside of his dear friend Lazarus, he said, "He who believes in me, though he die, yet shall he live, and whoever lives and believes in me shall never die."

(a) If this is true, it is the most excitingly relevant thing imaginable. If a man believes in the king of this eternal kingdom and by Christ's victory can enter into eternal life so that he never really dies, that is the most tremendously relevant fact that you can imagine.

(b) It means that we believe that the spirit triumphs and that we commend our souls to God. If we are able to do this and if we are able to enter into the triumph and victory of the Easter faith, then it will have everything to do with the nature of our daily life, for this is a faith to live by.

II. The very nature of eternal life is that it is a life of quality. Paul says, "If you are risen with Christ, seek those things that are above." This is a practical injunction. It means you are going to live on a higher level. Jesus never wearied of teaching in these terms—"to lay up treasures in heaven." When you are in heaven? No. When you are on earth. This is the way of life, the way to live: to lay up heavenly treasures now. You enter into a quality of life that is eternal while you are living in this world of time.

III. This begins to clarify in our thinking the great and ultimate distinction that is made between those who enter into heaven and those who do not.

(a) If you cultivate a taste for what is eternal, then you will be happy with the things that are eternal. You will be a joyful and contented citizen in the kingdom of life that lasts forever.

(b) If you do not have a taste for spiritual things, if the hour of moral decision leaves you untouched, and if the company of Christian believers is tedious to you, then you will find heaven a terrible bore.

(c) To enter into this great citizenship which is laid up for us in heaven, we have to cultivate a taste for things eternal every day in our life here upon earth. Our savior came into our human realm to teach us how to cultivate a taste for things that are eternal.

(d) Our savior is inviting us to come into eternal life in the only way that anybody can come into it with deep satisfaction and peace. It is to follow his way now, to learn to love the things of his kingdom that we really ought to love, and to prepare ourselves now for that eternal life which is our true fulfillment in his kingdom of life that lasts forever.—Lowell M. Atkinson.

ILLUSTRATIONS

TOO LITTLE TIME. Love makes people believe in immortality because there seems not to be room enough in life for so great a tenderness, and it is inconceivable that the most masterful of our emotions should have no more than the spare moments of a few brief years.—Robert Louis Stevenson.

THE GATEWAY.   Pearl S. Buck in her novel, *The Big Wave*, depicts a beautiful exchange between a boy and his father. "What is death?" Kino asked. His father replied, "Death is the great gateway." "The gateway where?" His father smiled. "Can you remember when you were born?" Kino shook his head: "I was too small." His father laughed: "I remember it well. Oh, how hard you thought it was to be born! You cried and you screamed." "Didn't I want to be born?" His father smiled: "You did not. You wanted to stay just where you were in the warm dark house of the unborn. But the time came to be born and the gate of life opened." "Did I know it was the gate of life?" "You did not know anything about it, and so you were afraid of it. But you see how foolish you were? Here we were waiting for you, your parents, already loving you and eager to welcome you. And you have been very happy, haven't you?" "Until the big wave came," Kino replied. "Now I am afraid again because of the death the big wave brought." "You are only afraid because you do not know anything about death," his father replied. "But some day you will wonder why you were afraid, even as today you wonder why you feared to be born."

TOGETHER FOREVER.   A group of Americans were sitting around a table in earnest conversation with Karl Barth, the Swiss theologian. One of them asked, "Dr. Barth, do you truly believe that there is a life hereafter where we shall meet the ones we love?" Quickly he replied, "Yes and some we don't love too!"—Clayton A. Pepper.

DARK TUNNELS.   When my daughter was a little girl, she was terrified by tunnels. When traveling with me on a train she would cling to me and press her face against me the moment the train entered a tunnel and would raise her head only when I assured her that we were once again out in the sunshine. A few years later her feelings changed entirely, and when

we would be driving over the Pennsylvania Turnpike, as we did frequently, she would become pleasantly excited as we approached one of the tunnels that extend under the mountains. "I like the tunnels," she explained one day. "They have light at both ends!" Those words have returned to me more than once when I have been going through some of life's dark tunnels. How true they are, if we will only look at the light at both ends of the tunnel.—Kathleen W. Welch.

INNER LIGHT.   People are like stained-glass windows. They sparkle and shine when the sun is out, but when the darkness sets in their true beauty is revealed only if there is light from within.—Elisabeth Kübler-Ross.

THE SHADOW.   I was driving with my children to my wife's funeral where I was to preach the sermon. As we came into one small town there strode down in front of us a truck that came to stop before a red light. It was the biggest truck I ever saw in my life, and the sun was shining on it at just the angle that took its shadow and spread it across the snow on the field beside it. As the shadow covered that field, I said: "Look, children, at that truck, and look at its shadow. If you had to be run over, which would you rather be run over by, the truck or by the shadow?" My youngest child said, "The shadow couldn't hurt anybody." "That's right," I continued, "and death is a truck, but the shadow is all that ever touches the Christian. The truck ran over the Lord Jesus. Only the shadow is gone over mother."—Donald Grey Barnhouse.

INSCRIPTION.   In the Grange Cemetery in Edinburgh is a gravestone which was erected at the close of World War I by a woman whose husband and three sons, her entire family, had given their lives for their country. She placed on it their names, ranks, the places where they fell, and underneath three words from the Bible: "But thou remainest." All else gone, she still had God. And with him were those dear to her, and in him they continued hers still, hers forever.—Robert J. McCracken.

NEARER HOME.   When we are young, heaven is a vague and nebulous place, but as our friends gather there, more and more it gains body and vividness and homeliness.—Arthur John Gossip.

GOD'S DAY.   Joseph R. Sizoo, referring to the words, "And the evening and the morning were the first day," pointed out that he would not have written it like that and that most of us would have turned it around and written, "And the morning and the evening were the first day." But we would be wrong and the book of Genesis right because God's day always ends in the morning. He never lets darkness have the last word. We can always depend upon the coming of the dawn. For God made a world like that. Isn't that our Easter faith? Isn't that good news?—Carl J. Sanders.

HIS OWN MEDICINE.   For whatever reason God chose to make man as he is—limited and suffering and subject to sorrows and death—he had the honesty and courage to take his own medicine. Whatever game he is playing with his creation, he has kept his own rules and played fair. He can exact nothing from man that he has not exacted from himself. He has himself gone through the whole of human experience from the trivial irritations of family life and the cramping restrictions of hard work and lack of money to the worst horrors of pain and humiliation, defeat, despair, and death. When he was a man, he played the man. He was born in poverty and died in disgrace and thought it well worthwhile.—Dorothy L. Sayers.

SONG AND GRIEF.   Instead of weeping when a tragedy occurs in a songbird's life, it sings away its grief. I believe we could well follow the pattern of our feathered friend.—Robert Sparks Walker.

NEAR AT HAND.   Wherever and whatever heaven is, it is not far away. If being in heaven means being near to God, then it surely stands to reason that we who are left on earth, whenever we are near to God, are wonderfully near also to those whom we have loved and lost awhile and who are nearer to God than we are.—R. Leonard Small.

PARAPHRASE.   The Lord is my pilot; I shall not drift. He lighteth my way across the dark waters; he steereth me in deep channels; he keepeth my log. He guardeth me by the star of holiness for his name's sake. Yea, though I sail mid the thunders and tempests of life, I will dread no danger: for thou art near me. Thy love and thy care they shelter me. Thou preparest a harbor before me in the homeland of eternity. Thou anointest the waves with oil; my ship rideth calmly. Surely sunlight and starlight shall favor me on the voyage I take, and I will rest in the port of my God forever.

NOT LENGTH OF DAYS.   In the Jerusalem Talmud is the story of a distinguished scholar, Rabbi Bun bar Hijja, who died at an early age about 325 A.D. His former teachers, who had become his colleagues, assembled to pay him honor, and one of them, Rabbi Ze Hera, gave his funeral oration in the form of a parable. He began by saying that the situation was like that of a king who had hired a great number of laborers. Two hours after the work began the king inspected the laborers. He saw that one of them surpassed the others both in industry and in skill. So he took him by the hand and walked him up and down until the evening. When the laborers came to receive their wages, each of them received the same amount as all the others. Whereupon they murmured and said, "We have worked the whole day, and this man only two hours, yet you have paid him a full day's wages." The king replied: "I have not wronged you. This laborer has done more in two hours than you have done during the whole day." So likewise, concluded the funeral oration, has Rabbi Bun bar Hijja accomplished more in his short life of twenty-eight years than many a grey-haired scholar in a hundred years. Therefore after so brief a span of labor,

God has taken him by the hand and gathered him to himself.—S. Robert Weaver.

READY.   During World War II Helmut Thielicke was pastor in Stuttgart, Germany. The city was ravished by Allied bombing. One morning Thielicke stood in combat boots and military fatigues before a gaping hole. It was a cellar which had sustained a direct bomb hit the night before. Some twenty men had been seeking shelter there. A woman approached to ask, "Are you Pastor Thielicke?" When he replied in the affirmative, she said: "My husband was down there last night. All they found of him was his cap. We heard you preach. I want to thank you for getting him ready for eternity."

FIRMLY ROOTED.   The best of God's saints must drink the wormwood; the dearest of his children must bear the cross. No Christian has enjoyed perpetual prosperity; no believer can always keep his harp from the willows. Perhaps the Lord allotted you at first a smooth and unclouded path because you were weak and timid. He tempered the wind to the shorn lamb. But now that you are stronger in the spiritual life, you must enter upon the riper and rougher experience of God's full-grown children. We need winds and tempests to exercise our faith, to tear off the rotten bow of self-dependence, and to root us more firmly in Christ. The day of evil reveals to us the value of our glorious hope.—Charles H. Spurgeon.

EMBROIDERED BOOKMARK.   Some years ago in a mine disaster in England forty miners lost their lives. The families, griefstricken and bewildered, gathered about the enterance to the mine. Someone asked Bishop Edward Stanley to say something that would help these hapless folk, and this is what he said: "We stand today in the face of mystery, but I want to tell you something I have at home. It is a bookmark, embroidered in silk by my mother given to me many years ago. On one side the threads are crossed and recrossed in wild confusion, and looking at it you would think it had been done by someone with no idea of what he was doing. But when I turn it over I see the words beautifully worked in silken threads, 'God Is Love.' Now we are looking at this tragedy from one side, and it does not make sense. Someday we shall be permitted to read its meaning from the other side. Meanwhile let us wait and trust."—John A. Redhead.

SECTION V. Resources for Lenten and Easter Preaching

SERMON SUGGESTIONS

Topic: Giving Up and Taking Up
TEXT: Matt. 12:43–45.

The important aspect of a Lenten pilgrimage has been misused, for when we give up some things we must complete this action by taking up other positive things in their places to fill the void of what we have given up. This is the point that Jesus makes in our lesson. The purpose of Lent is not to leave the person in worse shape when it is all over than he was at the beginning.

I. Give up not reading the Bible, and take up the Bible and read it.

II. Give up criticizing one another, and take up complementing one another.

III. Give up being in the dark, and take up walking in the light and being a source of light to those around us.

IV. Give up all vicious grudges, and take up the gracious act of forgiveness.

V. Give up hating, and take up loving.—Kenneth Merckz.

Topic: What Crucified Christ?
TEXT: I Cor. 2:8.

I. *Intolerance, racial and religious intolerance.* The Pharisees exemplified this. In the holy land in the day of Jesus the population was about one million persons and the Pharisees numbered 6,000. They were a very exclusive religious sect. They were the religious aristocrats. They were a minority group, but they exercised an influence far beyond their numbers. They believed in and defended the Mosiac law; they were the traditionalists. They observed all the various feasts and holidays and festivals. What was wrong with them? They thought they were better than anyone else.

II. *Political expediency.* Pilate had opportunities to save Christ from the crucifixion, but he was afraid to take the stand which he knew he should take because he thought Jewish authorities would report his actions to Rome. Thus he said he found no fault in him and washed his hands in their presence. He sent him out to be flogged and to endure the ugly crucifixion because it was politically expedient if he wanted to keep his position as procurator of Rome.

III. *The treachery and betrayal of his followers.* Probably one of the saddest verses in the Bible is "and they all forsook him and fled." One sold him for thirty pieces of silver. To go back on a friend is a common failing.

IV. *Public indifference and the mob spirit.* These are always present. The people had been coached by the agitators so that when the time came for Pilate to ask, "What then shall we do about Jesus, which is called Christ?" they cried out, "Crucify him." And there were people who had some sense of what was going on but were paralyzed by it all. They simply stood by and did nothing. Public indifference and the mob spirit are still at work in the actions of society.—William F. B. Rodda.

49

Topic: The Shape of the Cross
TEXT: Heb. 2:9.

I. There is irony in the cross. Examine its shape. It is a vertical, straight up and down. There is evidence that persons were sometimes impaled on poles, but a crossbar became part of general use. The two-way stretch, vertical and horizontal, made for maximum pain. Could this instrument have been tailor-made for the man from Nazareth? No other ever lived so completely by the shape of the cross.

(a) Jesus walked among men with his feet on the ground and his mind and heart in the heights. While walking with his feet on the ground, he heard a distant drummer and responded, "Not my will but thine." Vertically his life was stretched from earth to heaven.

(b) Life for Jesus would have been more comfortable had he only heard the distant drummer, but for him to hear was to respond. He must walk by the beat he heard. Because he loved God he listened, and because he listened he heard. His horizontal reach was all inclusive: Jews, Romans, Greeks, and even Samaritans. They accused him of eating with sinners. He counseled, "Love your enemies." Whom they would stone, he forgave.

(c) When they lifted this one to the cross he was ready—vertically stretched from earth to heaven and horizontally reaching with arms out-stretched toward the last and the least. Hear him, looking up to say, "Father, into thy hands," and looking out to a condemned criminal to say, "You will be with me." The stretch of the horizontal against the vertical was designed for maximum pain. And it was so.

II. The suffering becomes redemptive. There are many reasons why we suffer. All suffering is not healing. But when one voluntarily chooses to reach out to others, to lift them to the awareness of God, no matter the cost to himself, that suffering love becomes redemptive. Note two conditions that gave Jesus' life saving power.

(a) The first is the balance of the upward reach, seeking to know God's love, and the outward reach, God's love shared, poured out, and given. It is not God's love received that saves; it is God's love shared.

Not God's love for me but God's love through me. When the upward reach becomes an outward reach there is the shape of the cross and redemptive power.

(b) A second condition was his willingness to confine suffering to himself. He never sent another to die in his stead. "I lay down my life." Giving was his thing. They had accused him of healing a man with a withered hand. They never accused him of injuring a man's hand. Some ridiculed because he made the blind to see and the lame to walk. He never made another blind or another lame. It is no wonder that he said, "I'll do the dying."—Wesley P. Ford.

Topic: The Way of Suffering
TEXT: Mark 15:34.

Martin Luther sat motionless without food or water or sleep for many hours, pondering these words. When at last he stood, he exclaimed: "God forsaken of God! Who can understand it?" In the entire Bible one is hard-pressed to find words more difficult to explain than these. Who can fathom their depths? But fathom we must, for we are face-to-face with the gospel, overflowing with its summons to follow in the way of the cross.

I. These words from the cross testify to the reality of suffering. We so romanticize the beauty of Jesus' life that we forget the agony of his death. We see him walking among the lilies of the field, embracing small children with the love of a father, and touching the bitter infirmities of the most desperately ill with the grace of a physician, and overwhelmed by the glory of it all we suppose the cross to be another of those beautiful moments. But our sight is arrested by the agony of suffering, for we now see the man Jesus, brutally beaten and surrounded by enemies, passing from life to life through a death intensely painful.

II. These words from the cross testify to the real suffering of God. Often we suppose that he has insulated himself from the wretched trials and tragedies which disrupt the harmony of our lives. We imagine him laughing at our ridiculous follies or raging at our rank indiscretions.

But the sight of the cross arrests our attention. For there we see the gathering of God's enemies who laugh at the follies of his only Son and mock-rage at his extravagant claims for messianic authority. There in Jesus Christ we see God himself with nail-pierced hands and feet stretching out the pain of his last moments to the uttermost. Before our very eyes God himself suffers the excruciating pain of the cross.

III. These words from the cross testify to suffering as the way of the cross. This we deliberately try to forget. So often we limit our Jesus to the Christ of rose-colored kindness whose gentleness cradled sick children with the sweetness of love. But the cross arrests our attention. For there in the desolate suffering of our savior we see all the maimed and desolate creatures whose putrid bodies and festered souls craved the touch of Christ-like compassion. The ministry of Jesus Christ was no saunter down a country lane amid the lilies of the field. It was a pilgrimage up the main street of human history littered by the society's sufferers—the penniless poor, the hopeless mad, and the incurable ill. The way to the cross was among inescapable suffering.—Gary L. Wilson.

Topic: We Preach Christ Crucified
SCRIPTURE: I Cor. 1:18–25.

I. The cross demonstrates how far God would go to reveal his love for mankind. There was a cross in the heart of God long before there was one rooted on a hill outside Jerusalem. On Calvary it was not merely a man who endured the agonies of pain and death. It was God himself demonstrating how far he would go for mankind.

II. The cross demonstrates how far man would go in his rebellion against God. The cross is a window through which we gaze deep into the loving heart of God. It is also a mirror in which we see reflected our own rebellion against him. Calvary is the inevitable meeting place between the love of God and the sin of man. The horror of the cross is not merely pain and loneliness, thirst and death. Its full horror is revealed in the complete and unutterable stubbornness of men and women who will not come

to him. It is a symbol for all generations of our rebellion against God.

III. The cross demonstrates the total victory of God in Jesus Christ. Victory to the Greeks meant a hymn of praise to some deity who stirred human passions and imaginations, inspiring people to delight in the material things about them. Victory to the Romans meant a triumphant procession with marching soldiers, streaming banners, and cheering crowds. But victory to the Christian meant the decisive intervention of God in human history.

IV. The cross demonstrates what we as Christians are called upon to do. The church has often been described as "the way of the cross" and Christians as "followers of the way." God in Jesus Christ poured himself out in love for us. Therefore we are expected to do the same for the men and women of our own generation. We either accept our cross or we reject it. We cannot remain indifferent to it. —George C. Bonnell.

Topic: After the Hosannas
TEXT: Mark 11:11; 15–18.

With the cry of "hosanna" they greeted him. With the cry of "hosanna" in his ears he made his triumphal entry. And with the cry of "hosanna" began the last and most important days of his mortal life.

I. These eight days in the brief career of the man from Nazareth are the most important days in human history.

(a) It is not the "hosannas" that we remember; it is not the "hosannas" that interest us some nineteen and more centuries later. We know how fleeting and how transitory the greeting of the crowds was. We cannot view Palm Sunday nor any other day in Jesus' life apart from the drama that unfolded in the hours and days after the "hosannas."

(b) After the "hosannas" came the efforts of the authorities to trick Jesus into condemning himself; after the "hosannas" came Jesus' own warnings of the last days; after them came the last supper and Gethsemane, the betrayal and trial, the denials of Peter, the appearance before Pilate and the people, now no longer friendly; and after the "hosannas" came the crucifixion.

II. You may liken the "hosannas" of Palm Sunday to our weekly worship. Most of our living is not surrounded by "hosannas"; most of it does not take place in Sunday worship.

(a) Our living goes on after the "hosannas," after the Sunday service, on the next day and the next when we too must live out our faith and make our witness in the world.

(b) Such a witness is made in and through the economic, social, and political institutions of the world; there is no other way. It is on these days, after the "hosannas," that our discipleship is put to the test.

III. Ultimately the drama of life is not unlike the drama of holy week. There will be countless opportunities to witness and minister in the name of Christ, and each opportunity holds also a chance to avoid it, side-step it, or ignore it, if we choose to deny our Lord. And it is not easy to follow, to pay the cost; it is not even easy to know how to choose. After all, Peter denied Jesus three times before he realized what he had done.—Gregory T. Armstrong.

Topic: Death and Reconciliation

TEXT: II Cor. 5:19.

What does it mean that God was in Christ reconciling the world unto himself?

I. It will bring *forgiveness.* Man's problem is his sin. This sin stands between man and God and cuts off our relationship with him. The testimony of the New Testament is that in the atonement man's sins are forgiven and the barrier to fellowship with God is removed. Our sins have been covered with the blood of Christ, and God remembers them no more. (See Eph. 1:7.)

II. It will bring *liberation.* Man's problem is that he is in bondage to the powers of the world. Sin and death have us in their grip. The testimony of the New Testament is that in the atonement man is freed from these powers of the world. The Bible says that man is delivered from the curse of the law (Gal 3:13), from death (John 11:25), from corruption (Rom. 8:21), from condemnation (Rom. 8:1), from creaturely weakness (Rom. 7:24), and from the power of the devil (I John 4:4). Because of what Jesus did on the cross we can be free to become the persons God created us to be.

III. It will bring *sanctification.* Man needs hope for the future. Man's problem is that he has fallen short of God's ideal. He has missed the mark. He needs to be made over into a new person. The process by which we are refashioned into the image of God is called sanctification. And the testimony of the New Testament is that in the atonement man is started on the process of sanctification which will eventuate in his being like Christ. (See Heb. 10:10.)— Brian L. Harbour.

ILLUSTRATIONS

WORDS OF LIFE.   On the back wall of the Memorial Church at Stanford University is this inscription: "A noble ambition is among the most helpful influences of student life. No man can work well unless he can speak as the great master did of the joy set before him." Elsewhere in the form of a cross are found these words: "The cross is the emblem of faith, hope, and love, those ineffable virtues of the soul that abide forever, that can never be outgrown even on the loftiest planes of being in the mighty universe of God."—Harold Garnet Black.

THE SHADOW.   Holman Hunt on his third visit to the holy land sketched a carpenter shop and through the window of the shop pictured the hills around Nazareth. Every detail of that carpenter shop is done with great accuracy. The rack of tools and the tools also were purchased in Palestine. Inside the shop is Jesus with his mother Mary. Mary is rummaging in an old trunk where she keeps the gifts of the wise men—the crown, the censer, and the vase of myrrh which speaks of death. Jesus, wearied by a long day's toil, stretches out his arms to rest them, and the setting sun casts his shadow against the rack of tools which hangs on the wall in the form of a cross. Mary looks up and sees the shadow of a man on the cross and the vase drops from her hands. "Dear God, can this be prophecy? Must it be that my boy will die on a cross?" In that moment a sword pierces her heart, and a shadow rests on her life until that dread day on Calvary.— John Sutherland Bonnell.

BEYOND FAILURE. Jesus did not have to face failure in himself, but he did have to face it in respect of the hopes and desires he had formed for mankind. One of the chief elements in the agony of Gethsemane was the terrific and final adjustment of his spirit to the fact of the almost total failure of his call to his own beloved people. It is one of the grandest things in Jesus that he accepted this failure and went on to the cross with love and faith undiminished, so turning the failure, as we believe, into victory.—Herbert H. Farmer.

TURNING TO HIM. The cross is not and cannot be loved. Yet only the crucified Christ can bring the freedom which changes the world because it is no longer afraid of death. In his time the crucified Christ was regarded as a scandal and as foolishness. Today too it is considered old-fashioned to put him in the center of Christian faith and of theology. Yet only when men are reminded of him, however untimely this may be, can they be set free from the power of the facts of the present time and from the laws and compulsions of history and be offered a future which will never grow dark again. Today the church and theology must turn to the crucified Christ in order to show the world the freedom he offers. This is essential if they wish to become what they assert they are: the church of Christ and Christian theology.—Jurgen Moltmann.

GOD'S HAND. Mervyn Stockwood says that when he was a boy he used to go to the three-hour Good Friday services held at the church he attended. As the service moved on he kept hoping something would happen to save the situation. Surely somebody would intervene before the soldiers finished nailing Jesus to the cross. Certainly someone would break into the drama before circumstances became too desperate. Maybe God would take a hand in the affair and come to the rescue of his son before it was too late. The whole pageant was frightfully unfair. He shouldn't have "suffered under Pontius Pilate." Of course, God did have a hand in the affair. He shared it. He knew the pain and the anguish of it all. In his love he was crucified with Christ, and Jesus knew it. "Father, into thy hands I commit my spirit," he said, and he came through the worst with a word of forgiveness and of trust on his lips.—Harold Blake Walker.

THE ORCHID. In 1942 Singapore fell to the Japanese. Ethel Rogers Mulvaney, a Canadian working for the Red Cross, was one of 4,000 civilians who were imprisoned in Changi jail. As their first Easter in prison approached, Mrs. Mulvaney asked the Japanese prison commandant if they might sing in the courtyard on Easter morning. "Why?" he asked. "Because Christ rose from the dead on Easter morning," she replied. He barked his reply: "Request denied. Return to the compound." This drama of request and refusal was repeated twelve times. Then to their astonishment came the order, "Woman prisoners may sing for five minutes in courtyard number one, Changi jail, at dawn on Easter morning."

In the presence of one guard they sang for five precious minutes in which they praised God for the resurrection of Jesus Christ, the only hope to which they could cling as a living hope in the midst of their seemingly hopeless imprisonment. Silently they marched back. As Mrs. Mulvaney entered the passageway, the guard stepped up to her, reached under his brown shirt, and drew out a tiny orchid. Placing it in her hand, he spoke so softly that she had to bend close to hear. "Christ did rise!" said the guard. Then with a smart military about-face, he was gone down the passage way. Mrs. Mulvaney, her eyes brimming with tears, knew that she and the others need never again feel forsaken in Changi jail. Christ had not only risen; he had been recognized.—Adapted from *Guideposts*.

ALIVE OR DEAD? The five-year-old grandson of the senior pastor came to my office. His family had just moved from Washington, D.C. As we chatted about the nation's capital, we got around to Abraham Lincoln. The youngster spoke up: "He doesn't live there anymore. He's dead." After a moment he continued, "My grandfather has a picture of Mr. Lincoln, and in that picture he's alive." Do we picture our Lord as the historic Jesus of the poets and painters or as the risen Christ of the Emmaus Road and Damascus Way?—E. Paul Hovey.

CHANGE. A friend attended an Easter sunrise service at a Greek Orthodox church in Athens, Greece. As he entered the church he noticed that it was dimly lighted by candles. Heavy draperies closed all windows to the faint light of approaching dawn. The smoke of burning incense made the church even darker. The odor produced a funeral atmosphere. Rhythmically swinging the censers, the priests were chanting dirges in monotone. An atmosphere of mourning gripped the worshipers with a sense of depression. Then everything seemed to stop. A door suddenly was thrown open and someone shouted: "He is risen! He is alive!" Immediately the lights were turned up brightly. The window draperies were drawn, and the now fully risen sun came cascading in, flooding the sanctuary. The impact was startling and dramatic. The whole tenor of worship changed from melancholy to joy and expectation.—Gardner Koch.

HE GAVE HIMSELF. In his *Dialogues in Limbo* George Santayana pictures a stranger from earth, presumably a Christian, speaking with one of the spirits of antiquity about Jesus. Says the stranger: "If you asked me for my own opinion, I should say that there is one great gift which our Prophet has bestowed upon us, and that is himself. . . . It was divine love free from craving or decay. The saint and the blackguard alike were known to him at their true worth; in both he could see something disfigured or unattained, perhaps hidden from their eyes, and yet the sole reason and root of their being, something simple and worthy of love beneath their weakenss and perversity; and the assurance of this divine love. . . . lent them courage not wholly to despise themselves but to seed and to cleanse the pure pearl in their dunghill, on which his own eye rested, and not without reason to call him the savior of their souls."

SECTION VI. *Resources for Advent and Christmas Preaching*

SERMON SUGGESTIONS

Topic: Isaiah Names the Child
Text: Isa. 9:6.

A fourfold title is seen in the prophet's vision. Two titles—"Wonderful Counselor" and "Mighty God"—describe his nature, and two—"Everlasting Father" and "Prince of Peace"—tell of his work.

I. As "Wonderful Counselor" he is the fount of all knowledge, the source of all wisdom. Man has no cause to boast about what he knows, for God has given him the power to discern truth; and all truth inheres in him who said, "I am the truth."

II. As "Mighty God" he incarnates divine omnipotence. He who made himself subject to the tyranny of evil men "emptied himself" and became like us that we might become like him.

III. "Everlasting Father" describes his caretaking ministry. He loved us with an endless love, even while we lived in rebellion against him.

IV. As "Prince of Peace" he gave himself to bring reconciliation between God and man and between man and man.—L. D. Johnson.

Topic: The Hidden Glory
Text: Isa. 40:5.

God's glory can and does break into life in the most unexpected places, often where we least expect it and are least prepared to see what is there.

I. The evident glory of God can easily be seen and appreciated. (a) Consider the evident glory of the sunset, of the stars on a clear summer night, of the wide ocean stretching limitlessly in the distance, or of the breath-taking impressiveness of a vast mountain range. There come to all of us times when nature seems indescribably and almost unbearably beautiful.

(b) This is the evident glory that we usually associate with the Christmas scene. The familiar pictures of the nativity bathe the manger and the stable in an unearthly etherial radiance. Our annual community illuminations, our candles and Christmas trees, and the music of Christmas point us in this direction. For all this God must surely be praised.

II. The Christmas story points toward the hidden glory of a God who comes into human life through incarnation rather than through decoration. "Veiled in flesh," says the familiar Christmas carol, "the Godhead see!"

(a) Advent should remind us that, when God made himself known to man most fully, he entered the world through the birth of a truly human baby to an ordinary human mother in a place where nobody expected him. There was no room in the inn, and so they laid him in a manger. It was cold, rough, plain, dirty, and drafty there.

(b) The God and Father of our Lord Jesus Christ is found in the midst of human relationships. God's glory is found wherever the spirit of the life of that man of all men comes into being and whenever the love of God that was so fully expressed by him is expressed and reincarnated in the lives of men and women today.

III. We tend to look for the glory of God in the starry heavens, the mountain vastnesses, and the ocean's tides and waves when the Bible would teach us that he is most truly known and present in the hidden places of human living, in the places, for example, where people gather together in the awareness of his presence and then go forth to live their lives and to serve one another in his name.

(a) The glory of the Lord enters human life whenever a teacher labors long over a recalcitrant student, whenever a physician calms the anxious fears of a panic-stricken patient, whenever a businessman treats a hard-pressed and defaulting customer with courtesy and consideration, whenever a politician refuses to make an unethical but profitable deal at the expense of the electorate or takes an unpopular stand for a policy in which he believes, whenever a parent comforts his or her brokenhearted child or seeks reconciliation with an alienated son or daughter, whenever a young man dies in the service of peace and freedom and justice, whenever a housewife goes on assuming the same old burdensome responsibilities when it seems as if she couldn't face the same drudgery for another day, or whenever church people and churches speak and act in behalf of the poor, the unwanted, the despised, or the dispossessed.

(b) Only when God's word becomes flesh and dwells among us in this manner do we begin to behold his true glory, "full of grace and truth." Even you and I, by the way in which we live and respond to the situations in which we find ourselves, can open up a crack in the wall between earth and heaven and let the glory in for ourselves and for those around us, not just at Christmas but on any day of the year.—Edward C. Dahl.

Topic: On Being God's Elect

Text: Luke 1:38.

I. Mary was right. She did not deserve her election as the mother of Christ. It was God's grace, not her goodness, that determined her choice. God's favor reflects his goodness, not ours. To be his elect is an occasion not for pride but for humility. Fortunately it was in humility that Mary responded. She did not congratulate God for his wise choice as some of us might have done.

II. Mary learned that election by God is not only a glorious privilege but also a great responsibility.

(a) There is joy in being chosen, but let us never forget that God chooses us because he has a purpose for us, something he wants us to do or to become.

(b) Mary must have sensed this, for even as Gabriel was singing the glory of her election as the mother of the Christ, Mary replied humbly, "Behold, I am the handmaid of the Lord; let it be to me according to your word." What she means, as the NEB makes clear, is this: "Here am I . . . the Lord's servant." She sensed that her election meant servanthood.

(c) It is no less with us who are God's elect as the new Israel. As Peter puts it, "But you are a chosen race, a royal priesthood, a holy nation, God's own people." Why? "That you may declare the wonderful needs of him who called you out of darkness into his marvelous light." He chooses us because he has something for us to do—a purpose to fulfill and a mission to perform. We all glory in the privileges of his election and of receiving the favor of God. We need also to concern ourselves with the servanthood to which he has called us.

III. "You have found favor with God," she was told. Yet it seemed a strange kind of favor during all those obscure years in Nazareth, those months of embarrassing notoriety when her son pursued that brief and strange public ministry, and then that terrible day on Calvary. What kind of favor was that? The kind of favor God always gives to his faithful servants, his elect.

(a) Hardship and opposition are the strange rewards of those who are chosen by God. Instead of receiving the promise of immunity from difficulty and suffering, the person who embraces Christianity is more likely to suffer for his faith.

(b) To be one of the elect, one of God's people, means inevitable suffering, perhaps even a cross. The favor of God, Mary was to learn—as Israel had discovered before her and Christendom after her—is not the easy way to unbroken happiness. For between the favor of God's election and the vindication of his victory lies the road of the suffering servant.—Lawrence W. Althouse.

Meditation: The First Christmas Carols

Matthew related the disappointments of that first Christmas: the apprehensions of Joseph regarding full marriage to Mary with child, the wrath of Herod, the slaughter of the innocents, and the flight into Egypt. But Luke recorded the five thrilling carols of the first Christmas.

The first was the song of the angel who announced to Mary: "That holy thing which shall be born of thee shall be called the Son of God." It was the sweetest solo an angel ever sung. It was the song all humanity had been waiting breathlessly to hear.

The second Christmas carol Luke gives is the Magnificat: the song of Mary in her response to the angelic announcement. It was fragrant with devotion, sweet with humility, exultant in grace, and prophetic in tone. How fitting that God should choose a woman of such piety and simplicity to be the mother of our Lord and to sing about it so sweetly.

Luke's third Christmas carol is the song of Zacharias whose long silence broke forth in praises to God. He sang of the approaching Christ and of the expectant birth of his own son, the messiah's forerunner, for which Elisabeth and he had waited until their old age. He rejoiced in God's oath to Abraham now being fulfilled. He sang of holiness and righteousness of the knowledge of salvation and of the remission of sin.

The fourth Christmas carol was the glad "glory to God in the highest, and on earth peace, good will to men" sung by the angelic choir to humble shepherds the night Jesus was born. This was the carol supreme!

Luke's fifth Christmas carol was the song of the aged Simeon who blessed the infant in his arms—the savior for whom he had watched so many years.—Fletcher Spruce.

Meditation: The Christ of Christmas

Amidst the pastorals of sleighbells and snow frosted windows, twinkling lights and aluminum stars, the remnants of a nativity scene occasionally finds brief incarnation.

Somewhere in the array of department store bustle and jingle bell hustle, strains of a familiar carol faintly share their message of "peace on earth" and "glory to God in the highest." Ah, yes, "Christmas" celebration and the birth of the savior.

The birth of the savior seems somewhat removed from the present-day celebration of this rich tradition. If we did not know otherwise, we might well think that Christmas was an invention of Madison Avenue advertising agencies to promote business. The idea of the kingship of Christ has been all but lost from our Christmas horizons. Television Christmas specials rarely mention it, and public school's Christmas programs omit it as being too offensive.

Christ is offensive, not as that cute baby in the manger, where the world would like to keep him, but as the author and king of life who demands allegiance and would exercise authority over our lives. Is it any small wonder that "all Jerusalem was troubled" at that first Christmas? Or is it any wonder that this generation has edited out the authoritative Christ, the Christ of service, the Christ of mission? The baby grew up.

Christmas is a lovely time of year. It speaks of giving, of family ties, of harmony and brotherhood, joy and peace. These are the gifts of a loving God to a loved world, and it is Christ, the gift of God, who holds it all together. We must never fail to realize that the advent of that single solitary life is an ever-present reality which we must embrace with the totality of our being, even at Christmas time. Wise men know this.—Randal Lee Cummings.

Topic: Christmas Revelations

TEXT: John 1:14.

I. Christmas reveals something of the quality of God's mercy. It was God's active mercy that came to the world with the birth of Jesus. In that act we have the unmistakable evidence of a God who seized the initiative. In that act we see an Almighty who had compassion on his children. God visited man and assured him that he does not intend to forget him.

II. Christmas reveals something of the nature of God's grace. By grace I mean voluntary compensation, an outright gift. Grace is characterized by God's reaching down to help us in every aspect of our need. It is God's doing for us what we are unable to do for ourselves. It is at Christmas that we see a manifestation of the tremendous difference that God through Jesus Christ has made and continues to make in our lives.

III. Christmas reveals something of the quality of God's love. That one, grand invasion of God's love came in the personification of his spirit through his son Jesus. In Jesus the people of his day saw, and we now in spirit realize, the warm and tender interest God has in each of us. "The Father himself loved us." Therein is love in the superlative degree, not that we loved God but that he loved us and sent his son to be the propitiation of our sins.— George A. Sewell.

ILLUSTRATIONS

JOY AND TENSION.   The season of Advent has great irony within it, for no season has more joy and happiness and at the same time more tension and tightness between persons. Sadly, the church has oftentimes, through heavy scheduling of activities, helped to cause some of this tension. It is crucial to help free people to experience the deeper meaning of the season, rather than bringing tension through so many traditional and many times meaningless activities. Too often we keep people from relaxing and experiencing the joy of God's special gift of life. The task of the church is not to fight for more time but to free us to experience the simple gift of life that inspires us to take a chance, to open up and share our friendship, our love, and our hopes, and to experience God's love, rather than repay it with gifts.—L. Jim Anthis.

HEART'S DOOR.   A young Christian in New Guinea was asked to describe Advent. His explanation was simple and to the point: "At Advent we should try the key to our heart's door. It may have gathered rust. If so, this is the time to oil it in order that the heart's door may open more easily when the Lord Jesus wants to enter at Christmastime."

PARABLE.   John Donne tells a parable of the mountain. A man is climbing a mountain, at the top of which he hopes to find God. By ascending the heights, the seeker expects to leave all the cares and miseries of life behind in the valley. But while he climbs, God is coming down the mountain into the toil and grief. In the mists of the mountain God and the man pass one another. When the man reaches the mountaintop, he will find nothing. God is not there. What then will he do? He knows the climbing was a mistake, but in agony of that recognition, will he fall down and despair? Or will he turn to retrace his path through the mists and into the valley to where God has gone seeking him?—Bevel Jones.

GOD'S CHOICE.   Jurgen Moltmann suggests that the incarnation was not necessary. Moltmann's notion is that God did not become man because he was compelled to, but because he chose to do so. This is a radical theological departure. Traditionally Christians have interpreted the incarnation as a necessary act for man's salvation. The view is that mankind was so very sinful and alienated from God that eventually God had no choice but to become human in order to heal the breach and save his human creation. Moltmann reasons that the incarnation is God's free choice. He became man in the person of Jesus of Nazareth because he wanted to. He became incarnate not out of necessity but out of love for us.—K. C. Ptomey, Jr.

IMMORTAL CROWN. Some of us can see the light resting upon a bishop's crosier, but we cannot see the radiance on the ordinary shepherd's staff. We can discern the hallowedness of a priest's vocation, but we can see no sanctity in the calling of a grocer. We can see the nimbus on the few, but not on the crowd; on the unusual, but not upon the commonplace. The very birth-hour of Christianity irradiated the humble doings of humble people. When the angels went to the shepherds, common work was encircled with an immortal crown.—John Henry Jowett.

AGELESS STAR. Did you think the star was meant just for the magi and the shepherds—just for that one night alone? Oh, no! God hung it there against the ages; it is for all of us. Its radiance enfolds us all, knowing no bound of creed, color, or servitude. It guides the aged home; it is reflected in the eyes of babes, generation after generation, and in the eyes of mothers seeking in their babes the countenance of Christ. All of us are come once more under the spell of the star, come to take new hope in peace and the prince of peace.

WHAT IS CHRISTMAS. Christmas is a gift of love wrapped in human flesh and tied securely with the strong promises of God.

Christmas is angelic music in the form of carol and oratorio with a celestial descant.

Christmas is "glory to God," "good will to man," and "joy to the world."

Christmas is "peace on earth" for those who accept it and live in unity with God's will.

Christmas is a man on duty tending sheep or machine who senses the upward call and stops to worship.

Christmas is a tall green tree which serves as festive altar for any household which discovers the true meaning behind it all.

Christmas is a ringing bell calling a distraught humanity to gladness and hope.

Christmas is a glowing hearth gently placed in the winter of man's loneliness.

Christmas is an altar to which man can bring his heartache for comfort, his lostness for guidance, and his sin for forgiveness.

Christmas is the sparkle of anticipation and the steady light of faith in the eyes of a little child as he hears the old, old story.

Christmas is a shining star of hope in the sky of all mankind.

Christmas is more than words can tell, for it is a matter for the heart to receive, believe, and understand.—Carlton C. Buck.

LORD OF THE STUDENTS. And so the good news came to "wise men," shall we say to students?—busying themselves with the vast and intricate problems of the mind. And the evangel offered the students mental satisfaction, bringing the interpreting clue, beaming upon them with the guiding ray which would lead them into perfect noon.

Yes, our wise men must find the key of wisdom in the Lord. To seek mental satisfactions and leave out Jesus is like trying to make a garden and leave out the sun. "Without me ye can do nothing," not even the unraveling of the problems which beset and beseige the mind.

My mental pilgrimage must begin with Jesus, and pay homage to his kingly and incomparable glory. I must lay my treasures at his feet, "gold, and frankincense, and myrrh." Then he will lead me "into all truth," and "the truth shall make me free."—John Henry Jowett.

DILEMMA. Peter Breughel's "Nativity" in the National Gallery has been called the most cynical picture in the world, and it is certainly a great contrast with the tender version of the same scene by Botticelli or the joyful painting of Paolo della Francesca in the same room. Breughel shows us the stable at Bethlehem with Mary and Joseph and the holy child, while in the foreground the kings present their gifts. But the place is full of soldiers, and it cannot be accidental that around the head of Mary and at her side are men at arms with spears and cross bows. "He maketh wars to cease; he breaketh the bow, and he cutteth the spear in sunder." "Well, does he?" the picture asks. "Sixteen hundred years have passed and the followers of the so-called prince of peace fill the earth with clamor, cruelty, and violence!" In the foreground kneel two of the kings. They represent great power groups, as might be the Most Christian King of France and the Most Catholic King of Spain. It is clear that it is sheer self-interest which has brought them to make this gesture of humility, and as they kneel one looks over his shoulder at the other, as if afraid that even here, at this moment, his rival will outdo him. At the side of the picture—a modern touch—stands the third world ruler, an African, silent and disillusioned. Cynical or just realistic? At least it puts fairly and squarely the dilemma which Dorothy Sayers put on the lips of Melchior in her play *The Man Born to Be King* when he asked, "The riddle that torments the world is this, shall power and love dwell together at last when the promised kingdom comes?"—E. G. Rupp.

SOUNDS AND SIGHTS.   The world is filled with the sounds of Christmas. If you listen with your outer ears, you will hear carols, bells, laughter, and now and then a sob of loneliness. If you listen with the inner ear, you will hear the sound of angels' wings, the hush of inner expectation, and the sacred sound of the deepest silence, the vibrant whisper of the eternal word.

The world is filled with the sights of Christmas. If you look with your outer eyes, you will see gay trees, tinseled stars, flaming candles, and a creche. If you look with the inner eye, you will see the star of Bethlehem in your own heart.—Anna May Nielsen.

GUIDING CANDLES.   Long ago there lived a shoemaker. Though he was poor, each night he placed a lighted candle in his window to welcome travlers seeking shelter.

War came to his nation, followed by famine. The shoemaker suffered less than some others. His neighbors believed it might be because of his lighted candle. On Christmas Eve every house had a candle burning in the window.

By morning a mantle of snow covered the village. Soon a messenger, bringing news of peace, came riding into the village. "It was the candles," the villagers whispered to one another. "They have guided Christ to our doors."—E. Paul Hovey.

TWO QUESTIONS.   There are many questions asked in the Bible, but on in Genesis and another in Matthew are, I think, greatest of all. God asked Adam, "Where art thou?" Wise men from the east asked, "Where is he that is born king of the Jews?" In one, God was searching for the sinner; in the other, men were searching for the savior of the world.—B. J. Ratnam.

SHARING ONE'S GRACES.   The true meaning of Christmas is expressed in the sharing of one's graces in a world in which it is so easy to become calloused, insensitive, and hard. Once this spirit becomes a part of man's life, every day is Christmas and every night is freighted with anticipations of the dawning of fresh, and perhaps holy, adventure.—Howard Thurman.

SECTION VII. Evangelism and World Missions

SERMON SUGGESTIONS

Topic: By All Means Reach Out
TEXT: Acts 26:17-18.

I. The church evangelizes by the faithfulness of its proclamation, by the compassion of its service, and by the reality of its fellowship. How did Jesus evangelize?

(a) He did it by telling. (See Mark 1:14.) He was teacher and preacher par excellence.

(b) He did it by serving. (See Mark 1:34.) When he met a sick man, he healed him; a hungry man, he fed him.

(c) He did it by loving. (See Mark 2:16.) He was above all a friend and especially a friend to the needy and to sinners.

II. How did Jesus' disciples evangelize? They followed in the steps of the master. Their witness was by faithful proclamation. (See Acts 5:42.) Their witness was by compassionate service. (See Acts 3:6.) Their witness was by loving fellowship. (See Acts 2:44.)

(a) Our strategy must be the penetration of the whole world through the mobilization of the whole church and the utilization of every rightful method, the comprehensive use of every legitimate method.

(b) When Paul said, "I am made all things to all men, that I might by all means save some" (I Cor. 9:22), surely what he was urging upon us is flexibility, not duplicity. Total integrity must be ours whatever method we use. Trickery is an alien intruder in the tactics of the Christian church. "We use no hocuspocus, no clever tricks, no manipulation of the word of God" (II Cor. 4:2, PHILLIPS).—Myron J. Taylor.

Topic: Building Up Christ's Body
TEXT: I Cor. 12:27.

How else can we do our part to build up the body of Christ, which is the church, unless we realize that we are persons sent "out into the fields which are white unto harvest"? Our task is to tell people who Christ is and what he has done for all of us but particularly for ourselves.

I. The task is *evangelism*—bringing to a generation of persons, who have lost their identity and their way, the good news that there is one, Jesus Christ, who can and will save them.

II. The task is *mission*—living in the world but becoming the leaven of the spirit of Christ which can permeate the whole of society around us.

III. The task is *service*—calling us to give, to teach, to heal, to comfort, to encourage, and to help the other fellow bear his heavy load.

IV. The task is *ministry*—that to which all of us who name the name of Christ are called.—Hoover Rupert.

Topic: The Cause of Christ
TEXT: Rom 1:1 (NEB).

I. Those who make up what is called the Christian church are caught up in a cause, for by definition the church is a group of

61

men and women who are called out from the mainstream of humanity and called to an allegiance which transcends the ordinary concerns of men.

II. The apostle Paul went through countless beatings and imprisonments and harassments for his allegiance to Jesus Christ. Paul's commitment made him a missionary. So it must always be for those who constitute the Christian church. For the church's great task is to herald, to witness, and to demonstrate the meaning of God's reign. The church exists to call men and women to something greater than themselves and to the greatest cause of all, the cause of Christ. Therefore it needs to be a missionary church because to be otherwise would be to deny the very fact that has called her into being.

III. If you are a member of the church, if you claim to be Christ's disciple, and if you have given yourself to the cause of Christ, the meaning for you is obvious, is it not? You too are called to be a missionary. That is always the case when a man or a woman gives his or her life over to the savior. If you are Christ's servant, then it can't be helped. You become a missionary —perhaps overseas, perhaps in some particular community the Lord makes plain to you, or perhaps right where you live, in your work, and in your relating to your friends and neighbors. But to give yourself to the cause of Christ is to give yourself to the gospel, to God's good news, and to the spreading of it.—Arthur McPhee.

Topic: World Mission

TEXT: Matt. 24:14.

I. The spirit of God is summoning the church everywhere to the unfinished task of world mission.

(a) No one can listen to what is happening in land after land without hearing a renewed call to evangelism. Christians are having placed on their heart and conscience the millions of people who know little or nothing of Jesus Christ.

(b) If Jesus is the hope of the world, and this is the faith of a Christian, then it is intolerable that millions live and die without that hope. To do nothing about the spiritual starvation of masses of people is as unpardonable as to be doing nothing about the physical hunger of the world.

II. No longer is world mission an overseas task alone. In terms of need the world is one for people are as ignorant of the Christian faith in our own street and town as anywhere in the world. Everywhere children are growing up without any knowledge of the Christian faith. We can see them playing in the street where we live any Sunday, knowing that probably they come from homes which are two or three generations separated from any religious faith. Their souls are as undernourished and neglected as bodies were in the bad old days. World mission belongs to the street where we live.

III. The message of world mission is crucial. The world cries out not for half-a-gospel but the full-orbed gospel of Jesus Christ. There is no word of deliverance in a message carefully trimmed to the modern mind. The judgment of failure is falling on the humanist church and the secular gospel. The reality of the God-experience is the touchstone of faith. God is not a problem to be solved but a person to be known and enjoyed.—Alan Walker.

Topic: Christians Aflame!

TEXT: Luke 12:49.

I. Christians are a people kindled with divine fire. (a) Fire is the symbol of the Spirit of God. To be aflame is to have God the Spirit in you. The author of Hebrews says, "Our God is a consuming fire." God came to Moses at the burning bush; the place was holy because God was present. On Mt. Carmel God answered Elijah's prayer to send fire from heaven to consume the sacrifice. In the case of Jeremiah, God's word was "in your mouth a fire." After walking with Jesus on the way to Emmaus, the disciples asked, "Did not our hearts burn within us while he talked to us on the road?"

(b) Christians are aflame with God in them. John the Baptist predicted that Jesus "will baptize you with the Holy Spirit and with fire" (Luke 3:16). Elton True-blood describes the church as an "incendiary fellowship." The Holy Spirit comes to us as tongues of fire.

II. Christians can let the fire of God go out. The fire of God the Spirit is not necessarily an eternal flame. How can the fire of God go out of your life?

(a) The fire can be extinguished by the water of worldliness.

(b) The fire can be smothered by the cares of this life.

(c) The fire can be so encircled that it burns itself out in self-centeredness.

III. Christians need to keep the fire burning in their lives. (a) Fire is needed for cleansing. The fire of God's Spirit burns up the evil in our lives. Gold is refined by fire.

(b) Fire provides energy and power. The fire of the Spirit builds up steam to drive the engine which pulls the train of burdens. (See Acts 1:8.)

(c) Fire lights other fires and spreads. A fire feeds on what is next to it. It is contagious. If the person next to you at home, at work, at play, or in school does not catch on fire from your fire, then your fire must have gone out. Fire spreads as the wind blows. The Spirit is the wind of God that scatters the fire to others. Christians intentionally and deliberately put people on fire with God.—John R. Brokhoff.

Topic: What Is Evangelism?

TEXT: Isa. 52:7.

It is being present to another person, being there in the deepest sense of the term, knowing that God is present to you both, as present as each will permit.

It is listening, open-ended listening, prayerfully trying to understand what the other person is saying through his words and feelings.

It is being an overflowing bucket, in the midst of the dialogue telling what cannot be kept in—good news!

It is telling our story, the story of a pilgrim people, supremely the story of Jesus Christ, God's true man and true hope.

It is speaking from the bottom of the heart, not from the top of the head.

It is speaking more to the heart than to the head.

It is inviting others to a pilgrimage in discipleship to Jesus Christ.

It is the sharing and celebrating of beauty, truth, goodness, and love.

It is a joyful throwing of your faith into the air.

It is a healing word spoken and a healing deed done.

It is an act of reconciliation.

It is a cup of cold water given.

It is a life lived authentically and humbly.

It is a hope shared—a hope for this neighbor and every neighbor.—Gerald J. Jud.

ILLUSTRATIONS

MISSIONARY AWAKENINGS.   Right down through the ages you will find great missionary awakenings when you have the conjunction of these two factors—some fresh vision of the world opening up vast areas of human need and with this a spiritual awakening which makes one vividly conscious of a source that can satisfy that need.—Daniel J. Fleming.

SOUL PAIN.   Can you mention the names of people, two or three, perhaps, who are to you a real sorrow because they are not Christians? They are good people, they are your friends, but always when you think of them there is a pain in your soul because they do not serve Jesus Christ. Are there such people in your life? If not, you are not an evangelist.—D. T. Niles.

OBSCURE MISSIONARIES.   During the great age of expansion which followed the death of Paul, we do not hear the name of a single outstanding missionary. The real work was done by countless obscure men and women who made it their first duty to spread the message in their own circle of friends and neighbors.—Ernest F. Scott.

HOLDING THE ROPES.   In 1791 William Carey published a little book entitled *An Enquiry into the Obligations of Christians to Use Means for the Conversion of the Heathens.* Then in 1792 at the Nottinghamshire Baptist Association he preached his famous sermon based on Isa. 54:2–3. In October 1792, at the home of Widow Wallis, the first society for the work of foreign missions was formed and the modern mission movement was begun. In offering himself as a missionary, Carey said, "I will go down into the well if you will hold the ropes." In any successful effort there must be those who serve behind the lines, those who go down into the well, and those who hold the ropes.—James E. Carter.

CHRIST'S ARMS. While I was in the Army, my wife Glenna and I lived in Bangkok, Thailand, for nearly two years. During that time Glenna enjoyed the friendship of a young Thai woman named "Ow" who, like most Thais, was Buddhist.

Ow worked at a newspaper concession stand in the lobby of the hotel where the NCO Wives Club met, and Glenna often went a little early and stayed awhile afterward to talk with her. And occasionally they would talk about religion—Christianity and Buddhism.

Once, when Ow visited Glenna at our apartment, they somehow got around to discussing Mark 1:41 which says that Jesus "stretched out" his hand to heal a leper. Ow, who was just learning English, didn't quite understand the phrase "stretched out." So to illustrate my wife held out her arms.

Immediately Ow's face lit up with comprehension. "Oh, yes," she said, "I know what you mean. Your God is always doing that, isn't he?"

At first I was puzzled by her remark. But then I realized she had probably seen pictures that portray Jesus with arms outstretched, reaching out to feed, to heal, to comfort, to bless, to beckon the crowd, and to call his disciples to himself.

"Your God is always doing that, isn't he?" Yes, he is. And if we are Christ's church, his body, so will we.—Charles Michael Johnson in *The Disciple.*

TRAILBLAZERS. Where would any of us Christians be today

(a) if the disciples had decided to stay in Jerusalem and clean up their backyard first,

(b) if St. Paul had refused to accept the challenge to move from Asia Minor to Europe,

(c) if St. Augustine had elected to deal with local problems first,

(d) if Boniface had stayed in his English monastery instead of going forth to evangelize the barbarous people of Germany,

(e) if Count Nikolaus von Zinzendorf and his followers had been content to remain in Germany instead of founding their Moravian communities in the new world, and

(f) if David Livingstone had not been lured by the mystery of half-hidden Africa?

Our own heritage as Christians, our civilization, and the course of the world's history has been radically influenced by their calling to serve Christ somewhere other than home.—A. Theodore Eastman.

LIGHT FROM THE SUN. One of the amazing transformations on the mission field in the twentieth century was the conversion of a high caste Hindu into a devoted follower of Jesus. Sadhu Sundar Singh in one of his books tells how he prayed and practiced the presence of Christ. "After reading the word of God I spend time in prayer, and then I feel a wonderful atmosphere that I call heaven on earth. Psychologists have asked me about that experience. One said to me, 'You feel a kind of peace; that is a matter of temperament or the result of your imagination and meditation.' I answered: 'Before I give an answer I want to ask you a question. There was a man born blind who was made to sit in the sun on a cold winter's day. They asked him, 'What do you feel now?' 'I feel warm.' 'Yes, because the sun is shining.' 'Oh, no, that warmth is the result of my own imagination; there is nothing outside, no ball of fire hung in the sky. I cannot believe the sun is standing without a pillar under it. The heat is in my body and in the circulation of my blood.' The blind man could not believe in the existence of the sun. 'What do you think of that man?' 'He was a fool,' said the psychologist. 'And you are a learned fool. I have experienced meditation, and the imagination of hours could not give me that experience. Christ gave it to me when I never expected it, and you say, 'It is the result of your imagination.' Yes, when we are quiet with God, we receive heat and light from the Sun of righteousness; it is not the result of our imagination or meditation but a reality."

INGLORIOUS COP OUT. In the latter part of the thirteenth century Nicolo Polo, father of Marco, along with his brother, Maffeo, visited the court of the emperor, Kublai Khan. The Khan's kingdom reached from the Urals of Russia to the Himalayas and from the Danube River to the China Sea.

Kublai Khan had never before met Europeans, and he was delighted with the Venetian brothers. He was especially impressed with their religion and sent them back with letters to the pope urging the dispatch of a body of educated men to instruct his people in Christianity.

Upon returning, the Polos learned that no new pope had been appointed following the death of Clement IV in the previous year. After a long delay and tedious political wrangle, the new pope could supply but two Dominicans, who soon lost heart and turned back. When Rome failed, Kublai Khan fell back upon Buddhism as his chief civilizing instrument. You can't help but wonder what the outcome of history would have been had the emperor's request for missionaries been met. It is possible that all of China, Japan, India, the Middle East, and Turkey would be predominantly Christian today.—Claude Turner.

TESTIMONY. While I was a missionary in India, I was summoned to the bedside of a Brahman priest, who was apparently dying. Although I could give him no medical help, I told him I would gladly pray for him, that our living savior might touch his body with healing and his soul with salvation. On three successive visits within one week, I read to him the story of the death and resurrection of Christ.

On the third day, as I prayed, I heard Tiwari struggle to his feet. Closing my prayer, I saw him standing beside me with head bowed and hands clasped. I tried to make him lie down again, but this was his reply: "As you were praying today, I became conscious of Another in the room with us; and I knew in my spirit it was that Jesus of whom you read in your holy book. In his presence I could not remain lying down." Very shortly afterwards, Tiwari became a faithful follower of the Lord.—M. Murray Macleod in The Upper Room.

CARETAKER. An Englishman had, as a young man, gone out to one of the British colonies on the west coast of Africa. There he had built a profitable business trading with the natives. For some reason he had developed a strong dislike for missionaries and their work, and when he returned to England for a visit, he spoke out against missions at every opportunity. "The natives are happy in their own religion," he insisted. "All the missionaries do is spoil them."

Someone asked him who was taking care of his African business during his visit to England. "Oh," he responded, "I left one of the natives in charge." "How did you select the man?" "I picked a man who had attended the Christian school and was a leader in the native church," he replied. "Why did you pick a man like that?" "Well, I knew he wouldn't cheat me during my absence" came his surprising reply.—John W. Wade.

QUESTION. A missionary who had reached retirement age chose to spend the remaining years of his life in South America, the country he had served for many years. A young ministerial student asked him: "Sir, why are you going back to that country to give the remaining years of your life to those people who really don't care for you? Why don't you spend the balance of your life in the luxury of the United States?" He responded, "Son, don't ask me why I am going; ask yourself why you are not."—Billy Weber in Proclaim.

ACCEPTANCE. Have you met him? If you have, then you know how you came to recognize and accept his hand upon your shoulder, his yoke upon your neck, his goad behind your feet, his call within your heart.—D. T. Niles.

A LARGER EVANGELISM. The time is overdue for Christians to find a new, saner, larger evangelism. The new evangelism must express the fruits of biblical scholarship and appeal to the mind as well as the emotions of modern people. It must draw together the personal and social elements of the gospel, seeking at the same time the conversion of men and women and the building of a society fit for people to live in.—Alan Walker.

DIVINE CURRENT. Real revival is the spirit of God moving into and through yielded lives—a divine current that gives everything it touches either a charge or a shock. We might as well try to run a factory on a flashlight battery as to undertake the mission of the church on mere human energy, methods, and enthusiasm.— Vance Havner.

GREATEST THING. Someone asked Lyman Beecher, "Mr. Beecher, what do you count the greatest thing that a human being can be or do?" Without hesitation he replied, "The greatest thing is not that one be a scientist, important as that is; not that one shall be a statesman, vastly important as that is; not that one should be a theologian, immeasurably important as that is; but the greatest thing of all is for one human being to bring another to Jesus Christ the savior."

TOUCH OF THE GALILEAN. The most wonderful work in all the world is not to take iron and steel and make a locomotive or a watch. Nor is it to take pen and paper and write and *Iliad.* Nor is it to take paint and brush and paint and Angelus. An infinitely greater task than all this is to take an ignoble man and transform him into an upright man. Here we touch the creative power of the Galilean and bow before the mysteries of God.—George E. Wellington.

A MISSIONARY'S INTERPRETATION OF I COR. 13. If I have the language ever so perfectly and speak like a native and have not his love for them, I am nothing.

If I have diplomas and degrees and know all the up-to-date methods and have not his touch of understanding love, I am nothing.

If I am able to argue successfully against their religions and yet have not his wooing note, I am nothing.

If I have all faith and great ideals and magnificent plans and have not his love that sweats and bleeds and prays and pleads, I am nothing.

If I give my clothes and my money to them and have not his love for them, I am nothing.

If I can heal all manner of sickness and disease, but wound hearts and hurt feelings for want of his love that is kind, I am nothing.

If I can write articles or publish books that win applause but fail to transcribe the word of the cross the language of his love, I am nothing.—Lois Fitzgerald.

SECTION VIII. Children's Stories and Sermons

January 6. The Wise Men Came and Went (Epiphany)

Historians believe that the wise men came the twelfth day after Jesus' birth. By our calendar that would be on January 6, and on this day we begin one of the important seasons of the church year. We call this season Epiphany, which is the season of the evangel, the proclaimer, or the teller of the story. It was the wise men who found Jesus, and after they had found him, they went out to tell the world about what they had experienced. This is the theme of the season of Epiphany, and this is the time when we talk and study and think about missions and the importance of the missionary work of the church. We remind ourselves during this time that we must do what the wise men did. We must come to find Jesus; we must come into his presence, but then we must go, as they went, and become evangels, proclaimers, or tellers of the story of Christ.—J. Ben Cunningham.

January 13. Pulling Together

Years ago, in a burst of civic pride, the city of Richmond, Virginia, commissioned a statue to be made of their famous General Robert E. Lee riding on his horse, Traveler. When the statue arrived on a flat rail car, it would have been routine to transfer the statue to wagons and have it moved to the park. Then someone had an idea. He said, "Let's pull the statue ourselves." The day was set for moving the statue. The street was decorated with flags. Bands played. People joined together in pulling the rope. Rich and poor, leading citizens and the poorest servants pulled together. Then when the journey ended, someone took out a knife and cut off a piece of rope as a souvenir. The idea spread. A lot of other people did the same thing. Years later citizens of Richmond would take from their pockets an old piece of rope and say: "I had hold of the rope. Did you?" The load is too heavy for one person or a few, but we can pull together and with God's help we won't fail.—Joe A. Harding.

January 20. The Master's Plan

Little boys help the makers of oriental rugs in the Near East. While the rug makers stand in front of their rugs as they are stretched on their frames, the boys stand behind the frames. As the strands of wool are pushed through the web by the rug makers, the boys push them back. Every now and then one of the boys makes a mistake, pushing the returning strand through the wrong hole in the web. From their side of the rug the boys never see the pattern that the master rug maker is following. But when the day's work is finished the boys are allowed to go around to the front where they can see the beauty of the rug that they have helped to create. When they are working with a rug maker who is a true master of the craft, the boys discover that the master has been able to weave even their errors into the beauty of his overall plan.

January 27. Winter Visitor

Go almost anywhere in the suburbs or the country now, even to the edge of a city park if there is a bird feeder nearby, and you will see chickadees.

A full-grown chick seldom weighs more than half an ounce, about the weight of an ordinary letter. Inside that tiny body is a heart that beats close to 700 times a minute, so fast that through a stethoscope its sound is practically a buzz. Its body temperature ranges around 105 degrees, which accounts for that high-tension activity.

On a cold day a chickadee needs its own weight in food to keep the inner fires burning. Its small fraction of an ounce of feathers, which can fluff it to the size of a sparrow, helps hold warmth while the dark back and head gather additional heat from the winter sun.

But these are details. This bird is more than the sum of its anatomical parts. It is a lively spark of personality. It can be a ham actor, a bully, a wheedler, an acrobat. It loves a human audience and comes to the dooryard feeder as much for companionship as for a snack. As an entertainer, it is all pro, the feathered song-and-dance performer who gets, and deserves, top billing on the winter circuit of the dooryard feeders.—*The New York Times.*

February 3. Obeying Orders

More than a century ago an English farmer was at work in his fields when he saw a party of huntsmen riding about his farm. He had one field he did not want the hunters to ride over, as the crop was in a condition to be damaged by the hoofs of horses. He sent a boy in his employ with orders to shut the gate to the field and on no account permit it to be opened.

The boy obeyed the orders of his employer, and scarcely had the gate been closed when the hunters came and ordered that the gate be opened. The boy refused to do this because of his orders. The men threatened him and tried to bribe him, but he repeated that he had his orders and he would not disobey them. One after another of the hunters came forward to speak, but the boy refused to open the gate.

Then a man of commanding presence, evidently experienced in military life, came forward and said: "My boy, do you know me? I am the duke of Wellington, one not accustomed to be disobeyed, and I command you to open that gate that I and my friends may pass through."

The boy lifted his cap and stood bareheaded, a sign of respect which was customary in that day. Then he spoke with firmness: "I am sure the duke of Wellington would not wish me to disobey orders. I must keep this gate shut. No one is to pass through but with my master's express permission."

At this expression of obedience the old warrior lifted his hat to the boy and said: "I honor the man or boy who can be neither bribed nor frightened into doing wrong. With an army of such soldiers I could conquer not only the French but the world." Then he handed the boy a large coin and galloped away. The boy then told other workers on the farm: "Hurrah! Hurrah! I've done what Napoleon could not do. I've kept out the duke of Wellington."

February 10. The Scorpion and the Arrow

What do you do when you get boiling mad? Do you explode, try to bottle it up, go for a long walk, or what? Ruth Stull, a missionary to South America, tells of a custom the Indian women have when they get angry. She says that they paint a black scorpion on their faces. The scorpion is a signal to others that the woman with one painted on her face is "out of sorts" right then, and anyone who tries to communicate with her may well get "stung." When the time of anger is over, the scorpion is taken off and an arrow is then painted on. The arrow in their society is a symbol that the person wearing one is ready to engage in friendly conversation and feels kindly toward everyone.—Charles E. Ferrell.

February 17. Two Neighbors (Brotherhood Week)

Before the present custom of renewing hybrid corn seed each year had begun, a farmer secured some improved seed reputed to produce unusually large, rich corn.

His acquaintances heard of the good fortune, and a next-door neighbor came to the house, asking that a part of the seed be shared with him. This the farmer refused to do. Instead he turned his back on the petitioner, saying, "Everybody looks out for himself in such matters."

The neighbor, upset by this treatment, left without a word. Soon he planted the old-style seed in one field while across the fence the other farmer put his better-type corn into the earth. What happened proved surprising to the two men involved. At first everything seemed to go well with the corn from the better seed. But by the second year the plants in the two fields had cross-fertilized, giving rise to a variety much smaller than the new seed should have yielded.

One day late that fall the first farmer drove a wagon up beside the kitchen door, prepared to leave for the highway. His wife, busy at her stove, asked what he was doing. "I have brought some new, improved seed and am taking half of it to my neighbor," he replied, smiling. "I have learned it is impossible for me to be truly successful while he is not doing well. Our lives and fortunes go together."—*Moody Monthly.*

February 24. Chilo and the Christians (Lent)

Chilo, a character in *Quo Vadis* posing as a Christian, entered the homes of believers, reported their names to Nero, and led palace guards to their hiding places. Because of his treachery, scores were crucified, burned alive, or fed to starving lions. Day after day Chilo sat high in the Colosseum and saw Christians fall before the lions with a song on their lips or burn on crosses with joy in their faces. When the martyr Glaucus looked into the traitor's face and cried, "I forgive you!" Chilo was moved to stand and proclaim: "The

Christians are innocent of the burning of Rome. Nero is the guilty man." Chilo then met Paul, who assured him that Christ was merciful to even the worst of sinners. Caught by the guards and crucified, Chilo lifted his eyes to heaven and whispered, "Jesus, my Jesus."—Naomi Ruth Hunke.

March 2. The Greatest Gift (Lent)

On my desk rests a plastic paperweight in which seven Roman and Phoenician coins are embedded. All are interesting, but three recall special events concerning gifts. The largest is the shekel of Tyre, like the "thirty pieces of silver" paid to Judas for his betrayal kiss. That infamous gift to his loving master still appalls us.

The second is the denarius of Tiberias, the "tribute penny." Christ admonished the chief priests that some gifts indeed belong to Caesar but others, by virtue of creation, belong only to God. God claims his part.

The smallest coin is the lepton of Caponius, "the widow's mite." For me it has a three-fold message.

It speaks of confidence. The widow made no effort to conceal the coins. She was not ashamed of her gift. It was her expression of thanksgiving to God.

It speaks of values. In Palestine's monetary world the copper coin known as a lepton was insignificant. But in God's value system, it ranked first. The human eye sees the gift, but God sees the heart.

It speaks of giving, declaring that the greatest gift is that which entails sacrifice. The widow gave all that she had, and the one who witnessed it gave even his life.—Vernelle Ports Long in *These Days.*

March 9. Lump in the Throat (Lent)

E. Stanley Jones told about a little boy who was trying to grasp the understandings of Christian faith, especially at the point of seeking forgiveness and entering into deep fellowship with God. His teacher suggested an analogy. "When you do as your parents desire," he said to the boy, "you feel good inside. But what happens when you disobey and when you go against their will?" The youngster replied, "I have a lump in my throat." The teacher and the boy prayed together, the boy saying to God: "I've always felt I belonged to you, but I've been afraid to say so. Now I say so!" They concluded their prayers, and the little fellow said joyously, "The lump is gone from my throat."

March 16. The Little Box (Lent)

"The Cedar Box" by John Oxenham tells of a man who was very ill and had allowed himself to give up all hope of recovery. One day his physician brought him a little box made of cedar wood, ornately carved and beautifully polished. At first the box made small, if any, impression upon the man, but as he examined it carefully he saw evidences that it had come from the holy land. This led him to speculate as to its origin and history. With his days of speculation his zeal for life returned. Almost before he knew it he was growing stronger.

At length he was told the story of the box, how it had been passed from one generation to another since first it was made by Jesus in the carpenter's shop in Nazareth and given by him to his mother Mary. The significance of the cedar box was supposed to lie in the fact that it was something which our Lord's hands had fashioned. Whoever looked upon it or handled it felt a strange, miraculous power coursing through him to give him strength and courage to face life.

Whenever people come into the awareness that Jesus is present they find strength and courage for living. Life takes on meaning and "we are whole again."—Homer J. R. Elford.

March 23. The Weight of the Cross (Passion Sunday)

A prominent American businessman set out for Oberammergau, Germany, in order to see the Passion Play. He was enthralled as this great drama unfolded, depicting the story of the cross and Christ's great suffering on Calvary. At the conclusion of the play he went backstage in order to meet Anton Lang who played the part of Christ.

After taking a picture of the actor, the businessman noticed standing in a corner the great cross which he had carried in the play. "Here," he said quickly to his wife, "you take the camera. When I lift the cross on my shoulder, snap the picture."

Before the actor could say anything the man had stooped to lift the cross to his shoulder. To his amazement he could not so much as budge it off the floor. The cross was made from heavy oak beams. Panting from strain and frustration, he turned to the actor and said: "Why, I thought it would be light. I thought the cross was hollow. Why do you carry a cross so heavy?"

The actor replied, "Sir, if I didn't feel the weight of the cross, I could not play his part."—C. Thomas Hilton.

March 30. Beneath God's Tree (Lent)

An old minister told of a farm woman who in the summer months would sit under the shade of a particular tree in her backyard while she shelled the beans, peeled the potatoes, and the like. There were other trees in the yard with more luxurious shade. When asked why she sat under this tree, she told of a son who had gone away to war and who had not returned. While only a small boy, he had planted this tree. She now sat in its shade because of the one who had planted it. You and I have far better reasons for "sitting in the shade of this tree that Christ planted." It is an expensive "tree." It cost God his son. It cost Christ his life. Throughout the centuries, its roots have been moistened with the blood of martyrs. —Jerry Hayner.

April 6. The Butterfly (Easter)

With deliberate sureness the small form begins to emerge. Turning and twisting slightly to free itself from its silken prison, the shape is not yet clear. Only barely can be seen the shadowed hints of color, suggesting something more.

Suddenly, with wrenching force, the figure tries once more to loose itself from bondage. The cocoon splits wide, and in that breathless moment a new and unexpected frame comes into view. Mounting on widening wings of brilliant hue, the creature takes to the air with welcome ease and leaves forever the broken, tomblike shroud.

Is it any wonder that the early church used the butterfly as a symbol for the resurrection? In its transforming cycle from the lowly caterpillar and cocoon to the radiant brightness of one of nature's freest and loveliest creatures, it symbolized the bright promise of God's victory over the grave.—James O. O'Dell.

April 13. What the Seedling Said

We were climbing a mountain by the Columbia Ice Fields in the Canadian Rockies. High in the alpine area above the timber line we stopped to rest, and I leaned against a boulder, partly sat on it. As I looked down, I happened to see, just barely coming out from under the edge of the boulder, a tiny evergreen seedling.

I thought, I wonder if that plant knows where it is? I wonder what it would say if it could speak? And the seedling said to me: "By my seed I am destined to reach the skies and embrace in my arms the wind, the rain, the snow, and the sun and sing my song of joy to all the heavens. But this I know I cannot do for I have taken root above the timber line. And yet I do not want to die. I will not give up. I will find a way of life that will yield growth and development despite the hardships of which my life will partake. In the end I may not look like other trees, but I will be the best I can be. I will use every resource within me and answer life with life. In so doing I shall affirm that there is a God in this universe who sustains the life that is in it."

I saw a few other timber line trees, not straight like trees in the valley, but like huge vines crawling along the ground and twisted by the fight with the wind and the storm, yet in their own way very beautiful and very strong. I looked down at the tender plant, and in my mind I said, "Amen, timber line seedling, the kingdom will come in you."—Winfield S. Haycock.

April 20. Two Hands

It's impossible to clap with one hand. It takes the cooperation of two hands clapping. Here's how the Bible describes another kind of cooperation: "We know that all things work together for good to them that love God." You might say all things cooperate for good, like two hands clapping, when our hearts overflow with love for God.—Robert J. Hastings.

April 27. The Touchstone

From the ancient library of Alexandria has come the touchstone story. A magic stone, which allegedly could turn common metal into pure gold, was to be found somewhere on the shores of the Black Sea. Lying amid countless pebbles which looked exactly like it, the touchstone's only distinction would be its warmth.

Intrigued by the story, one man set out to find and utilize the touchstone. Camping on the seashore, he began picking up every pebble within reach, always feeling for the one that was warm. The first day passed while hundreds of stones were picked up and quickly discarded into the sea. A week passed, then a month, and eventually a year with not a trace of the touchstone. Yet the search went on and on while the seeker picked up pebbles only to cast them aside and reach for another.

One routine morning his hand fell upon a warm pebble, and he casually threw it into the sea. The monotonous habit of picking up pebbles and discarding them had left him insensitive and undiscerning.
—G. Othell Hand.

May 4. Links of Love (National Family Week)

A family gathered around the television for a show the children had waited all week to see. Janie shoved five-year-old Mark, and he began to cry. Janie's father warned her if she bothered him again she would be sent to her room. Mark inched too close to Janie, and she slapped him. An expression of sorrow appeared immediately on her face.

Her father said, "Go to your room, Janie." As she left the room silently, the family saw that she was crying. Mark, who hated to go to bed anytime, stood up. "Night," he said softly and left the room. Janie's older sister said, "Think I'll turn in early too." Then Janie's parents turned off the set and went upstairs to bed.

Janie had been wrong, but the members of the family loved her so dearly they couldn't let her bear her punishment alone. Although nothing was said, Janie heard her family come upstairs and felt their presence, love, and forgiveness.— Marion Bond West in *Home Life.*

May 11. His Mother's Song (Mother's Day)

G. Ernest Thomas tells a story from the early days of the frontier settlement of America. He describes an attack on a small town in Tennessee by a group of hostile Indians. "Some of the settlers were killed; many others were taken prisoner. Among those carried off was a three-year-old child. Twenty years went by, and the heartbroken mother never stopped wondering what had been the fate of her little boy. Finally peace was made between the Indians and the white men. As part of the celebration a group of warriors came back to the town where once they had burned and killed. The Indians were bronzed of skin, painted grotesquely, and carried weapons of war. The lonely mother who had lost her child twenty years before stood with the other settlers gazing at them. Suddenly she thought she recognized something in one of the tall and stately red men that reminded her of her son. She called him by name. Of course the warrior did not answer. But the more she looked at him the more she became convinced that he was her son. As a last resort she began to sing one of the lullabys which she had sung each night to her child before putting him into his crib. As she sang the young man seemed puzzled. Then he broke from the line of Indians, rushed to his mother, and fell at her feet. Her song had called him back from a life of savagery."

May 18. God's World

In a New York home I watched a fifteen-year-old boy wrestling with a problem in geometry. "This is hateful stuff," he said. "By the way," I asked him, "did you know that the universe around us has been con-

structed on geometrical lines?" Instantly he was all attention. I explained that as scientists penetrate ever deeper into the cosmos with giant telescopes they find laws in operation that their minds can understand and plot out and that the mind of the creature and the mind of the creator possess important powers in common and appear to work by the same laws. After our conversation I noticed that the young lad turned back to his school work with a new respect for geometry.—John Sutherland Bonnell.

May 25. The Treasures He Missed

A small boy found a bright copper penny in the grass. He seized it eagerly. It was his and had cost him nothing! Thereafter, wherever he went he walked head downward, searching for further treasure. During his lifetime he found 313 pennies, 61 nickels, 22 dimes, 14 quarters, 7 half dollars, and one lonely dollar bill—a total of $16.38. The money cost him nothing, but he missed the fiery splendor of 25,550 sunsets, the glow of millions of stars on innumerable nights, the singing of the birds in the trees, and the smiles of friends he could have had if he had not passed them by.—Floyd Coffee.

June 1. Helping the Helpless

In the teeming heart of Calcutta, India, there is a Lee Memorial Home for children. The Lees, who established the home, were missionaries in Calcutta. They had six children attending school at Darjeeling in the foothills of the Himalayas. One tragic night during the monsoon rains the whole mountainside, upon which the school was built, slipped and buried all six children at once.

The Lees were grief stricken and stunned. Instead of surrendering to bitterness and crying out, "Why did God do this to us when we are serving him in Calcutta?" they decided to care for homeless children. They turned from their sorrow to receive abandoned, homeless children off the streets. For seventy-five years that home has been filled with an average of 500 homeless children a year. A family of six became a family of thousands.

On the hillside they placed a monument to commemorate the memory of their six children. On the monument are the words, "Thanks be to God who gives us the victory through our Lord Jesus Christ."—Joe A. Harding.

June 8. Something New

Chad Walsh tells of something that happened at breakfast with his seven-year-old grandson. He said the boy, out of the blue, started shouting and pointing. On the window screen was a strange-looking creature that resembled a cockroach and a fat spider.

"Something's coming out of it!" the boy said excitedly. And sure enough, the boy was right. There was something almost shapeless, long and slender that emerged from the strange creature. The thing had a kind of crinkly appearance, a little like crumpled aluminum foil.

Then the shapeless foil took on a precise shape. The long body was straight and thin. There were two sets of wings on the creature as streamlined as an airplane.

The grandson exclaimed, "It's a dragonfly." And the boy was again right. The wings began to take on a new strength and substance. An hour later the dragonfly set his wings in motion and flew away.

June 15. God Cares

A nine-year-old boy was in a hospital because he had been burned rather badly. The wife of his school principal started visiting him and reading to him almost every day. One day they got to talking about God. "Do you really think God is here?" asked the boy whose name was Darrell. "Of course," said the woman. "It's God who helps the nurses turn you and who eases your pain. He's going to make you well again."

Sometime later an elderly lady mistakenly stepped into Darrell's room and, seeing the lad all puffed up with the burns and covered by layers of sterile gauze, said pitifully, "Oh, why does God punish a child like that?"

Darrell almost shouted at the woman, "Don't say that!" Then hiking himself painfully up on his elbows, he said: "Don't say anything bad about God! When it hurts, God cries with me!"

June 22. Five Salesmen

Several doughnut shops on the same city street were highly competitive. One day the owner of one of the shops placed a sign in his window that read, "Best donuts in town." Not to be outdone, a shop down the street brought out a sign that read, "Best donuts in this country." Across the street the sign appeared, "Best donuts in the world." About this time another owner posted a sign that proclaimed, "Best donuts in the universe." At this point the most enterprising owner of all printed his sign that read, "Best donuts on this street."—James E. Carter.

June 29. Forty-Five Stars (Independence Sunday)

On historic Pennsylvania Avenue in Washington, D.C., over a small bakery, flew a tattered flag with only forty-five stars. Someone remarked that it should be hauled down. The Viennese baker's eyes misted. "My father saved this flag at the risk of his life when the vessel on which he was emigrating to America was sunk at sea. I was then only ten. Later my father gave me this flag, saying: 'America is a country trusting in God from its beginning. You must go there some day to live in religious freedom.' I was a man before I could come to this land. That flag means something very special to me. I will fly it every holiday as long as I live!"—N. Z. Thompson.

July 6. Words of Encouragement

Some years ago an Olympic champion named Charley Paddock spoke to the students at East Tech High School in Cleveland. His message was this: "If you think you can, you can. If you believe a thing strongly enough, it can come to pass in your life." Afterward a tall, thin fellow went up to him and said, "Gee, Mr. Paddock, I'd give anything if I could be an Olympic champion just like you." Paddock assured the young boy that it was possible if he developed the right attitude and worked at it. The boy did, and in the 1936 Olympics held in Berlin he won four gold medals. His name was Jesse Owens. But that is not the end of the story. Some years later Owens was speaking to a group when a young boy came up to him. He too said that he wished to be an Olympic runner. Owens passed on the advice he had received from Paddock: "If you believe a thing strongly enough, it can come to pass in your life." In 1948 that same boy to whom Jesse Owens had spoken also won an Olympic medal. His name was Harrison Dillard.—Charles E. Ferrell.

July 13. Toil-Worn Hands

In the Lady Chapel of Liverpool Cathedral are two windows dedicated to some of history's outstanding women, but there is one among them whose name you almost certainly will not know. Kitty Wilkinson is pictured with the gnarled hands of a woman beaten by rheumatism. But they were also the tender hands of a woman who mothered the motherless. In all she fostered forty-five orphaned children and scrubbed floors in other people's homes to raise money to keep them.

The hands of Jesus were God's answer to hard work. They became toil-worn in the carpenter's shop at Nazareth, but they were also tender. They were pierced with nails—the cost of our redemption. Our hands should be given to the Lord Jesus in the service of others in love and devotion. —Maurice Barnett in *The Upper Room.*

July 20. The Time to Cross the River

Not many miles out of the beautiful town of Sylva, North Carolina, is the crest of the Blue Ridge Mountains where the eastern half of the American continent is divided by misty, majestic peaks. As one approaches that continental divide, a little spring by the side of the road can be seen. The water trickles forth and makes its way down lush, green hills. For miles along the way one may cross the stream with a single step.

Somewhere among the foothills that small stream is joined by another brook and becomes the Tuckaseigee River. The Tuckaseigee in turn travels on, merging with other rivers and eventually flowing into the mighty Mississippi.

Tourists have pondered the journey of waters from the roadside spring on the mountaintop. One in particular, becoming a bit pensive and philosophic, observed that "the time to cross a river is before it gets too wide." It is a truth life continually impresses upon us.—G. Othell Hand.

July 27. The Fallen Giant

On the slope of Long's Peak in Colorado lies the ruin of a gigantic tree. Naturalists tell us that it stood for some four hundred years. It was a seedling when Columbus landed at San Salvador and half grown when the Pilgrims settled at Plymouth. During the course of its long life it was struck by lightning fourteen times, and the innumerable avalanches and storms of four centuries thundered past it. It survived them all. In the end however an army of beetles attacked the tree and leveled it to the ground. The insects ate their way through the bark and gradually destroyed the inner strength of the tree by their tiny but incessant attacks. A forest giant, which age had not withered nor lightning blasted nor storms subdued, fell at last before beetles so small that a man could crush them between his forefinger and his thumb.—Harry Emerson Fosdick.

August 3. The Door

A group of tourists traveling throughout the eastern lands came across a shepherd tending his sheep. The shepherd showed them the fold into which the sheep were led at night. It consisted of four walls with an open gap. One tourist observed: "There is no door to close and shut out beasts of prey. How are they protected from danger?"

"I am the door!" was the emphatic reply. "When the light has gone and all the sheep are inside, I lie in that open space; and no sheep ever goes out but across my body; nor does anything enter without stepping on me."

When Jesus used the picture of the shepherd and the sheep, he capitalized on imagery woven into the thought and language of the people of his day. Again and again in the Old Testament, God is portrayed as the shepherd of his people. (See Ps. 23; 95:7; Isa. 40:11).—G. Othell Hand.

August 10. Tennessee Hero

There is on the steps leading up into the capitol grounds in Nashville the bronze statue of a youth named Sam Davis. They show him dressed in the crude butternut jeans and the homespun shirt of his backwoods life of his day. He was taken prisoner in the War between the States and accused of being a spy. It happened that he did have in his possession information which would have turned over to a firing squad his captain, who was also a prisoner. Sam Davis, true to his simple code of honor, would not tell, though he knew his life was a forfeit by the hard laws of war. He was offered his life again and again if he would divulge his information. This simple, unlearned country boy simply said, "I'd rather die a thousand deaths than betray a friend." So they shot him, and so Tennessee put him in bronze on the steps of her capitol that other Tennessee boys and youths everywhere may know that it is not the length of life that counts but its quality.—Nolan B. Harmon.

August 17. What One Man Discovered

In my hand you can see a cluster of sweet grapes. Nearly everybody likes sweet grapes, but until these modern days of refrigeration we had no way to keep grapes fresh. Most grapes grown in old days were made into wine.

Back in 1872 a terrible drought kept California grapes from growing big like these. The grape growers were saddened at the sight of their vineyards with such poor grapes. One grower sent a boxful of the shriveled grapes to a grocer in San Francisco. He instructed the man to sell at any price. Now what could a grocer do with a box of bad grapes?

That's a question God must sometimes consider. He sees boys and girls who do bad things. Can anything good come from children like that?

Well, you know what that grocer did with those dried grapes? He left them in the sun a couple days longer, and he discovered raisins. Dried grapes turn into raisins. In this way the grape-raising industry of California was born. What had seemed like a terrible disaster had turned into a wonderful discovery. Now grapes could be grown not to make bad wine but for good raisins.—C. W. Bess.

August 24. The Right Fielder

There was a certain right fielder who, having spent five innings in right field and having seen no action, no hits to his field of play, and no need for him to be out in right field, was tempted not to go out into right field for the next few innings.

He felt he could sit on the bench and just wait for the innings to be over, and then he would take his turn at bat. He could see no reason for staying in the hot sun and waiting out in right field if no one was going to hit the ball to him.

But when he came to himself and realized how important it was for him to take his place, he returned to right field. He resolved that he would stay out there every game even if no one ever hit a ball to him because ball games are played with a man in right field. And a long, high fly came his way in right field, and he caught it and saved the game.—David Ehrlin.

August 31. Working Tools (Labor Sunday)

In Jean Francois Millet's painting "The Angelus" two people are standing in a field at the close of the day as the distant church bells toll out the hour of prayer. One is a young woman with bowed head; the other is a young man who stands fumbling awkwardly with his hat. Beside them is a wheelbarrow containing the tools they have been using all day. The highlight of the picture is formed by the rays of the setting sun. Much to the amazement of many, those rays are neither found on the girl's prayerful posture or the uncomfortable lad. Instead they fall on the wheelbarrow and working tools, an artistic tribute to the dignity of the common task.—*Proclaim.*

September 7. The Burden

A king moved his people to a new location. He insisted on taking with him a young fruit tree which was much too heavy for any one man to carry. Everyone avoided it, except one young man not yet wise in the ways of the world. For the first few days he always reached camp completely exhausted long after everyone was settled for the night. But he seemed to grow stronger each day of the long journey. Finally they set someone to spy upon him to discover the source of his strength. What the spy saw was an amazing thing. Early in the morning the tree would blossom and by noon it would bear fruit, so that the youth carrying it could refresh himself during the journey. His burden thus became his bread.—Roy L. Minich.

September 14. A Good Reputation

The teenage boys and girls on the school bus were becoming rowdier and louder. They had a substitute driver and recognized an opportunity to misbehave and ignore the rules.

Someone in the back of the bus shouted an obscenity. The driver looked in his rear view mirror and saw a girl he was almost sure was the guilty one.

When they arrived at school, he took Nancy to the office and accused her. She began crying. Suppose no one believed her innocence? Would they take her word over that of an adult?

The principal was shocked. He listened to the accusation, then said: "I don't believe Nancy said that. I know her reputation."

Her friends and teachers heard of the incident and came to Nancy. They too said they knew her reputation and didn't believe that she had said those words.

People are still drawn to one with a good reputation even as they were in Christ's time.—Marion Bond West in *Home Life.*

September 21. Be a Scrambler

One of the reasons Fran Tarkenton and Roger Staubach are two of the finest quarterbacks in the history of American football is that, in addition to the ability to lead a team of men, to know what signals to call on given situations, to be able to pass with pin-point accuracy, they are known as "scramblers." That simply means they have the ability to run all over the field when a play goes wrong and somehow escape tacklers until they have made a substantial gain. What they had planned goes awry. The pass receivers are covered, the blitzing front-four opposing linemen are bearing down upon the quarterback, and he must either "eat the ball" which means a loss of yardage or try to scramble out of the predicament. Certainly that's true to life. We all need to be scramblers.— Hoover Rupert.

September 28. A Word for Obedience

For a long time the missionaries of Africa did not have a word for obedience. One day as a missionary was leaving a village his dog stayed behind. The missionary whistled, and the dog came running at top speed. An old native observing this said in admiration, "Mui adem delegave ge." Literally translated this is "Dog your ear is only." Put in smooth English it comes out, "Your dog is all ears." This is obedience—to be all ears.—Ralph Kelly.

October 5. Little Rewards

An Italian baker in 610 A.D. had some scraps left from his bread-making, so he twisted the scraps of dough to look like folded arms. Then after he baked them, he rewarded the children who never forgot their prayers by giving the goodies to them. They looked like the children's arms when folded across their chests while praying, which is the way the children in that country did when praying. The baker called the goodies *preticla*, which is the Latin word for reward or *little* reward, but gradually the name changed to the present one of pretzel.

The idea spread from northern Italy to Austria and Germany. At first the pretzels were soft. Then one day a young baker in charge of a big oven fell asleep and left a batch of them in the oven until they were golden brown and crisp. The children liked them better that way, and from then on that is the way they have been. And millions of them are sold all over the world every year. In the United States there are four hundred million pretzels baked every year with sales amounting to two million dollars. It is interesting to remember that children's prayers had an important part in the original making of these crisp goodies which most youngsters like.—Louise Price Bell.

October 12. Christ's Kingdom

A teacher asked his young students some questions. Pointing to a stone in his ring, a flower on the table, and a bird that flew past the window, he asked to what kingdom each of them belonged. The children gave him the right answers: the mineral, the vegetable, and the animal kingdoms. Then he asked, "To what kingdom do I belong?" This is a key question for our lives. For some people the answer is the animal kingdom because they live only on the appetite level and are controlled by their passions and physical desires. But most people rise above the animal level. They have a sense of right and wrong, a feeling of duty and decency, some ideals and purposes. Some rise to an even higher kingdom. No one can think of Christ as being animal. Though he took the form of man, he was divine. He belonged to a kingdom beyond the kingdoms of this world.—C. Thomas Hilton.

October 19. The Master's Touch

A little girl, who was staying at a hotel, was learning to play the piano. Every morning she got up early and did a half-hour of practice. To the disgust of many other guests, she always played a wrong note at the same point in one of the pieces. The mistake was so obvious that everybody except the child recognized it at once. It became so regular that all the guests waited for her to play it and then groaned.

Something had to be done. Among the guests was a famous pianist. He also heard the wrong note, and his sensitive ear was hurt by the constant error. He determined that it should annoy the guests no longer. The next morning he got up early and went to the lounge just as the little girl was about to start her practice. He did not rebuke her for her mistake or even sit down at the piano and show her how to play the piece. Instead he sat beside her, and while she played he improvised with beautiful chords and scale passages. He did this so skillfully that the wrong note no longer gave pain to the guests. It was still there, but he used it to produce a beautiful harmony.—Gordon Chilvers.

October 26. Through the Door

The small boy shuffled in and stood by his grandfather's bed, his eyes brimming with tears. "What's the matter, son?" the old man asked, reaching for the boy's hand. "I'm scared." "Scared of what?" With the honesty of young children, the lad said, "I'm scared you're going to die!" The old man patted the bed for the boy to sit down beside him. Then he spoke gently: "Look out the door at the garden where the walk turns toward the garage. If I went through that door and down that walk, soon you couldn't see me. But that wouldn't mean I wasn't there, would it?" The boy shook his head. "What we call death is like that for the Christian. We go through a door from one place to another. You can't see me as you do now, but I'll go right on living. And the great part is that I'll be living with Jesus."—Amelia Bishop.

November 2. Filling the Cup

A cup can hold as much dirty water as clear water. The same is true of people. We can hate as much as we can love. It's not that some are worse than others, but that the worst has taken over all that we are. Fill your cup with clear water, and muddy water will never be a problem.—Robert J. Hastings.

November 9. Building the World

An old legend in the Talmud reveals the preeminence of love. According to this story, when God created the world, he called his angels together and asked, "Who will build the world for us?" The angel of beauty said, "Let me build it," but God replied, "No, for if you build there will be no weakness to be helped." The angel of wisdom said, "Let me build," but again God answered, "No, for if you build the world it will be so perfect that there will be no room for progress in it." Finally the angel of love said, "Let me build the world." And God agreed. Into this world love put the beautiful and the ugly, the strong and the weak, the wise and the foolish, sickness and health, life and death, happiness and pain, and these things were tied together in such a way that only as human beings loved could they begin to understand the world in any way whatsoever. When the world was finished, the angels gathered together again to look at this strange creation. One by one they shook their heads saying, "What a failure." But the angel of love answered, "No, for in this world the children of men become the children of God through love and love never fails."—John H. Townsend.

November 16. Hands That Do Good

A teenager hurried to an elderly lady struggling with a sack of groceries. He carried the load to her home. Even the youth's hands seemed to smile.

A doctor placed his strong, reassuring, healing hand upon the shoulder of a lady whose mother had just come through a successful operation.

An elderly man's hands still had a lot of loving in them as they folded in prayer.

Many hands at a church's "workday" or preparing for an all-church picnic make the job easy and pleasurable.

Hands that touch, lift, love, comfort, guide, and bless are active and useful hands. They multiply joy and life.

How inspiring the words that depict Aaron ministering to the Israelites: "Aaron lifted up his hands toward the people and blessed them" (Lev. 9:22).—Harold A. Schulz.

November 23. Unclaimed Treasure (Bible Sunday)

Many years ago a poverty-stricken man in New Jersey opened an old family Bible and found, scattered throughout its pages, $5,000. The book had been in his possession for almost thirty-five years. The Bible was left to him by his aunt, a portion of whose will read: "To my beloved nephew, I will and bequeath my family Bible and all it contains, with the residue of my estate after my funeral expenses and just and lawful debts are paid."

The residue of the estate amounted to a few hundred dollars. When this money was gone, the nephew lived on a meager income and later grew too old to work. All this time the Bible that his aunt had willed him was left unopened. Only by accident one day did he discover the money but only after living in dire poverty for most of his life.

The Bible is without value unless its pages are opened, read, and appropriated. It is then that it gives light and life.—E. Schuyler English.

November 30. How Old Are You? (Advent)

A boy, when asked his age, unhesitatingly replied, "My mental age is 9.5, my physical age is 7.8, and my chronological age is 8." Apparently having been exposed to the educational testing system that uses these terms, the boy indicated that he was younger physically than chronologically, yet not as old in chronological years as in mental ability.

Spiritual maturity may be quite different from physical maturity. To maintain good physical condition, certain requirements are met such as proper diet, exercise, and rest. To maintain good spiritual condition, a proper balance of prayer, Bible reading, and Christian service must be maintained.—Fannie D. Moore.

December 7. What Is a Christian? (Advent)

After the death of Phillips Brooks, for many years the great pastor of Trinity Church in Boston and the composer of "O little town of Bethlehem," an appreciative congregation wanted to do something to honor the memory of their beloved pastor and friend. So they hired one of America's finest sculptors and gave him the assignment of erecting a monument in front of the church. For months the artist talked to people who knew Brooks. Eventually he unveiled the statue. It showed Phillips

Brooks standing behind the pulpit. But there was more. For standing beside the great minister with his hand on Brooks' shoulder was a statue of Christ. When asked why, the artist responded, "Brooks was a man whom you could not explain apart from Jesus Christ." What is a Christian? He is a person whom you cannot explain apart from Christ.—Jerry Hayner.

December 14. The Real and the Unreal (Advent)

A large department store had a huge papier-mache figure of Santa Claus on the roof of the covered passageway by the front entrance. The Santa was positioned in such a way that a child could be seated on his lap. When an attendant pressed a button, the figure would say, "Well, little one, what do you want old Santa to bring you for Christmas?" A grandfather, holding his little flaxen-haired granddaughter by the hand, pointed to the massive Santa. "Would you like to sit on Santa's lap?" The little one shook her golden curls. "No," she said, a little primly for a five-year-old. "Why not?" came the interested question. "I would rather sit on the lap of Jesus" was the solemn answer. "It is his birthday at Christmas. He loved the little kids, and my Sunday school teacher says that he took them on his lap and blessed them. Besides, that Santa's not for real." —Harold E. Dye.

December 21. Good News (Advent)

One year, after all the parts were assigned for the fourth-grade portrayal of the Christmas story, a problem was discovered. Young Timmy was having a hard time with his line. He was supposed to say, "I bring you good tidings of great joy." They told him that "tidings" was an old word for "news" or a "message." When the big moment came for him to say his line, it left him completely. So he said, "Folks, have I got some good news for you!"—Frank Pollard.

December 28. Old Faithful

The favorite of all the geysers in the Yellowstone National Park is Old Faithful. Every 64.5 minutes, with a loud roar, it sends a tall, graceful column of steam and water 150 feet into the air. Every time the geyser spouts, it uses ten to twelve thousand gallons of water in this wonderful display.

There are geysers that spout higher, but Old Faithful is the favorite. I think you can guess why. Its name is a giveaway. Boys and girls love it because it is faithful. That's a wonderful thing to be. I know men and women who are like that. Each one of them may be called Old Faithful. What a wonderful name to carry!—Rita F. Snowden.

SECTION IX. *Sermon Outlines and Homiletic and Worship Aids for Fifty-Two Weeks*

SUNDAY: JANUARY SIXTH

MORNING SERVICE

Topic: Too Slight a Task (Epiphany Sunday)

Text: Isa. 49:6 (NEB).

I. Few people have not had the experience of Isaiah which is reflected in today's text. All of us come to the time when we have to ask for help.

(a) In Isaiah's case it was completely understandable. He was a leader of the Jews exiled in Babylon. How was he to keep up their hopes while they toiled in slavery? How was he to convince them that God had not forgotten but was at that very moment working in their behalf to bring to pass better things than they could ask or think? How was he to assure them that they would return to their homeland and, more than that, that it would be a place of joy and prosperity and peace? What a task was laid upon Isaiah. No wonder he asked for help.

(b) Yet what a surprising answer he received to his prayer. "It is too slight a task for you, as my servant, to restore the tribes of Jacob, to bring back the descendants of Israel: I will make you a light to the nations, to be my salvation to earth's farthest bounds." Not just Israel but the world is your task.

II. Isaiah was a man of prayer, and prayer was not a retreat, a subtle way of avoiding the hard decisions or of withdrawing into one's self and letting the world go hang. There are people who use prayer that way, but Isaiah was not one of them. Nor Jeremiah, nor any of the prophets, nor Jesus. Prayer for Jesus and the prophets was not an escape but an empowerment. It was not the attempt to find a hiding place but the attempt to find that hidden spring welling up within to enable them to do the will of God. Prayer was power. Prayer is power to change people, to withstand the temptation to an easy life, to see clearly, and to act rightly.

III. What we think of as our task is too slight if we are the Lord's servant.

(a) Particularly should all who are in the church take this to heart, for how often we have conceived of our task in petty and even selfish ways? Here we are charged to be a light to the nations, to bring all men under the persuasive and enobling power of the gospel, and to be the salt of the earth. Yet if we hold the mirror up to our churches, what do we see?

(b) If when we hold the mirror up to our parish or ourselves we see preoccupation with the trivial and the transient, we ought to remember this answer of the Lord to Isaiah, "It is too slight a task." And if it was too slight a task for Isaiah to bring a nation of slaves out of bondage, you can see the scale by which we must weigh what we do.

(c) Yet the question will nag in our

minds, as it did with Paul, "Who is sufficient for these things?" We seem to have little power of our own that is able to cope with the fierce and boggling enormities of life. If God, who is power, is behind us to hurl our surrendered selves against the evils of our day, would we not also be instruments to slay the demons of our time? If the voice which spoke from the whirlwind could speak through us, would we not be able to calm the stormy blast and say effectively to our tumultuous world, "Peace, be still"?

IV. We do not even accomplish our lesser, slighter tasks rightly unless we see them as a part of the larger work to which we are all called.

(a) Some will push for court reform, a better way of selecting qualified judges, or arranging dockets. Others will want to improve police procedures. Others will work to ameliorate and redirect what the distinguished psychiatrist, Karl Menninger, has called the modern equivalent of the slave pens of the last century—our jails and prisons. All of this is important and necessary. And yet it is too slight a task unless it is done within the context of total justice to the offender and to the victim, justice that restores a right relationship to society, justice that is fair in the eyes of God.

(b) So it is with all of the great social evils of our time—racial prejudice, power blocs and the war system, the growing weight and threat to liberty of the Leviathan of bureaucratic government, the gross failure of our educational system. There is a task for everyone, but it is too slight a task if all we see is what is immediately before us, and we fail to look up to the larger universal plan of God's kingdom for our world. Our world's problems may drive us to our knees. Yet when we pray, the answer comes again, as it did to Isaiah, "It is too slight a task for you, as my servant."

(c) Each of us faces personal problems or family problems, and often these seem to be completely beyond any solution. We become depressed and discouraged, and when we are that way, nothing seems to hold out hope. Or we may be troubled with a restless conscience that will not let up on us or give us ease. Or we may have a battle with our health. And even if we have no heavy burdens, we each face the task of becoming a complete person and of making something worthy and significant of our lives.

(d) Only when we seek self-mastery and self-completeness for a large obedience to God and expanding service to our fellowmen is it a task big enough for us. Again this may drive us to despair. We may wonder if we will ever be rid of our anger, depression, envy, or smugness. Yet even in this we must hear again what the Lord said to Isaiah, "It is too slight a task for you, as my servant."—William Jackson Jarman.

Illustrations

HIS GLORY MANIFESTED. The sense of awe is rarely missing from the intimacies of the gospel story. The glory is manifested in many different ways: in the way Jesus spoke and in what he said, so that crowds listened to him and followed him; in his astonishing miracles of healing; in his confrontations with authority as well as in his gentleness with sinners; in those strange moments, as at the transfiguration when his disciples found themselves out of their depth and could only wonder at him; and supremely for all his friends in their traumatic experience of his passion and in the joy beyond belief of knowing that he is alive for evermore. When we speak of "epiphany" in relation to Jesus, we should be thinking of his whole life. It is the life itself which is the manifestation.—F. Pratt Green.

MOMENT BY MOMENT. As life is made up for the most part not of great occasions but of small everyday moments, it is the giving to those moments their greatest amount of peace, pleasantness, and sincerity that contributes most to the sum of human good.—Leigh Hunt.

Sermon Suggestions

THE CALL OF THE UNKNOWN. Text: Gen. 12:1. (1) The call of the unknown comes to those prepared to move at God's command. (2) We are challenged by visions of God's promise in the call of the unknown. (3) God's presence gives meaning and power.—Carl W. Segerhammer.

MEASUREMENTS FOR CHURCH PLANNING. Text: Luke 14:28. (1) Our attitude will be an important factor. (2) Our commitment will be decisive. (3) Our cooperation will be important. (4) Our faithfulness will be necessary. (5) Our prayer life will be needed. (6) Our spiritual health will be vital.—C. Neil Strait.

Worship Aids

CALL TO WORSHIP. "Great is the Lord, and greatly to be praised; and his greatness is unsearchable. One generation shall praise thy works to another, and shall declare thy mighty works." Ps. 145:3–4.

INVOCATION. Almighty and everlasting God, whom the heaven of heavens cannot contain, much less the temples which our hands have built, but who art ever nigh unto the humble and the contrite: grant thy Holy Spirit, we beseech thee, to us who are here assembled; that cleansed and illumined by thy grace, we may worthily show forth thy praise, meekly learn the word, render due thanks for thy mercies, and obtain a gracious answer to our prayers.

OFFERTORY SENTENCE. "Give unto the Lord the glory due unto his name: bring an offering, and come before him: worship the Lord in the beauty of holiness." I Chron. 16:29.

OFFERTORY PRAYER. Almighty God, may we trust more and more in thy kind providence, and may our submission to thy will be revealed in the deep devotion expressed through these gifts we offer in Christ's name.

PRAYER. Almighty and eternal God, we come, as did the wise men, to set our sights upon him, to see the wonder of divinity in human flesh, and to adore him.

O God, how can we adore him? How can we adore him, the prince of peace, in a world where peace is executed on the scaffold? How can we adore him, O God, who is the son of the just and righteous God in a world where men exploit their brother and, in the name of necessity and all things good, pour out injustice after injustice on their neighbors because they may look differently? How can we adore him, O God, who is the son of the God of love in a world where it is common practice to hate under subtle disguise in the name of profit or for the sake of the corporation or even in the name of the nation? How can we adore him, O God, who showed compassion to the rejected, who loved the unlovable, who was genuine, frank, and honest in the face of dishonesty, deceit, and hypocrisy?

O God, we confess that we do not adore him, not because we do not know how, but because we fear the high cost; we confess we heap up failure after failure to adore him, disobedience upon disobedience, because we will not take the risk, because it is hard and we prefer the easy way of singing praises to him with our lips but not in the voting booth and the easy way of reciting sweet-sounding phrases in the sanctuary on Sunday but not of having words of healing in our families or at work during the rest of the week.

Help us not to be like the wise men who came once with their presence but who were never heard from again. Help us to throw away our defenses to thy judgment; make us open to judgment, that we may see the necessity and reality of thy mercy and receive it.

Grant us, O Lord, those things and only those things that we ask that will increase our commitment to thee—Father, Son, and Holy Spirit—that will aid us in our relationship to our brother. Grant us also all those things for which we may not ask but for which we have a need for the health of our society and of our spirits.—Ralph W. Mueckenheim.

EVENING SERVICE

Topic: Making the New Year New (New Year's Sunday)

TEXT: Ezek. 11:19.

Someone has said that one of the lessons we learn from history is that we learn nothing from history. The gospel holds out the chance for new life, new beginnings, and new opportunities. How do we make the new year new and not just a repeat of the same old mistakes, habits, and attitudes that have gone before?

I. We make the new year new when we put the past in perspective. (a) Many of us do not deal adequately with our pasts. We carry the heavy luggage of yesterday into the present. There are sins that have not been forgiven, relationships left frazzled, and mistakes that we continue to make again and again.

(b) The Bible admonishes us to forget those things which lie behind. The Hebrews were told to take little when they made their journey toward the Promised Land. They had to travel light or the journey would be cumbersome and impossible. We too must shed the things that make the journey a hard one.

(c) Alongside the suggestion to forget the past is the idea that we must remember the past. Continually the Bible says, "Remember." In remembering the past we put it behind us. Then we can go beyond our mistakes with God's help.

III. We make the new year new when we reckon with the truth that we have a second chance.

(a) Take your 1980 calendar and look at it. The pages are all fresh and unused. The year is undecided. This new year provides us with a new set of alternatives.

(b) Robert Frost has a poem about the road not taken. Two roads diverged in a yellow wood, and the one that he took made all the difference. So options are not frozen. Things can be different. The time can be redeemed.

IV. We make the new year new when we reckon with resolution and commitment. Paul said, "This one thing I do." He pressed forward to what lay ahead. Commitment to the future depends on our intentions in the present tense. We begin to act. What is it in your life that you need to lay hold of? What actions does your church need to give itself to in the days ahead?

V. The new year becomes new when we revise our timetables. (a) Something new has entered the scene. We can begin to look at life a little more objectively. So 1980 begins inventory time.

(b) Have we been happy where we are? What kind of relationship have we had in marriage, with our children, or with other people? Have we grown in 1979, and what areas do we need to zero in on during this new year? How close has your church come to the intention of Jesus?—Roger Lovette.

SUNDAY: JANUARY THIRTEENTH

MORNING SERVICE

Topic: Contemporary Faith

TEXT: Heb. 11:1 (PHILLIPS).

The actions recorded in Heb. 11 were at the time of their occurrence experiences in a contemporary faith situation. The persons involved did not as a rule have an eye toward history. They were caught in situations in which they accomplished the seemingly impossible by faith, and the result helped make history. One never knows when his action of faith in a contemporary situation may become historic. Faith is a contemporary reality. It is meant to be an integral, elemental part of one's spirit and motivation; it is not something special from "out there" that one brings in at a moment of need; it is a normal factor in life. Faith is a positive factor which produces courage and strength so that one may forge ahead fearlessly in the midst of any difficulty or challenge.

I. *Definition of faith.* Heb. 11 begins with a definition of faith. (a) Faith is a hypothesis, a presupposition. The word translated assurance really could be more accurately translated assumption. Faith is assuming that that which we hope for is really true, and it is the conviction that that, though we cannot yet see it, actually exists. There is nothing wrong with beginning the spiritual order with a faith-hypothesis. You do not understand all of the things concerning God and the spiritual life: the deity of Christ, the efficacy of atonement, the power in prayer, etc. You begin with the assumption that it is true as the Bible, God's revealed word, says.

(b) Faith is belief. Here one engages in the personal aspect, which is elemental in spiritual faith. Faith is trusting implicitly the integrity and the word of a trustworthy person. When you accept the things of God you trust the word of God. That is the only assurance you have, at least to begin with, of your salvation. (See I Pet. 1:23.)

(c) Faith is confidence. When we speak of having faith in the face of the challenges and the trials of life, we sometimes mean that we have the courage, the confidence to move ahead. We cannot say that we have all of the answers; we do not have all of the loopholes plugged; but we will go ahead with what we have, believing God will enable us to meet the future needs. Some people will not move an inch until they have everything in hand; they will never do anything on faith, especially promising financial stewardship. But there are others who go out with nothing, except their lives, and they are willing to give all they have regardless of the sacrifice required. Their faith is the confidence that all will work out with the help of God. They have faced the challenge realistically and confidently, saying, I believe this is the way; I will walk in it.

(d) One final word completes the definition of faith. That word is obedience. Faith is "evidence"; it is "putting all our confidence" and "makes us certain of realities we do not see." The action that proves our faith in these realities is obedience to God who promises them. The proof of love is action. So faith becomes full in the action of obedience. Only he who obeys believes, and only he who believes obeys.

II. *Declaration of faith.* From definition we move quite logically to declaration, putting oneself on record, on the line, so to speak. (See v. 6.) This is how we begin the Creed, "I believe in God the Father . . . the Son . . . the Holy Spirit." That is what Paul said in the midst of the storm, "I believe God, that it shall be even as it was told me" (Acts 27:25).

(a) Faith in the fact of God moves next to a declaration of the fact of creation. (See v. 3, PHILLIPS.) This is a hypothesis that came by revelation. No one yet has discovered it through the scientific approach, although with every new advance in science we are seeing the evidence of the creator. It becomes increasingly clear that God created in the way the scripture says that he did: by the expression of his power, for everything consists of elemental energy. (See Ps. 33:9.)

(b) The declaration of faith involves dedication to divine principles. (See vv. 25–26, PHILLIPS.) At whatever cost, holding to God's principles is mandatory in the life of faith. The realism of the faith-life is declared emphatically through moral and ethical actions.

(c) Relating the contemporary to the eternal is the final declaration of faith. While the man of faith lives realistically in the social order of the day and does not merely wait for this life to conclude, he is convinced that life has infinite dimensions of time, space, and human fulfillment. There is a sense, in which this life is a threshold to eternal life. The faith heroes of Heb. 11 walked as "strangers and pilgrims" in this world. They were persecuted on the right hand and on the left. They did not draw back, but they moved forward because they looked for a homeland, a heavenly one; they moved in the direction of the eternal goal.

III. *Demonstration of faith.* It is not enough to define nor even declare faith. We are called upon to demonstrate it. This essentially is the message of Heb. 11. Three great men stand forth in bold relief: Enoch, Abraham, and Moses.

(a) Enoch walked and talked with God. He was sensitive to the divine fellowship.

(b) Abraham "obeyed when he was called . . . not knowing where he was to go . . . for he looked for a city . . . whose builder and maker was God." He was responsive to the divine call. Direction and purpose were followed unswervingly even when rationale was clouded.

(c) Moses "refused to be called the son of Pharaoh's daughter" or "to enjoy the fleeting pleasures of sin, choosing rather to suffer with the people of God." He was obedient to divine principles. His parents had demonstrated courageous faith to protect his life as an infant. They were rewarded when he identified himself with God's people.

IV. *Dimensions of faith.* Heb. 11: 32–38 is a gigantic pageant of heroism which depicts the dimensions of the faith-life in human history.

(a) The roster reads like the marshaling of mighty men of valor, men who acted upon their belief and thus proved the fact of faith. The dimensions of faith here are tremendous. Great men like Noah, Abraham, and Moses stand out. But there were common people too, both men and women, "of whom the world was not worthy." The record speaks in glowing terms. (See vv. 33–37.)

(b) This does not sound like victory, does it? But these were all people of faith. For them death was by no means defeat; it was a martyr's coronation. This was the demonstration of faith by the common, nameless people who were willing to live or die in faith. Theirs was the route to greatness.

(c) God is looking for men and women who will keep faith contemporary and who will live or die heroically in this generation. Believe in God—Father, Son, and Holy Spirit. Believe in his word of promise, and act as though it were true. Be the one who will stand with the sword of the Spirit and the shield of faith. Let us give our contemporaries the benefit of seeing a living faith relevant to our age.—Paul P. Fryhling.

Illustrations

INSIGHT. It would not be too fanciful to think of faith as in the first instance insight. Faith at this level is the capacity to see. It is the capacity to see for oneself the loveliness of what is lovely, to see the difference between justice and injustice, to see the stupendous importance of truth, and to see the point of a cup of cold water given in love or the point of a man dying on a cross. If we see what is there waiting to be seen in our life and in this strange world of ours, waiting not necessarily on the surface but just beyond it and then more beyond that, then we have faith. If we see even a little, we soon find there is more and more.—Wilfred Cantwell Smith.

WATCHWORD. Ours is a new age. It has new speed, new power, new values, new dangers and new opportunities, new fears and new hopes. Part of our problem is we remain old men in a new world. We need a new moral sensibility. Yet we cling to our old immoralities. We need a new awareness of spiritual reality, but we squeeze our materialistic values. What makes Christianity a gospel is its affirmation that neither man nor society need stay the way they are. Human nature can be changed. Alongside of education and legislation it sets its distinctive watchword—regeneration. If Christianity affirms anything at all, it is that human nature can be changed, genuinely, radically, and permanently changed.—Chevis F. Horne.

Sermon Suggestions

PUTTING ON CHRIST. Text: Gal. 3:27. (1) There is a mystery in life that we can never fully comprehend. We can only accept it. (2) There is pain in life for which there is never a complete explanation. We can only accept it and—after we have fought to temper it—possess it. (3) There is grace in life—moments of grace, events that are filled with grace, ceremonies that are filled with grace, graceful people bearing grace; these are beyond human understanding. We can only accept such grace with thankful hearts.—John B. Coburn.

HOW GOD IS KNOWN. Scripture: Ps. 19: 1–14. (1) The natural means of revelation. (See v. 1.) (2) The scriptural means of revelation. (See v. 7.) (3) The personal means of revelation. (See vv. 13–14.)—Stephen F. Olford.

Worship Aids

CALL TO WORSHIP. "They that wait upon the Lord shall renew their strength; they shall mount up with wings as eagles;

they shall run, and not be weary; and they shall walk, and not faint." Isa. 40:31.

INVOCATION.   O God of mercy, in this hour in thy house have mercy upon us. O God of light, shine into our hearts. O thou eternal goodness, deliver us from evil. O God of power, be thou our refuge and our strength. O God of love, let love flow through us. O God of life, live within us, now and forevermore.

OFFERTORY SENTENCE.   "This is the thing which the Lord commanded, saying, Take ye from among you an offering unto the Lord: whosoever is of a willing heart, let him bring it, an offering of the Lord." Exod. 35:4-5.

OFFERTORY PRAYER.   Our Father, open our eyes, we pray, to the glorious opportunities of sharing with others our blessed experiences of fellowship with one another and with thee.

PRAYER.   O God, our Father, in the beauty of this day, in the glory of this life, and in the quietness of this place, we come to seek your direction for our sometimes misdirected lives. We realize in the depth of our spirits that the goals that we have set for ourselves in this world—of success and advancement, of possession and riches—are frequently of a fleeting nature with no lasting contentment. Thus we search for permanence and staying peace in our transient lives.

Show us the way, O God. Lead us anew down the sure, firm highways of faith, hope, and love in which we invest ourselves in the deepending conviction that you are the ground of our being and of all being; that Jesus the Christ is in fact the hope of the world; and that our lives are empty and void until we grasp and show Christian love.

Thus, our Father, in our growing faith we offer our thanksgiving for you—for your power and care in our midst and for your gifts of mind, body, and spirit that offer to us the opportunities of growth and worth and value. We are thankful that you came to us in Christ so that our sins are taken away and death is no more. And we are thankful for Christian love in which you hold and sustain us and which challenges us to reach out and embrace our fellowmen in the manner and the way of Jesus himself.

Lift us this day to faith, hope, and love in our lives.—Arthur H. Bishop.

EVENING SERVICE

Topic: The Will of God
TEXT: Matt. 7:21.

The will of God is the primary pursuit of the Christian. It was the matchless motivation of the master. It was the driving desire of the disciples. A Christian is not just a person who makes religious noises or performs religious rituals or attends religious services. A Christian is a person who does the will of God.

I. What is the will of God? (a) *The will of God is personal.* God's will is for you to realize the unique potential which he planted within your life. God's will is that your practice might match up to your potential.

(b) *The will of God is present.* God does have a will for your future, but he also has a will for your present. God's will is for now.

(c) *God's will is progressive.* We do not discover all of God's will at once. The will of God is an open door which bids you to enter. The will of God is an appeal to obey what we know so that we might learn what we do not know.

(d) *God's will is perfect.* You'll never know the joy of the abundant life until you dedicate yourself to God's perfect will for your life. God has a purpose for you. Some of you are hiding from God's will. Some are running from God's will. You need to accept it for it is perfect for you.

II. What are our resources and where can we look to discover the will of God for our lives?

(a) *We have an eternal source.* The place to begin in discovering the will of God is with God himself.

(1) One way to tap this eternal source is the Bible, the record of God's self-disclosure to man.

(2) Prayer is an attempt to so align yourself with God and to so put yourself in

tune with him that you will begin to want what he wants.

(3) The purpose of worship is to help you know God more intimately and to understand his word more clearly.

(b) *We have an internal source.* In seeking to discover the will of God you can look inward for help.

(1) God has given us minds with which we can think. With our minds we can recognize our talents and skills. This knowledge will help us know what we should do with our lives.

(2) More important than our mind is the indwelling Spirit of God that every Christian has. And as we allow this Spirit to communicate with our spirit, we will gain insights into God's will and purpose for our lives.

(c) *We have an external source.* We should not only look up and look in, but we should also look out in seeking to discover God's will. There are many to whom we can talk who can share helpful insights out of their experiences.

(1) Listening to those who have been that way before will help.

(2) Reading helps. We live in the age of books. Some of my keenest insights into life have come as I read the biographies of God's great men of the past, and these have helped me to hammer out God's will for my own life.

(3) External circumstances are instrumental in helping us to discover the will of God. Many times a closed door has precluded a first choice but has led persons into a second choice which turned out to be God's perfect will for their lives.

III. G. Campbell Morgan asserted that we have three indicators as we seek to discover God's will: the truth of God contained in his written word, the purpose of God indicated by his indwelling Spirit, and the government of God exhibited in the opening and shutting of doors. Certainty comes not from one or the other of these but in a combination of the three. If we will study the word of God, if we will be open to the Spirit of God, and if we will be sensitive to the government of God, then we will discover his plan for our lives.— Brian L. Harbour.

SUNDAY: JANUARY TWENTIETH

MORNING SERVICE

Topic: How to Pray for Missions (Missionary Day)

TEXT: Acts 26:17–18.

As a Christian missionary Paul spent much time praying for others. From Acts and his thirteen letters we gather at least twenty instances of such intercession. But Paul also felt the need for others to pray for him. Sometimes he voiced that need in requests of a general nature, such as we find in Rom. 15:30 and I Thess. 5:25. But more often he zeroed in on specific concerns which his missionary labors brought to the fore. In doing so he gives us a guide for our missionary intercessions today.

I. We should pray for missionaries to "be delivered from unreasonable and wicked men" (II Thess. 3:2, cf. Rom. 15:-31). As we move toward the end of time scripture leads us to expect a great outburst of satanic opposition against all Christian endeavor.

II. We should pray that the missionary's service "may be accepted of the saints" (Rom. 15:31). The United States is little loved by most peoples of our world. The resentments produced by mistakes in our foreign policy often spill over into even Christian hearts and hinder full acceptance of the missionary's presence. Only prayer support can break down this barrier and give God's ambassador that loving acceptance by national believers which is so essential to the success of his work.

III. We should pray for God to open doors of opportunity for the missionary's witness (Col. 4:3). From his experiences in Jerusalem (Acts 22:17–21) and Antioch (Acts 11:25–26) Paul learned the difference between butting his head up against a stone wall and walking through an open door. The missionary's time is too short and his resources too limited for him to expend them on stone walls. He needs God's guidance to open doors.

IV. We should pray for God to give the missionary courage to witness boldly for his Lord in all circumstances (Eph. 6:19–20). It may come as a surprise to some to realize that the great Paul had a problem at this point. But many a modern missionary can testify that this is a recurring need for him. Such boldness comes only from the fulness of God's Spirit (Acts 4:31).

V. We should pray that God will enable the missionary to make his message plain (Col. 4:4). Such is the meaning of the KJV expression "make it manifest." Most missionaries have to witness in a second language. This request involves both language proficiency and the wisdom to know how to "put the fodder down where the sheep can reach it."

VI. We should pray for God to make the missionary's witness fruitful (II Thess. 3:1). A heart-rending aspect of most missionaries' furlough is the constant reminder of how few believers there are on his particular field of labor as compared with what he sees in the homeland. One cannot help but long for your prayers that "the message of the Lord may spread rapidly and be honored, just as it was with you" (NIV).

VII. There is one major difference between Paul and most contemporary missionaries. Paul was not a family man. If he had been, I believe that he would have added one more request to his list. So let me add it for him in the name of all my colleagues. Please pray for God to bless the parents whom missionaries leave behind as well as the children whom they take with them to the field and from whom, all too soon, they must be separated as they return to the States for their continued education.—James D. Crane.

Illustrations

CLAIMING HIS PRESENCE. It must remain very questionable whether a stay-at-home church that is withdrawn from the world into its own little Christian ghetto, disobedient to the great commission, and indifferent to the needs of the world is in any position to claim or inherit the promise of Christ's presence. But to those who go into the world as Christ came into the world, to those who sacrifice their ease and comfort and independence and safety and hazard their lives in the search of disciples comes the promise of the presence of the living Christ.—John R. W. Stott.

WHAT THEY SAW. The African Institute of London made a film to teach African villagers how to drain mosquito-infested ponds and how to practice good sanitation in order to improve the health conditions. After showing the film to some villagers, they were asked to describe what they saw. Someone said that he saw a chicken. All of the other Africans agreed that they too had seen the chicken. The producers of the film did not recall a chicken's being in the film. But as they scanned it again frame by frame, they saw in the lower right-hand corner of one of the frames a frightened chicken heading for safety. The Africans had all missed the main point of the film because of the chicken. Maybe it was because chickens meant something to them —eggs and food—while stagnant ponds and garbage and debris were not interesting or exciting. Yet these last things were the source of sickness and death. But the villagers' interest in the chicken had overshadowed whatever else was in the film.—Charles E. Ferrell.

Sermon Suggestion

WHEN WE PRAY. Text: Luke 11:2. When we pray we must always remember three things. (1) The love of God ever seeks and desires what is best for us. (2) The wisdom of God alone knows what is best for us. (3) The power of God alone can bring to pass that which is best for us.—William Barclay.

Worship Aids

CALL TO WORSHIP. "Lord, who shall abide in thy tabernacle? Who shall dwell in thy holy hill? He that walketh uprightly, and worketh righteousness, and speaketh the truth in his heart." Ps. 15:1–2.

INVOCATION. We turn our minds unto thee, O God, that thou wilt give us deeper insight into the meanings of the life of thy Son, our Lord. We turn our hearts unto thee that thy love may flow through them. We turn our wills unto thee that thou mayst guide us in all that we do and in all that we say.

OFFERTORY SENTENCE. "Whatsoever ye would that men should do to you, do ye even so to them: for this is the law and the prophets." Matt. 7:12.

OFFERTORY PRAYER. Accept, O Lord, these offerings thy people make unto thee and grant that the cause to which they are devoted may prosper under thy guidance, to the glory of thy name.

PRAYER. Like the first disciples we ask, "Lord, teach us to pray, for we know not how to pray as we ought." We know not how to pray as we ought, but we know we ought to pray. We know not how far our intercession reaches, but we believe that more things are wrought by prayer than this world dreams of and that the whole round earth is every way bound by gold chains about thy feet. We would make ourselves links in the golden chain by which the earth is bound to thee.

Teach us so to pray that our prayer deserves to be heard. We ask not to be made better than others. We ask to be made better than ourselves, changed from what we are to what we ought to be. What in us is dark, illumine; what is low, raise and support.

Help us not to forget what we ought always to remember—no matter who we are or what we are or what our past has been or what the future holds, thy grace is sufficient for us. Help us not to remember what we ought always to forget—the resentments that poison our minds and the unclean images that deface them. Help us to perceive that the decisive things are not what happen to us but what happen in us.

Give us each day with our daily bread power to win the victory over whatever weakens or defiles and power to live as they must live who know that they are sons of God, heirs of the eternal, fitted for communion with thee, with spirits as lasting as thine own.—Frank Halliday Ferris.

EVENING SERVICE

Topic: Christian Unity and the Holy Spirit (Week of Prayer for Christian Unity)

TEXT: Eph 4:3.

I. The Holy Bible establishes the undeniable relationship between Christian unity and the Holy Spirit.

(a) The outpouring of the Holy Ghost at Pentecost brought forth a living unity. The Holy Spirit endowed the church with the work of the ministry for the purpose of causing all to come into the unity of the faith, into confidence, and into the knowledge of the Christ of God. (See Eph. 4:11–13.)

(b) The Holy Spirit fosters a unity through Christ which far supersedes a fragmented, splintered, or narrow reference to brotherhood.

(c) The Holy Bible reveals that Christian unity incited by the Holy Spirit goes far beyond a master plan of mechanical uniformity. Because the believer has confessed his sins and has committed his life by faith in Jesus Christ, he partakes of a common bond which fuses all true believers into a spiritual company. The Holy Spirit produces similarity of nature.

II. The Holy Spirit is the power which enables the believer to keep the unity.

(a) To ignore the Holy Spirit is to ignore God. Wrongdoing naturally hurts and breaks the unity. Pride is the matrix of division. Envy separates friends. Anger instigates unregulated conduct.

(b) There can be no outward unity except there first be internal unity with respect to faith in the godhead. There can be no unity where differences exist about the integrity of the Holy Bible. There can be no real unity where there is doubt about the person and work of God. There can be no Christian unity where unbelief shrouds the deity of Jesus Christ. There can be no unity where the place and power of the Holy Spirit are ignored.

(c) In John 17:21 we see Jesus' deep concern for correct unity. The greatest obstacle to unity is not the diversity of denominations but the varying interpretations regarding the Christ, his salvation, and his church. When we accept the Holy Bible as the infallible word of God and from it and it alone find our message concerning Jesus Christ and his redeeming work, then shall we know spiritual unity.

III. The bond of peace is an adhesive force, and it does not require "stained-glass lingo" to portray its image. Christians are kinsmen, born of the same spiritual parents, filled with the same life, and clothed upon by the same Spirit, and members of the same body. The posture of Christian unity does not depict a fight-back-or-subdue-it attitude. Neither does it advocate that you "flee from it and you shall escape it." Nor does it insist that problem-solving group work will cause disunity to dissuade.

(a) Peace comes from a sense of sins forgiven. There can be no peace within until there is peace with God. Happiness is only momentary if sins are not blotted out.

(b) Peace is the direct result of trust and confidence in God. The peace of Christ is a prerequisite to purposeful living. It was this element of peace which enabled Paul to face with anticipation the critical end of his life. (See II Tim. 4:7–8.)—R. Leonard Carroll.

SUNDAY: JANUARY TWENTY-SEVENTH

MORNING SERVICE

Topic: Solving Inner Conflicts

TEXT: Matt 12:25.

I. There is the conflict between the higher and the lower self. (a) Jesus said the cure for inner distraction was to get all of our powerful energies faced in one direction and to subordinate all of our lesser loyalties to one master loyalty. (See Matt. 6:33.) Seek ye first the kingdom of God and his righteousness, and life and all these other things will be added to you."

(b) Many people cannot make up their minds as to whether they care more for character or for comfort, whether they honor their conscience more than they seek convenience, whether they love righteousness more than they love revenue, and whether they care more for outward show than they do for inner integrity and contentment.

(c) There are many selves and many instincts and many emotional drives seeking to gain expression in us. We can identify ourselves with our highest nature and not our lowest. We can channel our desires and sublimate them so that they satisfy our total personal life instead of tearing us apart and burning us up in anger or resentment or yearning or remorse.

(d) There are three things we can do in this conflict of the higher against the lower, the gentleman against the rogue, the spirit against the flesh.

(1) We can give in to the lower part of our nature—the man in the cellar. Many people do it. Their theme song is "doing what comes naturally." Let yourself go; obey your instincts. Why be bothered about consequences? But you cannot get yourself together on this basis.

(2) The second answer is to affect a compromise, to try to carry water on both shoulders, or try to play one side against the other to get what you want. But this eventually sends a rift of contradiction right down through the center of our lives. It destroys any sense of unity or of real purpose. We become seeds blown by the wind.

(3) We can give ourselves to the highest we know. This harnesses our lower instincts so that they serve us instead of weakening us. We become unified, integrated, and purposeful persons. This is what happened to the younger son in Jesus' parable. He "came to himself"; he saw that he had wasted his substance and his soul in riotous living; he was now just a keeper of swine, and he had acted like an ungrateful cad. If that were all, he would have stayed in that low condition. But he also saw himself as a son with a father who loved him and a home and a better self to which he could return.

(e) The conflict between the higher and the lower can be solved. The New Testament says with undiscourageable confidence that it can be done through the atoning power of Jesus Christ. St. Paul asked: "Who shall deliver me from this miserable, divided self? I thank God through Jesus Christ." He leads us into a cleansing, unifying experience that we call conversion or regeneration, so that we begin to live by the power of God for the highest things in life and not the lowest. When we surrender our lives unconditionally to God, we become whole persons.

II. A second conflict is that between the smaller and the larger self. (a) This is the conflict between egocentricity in which everything revolves around us and the larger life of maturity in which we forget ourselves for the sake of great aims outside ourselves.

(b) The self-centered person wants to be appreciated; he is like a spoiled child who wants all the attention to be lavished upon him. He is so acutely aware of himself that objective interests and facts have a hard time claiming his interest or concern.

(c) The egocentric person is really a specimen of arrested development for he has never grown up out of infantile self-centeredness into the maturity of a real person. Egocentric people are problems to themselves and to others, for they are habitually baffled, frustrated, and unhappy. The more they crave attention and admiration the less they get, because the more they express their self-love the less lovable they become to others. It is the selfless, the self-forgetting person who wins our admiration and our friendship.

(d) The important question is whether we live with a mirror mind or a window mind. The self-centered person lives in a mind which is like a room surrounded by mirrors. Every way he turns he sees his feelings, his desires, his touchiness, his hurts, his self-pity, and his desire for attention. He never sees people or facts as they really are because he sees them only as a reflection of his own interests. But the mature person changes the mirrors to windows through which he can look out to large interests that challenge him. He gets outside of himself and his own feelings and reflections into a real world of people and causes and truths and work that are worthful for their own sakes.

III. What can we do to solve our inner conflicts? (a) We must be willing to bring our conflicts up to the surface and face them. Otherwise we submerge them more deeply in the unconscious or subconscious mind. We don't want to recognize them.

(b) We must talk to someone about our conflicts so that we may get insight into what caused them and get assurance that they can be handled and conquered.

(c) We must recognize our responsibility. This is what we do not like to do. In fact, we will set up elaborate defenses to protect ourselves and to justify our feelings and our attitudes rather than face unpleasant facts which indicate our share or responsibility.

(d) We must make our decision as to what we will do. We can begin to reeducate ourselves. We can begin to rebuild our personalities and our lives and our relationships upon more constructive foundations.

(e) To win the war inside yourself you need to lose your multitudinous, clashing selves, each seeking its own satisfaction. You must lose them for his sake, and in the giving of yourself to the higher and the larger live in Christ your life will become unified, organized for action, happy, and satisfied.—David J. Davis.

Illustrations

STIFF AND PURE.   George Fox was often in trouble with the law because of his beliefs and practices as a Quaker. On one occasion he was arrested and badgered in an effort to get him to recant. The soldiers of King Charles reported they could not bend his spirit nor make him deny his faith. They said, "He is as stiff as a tree and as pure as a bell."—Hoover Rupert.

DECISION.   When Dietrich Bonhoeffer came to the United States to escape the Nazi terror, he had been persuaded by his friends he could do more as a Christian leader by staying alive than he could by risking death in his native Germany. There was much to commend that point of view. He was a distinguished theologian and philosopher just entering the height of his power. But after he arrived in the United States, he sat one afternoon in the garden of Henry Sloane Coffin and wrote: "Here in Dr. Coffin's garden I have had time to think and to pray and to have God's will for me clarified. I have come to the conclusion that I made a mistake in coming to America. My brothers in the Confessing Synod wanted me to come. They may have been right in urging me to do so, but I was wrong in coming." So Bonhoeffer went home to die at the hands of the Gestapo.—Harold Blake Walker.

Sermon Suggestions

FOUR WAYS TO RIGHT A WRONG.   Text: Matt. 7:2. (1) "If he hurts me, I will hurt him more"; that is vindictive vengeance. (2) "If he hurts me, I will treat him the same"; that is retribution, the old law of an eye for an eye. (3) "If he hurts me, I will ignore him, and have nothing to do with him"; that is indifference, disdain. (4) "If he hurts me, I will love him, and serve him"; that is the Christian way, and that is the way that brings reward.—Charles L. Allen.

HOW GOD HELPS.   Scripture: I Kings 19:4–13. What does God do to help Elijah? (1) He sends some hot food and a jar of water. (2) He listens. (3) He speaks.—Joe A. Harding.

Worship Aids

CALL TO WORSHIP.   "Let all those that put their trust in thee rejoice: let them ever shout for joy because thou defendest them: let them also that love thy name be joyful in thee." Ps. 5:11.

INVOCATION.   Out of our darkness we are come to thee for light; out of our sorrows we are come to thee for joy; out of our doubts we are come to thee for certainty; out of our anxieties we are come to thee for peace; out of our sinning we are come to thee for thy forgiving love. Open thou thine hand this day and satisfy our every need. This we ask for thy love's sake.

OFFERTORY SENTENCE.   "Lay up for yourselves treasures in heaven for where your treasure is, there will your heart be also." Matt. 6:20–21.

OFFERTORY PRAYER.   Our Father, forgive our indifference and neglect, and help us to hear thy call to partnership with thee in making a new heaven and new earth.

PRAYER.   Lord God, we know not what a day may bring forth of sorrow or of joy but only that each day is thy gift to us and an occasion to serve thee. Keep us from treating any day and its duties with contempt. Make us aware that no period of our life is time wasted except as we waste the hours entrusted to us. Remind us that "he who is faithful in little is also faithful in much" lest we dream of doing great things when we ought to be busy with the job before us. Train us to see thee back of every assignment and that doing it unto thee, our task, however common, shall be great and holy. To this end grant us thy blessing, through Jesus Christ, our Lord. Lord Jesus Christ, whose mighty love caused thee to become man and suffer a cruel death for us, we thank thee! Thou art acquainted with the pressures we confront as we seek to follow thee and sympathetic to our cry. Give us the will and strength we need. Thou, who didst stoop to serve us, make us so big that we shall not be afraid of losing our dignity by lending a hand. Thou, who didst once work wood as a carpenter, make us proud of the rough hands of honest toil. Thou, who hast borne with us in infinite patience, teach us not to despair of anyone committed to our charge nor let us grow weary in well doing. Give us the confidence that in following thee, eternal Lord, we are certain of ultimate triumph, for thine is the kingdom, the power, and the glory, forever.—Gilbert A. Jensen.

EVENING SERVICE

Topic: Set Free!
SCRIPTURE: Gal. 4:8–11; 5:1–10.
What is the true freedom found in Christ?

I. The freedom of Christ is a freedom from sin. When his words of forgiveness, "Thy sins be forgiven," are spoken, the burden of sin is lifted, and there is a spiritual freedom in knowing that he has taken away our sins.

II. The freedom of Christ is a freedom from being too anxious. (See I Pet. 5:7.) In Christ the burden of anxiety is removed.

(a) This is not to say that there is a lack of caring and concern. Paul Tillich said there is an ontological anxiety in our being. This is a built-in anxiety and concern. Christ gives a new direction to our caring and concern.

(b) We need to remember that we always have the limited view of any situation, but God sees the totality of it. Joseph's brothers sold him into slavery and meant it for evil. God meant it for good, and great good came from it.

III. Freedom in Christ is a freedom from meaninglessness. (a) Today many people seem to lack a sense of meaning and purpose in life. Increased urbanization and technology bring dehumanization. Christ will not change the industrial order back to what he knew in Palestine when he was on earth in the flesh. But he can change one's view of the technological order. He brings meaning and purpose to life in varied environmental circumstances.

(b) When there are inner frustrations and conflicts, almost any outward circumstance would be unsatisfactory. The converse is also true. When one's inner life is at peace and he has found the meaning of life in Christ, the most difficult situation can be met with the awareness that God is at work in it.

IV. True freedom in Christ means hope. (a) In the struggles of people for freedom there is always hope. If it were not for hope in achieving freedom, the struggle would cease. We should have an appreciation of other nations seeking their freedom. The struggle of the third world nations for freedom is fired by hope.

(b) The Christian man is a free man, and he is a man of hope. He believes the Christ who was victorious over the powers of sin and death on the cross is the sovereign Lord.—W. Aubrey Alsobrook.

SUNDAY: FEBRUARY THIRD

MORNING SERVICE

Topic: Christianity and the Body
TEXT: I Cor. 6:20.

I. The soul moulds the body, and no less does the body mould the soul. Bacon said that a healthy body is the soul's guest chamber; a sick body, its prison. Everything that injures the health of the body inevitably tends to injure the life of the spirit.

(a) There is a religion of hygiene, a morality of diet. Eating, drinking, and sleeping, ventilation, sanitation, and good housing are not outside the influence of our religious faith. They are as much a part of it as prayer and worship and work. The maintaining of health is an aspect of Christianity, for the aim of Jesus Christ is to impart fulness of life, and where there is most life there is less opportunity for the seeds of disease to take root.

(b) It is part of an individual's business as a Christian, not just as a responsible citizen, to keep himself as far as possible in a state of physical health. We are to provide God with the most effective instrument we can.

II. For centuries throughout Christendom the body was thought of as the prison of the soul. All its faculties were deemed impure. The body was said to cramp the soul and to be the principal hindrance to the enjoyment of God's presence and fellowship. It was taught that redemption meant the separation of body and soul, as of two elements that had been unnaturally conjoined. The longing for release from the body was at the very center of the hope of immortality.

(a) Lurking in the minds of many today is the thought that sin in its origin and essence is physical and that bodily instincts, appetites, and passions are evil. There is not a word in the teaching of Jesus to support the presupposition. The instincts, appetites, and passions, to be sure, are one main avenue along which sin makes it approach to us, but the New Testament nowhere says that sin can be traced for its source to the body. Paul does refer to the flesh as the seat of sin, but by the flesh he does not mean the physical body but the frailty and propensity to evil resident in our humanity, especially in our will.

(b) Never think of the body and its passions and appetites as evil in themselves. If you believe in God as the creator of human life, then they are divinely implanted. Temptation makes its approach to the soul through the body, but every passion and appetite is right and good in its own place and when kept under proper discipline and control.

(c) Our appetites and passions only become evil when they seek the aid of our reason, our will, and our freedom. It is in our inmost self-conscious being that sin has its center and core. Said Jesus, "Out of the heart of man [and by the heart is meant the total personality and character, not simply the emotional nature] evil things proceed." We are evading the issue if we put the blame on our bodies for a perverseness whose real seat is in our spirits.

III. The crowning proof that the body with its appetites and passions is not evil in itself is the fact of the incarnation.

(a) The supreme revelation of God is Christ who took upon himself a human body. When God wished to express himself most clearly and in a fashion that could be comprehended by men under earthly conditions, he sent his son to dwell among us. Jesus is the word made flesh. In him we see once and for all what the body may be—a veritable dwelling place of the divine.

(b) We get some idea of what Jesus thought of his body when the evangelist says, "He spoke of the temple of his body." That conception of the body as a shrine inhabited by God runs through the entire New Testament. Observe how it is phrased. "The temple of God is holy, which temple you are." And again, "Christ shall be magnified in my body." And again, "I beseech you, therefore, brethren, by the mercies of God, that you present your bodies a living sacrifice, holy, acceptable unto God, which is your reasonable service." And again, "Do you not know that your body is a temple of the Holy Spirit within you which you have from God? You are not your own; you are bought with a price; therefore glorify God in your body."

IV. We live in an age obsessed with sex.

(a) For the obsession advertisers and the proprietors of newspapers and picture magazines must carry a heavy load of responsibility. Sex today is romanticized. It is made an end in itself. There is as much of a cult of Aphrodite among us as there was in the old world.

(b) The Christian attitude toward sex is not unromantic, but the word that best describes it is sacramental. Reverence for the body is a foremost characteristic of our faith. The law against adultery and the law against murder rest on the sacredness of human nature. Christianity sees man as the child of God, not as the product of purely natural forces and motivated by basically animal desires. It is emphatic that the sexual nature is not something of which there is any need to be ashamed.

(c) It is not a case of guilty desires disposed of with propriety in matrimony. There is no taint attaching to the physical relationship, but it should never be merely physical or sensuous. It should be the symbol and expression of a deeper mental and spiritual relationship. Love should not be identified exclusively with sex since it is a self-giving of the total personality, a spiritual union of which marriage is the supreme sacrament.—Robert J. McCracken.

Illustrations

LOVE AND DIRT.   A bus was taking a group of visitors on a sight-seeing tour through New York City. At one of the stops a little lad with tattered clothes, un-kempt hair, and dirty hands and face stepped onto the bus. A woman asked the woman seated with her: "Where in the world is that boy's mother? Look at that dirt on him." The other woman re-sponded, "Well, I'm sure that he has a mother, and I'm quite sure she loves him, but evidently she doesn't hate that dirt." Then she added: "I can tell you that you hate the dirt, but I don't believe you love the boy. Until loving the boy and hating the dirt can be combined, I'm afraid the boy will remain the same." Jesus surely does hate the sins of the world which man commits, but at the same time he loved the heart of man enough to shed his blood on Calvary to prove that love to all mankind. —J. Walter Hall, Jr.

RECKONING. Malachi Martin in *Jesus Now* says that when Pope Urban VIII in December, 1642, heard of Cardinal Riche-lieu's death, he exclaimed: "If there is a God, the cardinal has a lot to answer for. But if there is no God, why, the cardinal has had a very successful life."

Sermon Suggestions

UNTURNED CAKES.   Text: Hos. 7:8. (1) Orthodoxy without life. (2) Piety without principle. (3) Morality without religion. (4) Zeal without knowledge. (5) Enthusi-asm without faithfulness. (6) Desire with-out decision.—W. W. Weeks.

THE PAIN GOD GUIDES.   Text: Eph. 12: 11. (1) God disciplines us to make us more teachable. (2) God disciplines us through pain to make us more resourceful. (3) God guides pain as a discipline to make us more helpful to others.—Ralph W. Sock-man.

Worship Aids

CALL TO WORSHIP.   "Sing unto the Lord, sing psalms unto him. Glory ye in his holy name: let the heart of them rejoice that seek the Lord." Ps. 105:2–3.

INVOCATION.   Most holy and gracious God, who turnest the shadow of night into

morning: satisfy us early with thy mercy that we may rejoice and be glad all the day. Lift the light of thy countenance upon us, calm every troubled thought, and guide our feet into the way of peace. Perfect thy strength in our weakness and help us to worship thee in the spirit of Jesus Christ our Lord.

OFFERTORY SENTENCE.   "Therefore, my beloved brethren, be ye steadfast, un-moveable, always abounding in the work of the Lord, forasmuch as ye know that your labor is not in vain in the Lord." I Cor. 15:58.

OFFERTORY PRAYER.   O Christ, may we walk constantly in thy way and work fer-vently for those causes which are dear to thee.

PRAYER.   Eternal and ever-blessed God, we ask thee to bless all those on whom thou hast laid great burdens of re-sponsibility and trust.

Bless all statesmen and ministers of state and all who serve in the government and administration of our country, our cit-ies, our towns, our counties, and our dis-tricts, and grant that they may take thee as their counselor at all times and that they have wisdom to think with clarity and to act with courage.

Bless those who are the employers of their fellow men and those on whose deci-sions the welfare and happiness of others depend, and grant that they may use their power to be the servants of their fellow men and that they may hold all things in stewardship for thee.

Bless those who wield great influence by their tongue or by their pen, those who speak and broadcast, those who write in books and newspapers and magazines, and those who mould and influence public opinion, and grant that they may corrupt no man's innocence and weaken no man's faith and that they may never sneer at vir-tue or make sin attractive but that they may ever commend to others beauty and goodness and truth.

Bless those who preach thy word in all the churches in all the countries of the world, that the witness of their words may be confirmed by the example of their lives, that they may be saved alike from pride and from despair, and that they may faithfully and wisely sow the good seed and leave the increase unto thee.

Bless all doctors, physicians, and surgeons, and grant them skill to bring health to men's bodies and sanity to men's minds, and grant that in their hearts there may be sympathy, understanding, and love for those whom it is their privilege and their task to help.

Bless all teachers in schools, in colleges, and in universities, and grant that they may have learning with humility and knowledge with simplicity, and grant that they may ever seek to make their scholars and their students into men and women whose minds are wise, whose hands are skilled, and whose hearts are pure.

Bless all parents, all fathers and mothers, that they may give their children tenderness and loving care, understanding and sympathy, that they may be to them an example unto all that is good, and that they may give back to thee the children who thou didst give to them.

Eternal God, so bless and help each one of us that none of us will ever fail in the trust that thou hast committed to our charge.—William Barclay.

EVENING SERVICE

Topic: God Can't Be Beat!

TEXT: Isa. 41:13.

The elderly gentleman's statement "God can't be beat!" made a lasting impression upon me.

I. God can't be beat when people need deliverance from sin. Medical science offers treatment to the alcoholic, but can it compare to the deliverance which God can give to the alcoholic who surrenders his life to him? In the military many more service personnel are delivered from drugs by the power of Christ than by any other means. Millions testify to deliverance from the bondage of sin through faith in the blood of Jesus Christ. Who else can deliver from sin except God?

II. God can't be beat when people need healing for their bodies. We constantly receive wonderful healing testimonies from people who were given up to die by medical doctors, yet God miraculously healed them. They are living witnesses of God's great healing power.

III. God can't be beat when people need a trustworthy and dependable friend. Every individual at some time in his life has the feeling that he is friendless. Also people become frustrated and disappointed at various times because someone whom they trusted betrayed them. Isn't it wonderful to know that God never betrays any of his children?

IV. God can't be beat when people need someone to relieve them of their burdens. Many Christians are weighted down with burdens that hinder their spiritual progress and their usefulness to God and his work. It is not God's intention that his children be drained of their spiritual victory by hindrances which he can remove. He just wants us to trust him. The Lord is our burden-bearer.

V. God can't be beat when there are problems to be solved. Many times our efforts to find the solution are feeble and unsuccessful. I recall many instances, when counseling others, that I did not know what advice to offer. However, after calling upon the Lord for guidance, he helped me in a marvelous way. I am sure that this has been the experience of many other ministers. Many laymen can also testify to the miraculous way in which God has provided the solution to problems they encountered.—O. W. Polen.

SUNDAY: FEBRUARY TENTH

MORNING SERVICE

Topic: The Gospel Is for Everyone (Race Relations Sunday)

SCRIPTURE: Rom. 10:1–15.

I. *The availability of the gospel.* (See vv. 5–8.) (a) Pious Jews in Paul's day thought that a strict moral life, obedience to the Mosaic law, was the way to God's favor. That had once been Paul's conviction too, but he had come to realize that this was an impossible way. We are saved, not without moral effort, it is true, yet not by moral effort either. To establish right relations with God we must rather respond to the God who approaches us in Jesus Christ.

(b) There is no need to search the heavens to find a savior for mankind and no need to search the deeps, for Christ, though crucified and buried, is risen from the dead. We do not need to search for saving truth about God, he continues in v. 8, and we do not have to work out our own salvation, painfully and uncertainly, for both are freely offered to us in the gospel which is preached throughout the world. Believe on the Lord Jesus Christ and you will be saved.

II. *The fundamentals of the gospel.* (See vv. 9–10.) (a) The gospel which Paul and the church after him proclaimed is based on the fact that in one supreme moment of human history God was uniquely present in the person of Jesus of Nazareth. In him "eternal love has become concrete and intelligible; in a life lived among us we see the nature of the transforming goodness with which we have to deal" (Gerald L. Cragg).

(b) This revelation of God in Christ reached its climax in the resurrection, which meant for the early Christians and those who have followed them, that Jesus Christ is a living Lord who demands their continuing allegiance, an ever-living companion who guides them as they face life's problems, who gives them courage and strength as they face the duties of life, a savior who enters into their lives with saving power.

(c) If we are to realize the power of this gospel, we must believe with our hearts, minds, and wills and confess with our lips. Why confess with our lips? Because, wrote James Hastings, "a faith kept to itself, confined within the soul, denied all expression, will soon cease to live."

III. *The universality of the gospel.* (See vv. 11–13.) (a) In v. 11 Paul quotes from the Septuagint translation of Isa. 28:16 with the alteration of one very significant word. As Paul quotes the passage it reads, "No one who believes in him will be put to shame." Paul adds the "no" to underscore the point on which emphasis is now being laid, the universality of the gospel, the fact that it is freely offered to all people without distinction.

(b) "There is no distinction between Jew and Greek," adds Paul, which to many of that day seemed as radical as it would if written to us: "There is no distinction between American and Asiatic or between communist and noncommunist or between black and white."

(c) In chapter 3 Paul had made the same point, meaning that all alike are sinners in the sight of God. He uses it here to indicate that the same invitation is extended to all, the same opportunity is open to all, and among all there is the same need. "The same Lord is Lord of all and bestows his riches upon all who call upon him." This, Paul adds, is in accordance with the well-known passage from Joel 2:32 which declares that "everyone who calls upon the Lord will be saved."

IV. *The obligations of the gospel.* (See vv. 14–15.) (a) Everyone who calls upon the name of the Lord will be saved, and therefore, Paul concludes, the conditions of such an invocation must be put within the reach of everyone. For people cannot call on him in whom they have not believed, they cannot believe in him of whom they have not heard, they cannot hear unless someone proclaims the good news, and preachers cannot proclaim the good news unless others provide the necessary means.

(b) There is no escape from Paul's logic. It is our responsibility to see that men and women are sent to preach the gospel at home and abroad. We do this best as we support the total program of the church which provides for the support of the local church, for missionaries at home and abroad, for Christian education in all its various aspects, and for other phases of the church's work, all of which are essential if people are to be won for Christ and trained in Christian living.—Ernest Trice Thompson in *The Presbyterian Outlook.*

Illustrations

LIVING IN LOVE.   In 1834 Dwight L. Moody traveled from America to England and had the opportunity to meet Henry Drummond, who participated in one of Moody's evangelistic services. Drummond was asked to choose some scripture verses, read them to the assembled crowd, and comment upon them. He selected I Cor. 13, reading these verses with such meaning and commenting upon them so significantly that Moody said he never would be content until he got Drummond to visit America to lecture on this classic description of love. In later years Moody said of Drummond, "Some make a casual journey into the thirteenth chapter of I Corinthians, but he lived there constantly."—John H. Townsend.

WITHOUT COLOR.   Knowledge is as necessary as light. In fact it is like light; it is in itself devoid of color, taste, and odor, and it should be kept pure and without admixture. If it comes through to us through the medium of prejudice, hate, or uncontrolled passions, it is discolored and adulterated.—Fulton J. Sheen.

Sermon Suggestions

WHAT IS LOVE?   Text: John 13:34. (1) Love is strength and courage. (2) Love is vulnerability. (3) Love is touching. (4) Love is action. (5) Love is discipline. (6) Love is God.—Ward D. Pierce.

CAN YOUR FAITH SURVIVE TRANSPLANTING? Text: Ps. 137:4. (1) A good many people seem unable to transplant their faith into everyday life. When they lift it out of the soil of the worship service and take it away from all ecclesiastical surroundings and into the ordinary relationships of life, it withers and fades. (2) A good many young men and women seem unable to transplant their faith from their hometown to a college campus. They cannot sing the Lord's song in the "strange land" of academic life. (3) A great many young couples lose interest in the church after they are married. Their religious devotion droops when transplanted to the soil of matrimony. (4) What kind of religion is it anyway that cannot survive transplanting? It cannot be the genuine article, for real Christianity is supremely a matter of the heart and is largely independent of external things like particular buildings and certain geographical locations. Wherever a person goes, his religion—if he really has any—goes with him. The Christian's first loyalty is to Christ and not to any particular preacher or local church.—William M. Elliott, Jr.

Worship Aids

CALL TO WORSHIP.   "Be strong and of a good courage, fear not: for the Lord thy God, he it is that doth go with thee; he will not fail thee, nor forsake thee." Deut. 31:6.

INVOCATION.   O Lord, who hast taught us that the love of money is the root of all evil, teach us to care for what money can buy—not security, but opportunity, not withdrawal from the world but a full participation within it, and not prestige but use. Help us to handle all the goods of life in the spirit of thy Son who out of his poverty made many rich.

OFFERTORY SENTENCE.   "We then that are strong ought to bear the infirmities of the weak, and not to please ourselves." Rom. 15:1.

OFFERTORY PRAYER.   O eternal God, may these gifts represent an inner commitment to love thee above all else and to love our brethren in need because they are loved by thee.

PRAYER. O God, we know that we do not need to search for thee or cry thy name, for thou art ever present. Help us to create the mood and atmosphere whereby thou canst make thyself known to us. Here we withdraw from the clamor and confusion of the world, yet we are ever nearer to the things that really matter.

Our gratitude to thee must be expressed anew with the rising sun of each new day. Without gratitude we know the channel to thee is closed. We have truly reaped where we have not sown, and we have entered into the labors of others. Life offers us dividends not of our making. Give us the insight to recognize these and then prepare ourselves for thy greater gifts. Keep our eyes open to the beauty of the earth, and make us truly thankful for the strengthening hands and hearts of friends, all the more welcome and inspiriting when unexpected.

We pray for forgiveness also, for we have fallen short often—even of our own best. Let us have the courage to rid ourselves of those things of which we are ashamed and that block the entrance of thy spirit. Forgive our heedless words spoken in anger. Help us to know that, as we approach the altar in reconciliation with our brother and ask forgiveness, in that instant thou hast granted it and made us new.

We pray for the peacemakers of the world and that we ourselves may become here and now the planks that must be provided for a platform of peace on which they may stand. Keep us mindful of those for whom there is no peace this day. Succor them and comfort them.

All this we ask not through any merit of our own but through the grace of our Lord Jesus Christ, to whom with thee and the Holy Spirit be all glory, honor, and dominion given, world without end.—Benton S. Gaskell.

EVENING SERVICE

Meditation: Leaping, Limitless Love (St. Valentine's Day)

SCRIPTURE: I Cor. 13.

Love is a mighty power, a great and complete good. Love alone lightens every burden and makes the rough places smooth. It bears every hardship as though it were nothing and renders all bitterness sweet and acceptable.

The love of Jesus is noble and inspires us to great deeds. It moves us always to desire perfection. Love aspires to high things and is held back by nothing base. Love longs to be free, a stranger to every worldly desire, lest its inner vision become dimmed and lest worldly self-interest hinder it or ill-fortune cast it down.

Nothing is sweeter than love, nothing stronger, nothing higher, nothing wider, nothing more pleasant, nothing fuller or better in heaven or earth, for love is born of God and can rest only in God, above all created things.

Love flies, runs, and leaps for joy. It is free and unrestrained. Love gives all for all, resting in one who is highest above all things, from whom every good flows and proceeds. Love does not regard the gifts but turns to the giver of all good gifts.

Love knows no limits but ardently transcends all bounds. Love feels no burden, takes no account of toil, attempts things beyond its strength. Love sees nothing as impossible, for it feels able to achieve all things. Love therefore does great things. It is strong and effective, while he who lacks love faints and fails.

Love is watchful and while resting never sleeps; weary, it is never exhausted; imprisoned, it is never in bonds; alarmed, it is never afraid. Like a living flame and a burning torch, it surges upward and surely surmounts every obstacle.—Thomas a Kempis.

SUNDAY: FEBRUARY SEVENTEENTH

MORNING SERVICE

Topic: Growing in Concern (Brotherhood Week)
SCRIPTURE: Gen. 37:42–45.
Life can be lived on several different levels. The easiest thing is to exist on the lowest level where one simply takes care of Number One without concerning himself about anybody else. On the other hand, a rich, full life includes a great amount of sacrifice. Judah's life is a study in the search for meaningful living.

I. *Selfish living.* (See Gen. 37:26–27.) (a) Self-esteem is necessary to a well-developed personality. Joseph's brothers were denied a good feeling about themselves because of their father's inordinate affection for Joseph. The scripture tells that Israel loved Joseph more than all his children.

(b) Joseph was a typical daddy's boy—a spoiled, goody-goody, tattle-tale. It would have been difficult to like Joseph at this point in his life, and because of their jealousy, the brothers made no effort to love the young Joseph.

(c) A person deprived of self-esteem turns inward and becomes self-centered and angry. When the brothers had the opportunity to vent their pent up anger, they seized it with open arms. The brothers, Judah included, had little or no concern for Joseph, but Judah, who had a cunning above all the rest, saw a way to make some money while getting rid of the despised Joseph. Instead of killing Joseph, Judah suggested that they sell him and make something on the deal.

(d) A person has reached the depths when he profits at the expense of others, especially his own family. It would have been a sad commentary on Judah if this is all that was ever written of him. God was good in allowing Judah to live long enough to overcome gross greed and deep-seated hatred. Life can be unfair along the way, but God is able to supply the grace whereby men are able to live above the injustice that life metes out.

II. *Responsible living.* (See Gen. 43:8–10.) (a) A later chapter in the life of Judah shows him with more compassion and growing maturity. During the intervening years Judah has developed a sense of responsibility. It would be interesting to know what caused Judah to change. Perhaps he was ashamed of his actions toward his little brother Joseph and therefore allowed God to make him a more caring person.

(b) The spotlight focuses now on Judah at a time of famine when the brothers need to buy grain in Egypt. On an earlier buying trip to Egypt Judah and his brothers dealt with the Egyptian leader, Joseph, whom they did not recognize. Joseph, wanting to see his full brother Benjamin, made Benjamin's presence a stipulation to their ever being able to buy more grain. Imagine Judah having to put his proposition to the aged Israel who had never entirely recovered from the loss of Joseph.

(c) Judah was ready to stake his life for the life of Benjamin. This was more than he had been prepared to do for the last favorite son of Israel—Joseph. In the very strongest words Judah promised to safeguard the life of Benjamin.

(d) Such responsible action was unknown to Judah only a few years before, but with experience and age comes compassion and understanding. It was to Judah's credit that he was prepared to make a contribution to the welfare of the family, where in the instance of Joseph he was unwilling to take a stand for a family member.

III. *Sacrificial living.* (See Gen. 44:30–34.) (a) Meaningful fulfilment is found at the level of selfless giving. Until one learns to live for others, he is not ready to live for self. Those who learn only to get and never to give find life to be as dry as sawdust and just as tasteless.

(b) Judah's journey toward a higher level of living met another challenge when the Egyptian official's cup was discovered in Benjamin's sack of grain. When Judah learned to his horror that Joseph would keep the alleged thief as his servant, he offered himself in Benjamin's place. Judah and his brothers were free to go home if they left Benjamin, but Judah had grown as a man since the last time he grieved his father. Not only had he become a responsible person, but he had also learned what it meant to offer self for the sake of another.

(c) Judah begged Joseph to let Benjamin go home with the rest of the brothers. He gave three arguments.

(1) The father, Israel, would die of grief if the young lad did not come home.

(2) Judah had sworn to bring the boy home safely. If he did not do so, he would bear the blame for his remaining life.

(3) Judah said he couldn't come before his father if the boy were not with him. Judah had learned a great lesson that there are some things more important than one's own life. In Judah's case the life of his little brother was more important than his own.

(d) Judah had grown from a selfish, callous, and vindictive man to a loving, caring, and giving person. Judah had a younger brother Benjamin to whom the father was partial. The circumstances had changed little since the selling of Joseph into slavery; the great change was in Judah.—Eugene Cotey.

Illustrations

LEARNING LOVE.   Some of us have written love on our Sunday cuffs so that we can give the right answer in church. However, we have not learned "love" as a way of life. Consequently, when we are caught off guard without time to peek at our sleeves, we give an entirely different and altogether wrong answer. The test of our character is seldom announced in advance. So we must indelibly learn that love is the answer. Only then can it become the automatic response in every trying situation or relationship.—Keith Huttenlocker.

SELF-LOVE.   For a long time I used to think this a silly straw-splitting distinction: how could you hate what a man did and not hate the man? But years later it occurred to me that there was one man to

whom I had been doing this all my life—namely, myself. However much I might dislike my own cowardice or conceit or greed, I went on loving myself. There had never been the slightest difficulty about it. In fact the very reason why I hated these things was that I loved the man. Just because I loved myself I was sorry to find that I was the sort of man who did those things.—C. S. Lewis.

Sermon Suggestions

CHRIST'S PREFERENCE FOR SINNERS. Text: Luke 15:2. (1) This man received sinners because they were lovable. (2) This man received sinners because they were valuable. (3) This man received sinners because they were redeemable.—Robert Menzies.

MORAL IMPERATIVES IN CHRISTIAN EDUCATION.   Text: I Thess. 4:9. (1) We must teach our young that all men are brothers. (2) We must teach them to know their brothers. (3) We must teach them to seek their brothers.—Oliver J. Caldwell.

Worship Aids

CALL TO WORSHIP.   "Thou wilt keep him in perfect peace, whose mind is stayed on thee: because he trusteth in thee. Trust ye in the Lord for ever: for in the Lord Jehovah is everlasting strength." Isa. 26:3-4.

INVOCATION.   Heavenly Father, we come before thee in trembling because we are conscious of our many sins and yet boldly because we know that thou dost love us. Forgive us our sins, and help us to become more worthy of thy goodness and love. May we gain that strength from communion with thee which will enable us to walk humbly and righteously before thee and uprightly before the world, manifesting in life's every experience that faith and courage which befit thy children.

OFFERTORY SENTENCE.   "Verily I say unto you, Inasmuch as ye have done it unto one of the least of these my brethren, ye have done it unto me." Matt. 25:40.

OFFERTORY PRAYER. Our Father, enable all Christians to know that their lives may be lived with Christ in God and that their gifts are means by which thy love in Christ may reach into the lives of wayward and needy persons everywhere.

PRAYER. Our most gracious heavenly Father, thou whose spirit meets us in the valley of shadows as well as on the mountaintop of triumph, we come before thee in this hour of worship, praying that thou wouldst sustain our spirits this day.

Sustain us as we seek to understand ourselves. We pledge ourselves to the cause for which thy son gave himself; but then in unguarded moments we reveal attitudes and actions that are unworthy of his love. Speak to our hearts of thy forgiving grace; set our minds on the lofty heights of fulfillment; and send us on our way.

Sustain us, O Lord, in our relationships with our fellowmen. Plant within our hearts the seeds of trust that will allow us to reach out unafraid to those around us. Give us vision to see the refinement that is a part of every heart, though it might not be perceived at first glance. Remove from us, O Lord, feelings of suspicion, bitterness, mistrust, and cynicism that rise against our souls like waves that pound the rocky shore.

Sustain us, O God, in life at home with our families. So often we close the door of our minds when we enter the sanctuary that is our dwelling place. Alert us, we pray, to the intimate needs that go unnoticed day after day because we are preoccupied with less important concerns. Let love flow unchallenged through the dry, parched land that we might glimpse what it means to speak of the redemptive love of Christ.

Sustain this nation, our Father, for we are fast becoming aware that the saving power is not within our grasp. Remove the weeds of bitterness that have strangled our sensitivity to the needs of other people. Show us what reconciliation really means and help us to understand it when we see it.

Sustain thy church, O Lord, and help us to prepare ourselves for the other that lies ahead within thy vineyard. Hold our tongues when we would speak pious but empty words. Let actions and attitudes stand side by side so that others will know that the church is indeed alive and at work in this world.

Sustain our spirits now as we come before thine altar in prayer. Hear our innermost thoughts and bring thy healing spirit forth to meet the uncountable needs that are ours this day.—Charles H. Sanders.

EVENING SERVICE

Topic: These Things Abide
TEXT: I Cor. 13:14.

I. Faith in Paul's thought means trust in God. This trust was based on Paul's memory of God's dealing with the Hebrew people from the time of Abraham to the time of Jesus Christ. Trust comes from our total history, especially from our parents. Unless a baby experiences what psychologists today call "basic trust," that child will not develop the kind of self-confidence and understanding necessary to become a normal human being.

II. Hope in Paul's theology means assurance that Christ has conquered death and that a person continues to learn about and to experience God forever. Hope is a view of the future that gives purpose to everyday events and provides a basis for making the decisions that we confront daily.

III. Love in Paul's analysis is a quality of life that is most like the nature of God. Jesus Christ was both an affirmation of God's love and a demonstration of what love would look like as lived out in everyday affairs. Although living a life in the spirit of love is not easy, Paul was convinced that this was the one thing every Christian could do regardless of vocation or educational background. No matter how complex and confusing human situations become, everyone has a small area in which he or she has control. There love can be achieved.

IV. In a world that has seen so much change, many people have come to think that whatever is new and causes change is good and is a mark of progress, but the

Christian believes that some things abide: faith which comes from the past, hope which directs us to the future, and love which characterizes our present human relations.

V. The greatest of these abiding things is love. Why? Because love is in the present and we can see and feel its effects. It

is the basis on which we judge everything else. There are false faiths, but a faith that produces a life of love is true. There are false hopes, but any view of the future that brings dignity to human beings and enlarges the joy of living is good.—C. Ellis Nelson.

SUNDAY: FEBRUARY TWENTY-FOURTH

MORNING SERVICE

Topic: The Kingdom of God and Our Missionary Task (Lent)

SCRIPTURE: Luke 12:32–34.

We stand today as the recipients of the precious gift of the kingdom of God, and as a result we have a corresponding missionary task. When Jesus says, "It is your Father's good pleasure to give you the kingdom," he proclaims that God has acted graciously toward us in that he has given to us his most precious gift, "the new life of his kingly rule." He has called us to live "the new life of faith," and we are called to the high privilege of living "as children of God" in the new fellowship of faith. This is the great gift which has come to each of us individually and to us as the body of Christ. But with this gift is the burden of a high responsibility.

I. *We are called to proclaim the good news of hope in the life of a despairing humanity.*

(a) The religious, moral, and social outcasts of Jesus day lived daily without hope. The peasant farmers, the *Am haaretzs,* of his day were locked out from sharing in the benefits of the religious resources of the Jewish faith. This was the ultimate in hopelessness, for it added to the deep social, economic, and political oppression which they shared and which was the common lot of the people of the little Jewish nation. They were drifting, as it were, in a dark night of nothingness.

(b) To his church God has entrusted this good news of hope. We must proclaim it to people in our own time. This is the great need of persons living in hopelessness, despairing of life in the midst of the tragedies and ambiguities of our times.

We have this gift from God, and in this hope we can proclaim with power that God's purposes will prevail. His will shall triumph. His truth is marching on.

II. *We are called to be a moral influence in the life of the world.*

(a) There is in every age the need for someone or some force which can exert a redeeming and reconciling influence so as to make for the best growth and development of persons and the improvement of the quality of the social character. Someone must show by being and actions the way that leads to the attainment of man's highest destiny and the establishment of the responsible society.

(b) In the contextual situation in which persons live and move and hope for being, we are often perplexed by the pervasive and abiding presence of the demonic which makes havoc with the lives of persons, precious in the sight of God. This was true in the time of our Lord's earthly ministry. Persons were poor, exploited, and oppressed. Persons were alienated and dispossessed as moral and social outcasts. Persons' bodies were diseased, afflicted, maimed, and deformed. Persons were emotionally and mentally disturbed, and their souls were caught in a malaise of inner conflict and vexation. Religious bigotry and exclusiveness were so pervasive that even through the channels of religion the people found no hope.

(c) Into this situation came the man from Nazareth preaching the new life of the coming kingdom of God. He was the antithesis to the prevailing religious, social, and moral climate of his time. To the moralists, the legalists, and the political accommodationists, who had social, political, and economic advantages, he was a threat and a menace to their vested interests. But to the dispossessed—the poor, the moral and social outcasts, and the women—he was God's power energizing itself to effect their salvation.

(d) God has placed his church in the midst of the human situation for just such a task as Jesus performed nearly two thousand years ago. We are his missionary presence in the life of the world. We are to symbolize in our lives what is right, good, and moral. We are to be that ever-present force for good in the midst of life. We must incarnate the righteous demands and embody the outbeaming of God's will. We are to be salt of the earth, the light of the world, the leavening influence, and the incarnation of those principles of life in the kingdom of God. We are to embody the truthful way that leads to life. This is our calling, our high task, for we have tasted of the powers of the age to come and experienced the joys of the kingdom of God.

III. *We are called upon to commit crucifixion on behalf of humankind so that out of our crucifixion persons may find life.* We are called upon, as Christ was called upon.

(a) "Without the shedding of blood, there is no remission of sins." This is one of the deep tragedies of human history, but men do not come to their senses apart from the shedding of blood.

(b) The cross demonstrated the depths of man's inhumanity to man, for what cruel forces conspired together to cause the savior's death. It demonstrated the depths of God's love for us in that it shows the extent to which God is willing to go in order to heal and restore broken and ruptured community. It is at the cross that we stand convicted. It is at the cross that we are compelled to repentance. It is at the cross that we make our deep surrender to God and accept his gracious gift to us, the new life of the kingdom.

(c) As Jesus went to his cross, we are to take up our crosses. Dietrich Bonhoeffer wrote, "When Jesus bids us, 'Come follow me,' he bids us to come and die." We cannot escape the terrible necessity of crucifixion if we would be faithful to our

discipleship. We are called upon to literally lay down our lives for the sake of persons who need to be redeemed. And it is over our battered, bruised, and dead bodies that people discover the path that leads to life. We are indeed crucified with Christ.

(d) The joys of the new life of the kingdom are not without suffering, but it is through the sufferings that we come into the fulness of his joy. It is by way of the cross that persons are saved. "The blood of the martyrs is the seed of the church." It is only through crucifixion that a resurrection can come. Apart from suffering there is no crown. The servant is not above his master. As he suffered, we must suffer; and as he was raised, so shall we be raised.—Robert Smith.

Illustrations

GOING HIS WAY.   You never hear of Jesus worrying about moving people out of the slums. He walked the squalid streets from end to end, getting the slums out of the people.—Paul Harvey.

ULTIMATE CONCERN.   To open oneself to another unconditionally in love is to be with him in the presence of God, and that is the heart of intercession. To pray for another is to expose both oneself and him to the common ground of our being. It is to see one's concern for him in terms of ultimate concern, to let God into the relationship.—John A. T. Robinson.

Sermon Suggestions

THE HOLY SPIRIT AND EVANGELISM. Text: II Pet. 1:21. (1) The Holy Spirit makes evangelism possible. (2) The Holy Spirit makes evangelism purposeful. (3) The Holy Spirit makes evangelism powerful.—John M. Drescher.

MARKS OF MATURITY.   Text: I Cor. 14:20 (RSV). (1) A mature person faces forward, forgetting much of the past. (2) The mature person has the ability to be genuinely interested in other persons. (3) The mature person learns to accept himself. (4) A maturing person keeps learning. (5) A maturing person has a growing faith in God.—David A. MacLennan.

Worship Aids

CALL TO WORSHIP. "They that wait upon the Lord shall renew their strength; they shall mount up with wings as eagles; they shall run, and not be weary; and they shall walk, and not faint." Isa. 40:31.

INVOCATION. O thou who art the light of the minds that know thee, the life of the souls that love thee, and the strength of the wills that serve thee, help us so to know thee that we may truly love thee and so to love thee that we may fully serve thee, whom to serve is perfect freedom.

OFFERTORY SENTENCE. "As we have therefore opportunity, let us do good unto all men, especially unto them who are of the household of faith." Gal. 6:10.

OFFERTORY PRAYER. O Lord, who hast given us the privilege of life, help us to magnify eternal values and to show forth by our lives and our tithes the Christ, whom to know aright is life eternal.

PRAYER. Ever-living God, we thank thee for the many ways thou hast made for us to know thee. The children of Israel felt thy splendor when they beheld a mighty mountain uplifted to the sky. Others have been touched with awe by the wonder of life beneath a microscope or the flaming grandeur of the sky at eventide. Some have known thy holiness by the stirrings of nobility and faith in the spirit of thy creature, man. Open the avenues of prayer unto us, O Lord, that in this hour of worship we may know that thou art God.

We remember, our Father, as we enter the doorway of the Lenten season with eyes open to the blackness of Christ's passion and the whiteness of his resurrection, that we are part of a company of millions in every land and of every race who share the despair of earth and the hope of the gospel. Let the observance of these holy days be rich and deep and alive. May the wonder of our common faith in Christ overshadow all our differences. Let the church be thy church united, strong, and true to her mission of peace.

O Lord of love and tenderness, draw near, we pray thee, to all thy children who are in trouble. Let those whose strength is spent find in this place a strength beyond themselves. Let our prayers carry our love through thee to all the homes of this parish where pain and fear and loneliness dwell. And grant that all those who have been forgotten of men may be assured that they are remembered of thee.

O God, recall us, we pray thee, to the main business of our lives. Long enough we have wandered in search of that which is neither bread nor true gold. Send us from thy house into thy world to be in it thy strong ambassadors. And in thine own way and time let thy kingdom come. We pray in the name and by the power of him whose life is given for the life of the world, even Jesus, our Lord.—Nathanael M. Guptill.

EVENING SERVICE

Topic: The Meaning of Ashes (Ash Wednesday)

TEXT: Isa. 61:1–3.

Lent begins with a powerful symbol: ashes. On Ash Wednesday the ancient tradition of placing ashes on the foreheads of Christians will be reenacted. Consider the meaning of ashes.

I. Ashes are a reminder of the way in which God creates. God formed men and women from the dust of the ground and breathed into them the breath of life. It is God who gives life, and that which is as lifeless as dust is the raw material for creation. Frederich Buechner has reminded us that just as there is buried in the lovely faces of our daughters the wrinkles and fears of an old woman there is also in the old woman the promise of new life.

II. Ashes are a reminder of the importance of confession. The penitent Christian who takes ashes upon himself is, despite popular opinion, not diminishing himself. "Quite the opposite. We have the feeling of having expanded" (Elizabeth

O'Connor). In confession life is enlarged for we become aware of the wounds of others, our place in the world, and those parts of ourselves which need God's love.

III. Ashes are a reminder that by God's power, seen in creation and experienced anew in confession, our wholeness is not in our goodness. Most of us hide many parts of our lives, and the cost of this is very high. The very things that we deny tend to control us. Our passion for pure goodness is actually a hazard and an indication that we have failed to hear the good news that in Christ we can acknowledge our brokenness. More than that, the evil in us can now be claimed and become a source of vitality. Shelson Kopp has pointed out that Hitlers succeed not because they are so evil but because we will not face the darkness of our own hearts. As children we owned all of ourselves— the good and bad. Part of becoming children again, as Jesus commanded, is knowing that we can embrace our failure and brokenness as well as our goodness. Our wholeness is knowing Christ's claim on the totality of our lives and not in our goodness.—Robert B. Wallace.

SUNDAY: MARCH SECOND

MORNING SERVICE

Topic: Nothing But Christ! (Lent)

Text: Acts 4:12.

The full significance of the text becomes manifest when we come to realize with C. Anderson Scott that the word "salvation" is here used for everything that the apostles found in Jesus Christ.

I. We need nothing but Jesus Christ for *reconciliation*. (a) The word "reconciliation" reminds us of our estrangement from God. According to the scriptures, our sins have separated us and God, and our iniquities have hid his face from us. (See Isa. 59:1–2.) As sinners we are the objects of God's wrath, we are men under condemnation, and all that awaits us is a fear of judgment.

(b) Our great need is to be reconciled to God, and the message of our text is that for such a reconciliation we need only Jesus Christ. Our good works avail nothing for they are not good enough, our church membership will not suffice for it has no value except as it is the expression of our faith, and our ritual will accomplish nothing for in itself it is mere form without any substance. Only Christ can take away the barrier of our sin because only Christ paid the price of sin and only Christ died the just for the unjust that he might bring us to God.

II. We need nothing but Christ for *regeneration*. (a) In reconciliation the problem is God's righteous reaction to our sin. In regeneration the difficulty is not God's reaction but our love of evil, our self-will, and our lack of desire for that which is high and holy.

(b) What can we do? Nothing by ourselves, but our God is able. All we need is Jesus Christ for when we accept him in faith his Spirit comes to dwell within our hearts, and we are quickened into newness of life, desire, and aspiration. We become new creatures in Christ. Old things are passed away, behold all things become new. (See Col. 3:1–3.)

III. All we need for *redemption* is Jesus Christ. (a) Redemption in the Old Testament is tied to the liberation of the Jews from their bondage in the land of Egypt. To Israel that was the decisive event in her history, the supreme act of God's intervention. (See Exod. 6:6; 15:13.)

(b) For us that Egyptian bondage is the bondage of sin. So often, even when we want to do that which is right, we do that which is evil. Thus one thinks of Paul's great cry of frustration in Rom. 3:15, 18, 25.

(c) In Jesus Christ there is a power, a reinforcement, and a strengthening that make for righteousness. Thus Paul answers his own question: "Thanks be to God through Jesus Christ our Lord!" (Rom. 7:25). And in making that confession Paul does not stand alone. Thousands upon thousands and thousands times ten thousands have found that to be true in their own experience. You see them marching across the pages of the New Testament and down the corridor of the centuries.

IV. Man needs nothing but Jesus Christ for *restoration*, for the triumph of righteousness, for the fulness of the kingdom, for the victory of God.

(a) Certainly that victory is not ours to bring. History tells us that human nature has ruined every Utopia and that there is no straight line from the efforts of men to the kingdom of God. We should have learned that truth from two world wars and from the division and chaos of the world today. The way of man is not in himself. Man by himself cannot bring in the kingdom of God.

(b) Only Jesus Christ can do that. That is the witness of his death and resurrection. He was taken by the hands of wicked men and was crucified and slain, but God made the evil which men do to praise him. Out of darkness he brought light, out of evil he brought good, and out of tragedy he brought triumph. (See Acts 2:36.) Since then that kingdom has grown from a grain of mustard seed until today it has become a tree that reaches out to the four corners of the earth. (See Matt. 13:31–32.)

(c) We have the assurance of scripture that God has a plan for the future when he will unite all things in Christ—things in heaven and things on earth. (See Eph. 1:10.) Our hope, our confidence, and our assurance for the future are not in ourselves but in Christ.—S. Robert Weaver.

Illustrations

IDENTIFICATION. St. Martin of Tours was seated in his cell when a knock came to the door, and a lordly presence entered. "Who are you?" asked the saint, and the figure replied, "I am the savior." The saint was suspicious and asked, "Where are the prints of the nails?" And the devil vanished.

SUNSHINE. E. Stanley Jones told the story of a girl who tried to describe to him how she felt about her recent conversion. She used a picturesque expression to say it: "I felt as if I had swallowed sunshine."

Sermon Suggestions

SIX LENTEN MASTERIES. Text: Luke 10:-19. (1) Master your mind. (2) Master your time. (3) Master your body. (4) Master your will. (5) Master your self. (6) Serve the Master.—*The Presbyterian Outlook.*

THE SOUND OF SILENCE. Text: I Kings 19:11–12. (1) Silence must be created by self-discipline. (2) The sound of silence is the sound of God's judgment. (3) Silence brings healing to us. (4) In the sound of silence God speaks to us and makes us creative.—John R. Brokhoff.

Worship Aids

CALL TO WORSHIP. "The Lord is exalted; for he dwelleth on high: he hath filled Zion with judgment and righteousness. And wisdom and knowledge shall be the stability of thy times, and strength of salvation: the fear of the Lord is his treasure." Isa. 33:5–6.

INVOCATION. O Lord of light, in this hour of worship in thy house make pure our hearts, and we shall see thee. Reveal thyself to us, and we shall love thee. Strengthen our wills, and we shall choose the good from the evil, and day by day manifest in the world the glory and power of thy blessed gospel, which thou hast made known to us through thy Son Jesus Christ.

OFFERTORY SENTENCE. "Every one of us shall give account of himself to God." Rom. 14:12.

OFFERTORY PRAYER. Our heavenly Father, help us to remember that though Christ does offer his companionship, yet to us belongs the decision as to whether or not we will follow him. May we through these gifts and our witness share with all the world the blessedness that comes to us through thy grace.

PRAYER. Wilt thou look upon thy people, our heavenly Father, with eyes of loving compassion. Wilt thou accept our humble prayers of love as we turn to thee in gratitude and devotion. Wilt thou meet us at the point of our deepest need and our highest aspiration as we open our hearts to thee in faith. May thy grace be our present possession and may we know in our heart of hearts that we truly belong to thee and that all is well for time and eternity.

We thank thee for thy wonderful graciousness toward us in days past, for the way thy providence has been over and above and around us, and beneath us the everlasting arms in every experience of this our life. We thank thee that we can turn to thee now as simply as a man turns to his friend to share with thee the thoughts of our hearts, the needs of our spirit, and the happiness that we enjoy in thy strengthening presence. We are grateful for the thought of a future that is filled with hope and promise and strength because we shall be with thee forever, and thou wilt never forsake us. For the wonder of a life that is filled with vitality and strength, with confidence and enthusiasm, with meaning and power, because of thy touch upon it and thy presence in it, we give thee our thanksgiving.—Lowell M. Atkinson.

EVENING SERVICE

Topic: What Is Special to Christianity?
Texts: Matt. 9:12; 18:15 (rsv).

I. The church is made up of a very special people who have come, aware of their sickness, and who celebrate their joy in being a part of the community called the friends of Jesus, the great physician and the bridegroom.

(a) People often say they feel better after worshiping. To some that may sound a bit selfish, but it is true. When you go to see the doctor, you surely hope you are going to feel better. And indeed you should feel better when you've been here to worship.

(b) No one of us would say that we are completely well. We are like the tax collectors and sinners who came to Jesus, and we know that there are many out there on the streets who call us hypocrites, and they're right. We are here as sinners. We need the great physician. He has opened

his "office" to us, and we are in his waiting room because we need him. We make no apology for that. If someone outside the church is healthier in spirit than we are, wonderful! If that person does not need the great physician, terrific! But we do. He has made us feel better about ourselves and about life.

(c) That calls for celebration. The physician becomes the bridegroom. When we are on the way to health, we do not go about sour faced and hard, as if we were still sick. We celebrate, as if we were at a wedding, full of good cheer and laughter and happiness.

II. We are to keep the health we gain and protect it. (a) We are part of what Jesus calls the new patch and the new wine. The church is not to become like the old piece of cloth. It is not to become like old wineskins for then it has lost its newness, vitality, and sparkle. If the patch goes limp and blends in with the used up cloth or if the wineskin bursts, then it is cast off and thrown out.

(b) In a biting little verse in one of Paul's letters he turns on his converts in Corinth and says, "Are you not behaving like ordinary people?" Paul could think of nothing worse to say than that. Jesus had been very clear about this. Jesus instructed his disciples to go to a brother, if he has sinned, and counsel him in his fault. If he doesn't listen, the disciple is to go again with two or three others and counsel him once more. If he still does not listen and persists in his error, it becomes a matter for the whole church. If that fails, said Jesus, the sinner should be separated from the body.

(c) The point is to keep the patch new and the wine fresh. Fading the patch to fit the old garment is to ruin the patch. Diluting the wine so that it won't stretch the wineskins is to spoil the wine. The church is to remain healthy in its witness to the world. The church—you and I, this celebrating fellowship that believes in Jesus who heals us—is not to become limp and faded like the world in which we live. We are not to dilute ourselves so that the bubbles of vitality no longer require change in us and others. The church is to transform life. It is to make all things new. Paul wrote, "Hold fast to what is good." Not everything is good. Not everything needs to be embraced.—Alfred T. Davies.

SUNDAY: MARCH NINTH

MORNING SERVICE

Topic: Three Roads (Lent)
Text: Ps. 25:4.

A good deal of the gospel story has to do with roads, for Jesus in his ministry went from place to place in Galilee and later in Judea, preaching, teaching, and healing, never really staying very long in any single city, town, or village. Much of his ministry took place, quite literally, on the road. The gospel story also has to do with roads in another sense. It is interested in the different roads that people took to come to Jesus. Some of these people took a particular road on purpose; they were trying to find Jesus. Others took a road for other reasons and only met Jesus along the way by accident, so to speak. And on one occasion at least two men took a particular road thinking it led away from Jesus only to have him overtake them as they walked and stay with them until they reached their destination.

I. The first was a road that was taken on purpose by men whose hope it was to journey to the place where Jesus was. This is the road of human aspiration.

(a) The wise men, eastern sages, watchers of the skies, had seen a new star in the heavens and had taken it to be a sign that the promised messiah of the Jews had come. When they set out from their homes in the east to find the place where the infant king had been born, there was only one road they could take. That was the great road that threaded its way for the entire length of the fertile crescent from the Euphrates in the east to the valley of the Nile in the west. It was the oldest road in the world, already ancient when the children of Israel followed it across the wilderness of Sinai in their flight from slavery in Egypt and northward toward the promised land. Indeed as early as that it even had a name—the King's Highway.

(b) If the wise men came to Jesus by a road that other men had made, so do we. Neither you nor I discovered the way to Jesus for ourselves. We were shown the way to reach him by our parents, our teachers, and our friends. And they in turn had been shown the way to them by their parents and teachers and friends, who had themselves been shown the way by others who had gone before.

II. The second is the road from Jerusalem to Jericho, which is the road of forgiveness.

(a) A certain man, said Jesus, went down from Jerusalem to Jericho and fell among thieves, who stripped him and beat him and went off, leaving him half dead. A certain Samaritan, as he journeyed, came where he was, and when he saw him he had compassion on him and went to him and bound up his wounds, pouring on oil and wine, and set him on his own beast and brought him to an inn and took care of him.

(b) That tiny masterpiece of storytelling was created as an illustration of the second of the two commandments on which Jesus based his teaching: "Thou shalt love thy neighbor as thyself." Jesus believed that love of neighbor was the key to the solution of the major problems that beset human society—injustice, inequality, discrimination, prejudice, and denial of basic human rights to life and liberty and the pursuit of happiness—and he gave himself to the kind of life that has been called the life lived for others. He also believed that the brokenness of the human family could be restored by means of forgiveness.

III. The third road by which people come to Jesus is the road from Jerusalem to Emmaus, which we may call the road of sharing.

(a) On the first Easter day toward evening two of Jesus' disciples were going home, walking westward from Jerusalem to their little village, facing the setting sun. Their hearts were heavy with grief, for they believed that with the crucifixion Jesus' life had ended once and for all and everything he stood for had been swept away. So they didn't recognize him when he caught up with them in the guise of a stranger and joined in their conversation. Only when they reached their village and invited the stranger to come inside with them and share their evening meal—a practice they had learned from Jesus—they recognized their companion as the still living Lord, as he took the bread in his hands and broke and blessed it, and then vanished from their sight.

(b) That loveliest of all the resurrection stories means that whenever Jesus' followers continue to live the shared life of love that he taught them they discover that his spirit is still present in their midst. In a very real sense that table in a house in a village near Jerusalem was the microcosm of the Christian church, the one institution that the world has ever known whose purpose is to call men and women to the living of the life shared in love.—Charles H. Buck, Jr.

Illustrations

HIDDEN SUNSHINE. There's a lovely line in John Wesley Powell's diary of his first momentous trip down the Colorado River through the Grand Canyon: "When the clouds 'get out of our sunshine,' we start again." To wait before we speak and to wait before we act until the clouds get out of our sunshine—that is of the essence of the Christian life. Clouds of selfishness, clouds of carelessness or of the wrong kind of caring that become the anxiety Jesus condemned, and clouds of going along with what others are doing, letting our standards slip, letting our dreams go —such are the clouds that hide the sunshine of God's own presence in Christ. Only as we wait to let those clouds get out of that sunshine do we have the chance to speak and act in the light of Christ's own speaking and acting, which we're always attempting to do as his disciples.—T. Guthrie Speers, Jr.

SO LITTLE TIME. A Persian prince desired to divide his life into four periods—the first for travel, the second for affairs of state, the third for friendship, and the fourth for God. But he died at the end of the first period.—Raymond M. Veh.

Sermon Suggestions

LENTEN DISCIPLINES. Text: Matt. 4:1. (1) Practice self-examination. (2) Practice self-discipline. (3) Practice self-commitment.—John N. Doggett, Jr.

GOD'S POWER IN US. Text: Phil 2: 12–13. God's power working in us enables us to emulate the mind of Christ. God's power working in us enables us to work out our salvation to its fullest. That power is released in our lives by some simple steps. (1) We must publicly profess that he is our God and that we belong to him. (2) We must participate actively in the life of his church. (3) We must pray daily as we seek to sensitize ourselves to the things of the Spirit. (4) We must study his word to learn its truth and apply it to our lives. (5) We must serve him on a daily basis. (6) We must be daily dependent on and sensitive to him.—Brian L. Harbour.

Worship Aids

CALL TO WORSHIP. "It is good for me to draw near to God: I have put my trust in the Lord God . . . God is the strength of my heart, and my portion for ever." Ps. 73:26, 28.

INVOCATION. Our heavenly Father, we thy humble children invoke thy blessing upon us in this hour of worship. We adore thee, whose nature is compassion, whose presence is joy, whose word is truth, whose spirit is goodness, whose holiness is beauty, whose will is peace, whose service is perfect freedom, and in knowledge of whom standeth our eternal life. Unto thee be all honor and all glory.

OFFERTORY SENTENCE. "Give unto the Lord the glory due unto his name: bring an offering, and come before him: worship the Lord in the beauty of holiness." I Chron. 16:29.

OFFERTORY PRAYER.   O living Christ, help us to know the ecstasy of thine everlasting lordship that we may more perfectly become cheerful givers.

PRAYER.   Eternal God, this could be our greatest hour this week if we could listen to thee. Or it could be our worst hour if we consult our desires and choose the way of self. Help us then to catch a glimpse of the possibilities for life available from thy hand.

Some are here with their faith shattered. Mend the brokenness and strengthen them.

Some are here with their hearts burdened. Lift the load and move beside them as a companion.

Some are here with deep wounds upon their spirits. Disappointments have halted their steps; discouragement has blurred their vision; depression haunts their soul. Speak, we pray, words that will lift them out of the valley to walk again in the light of thy presence.

Some are here, but they would rather not be. Duties are pressing them. Things are calling. The self is restless. Somewhere in this hour teach them the importance of spiritual things. Let us all see how empty we are without thee.

Make our worship meaningful. Break up our coldness with the warmth of thy spirit. Tear away our facade with the revelation of thy truth. Shatter our indifference by placing compelling causes upon our hearts.

A thousand things press us. All of them remind us how much we need thee. So we open our hearts. Come in thy way. Touch us anywhere. But touch us deeply with the things that will help us live another week. —C. Neil Strait.

EVENING SERVICE

Topic: Jesus as Divider of Men

SCRIPTURE: John 7:37–52.

Many thousands of pilgrims made their way to Jerusalem for the Feast of Tabernacles, the last of the three great annual Jewish festivals. It was designed as an occasion of thanksgiving for the concluded harvest, a commemoration of their wanderings in the wilderness, and a celebration of their deliverance from Egypt and settlement in the promised land.

I. *The proposition.* (See vv. 37–39.) Observing the multitudes moving about, the savior selected an elevated spot from which he could be easily seen and spoke. It was customary for teachers to sit while giving instruction, but on this occasion Christ stood. He spoke of their chief spiritual need in terms of one of their greatest physical necessities saying, "If any man thirst, let him come unto me and drink."

(a) *The appeal.* This expression, "If any man," marks the universality and the individuality of the appeal. This urgent appeal is extended to every person who hears it and thirsts, regardless of his race, country, age, or enormity of his sins.

(b) *The appetite.* "If any man thirsts." Thirst denotes a real and intense desire. Here Christ is referring to that intense longing for himself which only the Holy Spirit can create in the soul.

(c) *The approach.* "Let him come unto me." This verb "come" expresses action and signifies an approach to Christ. One who thirsts for salvation must come to Christ and fully trust him if his thirst is to be quenched.

(d) *The appropriation.* This expression "and drink" means to appropriate as a personal act. If one's spiritual thirst is to be quenched, he must come to Christ and trust him for himself.

II. *The problem.* (See vv. 40–52.) (a) A controversy arose as to the identity of Christ and what should be done with him. Many were impressed with the gracious words which he spoke and said, "Of a truth this is the prophet." Some thought he was the Christ. Others contended otherwise, asserting that the messiah would come from Bethlehem, according to the scriptures. Still others were hostile to the savior and wanted to arrest him and take him before the Sanhedrin.

(b) After hearing Christ the officers returned to the chief priests and Pharisees. The religious leaders demanded an explanation as to why the officials had not brought Christ with them. They explained they had never heard anybody speak as

Christ has spoken. Nicodemus reminded the Sanhedrin they should abide by the provisions of the law in dealing with a suspect. Unable to answer the logic of Nicodemus, they attacked him by asking if he were on the level of the ignorant Galileans against whom they were strongly prejudiced and highly critical.—H. C. Chiles.

SUNDAY: MARCH SIXTEENTH

SUNDAY MORNING

Topic: The Conquest of Grief (Lent)
TEXT: Isa. 53:4.

I. *Our Lord became acquainted with grief.* (a) Isaiah identified him as "a man of sorrows and acquainted with grief." John Calvin said of Jesus, "His life was a series of sufferings." Jesus said of himself, "They have persecuted me, they will also persecute you."

(1) He knew the grief of rejection in his own land, among his own people, and in his own family.

(2) He knew the grief of religious indifference to human need. At the synagogue in Capernaum there was a man with a deformed hand. The temple authorities looked at Jesus to see if he would heal on the Sabbath. Jesus looked at them angrily and said to the man, "Reach out your hand."

(3) He knew the grief of sorrow at the tomb of Lazarus where he wept.

(4) He knew the grief of anger. At Nazareth the words of Jesus so infuriated the mob that they took him to the edge of a hill to push him over the cliff. Twice he barely escaped the stones of those who would have killed him.

(5) He knew the grief of misunderstanding. When Jesus made that great affirmation, "I am the way, the truth, and the life; no one comes to the Father, but by me," Philip said, "Lord, show us the Father, and we shall be satisfied." Jesus said, almost with pathos in his voice, "O, Philip, have I been with you so long, and yet you do not know me?" (See John 14:6–9.)

(6) On the eve of his crucifixion he knew the grief of disappointment. The brothers James and John were involved in a hassle as to who should be first and second vice-presidents of the Kingdom of God, Inc., with home offices in Jerusalem. Judas made a deal with our Lord's enemies to sell him for the price of a slave. When a teen-age girl accused Peter of being a disciple, he swore with an oath, "May God strike me dead if I ever knew that man Jesus!"

(b) Grief is a consequence of sin. Had there been no fall, we should never have known grief. While Jesus did not know the grief of a sinner, he knew the grief of sin because he who knew no sin was made sin for us that we might be made the righteousness of God in him. (See II Cor. 5: 21.)

(c) Nothing in human experiences is foreign to Christ. "He was made like us in every respect." As the world's savior, he was acquainted with the world's grief in all its forms, from whatever source, and for whatever reason.

II. *Not only was Jesus acquainted with grief but he also did something about it.*

(a) Whatever may be the cause of your grief—sickness of disease, unhealthy relationships, or sin, your own or that of another which affects you—Jesus bore that upon the cross for you because he loved you. There is not one cause of human grief that he did not bear on your behalf.

(b) There is a vast difference between grief experienced in the Christian community and tears shed in the world of unbelief. The unbeliever carries his own grief, his own sickness, his own sins, and the weight of his own guilt. The person in Christ, though not spared life-shattering experiences, has full access by faith to turn to the Christ of the cross and know that there God himself lifts the burdens that cause estrangement, brokenness, and grief from the sinner onto the sin bearer.

III. *He expects us to bear the grief of others.*
(a) You really know that the God-given

release has been redemptive in your life when in gratitude you identify with the grief of others. Think of what Christ has done for you and then, as Martin Luther put it, be prepared to become a "little Christ" to another. (See Gal. 6:2.)

(b) Surely we must bear the burdens of others and so fulfill the law of Christ. Through the power of Calvary love the burden of our grief is lifted, making our shoulders free to bear the grief and suffering of those at our elbows and around the world.—Walter L. Dosch.

Illustrations

COMMITMENT. A man was in the hospital with a tragic terminal illness. His family was emotionally drained. His life had been one of a quiet, growing, often questioning commitment to God; his was not a blind faith, a closed system of commitment. Day by day his bodily strength and vitality ebbed away. The awful disease was destroying him. At times he gave in to anger and anxiety, but he always returned to that solid commitment developed through his life. It was there for him to draw on as the end of his life approached. He was upheld with what the Prayer Book calls "the comfort of a rational, religious and holy hope" —a hope which acknowledged his disease and imminent death but meant so much more than that. When he died several people remarked on what an exceptional person he had been in the way he faced death. But outside of his family no one caught the clue of what had made him that way. It was not sheer bravery and courage. It was not an intellectual stoic coming to terms with what he could not change. The man had a solid, not a casual, commitment. He had grown into it. He had built in his healthy days a strong relationship with God, and this was his resource not only at the end but along his way through the ordinary trials and tribulations of the day to day.—Robert P. Patterson.

CALM ASSURANCE. Do you remember the incident related by Robert Louis Stevenson who was crossing the Atlantic in a severe storm? Most passengers stayed fearfully to their cabins trying to ride through the storm. Stevenson, unable to stand the confinement any longer, made his way on deck and, clinging to the railing along the cabin, pushed forward to stand on the rolling and pitching deck. Seeing the mountainous waves and feeling the strength of the winds, a panic gripped him. But at that moment he happened to glance up toward the bridge. There was a flash of lightning, and for a passing instant the face of the captain was disclosed. On it was no sign of panic but a steady calm and assurance. Stevenson said that his own fear was stayed by that momentary vision of the face of the captain on the bridge. He knew they would ride the storm through.—Gene E. Bartlett.

Sermon Suggestions

THE MINISTRIES OF PRAYER. Text: Luke 18:1. (1) Prayer revives. (See Acts 4:29–32.) (2) Prayer restores. (See Ps. 51:12.) (3) Prayer removes sin. (See Isa. 6:6–7.) (4) Prayer reconciles. (See Gen. 32:9; 33:4.)—Gordon W. Johnson.

GOD AND THE FACT OF SUFFERING. Text: Heb. 5:8 (MOFFATT). (1) It takes a world with trouble in it to make possible some of the finest qualities of life. (2) It takes a world with trouble in it to satisfy man's demand for a dangerous universe. (3) It takes a world with trouble in it to train men for their high calling as sons of God and to carve upon the soul the lineaments of the face of Christ.—James S. Stewart.

Worship Aids

CALL TO WORSHIP. "Having therefore, brethren, boldness to enter into the holiest by the blood of Jesus, by a new and living way, which he hath consecrated for us, let us draw near with a true heart in full assurance of faith." Heb. 10:19–20, 22.

INVOCATION. O God, in glory exalted and in mercy ever blessed, we magnify thee, we praise thee, we give thanks unto thee for thy bountiful providence, for all the blessings of this present life, and all the hopes of a better life to come. Let the memory of thy goodness, we beseech thee, fill our hearts with joy and thankfulness.

OFFERTORY SENTENCE. "If thou draw out thy soul to the hungry, and satisfy the afflicted soul; then shall thy light rise in obscurity, and thy darkness be as the noonday." Isa. 58:10.

OFFERTORY PRAYER. O God, in whose sight a contrite heart is more than whole burnt offerings: help us with these our gifts to dedicate ourselves, body, soul, and spirit, unto thee, which is our reasonable service.

PRAYER. O Lord most holy, who has found us wanting and yet has not forsaken us, deliver us in these days of Lent from all the littleness of heart, shallowness of mind, and smugness of spirit that would keep us from entering into the full dimensions of thy love and purpose revealed in the life and passion of Christ. Search us deeply that in fellowship with him we may be cleansed from all insincerities: pious poses, cheap securities, careless devotions, and thoughtless prayers.

As in these days we walk again the battlefield of Christianity, may we seek to comprehend the meaning of the cross that is so central to our faith. As with Jesus we "set our faces steadfastly toward Jerusalem," may it be in a whole-hearted commitment to the doing of thy will even when it means the bearing of a cross. In our looking unto him who is the pioneer and validator of our faith, may we discover our drooping hands being lifted and our sagging knees being strengthened. Strengthen us to resist temptation in all of its enticements and to walk in the narrow way of discipleship, holding back nothing for ourselves. May our love for others be such a compassion that, taking upon ourselves their burdens, we may experience joy in bearing this cross. May we discover in thy "foolishness" that wisdom which makes us wise unto salvation.

With seeing eyes, sensitive minds, and open hearts may we be thrust into the life of our time to bear the suffering of humanity as Christ has shown us the way. In obedience unto death may the drops of our life's blood be mingled with his for the redemption of the world. For such a high calling we can never be worthy, O Lord, but make us faithful even as he was. For thy sake and for the sake of all of those for whom we have responsibility.—John Thompson.

EVENING SERVICE

Topic: Savior
TEXT: John 4:42.
I. Jesus is my savior because he saves me from a static existence and leads me to one that is dynamic and ever new. The night Jesus talked with the Pharisee, Nicodemus, Jesus told him, "Unless one is born anew, one cannot see the kingdom of God" (John 3:3). Unless we are born anew we cannot experience the wholeness of being that comes as we live in God's will and under his rule. That newness comes to me to the extent that I am able to open my life to Christ and to the truths of God he has revealed.

II. Jesus is my savior because through his life and death he has revealed to me that God is like the loving, patient, and forgiving parent, and this changes my life. It brings a continual renewal to my life.

III. Jesus is my savior because he saves me from despair. He said before leaving his disciples, "Lo, I am with you alway" (Matt. 28:20). I have found that this presence continues with us. Jesus as savior does not remove all anxiety and pain, but he enables us to endure it because he shows that God's concern is always with us.

IV. Jesus is my savior because he releases us from a fear of death. From him comes the truth that beyond death there is some kind of existence with God. The assurance of this helps to overcome our fears.

V. Jesus is my savior because he saves me from purposelessness in life. He said, "I am the way, the truth, and the life" (John 14:6), suggesting that as we follow this way we experience true life. Regardless of what tomorrow might bring, through Jesus I discover that there is meaning and purpose in living today.

VI. Jesus is my savior because he saves me from myself. He said, "If any man would come after me, let him deny himself and take up his cross and follow me" (Matt. 16:24). To the extent that I heed this challenge and do this, I find that I am able to break away from self-centered living, which is sin.

VII. Jesus is my savior because, when I respond to him, I am saved from sin and from centering life around myself.

VIII. Jesus is my savior not merely because he died on a cross 2,000 years ago but because his death and his life reveal much about the love of God which we can experience now in our lives.—Robert A. Langston, Jr.

SUNDAY: MARCH TWENTY-THIRD

MORNING SERVICE

Topic: The Cross Before the Cross (Passion Sunday)

SCRIPTURE: Matt. 26:36–46.

The moral grandeur of Gethsemane is one with the moral grandeur of Calvary. We must recognize Gethsemane as being the cross before the cross. Calvary was a cross of physical suffering. Gethsemane was a cross of mental and spiritual suffering. The second cross was made bearable and understandable because Jesus had been victorious with the first cross. Gethsemane was the cross of acceptance. Calvary was the cross of completion. If anything, it was the easier of the two. There is no incident in the trial or anywhere else where Jesus debates, deliberates, or shrinks from the cross after Gethsemane. From this moment on there is no decision to be made, only acceptance on the basis of the decisions already made.

I. In Gethsemane we get a magnified glimpse of the humanity of Jesus. (a) He was tempted, and he prayed for deliverance. Here it was not simply a question of his fear of death. His temptation was the temptation to doubt his messianic vocation in view of his imminent death on the cross.

(b) His mission was to set in motion the kingdom of God on earth. To this end he had lived and preached and performed mighty works. Was it all to be in vain? Was it to end in catastrophe? On the contrary God designed for him a crown of thorns. God had chosen to exalt him not on a throne but on a cross.

(c) Jesus was tempted to resist, but the moment of resistance was resolved in surrender. The hour of agony passed. Completely composed and serene, Jesus went forth to meet his captors and confront the cross.

II. Gethsemane is a drama that is enacted in every life for Gethsemane is representative of the conflict that is seen on all levels of life.

(a) The great conflict of life is the conflict of wills. Whose will is supreme? We see this conflict of wills wherever human beings intersect one upon the other. How are these conflicts of wills to be resolved?

(b) Obviously to attempt a detailed answer would carry us far afield. May two generalizations suffice.

(1) One is that God himself has endowed man with the kind of will that is capable of being in conflict. Free will, we call it.

(2) The second thing is that God's will is the supreme will, and all conflicts of lesser wills must be resolved in the light of God's all-inclusive will.

III. From Gethsemane let us learn these lessons about the conflict of wills.

(a) Even Jesus, the God-man who was not man in any way that kept him from being God and not God in any way that kept him from being man, felt compelled to subordinate his will to the all-inclusive will of God. And that will was not immediately known. Jesus had to ask and seek and knock until the door was opened and God's will became known to him.

(b) The great lesson of this cross before the cross is that the conflict of wills is resolved in submission to the highest will. The triumph of life for Jesus was in the yielding of his will to God's will. The final triumph in the conflict of life for each of us is the yielding of our wills to his.—Allen D. Montgomery.

Illustrations

SYMBOL OF FAITH.   Several years ago I visited a church in Manheim, Germany, that had been virtually destroyed during one of the Allied raids in World War II and then rebuilt when the peace was finally secured. What impressed me most was how the people had reinterpreted their symbols of faith following the horror of the war. In the chancel there was a cross which was nothing more than a crude piece of wood blistered and charred from intense heat, splintered and torn by fragments that had embedded themselves in the bark. The artist made no attempt to remove the debris. The cross had been carved from a tree that had been blown down by exploding bombs. It was a proper symbol for a congregation that believed that their death and misery had been absorbed into the very life of God and that was their hope.—Robert W. Tabscott.

LEGEND.   Hendrik Van Loon recalled a legend which says that humankind once lived in the Valley of Ignorance. The people regarded the everlasting hills which circled their peaceful valley as the end of the world. There was nothing beyond. Anyone who questioned this was shown the bleaching bones of others who had persisted in raising questions about the traditions and beliefs of the elders.

One day a young man went out in search of the beyond. He returned to describe the glorious world beyond the everlasting hills, the green fields and the lush foliage, the clear water rivers, and the lovely woodlands. But they didn't believe him and killed him as a blasphemer of the tradition of his people in the Valley of Ignorance.

One day when a famine came in the Valley of Ignorance, the elders remembered what the dead pioneer had said about the fertile fields and the productive acres beyond the end of their world. They sent a scouting party who returned to verify the blasphemer's report. So humankind left the Valley of Ignorance and dwelt in the land beyond the horizon of the everlasting hills. Only then did they think to send back a committee to raise a monument to their martyred pioneer. On it they put the inscription, "To the memory of one who dared to make us believe in the future."—Hoover Rupert.

Sermon Suggestions

A NEW LOOK AT LIFE.   Text: John 17:3. (1) Eternal life begins in getting the relationships right. (2) A new look at life will bring us nearer God. (3) A new look at life will motivate life's investment in that which will outlive life itself.—Carl W. Segerhammer.

BELIEFS DO MATTER.   Text: I John 5:1. (1) Belief changes the whole aspect of our life toward God. (2) Belief in God influences ourselves. (3) Our creative belief in God and in Christ influences our attitude and relationship to others.—Fred R. Chenault.

Worship Aids

CALL TO WORSHIP.   "Worthy is the Lamb that was slain to receive power, and riches, and wisdom, and strength, and honor, and glory, and blessing." Rev. 5:12.

INVOCATION.   Most gracious Father, who withholdest no good thing from thy children and in thy providence hast brought us to this day of rest and of the renewal of the soul: we give thee humble and hearty thanks for the world which thou hast prepared and furnished for our dwelling place, for the steadfast righteousness which suffers no evil thing to gain the mastery, for the lives and examples of those who were strangers and pilgrims and found a better inheritance in peace of soul and joy in the Holy Spirit, and above all for the life, teaching, and sacrifice of Jesus Christ.

OFFERTORY SENTENCE. "Greater love hath no man than this, that a man lay down his life for his friends." John 15:13.

OFFERTORY PRAYER. We give thee thanks, O Father, that through our tithes and offerings thou dost give us an opportunity to illuminate the dimness of the future and to glorify our present life with the word of him who is the light of the world.

PRAYER. Almighty and eternal God, we come to thee because we need thee. Without thee we are poor and weak. Our hungry souls long for food which this world cannot give. Our thirsty souls cry out for the water of life. We do not see the way we must go. The clashings and clamor of the world ring in our ears, and we have moments when we wonder why we were born. We are weighted down with discouragement. Despair rules our lives. Have pity upon us. Our lives are eaten away with sorrow and our years with sighing.

Teach us, O thou great redeemer, that with thee we may be lifted up. Let us see thee clothed in kindness and imparting the words of life. Let us see thee in white raiment, bringing light to our darkness. Let us see thee in thy high tower, commanding all upon earth to heed thee and follow thy voice. Come to us. Be our sure abode, and may we trust in thee.

Thou didst come to us in Christ. He knelt in the garden alone. He saw his trusted disciples betray him. He was led before his enemies. He went to the cross. Clouds hung over him. Could ever man reach such depths! His sorrow was like unto our sorrow and his cry like unto our cry.

But from the cross Christ cried to thee. From the tomb he rose to live eternally. Suffer us not to despair. We too may utter Christ's word of faith. Through him we may find victory.

Help us to understand thy ways. Even as thou didst overrule the cross for victory, so wilt thou overrule for good the cruel weights that enslave us. This is thy providence, O Lord our God. Thou wilt turn our night into morning. Thou wilt give us beauty for ashes, the oil of joy for mourning, and the garment of praise for the spirit of heaviness. O Lord God, we trust thee and honor thy name forevermore.— Albert Buckner Coe.

EVENING SERVICE

Topic: Father, Forgive

TEXT: Luke 23:34.

I. Usually when men died on crosses, they shrieked, railed, and cursed those who crucified them. But Jesus prayed. Not for himself but for others.

(a) "Said" is a verb tense which means he "kept on saying." Perhaps he began as they nailed him to the cross and continued to do so.

(b) His prayer to the Father was to forgive, not to curse, those involved. "Them" certainly included all who were involved in the event: Sanhedrin, Pilate, soldiers, and mob. But in the long run he prayed for us—the "crucifiers, then and now"—for we were there in our sins when they crucified the Lord.

II. How may we understand "forgive"? (a) The exact Greek verb is used as "suffer" or "permit" in Luke 18:16. Thus we may see a prayer that the Father will let the crucifixion continue. (See Matt. 26: 52-53.) Do not let the twelve legions of angels rescue me (v. 53).

(b) In a similar vein this very verb form is found in Matt. 27:49. When a soldier was about to press moisture to Jesus' lips, the others said, "Let be, let us see if Elias will come to save him." They had mistaken Jesus' word "Eloi" (Mark 15:34) for "Elias" or Elijah. "Let be" or "wait" renders this verb. Wait until after the resurrection before condemning.

(c) In Matt. 18:27 the verb is used of forgiving a debt by absorbing the loss of yourself. (See Matt. 9:2; Rom. 4:7.) So the verb may mean permit, wait, or forgive at one's own expense. We can see "forgive" in all these meanings.

III. This prayer is based on the fact that the people did not "know" or "really know" what they were doing. They did not know or believe that Jesus was the Son of God.

(a) Paul says that "had they known it, they would not have crucified the Lord of glory" (I Cor. 2:7–8). But after his resurrection they will know. Then their sin will be unforgiven apart from repentance and faith.

(b) It is not simply what we know but how we react to it. The Sanhedrin knew about the resurrection, but lied about it. (See Matt. 28:11–15.) Saul of Tarsus believed this lie until he met Jesus on the Damascus road. Knowing he was alive, he believed in him. (See Acts 9:3–6.)

(c) Jesus could pray this prayer because of his redeeming work. Almost two thousand years of Christian history testify to the fact that Jesus is God's Son and man's savior. So we really know. Forgiveness for us rests in our will to receive Christ as our personal savior.—Herschel H. Hobbs.

SUNDAY: MARCH THIRTIETH

MORNING SERVICE

Topic: The Kingdom Vision (Palm Sunday)

SCRIPTURE: Matt. 21:8–9.

I. The Palm Sunday experience is subject to a number of interpretations, and it reveals many truths about the human situation.

(a) It offers one insight to the human predicament that seems especially relevant to our own times. When Jesus entered Jerusalem there was a great burst of enthusiasm, a spontaneous and contagious response that became a strikingly colorful procession of all kinds of people. They sang and shouted with great joy because they thought that Jesus would bring them a triumphant victory, and they believed that in that victory he would resolve every social, political, and economic problem in keeping with their ideas.

(b) His entrance into Jerusalem signified for them that the kingdom of God would be established immediately upon the earth. Of course they had their own concept of the nature of the kingdom of God. It should not surprise us that they expected it to be in accord with their own desires.

II. It was not to be. The tensions increased as the tragic events of the week developed. In a matter of hours the ominous shadow of the cross fell upon the earth, pointing the way to the stark desolation of Good Friday. Swift were the changes from joy to sorrow and from triumph to defeat. The promise of his coming had been so high no wonder their spirits were left so low when the promise was left unfulfilled.

(a) They had their own ideas as to what God would do when he finally established his reign over all the earth, and those ideas bore a remarkable resemblance to what they wanted it to be. It took a crucifixion and a resurrection to finally establish the fact in human history that man's concept of a kingdom is almost always quite different from the nature of the kingdom of God.

(b) We have trouble with this ourselves. This is why periods of enormous enthusiasm are frequently followed by times of disillusionment which in turn breed apathy and even cynicism.

(1) The United Nations was launched into history with enormous enthusiasm as the parliament of nations which would usher in an era of peace for all people. That kingdom did not come as expected.

(2) The social activism among youth in the late sixties sputtered and then practically stopped. The kingdom did not come as they had expected.

(3) Churches throughout this land in the late fifties experienced the most rapid growth and the greatest expansion in our history as a widespread euphoria settled over the nation. But the kingdom was not realized, so the "sunshine patriots" gradually drifted away.

III. What has to be seen is a hard truth at the very center of Palm Sunday: God does not always act in human history according to our desires nor is he confined to our time schedules.

(a) When we grow weary or when we become disillusioned with whatever "cause" we may espouse, it does not mean necessarily that the cause is wrong. It may mean simply that we think in hours, and God thinks in centuries. What we verily believe calls for our support quite apart from the question as to whether fulfillment will come in our lifetime.

(b) We should not drift lazily in the wind, first this way and that, like sea gulls in a busy harbor. We need to land on solid convictions and set up a standard, believing that in God's good time our convictions will eventually find historical fulfillment, perhaps in ways yet to be known.—Charles L. Copenhaver.

Illustrations

MAN OF HOPE. Cardinal Leon Joseph Suenens of Belgium, in reply to somebody who asked him how he could hope in the present dire times, responded, "I am a man of hope, not for human reasons nor from any natural optimism but because I believe that the Holy Spirit is at work in the church and in the world, even where his name remains unheard. To hope is a duty, not a luxury. To hope is not to dream but to turn dreams into reality. Happy are those who dream dreams and are ready to pay the price to make them come true."

GOD'S VOICE. It is a mistake to assume that God's communications to us are limited to technical speech, whether of the written or the spoken word. Even our friends who walk by our side have many languages other than words. They speak to us in gestures, in the glow or the gloom of their faces, in a touch of the hand, and in a token secretly left where we shall find it. Often their most meaningful communication is by the way of silence. So also God speaks to us in the multitudinous voices of nature, the blessings of his providence, and the turning of an event. All our environment is vocal with his goodness, and those voiceless promptings from out of the silence of our soul are the fleet messengers of his will.—*The Daily Altar.*

Sermon Suggestion

WALKING WITH CHRIST. Text: Matt. 8: 19. (1) The Damascus Road—the road of conversion. (2) The Jericho Road—the road of service. (3) The road to Calvary—the road of suffering. (4) The Emmaus Road—the road of fellowship.—Charles L. Allen.

Worship Aids

CALL TO WORSHIP. "Hereby perceive we the love of God, because he laid down his life for us: and we ought to lay down our lives for the brethren. Let us not love in word, neither in tongue; but in deed and in truth." I John 3:16, 18.

INVOCATION. Our Father, thou who wast received amid the shouts of an earlier day, open our hearts and journey into our inward parts. Help us to lay aside all prejudices, forsake all sins, and overcome all biddings that might bar thy entrance. Let thy entrance into our hearts be triumphant. Conquer our fears, silence our unbelief, and quicken our faith. Lead us through thy Spirit to spiritual victory and conquest.

OFFERTORY SENTENCE. "If any man will come after me [saith Jesus], let him deny himself, and take up his cross daily, and follow me." Luke 9:23.

OFFERTORY PRAYER. As thy faithful disciples blessed thy coming, O Christ, and spread their garments in the way, covering it with palm branches, may we be ready to lay at thy feet all that we have and are, and to bless thee, O thou who comest in the name of the Lord.

PRAYER. O God, you are the Father of all men, and you can never be content until all your children come home to you and until your family is complete. We ask you to put into our hearts your own concern for those who still do not know you and love you.

Give us patience and skill to appeal to those whose hearts are hard and whose minds are shut. Give us wisdom and understanding to enlighten those who do not know the truth. Help us to prove the worth, the value, and the power of your word to those who despise it, not only by the arguments of our words but also by the quality of our life. Help us so to live that they will be compelled to see that we have a secret they do not possess.

Fill us with missionary desire to win those who have never heard the message of the Christian faith, and give us such a grasp of the truth and such a skill to commend it and defend it that we may be able to counsel, convince, and persuade those who have refused it or misunderstood it or perverted it.

So grant that the day may quickly come when all men will be united in the one family of which you are the head and in the one flock of which Jesus Christ is the chief shepherd, the day when the knowledge of you shall cover the earth as the waters cover the sea, the day when all men shall know you and love you from the least to the greatest, the day when the kingdoms of the world will be the kingdom of the Lord.—William Barclay.

EVENING SERVICE

Meditation: Why Do We Celebrate Palm Sunday?

On Palm Sunday Christians celebrate a strange event that has found its way into their religious heritage. Christians over the entire world center their thoughts upon the festal procession that accompanied Jesus as he entered Jerusalem long ago.

It is not easy to recapture exactly what happened on that day. There was probably a simple and spontaneous outburst of enthusiasm as pilgrims from Galilee accompanied their prophet to the feast in their holy city. They had seen his wonderful works among them, they had heard his teachings, and now under the spell of coming to the great religious feast of the year they hailed him with shouts of praise and with acts of acclaim.

When passersby inquired about the meaning of this demonstration, the crowds replied, "This is the prophet Jesus from Nazareth of Galilee."

It all happened very quickly and seemed to have been forgotten almost as quickly. In the gospel records and in the Christian correspondence that is preserved for us in the New Testament neither friend nor foe referred to this event again.

So far as we know Jesus himself never alluded to it again. It was not used as evidence against him at the time of his trial, where they were attempting to prove that he made extraordinary claims of his relation to God.

As time went on the members of the Christian group found something in this experience of Jesus that made them want to preserve the memory of it. It stood for something important in their religious experience. Every gospel writer included it in his record.

A slave in a modern novel makes a suggestion that sheds light on the persistence of this celebration in the Christian year. In Lloyd C. Douglas' book, *The Robe*, the slave Demetrius pushes his way through the crowd on the occasion of the triumphal entry, trying to see who is the center of attention. He comes close enough to look upon the face of Jesus. Later another slave asks him, "See him—close up?" Demetrius nodded. "Crazy?" Demetrius shook his head emphatically. "King?" "No," muttered Demetrius, "not a king." "What is he then?" demanded the other slave. "I don't know," mumbled Demetrius, "but he is something more than a king."—Rolland W. Schloerb.

SUNDAY: APRIL SIXTH

MORNING SERVICE

Topic: God's Body Language (Easter)
TEXT: I Cor. 15:54-55, 57.

I. A thrilling and inspiring text unfolds as Paul writes these words at the conclusion of his great chapter on the meaning of the resurrection of Jesus.

(a) These words communicate to us the best news ever heard on planet earth. Here is announced the possibility of a new posture, a new stance for everyday living. It is an exciting and hopeful approach to living, a leaning forward in joyous anticipation. It is something that lasts longer than a day. It lifts and inspires for a lifetime. It is a communication we cannot afford to miss.

(b) Communication experts tell us that we are constantly sending messages not just with words but also with our gestures, by what we do with our hands, our shoulders, our heads, and our eyes. It is possible to miss the message of the resurrection because we hear only the verbal message which we read in print in the gospels. We have to hear the tone of the voices. "He is not here! He is risen. Christ is risen. He is alive."

(c) We are here not just to hear the words but to see the faces of women radiant with joy and tear stained with gladness and of men breathless from running to the empty tomb, amazed that the tomb is empty, then filled with wonder and utter astonishment of the living one who comes to them.

(d) There is in the New Testament a subtle shift in the body language of ordinary people that occurs at the resurrection. No longer are they frightened, timid, and fearful. No longer are they bent with guilt and grief. No longer are hands twisted in anxiety and despair or brows furrowed in despair or eyes downcast in defeat.

(e) There is a new look that signals a new inner reality. There is in fact a new hope, a new inner birth, and a new certainty. Eyes are lifted, faces are upturned, shoulders straighten, hands relax, and the tension leaves. The tone of voice changes. There is a new expectancy, a new love of life, and a definite leaning forward in hope.

II. The resurrection is the sign that God is not defeated in his creation. The resurrection is the sign that he succeeds.

(a) Death is swallowed up in victory. Fear is defeated by radiant faith. Guilt is removed by the fact of God's grace, his forgiveness seen in the death and resurrection of Jesus. The resurrection deals with something that happened to a physical body. We don't understand it all. But a body that was cold, lifeless, and dead was transformed, made alive, radiant, and victorious.

(b) God wants to begin his resurrection victory in our bodies right now. God wants you to feel the uplift of the resurrection posture and to have the comfort of knowing death is not the end. Our separations that seem so long to us now are not final. There is going to be a joyous reunion.

(c) He has answers to our fears and our guilt. God himself is with us and for us. God wants to let us know that he cares. He hasn't left us. He will never desert us.

(d) Do you feel the tone? Do you see God's body language? God's body language is the risen Christ.

(1) God's body language is the risen radiance who said to broken-hearted Mary Magdalene, who knew sorrow, fear, and guilt, "Why are you weeping?" At first she thought he was the gardener. Then he said to her "Mary." It was the tone, not the word, that communicated.

(2) Today God speaks your name with a tone that invites us to look up from our heartache and our despair. Mary, Bill, Elizabeth, Bob, Lucy, Joe, John, Sarah, and Philip. He speaks your name.

III. What is our response to God's body language in the risen Christ? (a) I feel increasingly drawn to want to thank him for this gift. I understand the words of scripture at a new depth dimension. "But thanks be to God, who gives us the victory through our Lord Jesus Christ" (I Cor. 15:57).

(b) I find that I want not only to give thanks but also to listen. Once I experience the reality of God's communication and God's body language is known in the cells of my body as well as the surface of the brain, I long for more communication. I find this in the scripture where I now hear God's word spoken each day.

(c) My third response is to want to live in hope. That's the message of the resurrection. It's God's body language that says you can begin again. You can plan for the future knowing the harvest will not fail, for death is swallowed up in victory.—Joe A. Harding.

Illustrations

ABOVE ALL NAMES.   Jesus of Nazareth, without money and arms, conquered more millions than Alexander, Caesar, Mohammed, and Napoleon; without science and learning, he shed more light on things human and divine than all philosophers and scholars combined; without the eloquence of schools, he spoke such words of life as were never spoken before or since and produced effects which lie beyond the reach of orator or poet; without writing a single line, he set more pens in motion and furnished themes for more sermons, orations, discussions, learned volumes, works of art, and songs of praise than the whole army of great men of ancient and modern times.—Philip Schaff.

INSPIRATION.   A young woman who had been stricken with polio when she was a child was taken to church by a friend on an Easter Sunday morning. It was a beautiful service. The flowers were lovely, the music was stirring, and the sermon was both inspired and inspiring. When it was time for the congregation to stand during the service, the girl would take her crutches, struggle out of her wheel chair, and stand with the other worshipers. Each time the man who was seated immediately behind her would place his hands under her elbows and help her to stand. When the service was over and they were back at home, the friend asked the young woman, "What in the service impressed you most?" She replied, "The man sitting behind me who helped me get to my feet each time we needed to stand."—Harold P. Lewis.

Sermon Suggestions

BUT EASTER COMES.   Text: Matt. 28:1. (1) Easter comes to remind us that God intervenes in human affairs. (2) Easter comes to remind us that God has the last word and that last word is life, not death. (3) Easter comes to remind us that there was another time when darkness seemed to have covered the earth. (4) Easter comes to remind us that the darkness ended "when it began to dawn." (5) Easter comes to say that death is not final, for God's day won't be over until day breaks again. (6) Easter comes to remind us that it is not darkness that wins the victory but the dawn. (7) Easter comes with a break in the darkness.—Carl J. Sanders.

SIGNPOSTS TO IMMORTALITY.   Texts: I Cor. 15:54; II Cor. 5:4. (1) The fact of the reality of the unseen. (2) The rationality of the universe. (3) The character of God. (4) The Christian experience of regeneration. (5) The resurrection of Christ.—James S. Stewart.

Worship Aids

CALL TO WORSHIP.   "Blessed be the God and Father of our Lord Jesus Christ, which according to his abundant mercy hath begotten us again unto a lively hope by the resurrection of Jesus Christ from the dead, to an inheritance incorruptible, and undefiled, and that fadeth not away, reserved in heaven for you." I Pet. 1:3–4.

INVOCATION.   O God, we thank you this Easter morning for the eternal beauty and everlasting power of the resurrection of Jesus. We pray that these days shall see our Christ emerging from the tomb in which our generation has placed him—a tomb which we have closed with the stone of our selfishness and sealed with our hardness of mind and heart. Fill us this day with the spirit of reverence and humility because we are permitted to sing your praise. Help us to remember that we are your children living in your divine presence in our human lives. Make us faithful to duty and worthy of your love, through Jesus Christ our risen Lord.

OFFERTORY SENTENCE. "For ye know the grace of our Lord Jesus Christ, that though he was rich, yet for your sakes he became poor, that ye through his poverty might be rich." II Cor. 8:9.

OFFERTORY PRAYER. As we bring our offering today we thank thee, O God, for the happiness of our earthly life, for peaceful homes and healthful days, for our powers of mind and body, for faithful friends, and for the joy of loving and being loved. We pray that these blessings may come to abound throughout all the world and to all people.

PRAYER. Father of our risen Lord, we rejoice today in the victory of thy Son our savior, who by his resurrection provides hope for eternity and who through conquering affords assurance of our eventual triumph over sin and death and the expectation of endless life in unity with thee.

Mixed with our gladness, our Father, is the disturbing realization that the day seems far from dawning when every knee shall bow and every tongue confess thee Lord. Materialism enslaves the souls of men. Vast treasure and ceaseless research are devoted to development of more powerful weaponry; man is bent upon his own destruction. The forces of evil are rampant; wickedness reigns in high places. The meek do not possess their inheritance.

In this day of doubt and darkness, O Lord, we crave a renewal of our faith. We look to thee for succor. To whom else can we go? We implore thee for a new cause for hope, for understanding and compassion, for the spirit of intercession that we may pray consistently for the revelation of thy will and the strength to follow it. Give unto us a sacrificial spirit that we may witness to thy love without counting the cost.

Thou whose breath is life and whose life is love, deliver us from lives unshared, unsurrendered, and unredeemed, lest we die without ever having lived.—Benjamin C. Jones.

EVENING SERVICE

Topic: The Agony and the Ecstasy
TEXT: Matt. 20:18-19.

Before there could be the ecstasy of Easter there had to be the agony of Calvary. There could be no overwhelming joy of the Easter morn unless there had been the suffering, pain, and death of Christ on the rugged cross. There could be no rapturous delight of victory over death until Christ had tasted death for every man. As the rainbow follows the storm and as smiles follow tears, so the ecstasy of Easter follows the darkness of the crucifixion and the tomb.

I. *There was agony preceding the resurrection.* (a) Christ told his followers, "I go away" (John 14:28; 16:7) and "Whither I go, thou canst not follow me" (John 13:36). Such an announcement of a parting, a separation from their leader, teacher, and comforter brought intense pain to their hearts. Jesus was talking about a separation that seemed so final that even the thought of it produced a sudden, strong display of suffering—the agony of parting.

(b) The agony of his pronouncement in the text left them stunned, dismayed, and in great mental strain. They failed to hear the last part of his statement that on "the third day, he shall rise again."

(c) The agony in the garden preceded the ecstasy of the Easter morn. The four evangelists faithfully recorded the intense sufferings endured in the garden. (See Matt. 26:37; Luke 22:44.)

(d) Adding to the agony of Christ was the awful shame of public desgrace in being condemned to die on a Roman cross. The cross was for the outcast, and "cursed is every one that hangeth on a tree" (Gal. 3:13). To make it even more humiliating, the condemned was compelled to bear his own instrument of torture. After a night of ridicule, torture, flogging, and physical suffering, Jesus was forced to bear his cross amid a jeering, taunting mob. The agony of pain, the mockery of the howling populace, and the weight of the heavy cross could be endured, but the greatest agony of all was that "the Lord hath laid on him the iniquity of us all" (Isa. 53:6).

II. *The ecstasy of Easter came in the early morning of the third day.* (a) The angel proclaimed, "He is not here: for he is risen" (Matt. 28:6). The stone which was rolled away, the empty tomb, and the linen grave-clothes—no longer needed—all shouted eloquently of his complete triumph over death, hell, and the grave. Jesus met the two Marys as they left the empty tomb, and he stopped to talk with them. With overflowing joy they ran into the city to tell the disciples that they had seen the risen Lord.

(b) What overwhelming joy fills our heart when we realize the magnitude of Christ's victory over death! (See I Cor. 15:20.) All past victories seem to pale in importance in the triumphant fact that Christ won the victory over man's worst enemy. Shadows flee and darkness is banished in the light of the glorious new morn of the promise of eternal life.

(c) The ecstasy of Easter was intensified by the exultation of Christ in his triumph. (See Phil. 2:9.) He who was despised, shamed, beaten, and crucified is now raised by the hand of God to a position of glory and honor. They who formerly reviled him must bow down before him and confess that Jesus Christ is Lord. He was beside us, but he is now above us at the right hand of God. The bliss we enjoy in knowing that he is coming again for us is most satisfying on this Easter day.— James A. Cross.

SUNDAY: APRIL THIRTEENTH

MORNING SERVICE

Topic: But What Is He Doing Now?
TEXT: Heb. 9:24.

Now "in the presence of God for us" Jesus ministers according to our most fundamental spiritual needs.

I. *He is mediator of the new covenant.* (a) According to the abundant typology of the Old Testament, a lamb with neither spot nor blemish was required as offering for sin. Vicarious atonement under the old economy received its most forceful projection in the blood that was shed in Passover (Exod. 12) and Day of Atonement (Lev. 16) experiences. Jesus instituted the Last Supper in prospective commemoration of his own imminent sacrifice as God's supreme lamb par excellence when he told the disciples that "my body . . . is given for you" and that "this cup is the new testament in my blood, which is shed for you" (Luke 22:19–20).

(b) The writer to the Hebrews insists upon the precedence of Christ's shed blood. He now ministers not in an earthly tabernacle but in the very presence of God himself; he offers his own blood, not that of any animal, as atonement for sin; and he obtains thereby eternal, not mere provisional, redemption for us. (See Heb. 9: 11–13.) These realizations constitute the "how much more" (Heb. 9:14) dimension of "the precious blood of Christ" (I Pet. 1:19), for God "raised him up from the dead, and gave him glory" (I Pet. 1:21).

II. *He is intercessor when we pray.* (a) "It is finished" was one of Jesus' seven recorded sayings during the agony of the cross (John 19:30). Surely he meant much more than simply, "I am about to die" or "Three and a half years of ministry are nearing termination." But rather he must have reflected upon the historic record of the Old Testament economy, announcing that all of that now had been superseded by the offering of his own body upon the tree. The veil in the temple was rent in two at the instant of expiration (Mat. 27:50–51), symbolic of believers' immediate access into the presence of God through their prayers. Since the death and triumph of our Lord, there has been but "one mediator between God and men, the man Christ Jesus" (I Tim. 2:5).

(b) Not only has the provision of entree

into the holiest been secured by the blood of Jesus, but believers are invited—urged —to avail themselves of this access. Our "great high priest, that is passed into the heavens" (Heb. 4:14) has bidden us come boldly—expectantly but reverently—to the throne of grace "that we may obtain mercy, and find grace to help in time of need" (Heb. 4:16). He assures his own that, because he suffered as man and because he continues as glorified man, there is a fellow-feeling, an eternal rapport, established between him and us that renders him sensitive and empathetic to our weaknesses and temptations. (See Heb. 4:15.) And this is no tenuous relationship, for "he ever liveth to make intercession" for us (Heb. 7:25).

III. *He is advocate when we sin.* (a) While the penalty of sin has been remitted and its power broken for the recipient of grace, the presence of sin and possibility of sinning remain very real. This tension must necessarily be the experience of every believer. It is precisely to this tension that the apostle John directs his first general letter. Having insisted that his "little children" sin not, he hastens to announce a gracious provision for any who should do so. (See I John 2:1–2.)

(b) Victory over personal sin depends upon the present ministry of Jesus, called here our "advocate" or "lawyer." The Greek word is rendered paraclete, used by John also of the Holy Spirit in 14:16; 16:7. Sustaining his own through a continuum of cleansing, he pleads their cause before the Father. Christ saves from sin; and Christ keeps from sinning.—Donald N. Bowdle.

Illustrations

PERCEPTION. It was Easter and the chancel was filled to overflowing with great baskets of fresh-cut flowers, and fragrance permeated the sanctuary. Two kindergarten girls gazed in silent wonder at this glorious sight. Suddenly they turned to each other and spoke at the same instant. "It looks like a wedding!" said one. "It looks like a funeral," said the other. God gives blessings which he has already seen are good. It is not the situation or the gifts alone which are significant but how we perceive and respond. —Mary Love.

KNOWING THE COLONEL. In *The Hardest Part*, G. A. Studdert-Kennedy wrote about a question he encountered during the First World War. The young officer said: "What I want to know, Padre, is—what is God like? I never thought about it much before the war," he added. "I took the world for granted. I was not religious, though I was confirmed and went to communion sometimes with my wife. But now it is different. I have come to realize that I am a member of the human race with a duty toward it and that makes me want to know what God is like. When I am transferred to a new batallion, I want to know what the colonel is like. He bosses the show, and it makes a lot of difference to me what sort of chap he is. Now I'm in the battalion of humanity. I want to know what the colonel of this world is like. That is your business, Padre. You ought to know."

Sermon Suggestions

WHAT DIFFERENCE DOES IT MAKE? Text: I Cor. 15:20. (1) Jesus' resurrection is the great confirmation of Jesus' divinity. (2) The resurrection of Jesus Christ reversed the processes which had been set in motion by the fall of man into sin. (3) Jesus' resurrection made even more difference. Through it, death is destroyed. (4) The resurrection of Jesus provides those who believe in Jesus with power that enables them to build a new life for themselves right now.—Joel H. Nederhood.

THE WAY OF FAITH. Scripture: Ps. 16: 1–11. (1) The life of faith: "Preserve me, O God, for in thee do I put my trust . . . their sorrows shall be multiplied that hasten after another god" (vv. 1–4). (2) The legacy of faith: "The Lord is the portion of mine inheritance . . . I will bless the Lord, who hath given me counsel" (vv. 5–7). (3) The look of faith: "I have set the Lord always before me . . . at his right hand there are pleasures for evermore" (vv. 8–11).—Stephen F. Olford.

Worship Aids

CALL TO WORSHIP. "O send out thy light and thy truth: let them lead me; let them bring me unto thy holy hill, and to the tabernacles." Ps. 43:3.

INVOCATION. Almighty and everlasting God, in whom we live and move and have our being, who hast created us for thyself so that we can find rest only in thee: grant unto us purity of heart and strength of purpose so that no selfish passion may hinder us from knowing thy will and no weakness sway us from doing it and that in thy light we may see light clearly and in thy service find perfect freedom.

OFFERTORY SENTENCE. "If there be first a willing mind, it is accepted according to that which a man hath, and not according to that which he hath not." II Cor. 8:12.

OFFERTORY PRAYER. O God, who hast given us thy son to be an example and a help to our weakness in following the path that leadeth into life, grant us so to be his disciples that we may walk in his footsteps.

PRAYER. O Lord our God, we thank thee that thou hast created an orderly universe in which we can depend upon the coming of spring: the reawakening of the seemingly lifelessness of winter, the evidence of which we see now in the budding of the shrubs, and the coming forth of the tulips and narcissi.

We thank thee too that in thy plan for us, as thy children, there is an orderliness in our lives that thou wouldst have us follow: an orderliness set before us by thy son, our Lord Jesus Christ. It assures us that, where the seeds of faith are sown, there will follow trust, confidence, and obedience; where the seeds of hope are sown, there will follow encouragement, anticipation, and dedication; where the seeds of love are sown, there will follow harmony, cooperation, and goodwill. Blessed art thou, O God, for thou hast made it so.

There are those among us today who have special need of thy help: perhaps to overcome a temptation, to make a decision, to stop a quarrel at home, to be comforted in sorrow, illness, or pain, to make prayer more meaningful, or to make life more worthwhile. May the living presence of Jesus Christ enter into each heart that is seeking help for these or other needs. Thou, who art great and merciful, loving and kind, surely wilt minister to our needs as we sincerely pray about them.

There are many troubled spots in our world today that are sparked by turmoil, tyranny, or freedom-seeking drives. As these forces grow strong, may there rise up leaders intelligent enough to cope with the problems, wise enough to seek proper counsel, and faithful enough to know thy will in matters of state.

May we too be intelligent, wise, and faithful in order to be as leaven: to work within our homes, our community, our nation, and our world to raise the level of each until it becomes more of what thy kingdom on earth should be.

To this end we would dedicate ourselves in these moments and commend body, mind, and spirit to thy love, thy care, and thy guidance, in the name of Christ Jesus our Lord.—Donald A. Wenstrom.

EVENING SERVICE

Topic: Christ Risen and Reigning
TEXT: John 12:24.

I. The risen Christ is Christ's attestation to the reality of his claims. Again and again he said that he would rise again from the dead. (See Matt. 20:19; 27:9; Mark 9:9, 10; Luke 24:7.)

II. The risen Christ is the clue to the understanding of scripture. "For as yet they knew not the scripture, that he must rise again from the dead" (John 20:9). (See also John 2:22; Acts 2:24–32; 13:32, 35.)

III. The risen Christ is the fulfillment of his own word concerning the necessity of his resurrection to complete his atoning work. (See Matt. 26:21; Acts 3:18.)

IV. The risen Christ is the channel of blessing. (See Acts 5:30, 31; 10:40; 13:37, 38.)

V. The risen Christ is the object of our faith. (See Rom. 10:9; I Pet. 1:21.)

VI. The risen Christ is the assurance of our justification. (See Rom. 4:25.)

VII. The risen Christ is the answer to every accusation. (See Rom. 8:34.)

VIII. The risen Christ is put to the believer's account. (See Rom. 6:5; Col. 2:12.)

IX. The risen Christ is the model, aim, and end of the believer's life. (See II Cor. 5:15.)

X. The risen Christ is the ground of Christ's claim to the believer and his protection of him. (See Rom. 14:8–9.)

XI. The risen Christ is the pledge of our inheritance. (See I Pet. 1:3.)

XII. The risen Christ is the earnest of our being glorified with him. (See Rom. 8:11.)

XIII. The risen Christ is the guarantee that our loved ones, who have fallen asleep in him, shall be raised. (See I Cor. 15:20.)

XIV. The risen Christ is God's bond that we shall see our loved ones again who died in him. (See I Thess. 4:13–14.)

XV. The risen Christ is the exhibition of God's power. (See Eph. 1:20.)

XVI. The risen Christ is the worker's theme in testimony. (See Acts 3:15–16; 4:-10.)

XVII. The risen Christ is our commissioner for service. (See Gal. 1:1.)

XVIII. The risen Christ is the positive proof that God will judge the world in righteousness. (See Acts 17:31.)

XIX. The risen Christ should be the desire of all our life. (See Phil. 3:10.)—F. E. Marsh.

SUNDAY: APRIL TWENTIETH

MORNING SERVICE

Topic: Christian Hope

Text: Rom. 8:24

Hope is one of the words which takes its true meaning from Christianity. Dean Inge rightly said that "hope as a moral quality is a Christian invention." It was from the religion of the Old Testament that Christianity inherited this good hope, this expectant outlook on future time. Hope was the very life of Israel. "Our fathers hoped in thee." "The Lord will be the hope of his people." The prophets speak of the coming of a new era, an age of righteousness, justice, and peace. When we pass into the New Testament we find the belief that the prophecies have been fulfilled. The promised kingdom is at hand, and the promised messiah has come in the person of Jesus of Nazareth.

I. *Hope liberates. It is a door.* There is a phrase in the prophecy of Hosea which says: "I will give the valley of Achor for a door of hope."

(a) The valley of Achor was the place where Achan took part of the spoil at the destruction of Jericho and hid it. He and his property were destroyed and buried in that valley. The very place which was the scene of Israel's defeat and Achan's shame and sin was the place which God gave to his people as a door of hope. God points us back to our valley of Achor, to the place where we have already failed and fallen, and he says: "There is your door of hope. Go back and try again." And those who go back in his strength are enabled to write a new memory upon the old shame.

(b) The word "Achor" means literally trouble, and it is a great thing for us when we have learned that even in trouble God has for us a door of hope. How many a devout servant of Christ owes the beginning of his allegiance to his Lord to a serious illness, to some crippling disappointment, or to an overwhelming sorrow. Many have been able to say with the psalmist, "It is good for me to have been afflicted." There is a door of hope even in the valley of trouble, and those who tread it in God's company will not fail to find it.

II. *Hope protects. It is a helmet.* Hope is part of the armor of the Christian preventing him from being smitten down.

(a) Paul in one of his earliest letters writes, "Let us be sober, putting on the breastplate of faith and love, and for a helmet the hope of salvation." If we keep our faith in Jesus Christ, if our hearts are set with confident hope on that salvation which is to be brought to us as Christ's appearing, we need fear no evil. No foe can touch our life.

(b) Without hope no man can hold up his head in the battle. The forces of evil are mighty, but God is on the side of the good. Our souls may be distressed when we see the power and arrogance of the wicked but, echoing down the ages, comes the clarion call of the saints, "Hope thou in God."

(c) God is still on the throne. Righteousness and justice shall not vanish from the earth. God will never leave us nor forsake us. The cross is the pledge of that. Calvary is the ground of unquenchable hope. When the shallow hopes of the world are all dead, we can hope on in God.

III. *Hope holds. It is an anchor.* "We have fled for refuge," declares the writer to the Hebrews, "to lay hold upon the hope set before us: which hope we have as an anchor of the soul, sure and steadfast."

(a) As long as a man has hope in his heart life cannot destroy him. It may hurt him, but it will not break him. As long as hope holds out he will weather the roughest storm. Hope is an anchor—only, mark you, it must be Christian hope. What is Christian hope? It is the attitude of a man who has gazed upon the face of God the Father.

(b) In days of brightness hope can be the sail which the soul spreads to catch the favoring breeze, a sail which carries the ship over a sunlit sea towards a sure haven. But in the dark night of storm hope is an anchor that plunges down through the heaving waters and holds so firmly to the rock beneath that not all the fury of the storm can drive the vessel from its place of safety. Such is the hope that comes to us in Christ.—John Bishop.

Illustrations

LOSS.   When faith in God goes, man the thinker loses his greatest thought, man the worker loses his greatest motive, man the sinner loses his strongest help, man the sufferer loses his securest refuge, man the lover loses his fairest vision, and man the mortal loses his only hope.—Harry Emerson Fosdick.

CHAPTERS.   I keep thinking of the wisdom of Aristotle when he affirmed that happiness cannot be achieved in less than a complete lifetime. This means that the last chapter is just as important as is any other. It is good to be young, and it is also good to be old. Life is lived best if it is lived in chapters, the point being to know in which chapter one is and not to pine for what is not.—Elton Trueblood.

Sermon Suggestions

DARE WE HOPE?   Text: Heb. 6:19. It is important for us to find ways to open our lives that God may do his work in us and restore our hope. (1) One of the important ways is tying in with a fellowship of faith. That's why the church is important to your life. It is the fellowship of renewal. (2) It is important to act upon such hope as you have. It may seem little, but it will grow as you use it. (3) It is not enough to tie in to a fellowship or act upon the hope you have. There is a deeper part of Christian hope which we can call exposing life to the mind of Christ. Men have discovered—and the New Testament is full of it—that when one daily exposes his life to the mind of Jesus Christ something profound begins to happen.—Gene E. Bartlett.

THE GREAT HOPE.   Text: John 14:3. (1) The great hope is to discover him. (2) The great hope is to experience him. (3) The great hope is to share him.—Derl G. Keefer.

Worship Aids

CALL TO WORSHIP.   "Make a joyful noise unto the Lord, all ye lands. Serve the Lord with gladness: come before his presence with singing. Enter into his gates with thanksgiving, and into his courts with praise: be thankful unto him, and bless his name." Ps. 100:1–2, 4.

INVOCATION.   Our Father, we give thanks for Jesus Christ our savior. Help us to receive the fulness of thy salvation. Grant us grace to live joyful, obedient, and triumphant lives as thy children in this thy world. May the spirit of peace reign within our hearts and invade the nations of the world.

OFFERTORY SENTENCE. "Give unto the Lord, O ye kindreds of the people, give unto the Lord glory and strength. Give unto the Lord the glory due unto his name: bring an offering, and come into his courts." Ps. 96:7–8.

OFFERTORY PRAYER. Our Father, help us to love thee so well that we shall have all thy kingdom interests and all thy children at heart.

PRAYER. Almighty God, our Father, we praise thee for thy wonderful works to the children of men; we praise thee for thy gracious kindness, mercy, and love. We thank thee for the blessings of health and the bounties of the good earth, for homes that shelter our bodies, and for loved ones who gladden our hearts. We are thankful for thy tender mercy which reaches out to forgive our sins and misdoings. But we obediently acknowledge that we have not loved thee with all our heart and soul and mind and strength, and we have not loved our neighbor as Christ loves us. We have lived by sight and not by faith. We have resisted thy principle, "All things whatsoever ye would that men should do to you, do ye even so to them."

Teach us to pray, our Father. May we realize more perfectly how much we need thee. Endow us with a sense of thy presence, and keep thy ways ever before us. Create in our hearts the movement of thy Spirit so that we may know that we have passed from death unto life.

We pray for ourselves individually and for all collectively. We pray for the church; may it ever hold first place among the institutions of the world. We pray for the homes; may the families keep the altar lights ever lighted. We pray for our national leadership; may thy power be their power to save the world. Let not the darkness that men have created dim the lights

that thou hast set in thy world. Keep alive the beacons of hope until we find our way to the harbors of a better world.

Lead us, our Father, in paths so straight that young children may walk therein and not stumble. Lighten the yokes that are too heavy to be borne, and lift those who have fallen through weakness, failure, or sin. Guide us the long day through in this disturbed world, and at eventide stay thou by our side.—E. Allen Bailey.

EVENING SERVICE

Topic: What Are Your Priorities?
TEXT: John 21:15.

This was Jesus' last face-to-face meeting with Simon Peter. There were probably many questions Jesus wanted to ask Simon, but he asked him only one. "Simon, son of Jonas, lovest thou me more than these?" Jesus was getting at Simon's priorities.

I. Capernaum, a town on the northwest shore of the Sea of Galilee, was Simon Peter's home. He had been away from it much of the past three years, but now he was home again.

(a) There was no sand so shimmering, no waters so lovely, and no skies so blue by day and brilliant by night. How he loved that place! His life was bound to it by a thousand sentimental ties. Jesus is asking, "Do you love me more than these sentimental things?"

(b) Sentiment can be a lovely, human thing. Yet, sentimental attachments can get between one and his Lord. Christian discipleship is not so much sentiment, not so much a matter of feeling as it is of the will.

II. Simon Peter stood by his boats, nets, and fishing tackle. These were his possessions and his means of livelihood. His trade was an honorable one. The fish he caught found their way to hundreds of tables in Galilee.

(a) If Jesus had asked Peter if he loved his nets, fishing tackle, and boats, he would likely have denied it. But he did!

(b) We love things, and things within themselves are not bad. They can be put to good purpose. Yet here is one of our great dangers: things can be our gods, and we are never safe with them unless we have given priority to Christ.

III. Jesus was with six friends. He loved them, and they loved him. So much of his life had been fulfilled in the lives of these six men.

(a) Social relations with friends, in the family, or wherever are important. We can never be whole persons except in healthy, social relations.

(b) But we need a priority over these. Only as we answer this basic question affirmatively can the friend be safe with the friend, the wife with her husband, the husband with his wife, and the child with his parent.

IV. Finally there was Peter's own life. He was a strong man with many gifts. There was much about himself in which he could take justifiable pride. Yet Jesus was asking, "Simon, do you love me more than your own life?"

(a) Tradition has it that Simon Peter died in Rome. One day the officials were after him, and Peter began fleeing the city to the south along the Appian Way where he met Jesus Christ. Jesus stood in his way and asked, "Simon, will you deny me again?" And he answered, "Never again, Lord." And with that he returned to the city, gave himself up to the officials, and requested of them: "Crucify me head downward. I am not worthy to be crucified like my Lord." With that Simon Peter vowed that he loved Jesus Christ best of all, not with words, but with his life.

(b) If Jesus Christ should ask you that question, what would your answer be?—Chevis F. Horne.

SUNDAY: APRIL TWENTY-SEVENTH

MORNING SERVICE

Topic: Advice to a Young Man

TEXT: II Tim. 2:8 (NEB).

I. One piece of advice urged on Timothy was to "remember Jesus Christ, risen from the dead."

(a) Since the gospels had possibly not been written at this time, most of what Timothy learned about Jesus had come from those who knew Jesus personally or had heard about him from others. The story of Jesus' three temptations in the wilderness must have been common knowledge among the early Christians. Even better known was the temptation in the garden of Gethsemane, the last one in Jesus' life. There the options before him were two: to leave the garden by the rear entrance and thus secure his freedom, or to stay with his friends and face arrest, even a cross.

(b) In each case Timothy knew the outcome. He knew the decisions made by Jesus, the dedication and courage it took to make them, and the peace of mind that was his afterward. And since temptation is the common lot of humanity in one form or another, there certainly must have been times when Timothy needed the inspiration of the one who so adequately met it.

(c) The early Christians must also have been familiar with what Jesus did when people hurt him. His family misunderstood him, his friends deserted him, and his enemies caused him intense mental and physical suffering. Yet who could ever forget his words, "Father, forgive them"? So if Timothy was inclined to hold grudges against those who hurt him or if he considered getting even with them at any time, he had only to remember those words of forgiveness and act upon them. In consequence he would be a better man, and others would be better because of his spirit of forgiveness.

II. Timothy was told to compensate for his limitations. (a) Being human he had his problems. Some may have grown out of his racially mixed parentage; some out of a sense of inferiority or inexperience; some out of his frequent physical ailments. Doubtless there were tensions resulting from his commitment to be a Christian in a non-Christian world. He could well have understood what Paul meant when he said in Philippians, "I have been very thoroughly initiated into the human lot with all its ups and downs."

(b) Timothy could not simply regret his difficulties and wish them away. He would have to deal realistically with each one and then do something more. He must bring out of his liabilities something good and worthwhile. He must redeem his tensions, his infirmities, and his weaknesses. He must give God a chance to use him by means of the very things in his life that disturbed him.

(c) The suggestion was that he not busy himself contemplating what people thought of him or be overly concerned with his handicaps. On the other hand, he was urged to do something for others in a positive way. "Let no one look down upon you because of your inexperience, but set believers an example in speech, conduct, love, faith, purity."

(d) Timothy could never say to anyone, "I am setting you an example in Christianity." Nor can you today say that to others. You would immediately be in trouble if you did. Example is never a goal; it is a result, a consequence. The goal is in terms of speech and conduct as befits a Christian. It is love as expressed in human relationships. It is faith believing in what often cannot be seen. It is purity in one's life, attitudes, and actions.

III. The third suggestion to Timothy—more a charge or command than a suggestion—was that he work hard at his profession. "Preach . . . be urgent, convince, reproach, encourage, teach with patience."

(a) To do any of these things adequately calls for much preparation, much self-discipline, and much hard work. There is little place in the Christian world today, as was the case then, for one unwilling to prepare, to discipline, and to work. Jesus had said to some in his day, "My Father works and I work." We sometimes refer to the work ethic by way of understanding our American democracy. However regarded or localized, the work concept has its blessing in the New Testament.

(b) We can only surmise the degree to which Timothy took the advice of his older friends. Did he actually remember Jesus Christ when some temptation was thrust upon him? Did he consciously seek to let God use him and so convert his weakness into strength? Did he work so hard at his chosen way of life that many in the first century sought to imitate him? Certainly it is possible. It is possible that he was the most highly regarded man in his town of whom it could be said, "Well done, good and faithful servant."

(c) What of our time? Are there not countless faithful Timothys today? Some are in Burma; some are in the Soviet Union; some are in Brazil; some are in the United States. We know a few of them, certainly not all. Later generations will know them better than we do, seeing the results of their faithfulness, even as we see the works of those who have gone before us.—V. Carney Hargroves.

Illustrations

PARISH FIRE.   An English bishop visited a minister under his supervision and asked how the new parish was coming along. "Well, I can't put the Thames on fire!" the minister replied. "What I want to know," shot back the bishop, "is if we take you out and drop you, will it sizzle?"—Ken Bazyn.

HEALTHY FEARS.   Only fools are not afraid. Landlubbers, summering on the Maine coast, are singularly free of dreads. They have no idea what a tide can do, or what a heavy sea can mean, or what being lost in the fog without a compass feels like, or how great the difference may be between the true channel and ten feet to one side. The experienced natives of the coast, however, who understand the sea, have a healthy awe of it.—Harry Emerson Fosdick.

Sermon Suggestions

AS HIS CUSTOM WAS.   Text: Luke 4:16. (1) As his custom was, he went into the synagogue on the sabbath day and stood up to read. (2) As his custom was, Jesus surrendered his life to the will of his Father. Facing the death of the cross, he declared, "Not as I will, but as thou wilt" (Matt. 26:39). (3) As his custom was, Jesus loved and cared for all mankind. Matt.

9:36 says: "Jesus was moved with compassion, because they fainted and were scattered abroad as sheep having no shepherd." He cared—he cares—for the individual. He felt the pain of those who suffered physical affliction. He understood sorrow when death came. (4) As his custom was, he went about doing good. About the leper, an outcast of his day, the scripture says, "Jesus, moved with compassion, put forth his hand, and touched him, and saith unto him . . . be thou clean."—Mrs. Daniel Boyer.

THE ELDER BROTHER.   Text: Luke 15: 25. (1) We see him as a man who was utterly unappreciative of his privileges. (2) Our Lord reveals him as a man who was utterly hardened toward his brother. (3) We see this man, for all his excellences, utterly out of sympathy with his father. (4) We should never forget that the father loved that elder son.—George H. Morrison.

Worship Aids

CALL TO WORSHIP.   "God hath exalted him, and given him a name which is above every name: that at the name of Jesus every name should bow, of things in heaven, and things in earth, and things under the earth; and that every tongue should confess that Jesus Christ is Lord, to the glory of God the Father." Phil. 2:9–11.

INVOCATION.   Heavenly Father, we are grateful for this beautiful world thou hast created for us; for the singing birds, the radiant flowers, the blue sky, the soft breeze; for the dark night which gives way to a bright dawn; for the good earth which, when tilled by the plow, shoots forth the wheat, the corn, and the beans that our hungry bodies may be fed; for the trees which will fruit and a thousand gifts which come from thy bountiful hand. Help us to share this wealth, this treasure, with all who are in need.

OFFERTORY SENTENCE.   "Bring ye all the tithes into the storehouse, saith the Lord, [and I will] open the windows of heaven, and pour you out a blessing." Mal. 3:10.

OFFERTORY PRAYER.   Our heavenly Father, may thy kingdom be uppermost in our minds, our hearts, and our lives. Accept our gifts and with them the rededication of all that we are and have to thy greater glory.

PRAYER.   O Lord our God, who has created us and who knows our every thought and mood, we set aside this quiet time from our busy lives to give thought to our relationship with you and to reflect upon the meaning of our lives.

It is in these times of public worship that we realize how often we have neglected you in our private lives. We have so established our patterns of self-reliance and problem-solving and celebration that we have not turned naturally to you during the busyness and routine of the week. We feel badly about that. For we are not sure that we have made the right decisions in relying only on our wisdom. We are not sure that our actions have been as loving as they could have been if we had been more aware of you during the week. And we have that uncomfortable feeling that we have neglected some important things which were forgotten because we were out of touch with you.

O God, because we are weak and undisciplined in matters of the spirit, we pray that you would come more forcefully into our lives. Confront us in new and unavoidable ways that we may develop a sensitivity to your presence in the commonplace. In the people that come into our lives in the week before us, help us to see you challenging us to make the loving response.

Our Father, we intercede this day for all those who are dear to us. Because we know that you intend that life should be good and filled with happy moments and joyful relationships, we are pained when we see those we care about sorrowing, ill, troubled, in conflict, or misunderstanding. Enable us to be helpful and supportive in their time of need. And enable us in our own relationships to be constructive rather than destructive. We would contribute to an atmosphere of understanding and acceptance rather than of judgment and condemnation. Help us to see beneath the surface of one another to the intentions of the heart that we may be free from the restrictions of custom to do the loving thing in every situation.—Thomas R. Tupper.

EVENING SERVICE

Topic: Are You OK With God?
TEXT: Rom. 3:23–25.

I. Without Christ you are not OK with God. (a) This is based on the nature of God—"the glory of God." As his creation, God expects me to be like he is. "Be holy as I am holy." Some say, "God does not expect a man to be perfect." But he does! Because you and I are not perfect, we are not OK with God.

(b) This is based on the nature of man —"all have sinned." The liturgy has us confess, "We are by nature sinful and unclean." This is true with everyone. Because of this rebellion of sin, we are not OK with God.

(c) This is based on the nature of sin. From the garden of Eden and Adam's expulsion until now, sin separated God from man. Sin binds and blinds man to a state of bondage. He is subject to the wrath of God. How can you be OK with God when you are worlds apart from him?

II. With Christ you can get OK with God. (a) The way of the ladder. It represents making yourself acceptable to God. Climb toward God by moral effort as though you were on a ladder extending from earth to heaven. It is the impossible way of self-effort, works, and righteousness.

(b) The way of the escalator. This is the way of getting OK with God by contributing your bit to the salvation process. It is like using an escalator but walking up the escalator while it is in motion. It is known as "synergism." You think you can do it on your own, but you need God's help. It is an impossible possibility, for your most is too little to get right with God.

(c) The way of the elevator. Here is God's way. There is no moral effort on man's part to get OK with God. God comes down to earth in Jesus Christ, the elevator. By faith man is lifted and restored to God through love. "Love lifted me." The shaft of the elevator is the cross. In the cross man is made right with God. Atlanta boasts one of the highest hotels in the world—seventy stories high. If one has faith to get on the glass-enclosed exterior elevator, he is lifted 750 feet high in ninety seconds. Think what God can do for you in lifting you in Christ to himself.

(d) We are in a world filled with people yearning, searching, and crying for life, for peace, and for God. Some try to get OK with God by the ladder of self-effort. Others try to run up an escalator in vain. But there is only one way, the elevator of grace. When we persuade the unchurched to put their faith in Christ, they are lifted up by God to God where they can say. "I'm OK with God." And this is what the evangelical outreach is all about.—John R. Brokhoff.

SUNDAY: MAY FOURTH

MORNING SERVICE

Topic: Some Ideas We Need to Correct
SCRIPTURE: Phil. 1:9–10.

I. It is unrealistic to believe that everyone is going to agree with us all the time, like us all the time, or love us all the time. We should not expect it. We are grateful for those who do. We need not be defeated by those who don't.

II. It is unrealistic to believe we can be successful in every venture or that we can be perfect in all we attempt to do or be. No one ever has been; no one ever will. It is good to strive for improvement. We should strive for our best. But that's all we can do. It's a great feeling to do well, but we are not expected to be perfect. If a task or a project or something goes wrong, it does not mean we as persons are unworthy.

III. It is unrealistic to believe that there is any job or any task that doesn't have its frustrations, its discouragements, and its disappointments. Some do more than others; some less. But they are always there. If fifty percent of our tasks are enjoyable, that's a pretty good percentage. Appreciate the good parts of every task. Accept the discouragements. Be grateful for the opportunities.

IV. It is unrealistic to believe there is any relationship in home, work, or play that doesn't have some tension, some stress, or some differences. As long as we deal with people we will deal with some problems. They are not always going to act the way we want them to. Make an honest effort to see the good in people and situations as well as the frustrations.

V. It is unrealistic to believe there is any place, city, church, or neighborhood that is ideal or completely free from problems or that there is any place or situation that does not need change or improvement. There is no such thing as utopia. It is also true there is almost no place that does not have some advantages and some good points. Learn to see them and be grateful for them.

VI. It is unrealistic to believe that we will ever be completely free from feelings of guilt, doubt, inadequacy, anxiety, or anger. They are part of being human. They need to be understood and controlled, but they are always present. Accept your own fallibility and your own humanity. Be as gracious and understanding with yourself as you would be with others.

VII. It is unrealistic to feel that others should be blamed for all they say and do. All people have their own problems and tensions. Most people want to do better. If we understood the background we would probably understand the behavior. Try to understand and be kind.

VIII. It is unrealistic to avoid life and to refuse to face life realistically and honestly. Life is not easy, but it does have meaning. We can face it with dignity and courage.

IX. It is unrealistic to believe we can achieve anything significant quickly or that we can change in a hurry. Achievement and change are possible, but they usually come slowly and in small steps. The past does not need to control the future. We do have choices we can make. Recognize the possibility of growth. Keep moving in a healthy direction.

X. It is unrealistic to feel that there is only one solution to any given situation or that things are catastrophic if we do not find our solution. Seek help when needed. Keep trying. Always maintain the faith.—Charles F. Kemp.

Illustrations

ENDURING WORDS.   Children who have been brought up in a home where this certificate is on the walls will remember more than portraits or ornaments the words: "I have this day dedicated to God this home and all who dwell in it; to the deep affections of the family circle and to all friendly hospitalities; to courage, patience, and self-control; to all beautiful things of heart and mind and that lead the soul to wider vision and higher aims; to happiness, hopefulness, and health that it may ever be a dear haven of peace and joy."—Nolan B. Harmon.

ALTAR AND KITCHEN.   If our religion does not lift the level of our family life, it is not likely to be sincere or really effective at any other point. What occurs at the altar is insignificant unless what occurs there is supported by what occurs in the kitchen. The sermons by which Christian men and women may be rightly judged are the silent sermons of cooperative affection.—Elton Trueblood.

EVIDENCE.   Harvard psychologist Petrim Sorokin has written that two out of five marriages in the United States end in divorce. However, in Christian marriages where Bible reading, prayer, and church attendance are practiced, there is only one divorce in 1,015 marriages.

Sermon Suggestions

FAITH THAT DISTURBS.   Scripture: II Pet. 1:3–9. (1) That faith has been a real source of comfort and strength to man not found elsewhere, there can be no doubt. (2) Faith, as it is expressed in the Bible, is no less than a confident trust in the power of God, coupled with a wholehearted commitment to obey him at whatever cost. (3) Ours is a call to obedience to the will and way of God. It is a call not to retreat from the arena where the fierce battles are fought for the well-being of God's children but to engage in the battle even if it proves costly.—David H. McKeithen.

THE HABITUAL VISION OF GREATNESS. Text: Prov. 23:7. (1) It is a Christian duty to contemplate the best, to turn one's thoughts daily to what is fine and noble, and to be an admirer of worthy deeds, splendid generosity, magnificence in life and majesty in death. (2) It is a Christian duty to love the highest when we see it in men and women who make it easy to believe in God and goodness and in the shining virtues, heroic courage, warm magnanimity, patience that never wearies, readiness to forgive, and kindness to the erring. (3) It is a Christian duty to take a lofty view of what it means to be a human being and to side with all who take the lofty view. (4) It is a Christian duty to strengthen this inborn preference and make of the virtues of the great a mirror in which we see how to enrich and ennoble our lives.—Robert J. McCracken.

Worship Aids

CALL TO WORSHIP. "And we declare unto you glad tidings, how that the promise which was made unto the fathers, God hath fulfilled the same unto us their children." Acts 13:32–33.

INVOCATION. Grant, O God, that because we meet together this day life may grow greater for some who have contempt for it, simpler for some who are confused by it, happier for some who are tasting the bitterness of it, safer for some who are feeling the peril of it, more friendly for some who are feeling the loneliness of it, serener for some who are throbbing with the fire of it, and holier for some to whom life has lost all dignity, beauty, and meaning.

OFFERTORY SENTENCE. "Take heed what ye hear: with what measure ye mete, it shall be measured to you: and unto you that hear shall more be given." Mark 4:24.

OFFERTORY PRAYER. Eternal God, give us a vision of thy glory that no sacrifice may seem too great, and strengthen us in every step we take from selfishness to generosity.

PRAYER. Eternal Spirit, ever-creating, in whom we have life now and forever, we lift our thoughts in reflecting meditation.

As we think back over the past week's activities with its highs and lows, its joys and sorrows, we realize anew our constant need for your direction and guidance in our lives. Lead us in paths of building up instead of tearing down, in ways of loving instead of neglecting, and along highways of all-embracing instead of excluding.

We pray for courage and increased ability to do well the tasks that stand before us, knowing that in everything we do we witness to our faith or lack of faith in your living presence. We pray for an awareness of you upon all who worship here today that each of us may have our needs met, that our visitors may find friendship and acceptance among us, that the sorrowful may know the brightness of hope in Christ, that those caught up in monotony and drabness may see the challenge of some new service to their fellowmen and neighbors, and that those who have found some new joy may share it in giving light and inspiration to others.

O God, lead us in making this church a home for all of us that indeed we may be a fellowship of concern and compassion, a bulwark of peace and understanding, and a storehouse of nurture and guidance. Lead us forward, our Father, that assuredly your kingdom may come in each of us as we endeavor again and again to do your will.—Arthur H. Bishop.

EVENING SERVICE

Topic: The Dark Companion
SCRIPTURE: Matt. 10:26–33.
Fear is the dark companion of every human life. It is one of the things which isolates us from one another, and paradoxically because it is common to all of us,

it is also one of the things which binds us together in our humanness and our need.

I. There are two kinds of fear—healthy fear and unhealthy fear. (a) Healthy fear is the fear that a child learns regarding hot stoves and sharp knives. Healthy fear is that which we learn year by year as we grow and which protects us from the genuine dangers that threaten us, dangers to mind and body, to the relationships which we have with others, and to the world in which we live.

(b) Healthy fear is what makes courage possible, and unhealthy fear is another kind of experience entirely from that act of will and deliberation which is true courage. We are both fearful and courageous at the same time. It is part of the shifting mix of gifts and weaknesses and feelings which make us human. What we need to be concerned with is the fear which is neither helpful nor profitable. We need to face our dark companion, and we must understand that our faith gives us the resources to do so and to prevail.

II. Our dark companion is nourished by our feelings of worthlessness: I'm not good enough to succeed, not strong enough to bear responsibility for my life, and not clean enough to allow anyone even the smallest glimpse into the real me. I am not, here or there or perhaps everywhere across the range of my personhood, acceptable, and so the fear drives and so the fear compels. This is the fear that is unacknowledged, whose presence is known only by its effects upon us, those things which we do and feel which we don't want to do and don't want to feel, which we know drain and limit us, yet which we keep on doing in spite of ourselves.

III. What rescues us from this dead end is faith. "Fear knocked at the door. Faith answered. There was no one there."

(a) What makes it happen is the overwhelming fact that we are accepted. Our fears are known, and the pain and waste and misdirection which they produce are known by the God who knows us better than we know ourselves and who nonetheless finds us worth the effort of sending his son to live and die and live again that we might have the best possible assurance that he will receive us, however he finds us. We are good enough, and before that fact our fears begin to evaporate like mist in the sun. "Only when we feel accepted are we free to become ourselves" (Paul Tournier).

(b) Amid the wonder of the Christmas story, the most important words are those spoken to the shepherds: "Fear not." Jesus came through the storm on the Sea of Galilee to the disciples saying, "Take heart, it is I; be not afraid." To those who fall on their faces unable to look, he says, "Arise and have no fear." As he faced torture and death on his last night on earth, he said to his friends, "Let not your hearts be troubled, neither let them be afraid."

(c) We are understood by a power and a compassion beyond ourselves which challenges the strange affections which we have for our dark companion and encourages the desire to turn from that companion and walk at last in the light, healed and made whole.

(d) Whatever else we may be destined for, everything we know about Christian faith and everything for which this house stands declares that it is not for the shackles and the trammels of fear. For while the dark companion may be on our left hand, upon our right there journeys with us no less than the son of God.—Peter Hunt Meek.

SUNDAY: MAY ELEVENTH

MORNING SERVICE

Topic: Christian Motherhood (Mother's Day)

SCRIPTURE: Prov. 31:10–31.

I don't know if it is possible to teach someone how to be a good mother. Some things can be passed from mother to daughter and learned from books, but most of what makes a mother good comes from a deep love for her husband and children. Is too much expected of women today? Many mothers work to help with the family budget. They are expected to be beautiful, appealing, and intelligent at all times. They are expected to be up to date, provided that they are not too up to date. They are expected to guess what we want without any hints from us. Perhaps we expect too much from our wives and mothers because we don't know what makes a good wife and mother. What is a good mother?

I. A mother is realistic in her expectations. Often our world encourages unrealistic expectations. An example is that commercial which says you have one chance at life and you have got to hit it with all the gusto you can. This is certainly not very encouraging to someone who is tied to a house which needs cleaning. Years ago married people were often pleased just to survive. Making ends meet took lots of time and energy, and it gave a great deal of satisfaction. These days we are told that if a marriage is good we must feel good all of the time. But this expectation is not realistic, for nothing—job, school, motherhood, or marriage—is good all of the time.

II. The Christian mother should show the two basic Christian standards of love and forgiveness in her life.

(a) This is not the way the world lives. By love we mean the kind of love Jesus Christ had, love which loves those who do not deserve to be loved. This is the kind of love he had for us, who hurt feelings needlessly and disregard the love of others.

(b) We think of forgiveness when we say, "Forgive us our trespasses as we forgive those who trespass against us." Can the Christian home be less than this? Can the Christian accept God's love and forgiveness without letting it spread in his own life? Husband and wife forgive both the big and little things. Children forgive parents, and parents forgive children. We teach each other by word and by deed, and sometimes the deed leaves a deeper impression.

III. The Christian mother invests in the future. (a) Too many people make the mistake of not keeping their husbands first in the home, just as too many men make the same mistake about their wives. Problems arise at retirement and when children grow up and leave home. Husbands and wives have got to keep time for a walk in the park, a night on the town, or an evening alone at home. So often we are so busy pleasing friends that we lose touch with each other.

(b) The way you treat each other is important. It is easy to forget the simple courtesies of courtship. Those courtesies often slip because of the husbands, and it will not be good for any long-term relationship.

(c) Be aware of your partner's needs. Husbands, don't forget that your wife has problems with house and children. Sometimes when a child leaves home mothers have hard times. Be considerate of your wife. Wives, remember your husbands who face tension at work. Sometimes the worst tension may be due to advancing age and the fear of competition which is more energetic. Don't be careless of your partner's needs.

(d) Don't let problems with your children affect your marriage. When the children are gone, you two will be alone together, and you want to have a decent marriage left. In a similar fashion, do not let the children run the home. If you disagree on how to raise the family, talk it over and let the children know how you feel.

(e) Keep attractive your personal appearance. Americans joke about going to pot. Keep yourself looking as good as you can for your partner. Don't let your guard down because you are married.—Theodore W. Eisold.

Illustrations

A MOTHER'S PRIDE. During her son's term of office, the mother of President Eisenhower was interviewed on a television talk show. When the host asked, "Aren't you proud of your son?" Mrs. Eisenhower surprised him by saying, "Yes, I am, but which one are you referring to?"

ENDURING INSTITUTIONS. Families are enduring institutions. They have been the foundation for virtually every society known to history. They possess incredible strength and resiliency, especially when faced with adversity. The American people are a loving people. We cherish family life. I am confident that we can help shape an environment that strengthens and supports American families.—Walter Mondale.

Sermon Suggestion

THE KIND OF MOTHER GOD CHOOSES. Scripture: Luke 1:26–31. (1) The kind of mother God chooses is a mother kind of woman who deems it a high calling and privilege to have a supreme responsibility in shaping the lives of creatures made in the image of God. (2) The kind of mother God chooses is a woman of character who well knows that the best teaching is by example. (3) The kind of mother God chooses is a woman submitted to God who can look at all the temptations of a one-world view and see them for what they are, detours that lead away from life's greatest happiness and life's highest best.—Frank Pollard.

Worship Aids

CALL TO WORSHIP. "Wait on the Lord: be of good courage, and he shall strengthen thine heart: wait, I say, on the Lord." Ps. 27:14.

INVOCATION. O God our Father, creator of the universe and giver of all good things: we thank thee for our home on earth and for the joy of living. We praise thee for thy love in Jesus Christ who came to set things right, who died rejected on the cross, and who rose triumphant from the dead. Because he lives, we live to praise thee, Father, Son, and Holy Spirit, our God forever.

OFFERTORY SENTENCE. "If ye then, being evil, know how to give good gifts unto your children: how much more shall your heavenly Father give the Holy Spirit to them that ask him?" Luke 11:13.

OFFERTORY PRAYER. O Lord, upon whose constant giving we depend every day, teach us how to spend and be spent for others that we may gain the true good things of life by losing every selfish trait.

PRAYER. Our heavenly Father, we would ascend to thy holy hill to worship and adore thee, and as we contemplate thy faithfulness, we are condemned by our faithlessness: we have confessed to love thee, but we have not obeyed thee; we have said that we loved our fellowman, but we have not ministered to him according to our opportunity. As we confess our negligence and our carelessness, may we come in the spirit of true repentance and in the confidence that thou art faithful and just to forgive us our sins and to cleanse us from all unrighteousness.

O Father, we thank thee not only for life but also for all of life's extras. Thou hast not only created the world and the people in it, but also thou hast given to us loved ones and friends. Thou hast not only given us houses but also homes. As today we honor our families, we give thee thanks for the homes in which we share and in which we have shared; for the opportunity of Christian training in the formative years of our lives; for guidance in decision when we have lacked the experience to choose wisely; for security in our instability; for understanding in our foibles; for encouragement in our defeats; for love that has cared enough to discipline us. We give thee our humble thanks that thou "hast ordained the family for the welfare and happiness of mankind."

As we contemplate our responsibilities in the home, in the community, and in the world—although at times we are tempted to shrink from these—we do not ask for lesser tasks but for faith equal to our tasks. May this experience of worship be a season of refreshment for each of us. May we drink deeply of that well of water that springs up into everlasting life. As we wait upon thee, enlarge our hearts that we may receive the fulness of thy love. Stretch the imagination of our minds that we may find ways in which this love may be expressed in all of life's relationships. May we be faithful to our high calling in Christ Jesus to be instruments of thy reconciliation in our day.

O thou who art our Father, we lift before thee every family of our congregation and every member of each family: to those who suffer the pain and discouragement of illness, grant health according to thy perfect will; for those who are low on hope, rekindle the flame of expectancy; to those who find it difficult to let go of everything that they may trust only thee, grant the blessedness of this release; for those who have leadership responsibility in the family of the nations of this world, grant faithfulness to seek truth and justice for all rather than privilege for a few.

Now, O God, grant us the courage to go forth to live as we have prayed. For thy sake and for the sake of all of those for whom we have responsibility.—John Thompson.

EVENING SERVICE

Topic: Learning to Fail
SCRIPTURE: Mark 15:27–31, 66–72.

I. There are few focuses which dominate our lives like the fear of failure. Our compelling need is to succeed, even though we may not know what that is. Be it school, job, marriage, church, or even play, we must be a success. Yet the reality is that we all fall. Mark's story of Peter's great intentions and utter failure embodies a crucial word which we need to hear.

II. Failure is necessary for whole people. At the heart of life is a tension between our limited, finite self and the impulse to fly as eagles. We reduce life by only going after obtainables. Peter could have avoided failure by staying at the lake, but he put himself into a situation where he could fail. As long as we worship success we will see the human spirit getting smaller and smaller.

III. Failure needs to be incorporated into our lives. Despite the fact that failure is such a normal human experience, most of us have great difficulty integrating it into life. We spend a lot of time denying it. The story of Peter is all the more significant when you remember that Mark was essentially reporting for Peter. At this point Peter is not attempting to hide his failure toward the one who meant the most to him. He is a mixture, as we are, of courage and cowardice. He is, as in *The Wizard of Oz*, the cowardly lion. But let us remember that it is precisely the cowardly lions that change the world, for they have learned to integrate the forces of their life.

IV. We ought to ask ourselves whether being a Christian makes failure quantitatively a different experience. The issue is not whether we fail or succeed but whether we have risked enough so that failure is possible and whether we are willing to let God love our lives in both the successes and the failures. This story of Peter is a critical event in the life of Jesus. It also speaks of a basic spiritual task: dealing with our understanding of success and failure in the light of Christ.—Robert B. Wallace.

SUNDAY: MAY EIGHTEENTH

MORNING SERVICE

Topic: Trusting in God
SCRIPTURE: Ps. 23.

I. *God provides.* (See vv. 2–3.) (a) The representation of God as shepherd was natural in a pastoral country like Palestine. It is the shepherd's provision for his flock that is in evidence here, and that leads to the psalmist's first great affirmation, "I shall not want."

(b) The needs of the sheep can be reduced to three—pasture, water, and rest. Elmer Leslie writes: "To find these three together is not easy in Palestine. But the shepherd knows where to find the fresh shoots of green grass and where he may let the sheep graze and lie down. He knows how to lead the flock along the currents of the torrential mountain waddies until he finds a clear, placid pool of still water where the sheep may drink with comfort and safety."

(c) Grass is short-lived under the eastern sun; patches of herbage have to be sought daily. The clause, "He makes me to lie down in green pastures," suggests both rest and abundance. The sheep that lies down in a grassy field is fully fed and fully satisfied. The expression, "He restores my soul," means that he renews and sustains my strength with rest and nourishment. The once-weary sheep is ready to travel again.

(d) Carried over into the spiritual life, this first section says that God provides for every vital need of the soul, rest from the toil and sorrows of life and strength for its duties. "The Lord is my shepherd, therefore, I shall not want."

II. *God guides.* (See vv. 3–4.) (a) God provides not only food and rest; he also guides. We have the word "leads" in v. 2, but the word in v. 3 is a different word in the Hebrew and is rightly translated as "guides" in NEB and TEV. The "leads" in v. 2 refers to the shepherd going before the sheep that he may bring them to a place of rest and refreshment. The "guides" of v. 3 tells what happens when the sheep leave the green pasture and travel on the weary road with its heat and dust.

(b) Leslie writes, "The shepherd leads his sheep in 'right tracks,' for this shepherd knows the paths over rocky highland and open valley, and his reputation as a shepherd is at stake." (See Jer. 14; Ezek. 20:9.) When the sun is sinking and the deep shadows fall upon the valley and gorges, bringing peril of attack from wild animals or robbers, the sheep are not afraid. There is their guardian with his club (rod) heavily nailed at the end and with his staff with which he beats down leaves for his sheep. With such protection, the sheep are made comfortable.

(c) The "righteousness" in v. 3 is the righteousness of God. The paths which God assigns are righteous; right and safe paths, we might say. The valley of the shadow of death is properly, according to the Hebrew, "the valley of deep darkness" (as in the RSV margin), the reference being to one of those dark ravines which abound in Palestine in which wild beasts and other dangers often threatened. Death is one of those dangers that lurk in the shadows, but there are others. All such dangers the psalmist has in mind, particularly, it may be, the danger of the unknown.

(d) The shepherd care of God, let us note, is grounded in his very nature. "For

his name's sake" (v. 3) means that God's honor is at stake in caring for his own. The good shepherd will not be false to himself.

III. *God blesses.* (See vv. 5–6.) (a) In these two verses the figure changes. God becomes a host who bountifully entertains his guest at his table and provides him with lodging in his own house, as Oriental monarchs entertained those to whom they wished to show special favor.

(b) In the Orient to eat at a man's table meant to be under his protection. What gives particular zest to this picture is the fact that the host offers the guest his hospitality in the presence of his enemies. This is a more signal token of care and power than the green pastures are. The anointing refers to the unguents and perfumes which were the regular accompaniment of an Oriental banquet. A cup running over is handed him.

(c) "Surely" might better be translated as the RSV margin "only." Nothing but goodness and mercy shall follow me. There will be no pursuit by the enemies mentioned in v. 5. The psalmist as he goes on his way is conscious of a beneficent following. God's goodness and mercy follow his footsteps, assuring him of perpetual safety.

(d) The last clause seems to mean, "I will return to dwell in the house of the Lord forever." The words are meant to be understood figuratively, not literally. He is not thinking of perpetual residence in the temple but perpetual fellowship with God. The psalmist was thinking, it may be, only of the divine fellowship in this life. The Christian with his fuller revelation will think of the eternal mansions which the Lord has prepared for his true disciples.—Ernest Trice Thompson.

Illustrations

THE FOUNDATION. In New York City, down in the financial district, workmen were digging the excavation for a skyscraper, a sixty-story bank building, but they came on some quicksand. The engineers were amazed because most of Manhatten is solid rock. But there was this quicksand, which as everybody knows is hardly the ideal thing to build anything on, let alone a sixty-story building. They tried to pump it out. They tried to fill it in. They called a learned professor of geology and asked him how long it would take that quicksand to turn into sandstone? "About a million years," he said, "more or less." The building committee decided that they didn't want to wait a million years. Then someone suggested a chemical soil solidification company. When representative came, they asked him how long it would take to change the quicksand into sandstone. "Well," the man said, "we're rather busy this week, but we can take care of it next week, if that's all right with you." This firm brought some trucks loaded with sodium silicate and calcium chloride, and they dumped these chemicals into the quicksand, and it turned into a substance strong enough to hold a mighty skyscraper and is part of the foundation on which that skyscraper today stands.—Winfield S. Haycock.

A JAPANESE PARAPHRASE.   The Lord is my pacesetter. I shall not rush.

He makes me stop for quiet intervals.

He provides me with images of stillness which restore my serenity.

He leads me in the ways of efficiency through calmness of mind and his guidance in peace.

Even though I have a great many things to accomplish each day, I will not fret, for his presence is here.

His timelessness, his all-importance will keep me in balance.

He prepares refreshment and renewal in the midst of my activity by anointing my mind with his oil of tranquility. My cup of joyous energy overflows.

Surely harmony and effectiveness shall be the fruit of my hours, and I shall walk in the pace of the Lord and dwell in his house forever.

Sermon Suggestions

ACCORDING TO YOUR FAITH.   Text: Matt. 9:29–30. What did Jesus Christ mean when he said, "According to your faith, be it done to you"? (1) Rather than being the contradiction of intelligence, faith is the foundation and fulfillment of intelligence.

(2) Rather than being a substitute for the common sense of doing what we can for ourselves, faith is incentive and empowerment for our best endeavor. (3) Rather than being a luxury, faith is a basic necessity. In a fundamental sense we live by faith. This is a faith-demanding universe. Everywhere we turn it says to us, "According to your faith, be it done to you."—Everett W. Palmer.

JUST BE PATIENT.   Text: Gal. 5:22. (1) Patience brings hope. (See Rom. 15:4.) (2) Patience bears fruit. (See Luke 8:15.) (3) Patience inherits God's promises. (See Heb. 6:12.)—Cecil B. Knight.

Worship Aids

CALL TO WORSHIP.   "If a man love me, saith Jesus, he will keep my words: and my Father will love him, and we will come unto him, and make our abode with him." John 14:23.

INVOCATION.   Father God, you are known to us through loving persons who affirm the faith. May we be loving too. Father God, you are known to us through trusting acts which proclaim the truth. May we be loving too. Father God, you are known to us through trusting acts which proclaim the truth. May we be trusting too. Father God, you are known to us through the joyous story which celebrates your son. May we be joyous too. For we are here to affirm, to proclaim, and to celebrate. We believe! Help thou our unbelief! Amen!

OFFERTORY SENTENCE.   "Offer unto God thanksgiving; and pay thy vows unto the most High." Ps. 50:14.

OFFERTORY PRAYER.   Dear Father, may we ever give thee a definite, consistent, and heartfelt service.

PRAYER.   Our Father, we are thankful for thy abiding presence in every time of human need. Even though we dwell temporarily in life's valleys amid shadows, we know that our journey does not end in a darkened valley. Through thy steadying power, we are enabled to pass through life's depths and emerge victorious on the other side. Just as it always takes light to make a shadow, so we are confident that beyond disappointment, hardship, tragedy, and even death, there lies the light and reality of eternity. For the vision of a clear dawn and the assurance of a brighter tomorrow, we give thee thanks.

We are grateful, our Father, for thy presence with us not only in times of crisis but also in those times when we experience joy and when our cup overflows and we partake of life in all of its fulness. For thy presence with us on the day of graduation and the realization of life's vocation, we give thee thanks. For thy presence with us on our wedding day and the actualization of the marriage vow, we give thee thanks. For sharing in the welcoming acceptance of the newborn babe, we give thee thanks. For thy indwelling Spirit at the time of our rebirth and entrance into salvation, we give thee thanks. For the continuous witness of thy Spirit which causes us to experience gladness and to approach each new day with expectancy, we give thee thanks.—W. James Cowell.

EVENING SERVICE

Topic: Gifts and Their Uses
Scripture: I Cor. 12:4–7.

I. *There are varieties of gifts or abilities.* (a) Paul's emphasis seems quite obvious, but it is no less important today than it was in Paul's time. It means that everyone in the Christian church cannot do the same things and should not be expected to. The range of gifts or abilities in the church is wide.

(b) The idea of diverse gifts applies to pastors. Some are strong in preaching and weak in other matters. Some are strong in administration and weak in preaching. One of the things a pastor must come to terms with is his own strengths and weaknesses, hopefully seeking to improve his weaknesses. But Paul was not writing only to pastors. Paul was calling all Christians to recognize and acknowledge their particular abilities.

II. *All gifts alike are from God.* (a) These abilities are given, not created by the individual. Paul is concerned that Christians clearly recognize that their talents are God-given.

(b) We assume that there was a tendency in the church at Corinth for some members to rank their gifts above those of other members. Paul hoped to correct this tendency, which is also common in our time. Some are more gifted than others. Some have better minds, some greater imagination, and some greater physical endurance. This is true in all of life, no less in the Christian community than anywhere else.

(c) Paul wanted to impress on his readers that no person's gift was necessarily more important than that of another. When some wanted to argue about relative gifts, Paul was quick to say that all abilities are important to the life of the Christian community. No one possesses a talent except from God. It is God who gives the ability; therefore no one's ability is unimportant.

III. *Gifts are to be used for the common good.* (a) Paul argues that gifts are of little value if they are not used for the strengthening and upbuilding of the fellowship. He poses a question: What good are abilities if they do not improve the church?

(b) There are questions that all ought to ask. How do my abilities affect the life of my church? Is the church enriched by my gifts? Is the church better because of my contribution? Are my abilities helping the church? Are my talents used for the common good?

(c) Whatever our abilities, we are to use them in the service of Christ. Our responsibility is to recognize that we have something to contribute and that we are expected to exercise stewardship in our use of it. It is not a sin to have small abilities, but it is sinful not to use what we have and what we are for the upbuilding of the church. Whatever talents we have, we have a responsibility to use them in extending the cause of Christ in our world.—John Rutland, Jr.

SUNDAY: MAY TWENTY-FIFTH

MORNING SERVICE

Topic: The Church's Priorities (Pentecost)

TEXT: I Cor. 14:12.

I. We need a preaching and teaching ministry that faithfully expounds the text of scripture at the same time it relates to the burning issues of the day. Evangelical preaching tends to be biblical but not contemporary; liberal preaching contemporary but not biblical. Why must we polarize? It is the combination of the two that is so powerful. It is a rare phenomenon.

II. We need a warm, caring, supportive fellowship. Young people hunger for the authentic relationships of love. Hobart Mowrer, professor of psychiatry, described himself as having "a lover's quarrel with the church." Asked what he meant, he replied that the church had failed him when he was a teenager and continued to fail his patients today. How? "Because the church has never learned the secret of community," he said. Unfair perhaps, because some churches are genuine communities. But it was his opinion, which was born no doubt of bitter experience. I think it is the most damaging criticism of the church I have ever heard.

III. We need worship services that express the reality of the living God and joyfully celebrate Jesus Christ's victory over sin and death. Too often routine supplants reality, and the liturgy becomes lugubrious. Public worship should always be dignified, but it is unforgivable to make it dull. "The longer I live," said Geoffrey Fisher, "the more convinced I am that Christianity is one long shout of joy." He was right. And the joy of worship needs to be more uninhibited than is customary, at least in some of our more stolid historic denominations.

IV. We need an outreach into the secular community that is imaginative, sensitive, and compassionate. The true eccentricity of the church is seen when it turns toward the world. Such an outgoing concern would combine evangelism and social action and would overcome the sterile polarity that has developed between the two. It would insist that if faith without works is dead, then good news without good works lack credibility. It would also involve a renunciation of "clericalism," that is, the clerical suppression of the laity. Instead, all the members of the body of Christ would be active, their different ministries determined by their different gifts.

V. These four major signs of spiritual renewal in the church were exactly the characteristics of the newborn church on the day of Pentecost. Those first spirit-filled Christians "devoted themselves to the apostles' teaching and fellowship, to the breaking of bread and the prayers . . . And the Lord added to their number day by day those who were being saved" (Acts 2:42, 47, RSV). Wherever the Holy Spirit is present in power, the church is always characterized by an apostolic doctrine, a loving fellowship, a joyful worship, and a continuous evangelism.—John R. W. Stott.

Illustrations

CHURCH'S MINISTRY. The ministry of the church as a whole should be manifestly and explicitly both a ministry of love and service and compassion and also a ministry of proclamation of the coming of the reign of God in Jesus and the enlistment of persons for the service of that reign. Within that total ministry there is room for a variety of special callings, but the world should be in no doubt that the church stands for both these things and that they belong together.—Leslie Newbigin.

TWO VIEWS. In 1912 the great new ship, the *Titanic*, on her maiden voyage struck an iceberg and sank with hundreds of lives lost. After that tragedy one of our American papers carried two illustrations. One was a drawing of the ship striking the iceberg and crumpling like an eggshell.

Underneath the picture were these words: "The weakness of man, the supremacy of nature." The other drawing was that of one of the passengers, W. T. Stead, stepping back to give his place in the last life boat to a woman with a child. Underneath that picture was this line: "The weakness of nature, the supremacy of man."—Ralph W. Sockman.

Sermon Suggestions

THE MEANING OF MISSIONS IN THE EARLY CHURCH. Text: Matt. 28:18–20. (1) They preached an uplifted Christ. (2) They had an audacious faith. (3) They participated in the missionary task. (4) The early Christians relied upon spiritual means. Prayer pervaded the life of those early churches like a fragrance. (5) They were willing to suffer and if need be to die for the faith's sake, for Christ's sake. (6) There was about that group of early Christians a buoyant hopefulness.—James H. Landes.

THE GLORY OF GIVING. Text: Acts 20: 35. (1) A man's giving is the reflection of his interest. (2) It is what one gives away that he keeps and what one keeps that he eventually loses. (3) Giving measures the girth of your soul. (4) Giving brings joy to the spirit. (5) To give is Godlike.—Harold G. Cooke.

Worship Aids

CALL TO WORSHIP. "We have thought of thy lovingkindness, O God, in the midst of thy temple. According to thy name, O God, so is thy praise unto the ends of the earth." Ps. 48:9–10.

INVOCATION. Eternal God our Father, who art from everlasting, thou hast made us and not we ourselves. Thou hast sent us never far from thee that we, thy children, may learn the ways of freedom and choose thee with all our hearts. Grant us now thy Holy Spirit that, confident in prayer, we may worship thee with gladness and become as little children before thee.

OFFERTORY SENTENCE. "Every man shall give as he is able, according to the blessing of the Lord thy God which he hath given thee." Deut. 16:17.

OFFERTORY PRAYER. God of our fathers, dearly do we cherish the blessing which they church brings to us and dearly do we covet the privilege of sharing through these gifts the proclaiming of thy word until all of the earth shall praise thee.

PRAYER. Lord God our Father, for the church of Jesus Christ we thank thee: for her birth at Pentecost when the Holy Spirit descended upon the disciples with tongues of fire as with a rushing mighty wind, and they knew that Jesus lived and the things for which he stood were not dead. We bless thee for the martyrs whose blood became the seed of the church, and for the conservators who through the centuries kept the faith bright and shining in darkest of days. We rejoice in the reformers who turned again the hearts of true believers to the essentials of the prophetic proclamation and the simplicity of early Christianity and who knew the just lived by faith and found the real presence in the breaking of bread.

We bless thee too, Lord God, for the church of our day that has carried the gospel to all lands, recaught the vision of a just society for men of every color, race, and condition, and dedicated itself to implementing the dream of the ancient seer that nation would not lift up sword against nation, neither would they learn war any more.

May the members of every local church remember their high heritage, and may each one do his part in witness and work, prayer and support, and surely in vision, that every unit of the church universal may be worthy of the whole. We pray in the name of Christ Jesus our Lord, the bridegroom, whose church is his bride.—Hillyer H. Straton.

EVENING SERVICE

Topic: Why Did You Doubt?
TEXT: Matt. 14:31 (RSV).
I. Why did Peter doubt? Perhaps be-

cause he leaped into an experience mostly as a way of testing Jesus. "Lord, if it is you, bid me come to you on the water." Some of the disciples had earlier said that the figure they saw walking on the water was a ghost, but Peter decided to test Jesus in a radical way. There doesn't seem to have been much point in Peter walking on the water except to get some proof about who it was out there.

II. Why did Peter doubt? Perhaps because he ventured out impulsively beyond the range of experience where he was capable of believing. Peter was ready to trust his Lord and to follow him, but Peter wasn't ready for the risks and threats of walking on the deep waters of the sea. We grow and mature in our faith, and when we venture too far beyond the level to which we have grown, we are vulnerable to disastrous doubt. We live with the assurance that God will bring us to a faith adequate for the life he intends for us.

III. Why did Peter doubt? Perhaps because he left the boat to go out on his own. For the early Christians the boat was a symbol of the church, of the community of faith. Peter leaped out into the sea all by himself, and doubts engulfed him. He separated himself from the others, and when he found himself alone in the midst of the storm, the doubts assailed him.

IV. Why did Peter doubt? Perhaps because he focused on the threats. "But when he saw the wind, he was afraid, and beginning to sink he cried out, 'Lord, save me.' " Peter became aware of all the threats in his situation and panic struck, and he began to doubt and he began to sink. Each of us faces threats and dangers. There is evil in our world which can hurt us and others. There is illness which can shatter us. There are disasters which can overtake us. Certainly it is right to take proper precaution in the face of such threats. But if our attention is focused on the threats, we miss the evidence of the loving, sustaining care of God.

V. The question of Jesus to Peter confronts us: "Why did you doubt?" Surely it is appropriate to bring a measure of doubt and skepticism into our world, even into the religious dimensions of our lives. But the question of Jesus probes and exposes our failure to nurture the faith which can sustain and strengthen us. In his grace and mercy God still makes himself known to us that we may believe and that we may know the saving acts of the Lord.—Harry B. Adams.

SUNDAY: JUNE FIRST

MORNING SERVICE

Topic: Lessons from Zacchaeus
SCRIPTURE: Luke 19:1–10.

I. Jesus said to Zacchaeus: "Come on down." (a) Jesus is saying: "Enough of your evasion, rushing, grabbing, and getting. Enough of your climbing and avoiding. Enough of exploiting others. Enough of the spectator role. Enough of your wondering why something doesn't really get to you. Come down off your perch and look at yourself. Now is the time to start looking at where you have been and what your life-style is doing to you. Come on down for you must now meet yourself and review your direction of life. This is the end of everything and the beginning of everything else."

(b) In our achievement-oriented society, heart attacks and hypertension are on the increase. Is this the price we are prepared to pay for getting ahead and climbing to the top? You might own the whole world but die an empty soul. Come on down and review your life-style and what you think is important.

II. Jesus said: "Quickly." Do it now. Today salvation has come. It is most important that we do not go on procrastinating. You can dwell on the past hurts. You can bring up 100,000 reasons why you are as you are and another 100,000 reasons to defend your stance and your life-style. You can also think up another 100,000 obstacles that stand in your way to a different future. Put the history book away. Scrap the long-range plan. Be grasped by the great moment.

III. Jesus said: "Salvation has come to

you." Zacchaeus was a getter. Now he was told that this is not something you get and not something you even deserve. It is given by the generosity of one outside yourself. Independent of all your efforts, salvation has come to you. No more push for performance. Now it is essentially a matter of realizing something has happened and being something different.

IV. Jesus said: "Don't forget what you are. You are a son of Abraham, a Jew." How often you want to hide your religion or evade its illumination. Do not forget your roots. Do not forget you belong. Do not try to paralyze the power of your religion; for when you are least expecting it, it comes to remind you. Jesus realized how Zacchaeus' religion had been pushed aside, but he reminds him of its importance.

V. Jesus said: "I have come to seek and save what is lost." Though you are a son of Abraham, you have been a lost cause to yourself. He could have said it to us. Though you have been part of the Christian church all your life, you have not realized its significance for your living. Though you have been part of the Christian church for so long, you still find it hard to believe in yourself, to accept yourself, and to accept that God has accepted you.

VI. Jesus said: "What is more, I am coming to stay with you." (a) The good tidings of the incarnation is that God in his great generosity sends his son to an alienated and directionless mankind. He comes to dwell among us and to guide us into the way, the truth, and the life.

(b) In effect Zacchaeus says: "My God, something is happening to me. Here and now my little life becomes a life of generosity. Here and now what I have been holding against people, I will forgive. Here and now while I have been so jammed up in myself, I am going to let go. And if I am about to become part of a new being, I am ready."—Francis A. Macnab.

Illustrations

TO BE AT PEACE.   Humility is perfect quietness of heart. It is for me to have no trouble; never to be fretted or vexed or irritated or sore or disappointed. It is to expect nothing, to wonder at nothing that is done to me, and to feel nothing done against me. It is to be at rest when nobody praises me and when I am blamed or despised. It is to have a blessed home in the Lord where I can go in and shut the door and kneel to my Father in secret and be at peace as in a deep sea of calmness when all around and above is trouble. It is the fruit of the Lord Jesus Christ's redemptive work on Calvary's cross, manifest in those of his own who are definitely subjected to the Holy Spirit.—Andrew Murray.

REFLECTION.   In New Hampshire is a cliff whose profile resembles the craggy brow, the sharp nose, and the stubby beard of a man, and it is called "The Old Man of the Mountains." That resemblance was discovered by some hunter seeing the reflection of the mountain in Profile Lake at its foot. We can catch the reflection of Christ in the adoring eyes of little children as they listen to a Christmas story, in the grateful eyes of devout sufferers as they hear his comforting words, and in the reverential gaze of sincere worshipers as they sing his praise and pray at his altar.— Ralph W. Sockman.

Sermon Suggestions

THAT OLD-TIME RELIGION.   Text: Prov. 22:28. (1) Old-time religion is simple. (2) Old-time religion is spontaneous. (3) Old-time religion is scripture based. (4) Old-time religion is spectacular. (5) Old-time religion is supernatural.—H. B. Thompson, Jr.

TRY THIS SIMPLE TEST.   Text: Matt. 25:-40. (1) Where do I begin to be Christian? (2) How do I bear my witness? (3) How do I grow into the full experience of my faith? —Gene E. Bartlett.

Worship Aids

CALL TO WORSHIP.   "Ho, every one that thirstest, come ye to the waters. Incline your ear, and come unto me: hear, and your soul shall live; and I will make an everlasting covenant with you, even the sure mercies of David." Isa. 55:1, 3.

INVOCATION. Almighty God, regard, we beseech thee, thy church, set amid the perplexities of a changing order and face to face with new tasks. Fill us afresh with thy spirit that we may bear witness boldly to the coming of thy kingdom and hasten the time when the knowledge of thyself shall encircle the earth as the waters cover the sea.

OFFERTORY SENTENCE. "And they came everyone whose heart stirred him up, and every one whom his spirit made willing, and they brought the Lord's offering to the work of the tabernacle of the congregation, and for all his service." Exod. 35: 21.

OFFERTORY PRAYER. Help us to remember, O Lord, that a life is a more persuasive testimony that words, that deeds are more effective than argument, and that these gifts are only a portion of the loyalty thou dost require of us.

BACCALAUREATE PRAYER. We pause in these moments, our heavenly Father, to ask strength, guidance, help, and vision for these graduates gathered here. They are facing disillusionment and bitterness abroad in our world, a world they will find soon enough as a bleeding, stumbling world going from blunder to blunder, hollowed with graves, and hard with hate. May we, who take thy name upon our lips so easily, pause and learn again the lessons of life and hope.

May this class of graduates find in their education, both past and future, a broader vision of the needs of mankind and a deeper compassion to fill those needs. We pray for the planting of the seeds of concern for all humanity in their hearts and the humanity to tap the wells of mercy. Help them to stand for what is right, and, as they so stand, move them to be as anxious that the rights of others shall be recognized as they are that their own shall

be established. Encourage them, as they live and learn through a God-given sensitive conscience, to be as eager to forgive as they are to seek forgiveness.

As this class takes their place of leadership in the world that has found it easier to put men on the moon than to walk across ethnical, racial, and cultural barriers, let them give us the leadership our nation needs on these barely-touched frontiers. Let them step to a drummer's beat more noble than those heard by their forefathers as they face the hard roads before them of human relations, peace, ecology, and man's needs.

Bless this class with all of their latent possibilities, dreams, hopes, and talents; may their unique gifts flourish. Bless this school and this nation; may each more worthily form and nurture our youth as ministers of mercy and mold them as ambassadors of truth. May the touch and influence of this class be one of healing the wounds of heart and mind of our times wherever they scatter on this our world, as long as they shall live. Give them the courage and a dream of the future of what might be and the fortitude to lend their strength to that purpose.—W. Lee Truman.

EVENING SERVICE

Topic: Guidelines for Graduates (Commencement)

TEXT: Eccl. 9:4.

I. *Make the most of what you have.* Don't envy others their talents or possessions. You are a unique person, and you can make a contribution to the world which no one else can make. The apostle Paul admitted his human failings, but then he added, "By the grace of God I am what I am." He was willing to give the best that he had to Christ.

II. *Keep young in heart.* "Except you become as a little child you shall not enter the kingdom of heaven." The child lives with spontaneity, naturalness, and faith. We are apt to lose these traits as we grow older.

III. *Set reasonable goals for yourself.* Everyone needs to have objectives. Jesus said,

"For their sakes I sanctify myself." He was living for others. What goals do you have? These will help or hinder you in your progress toward the good life. Gordon Allport writes, "To understand a person we have to know what he is trying to accomplish, what he is trying to become, not merely how he got the way he is."

IV. *If the world hands you a lemon, make lemonade.* Life's sour situations can be sweetened if you try. Bing Crosby walked into his home one night to find that his children were wearing long faces. Their pet turtle was sick. Bing said, "Boys, it looks bad, but if the turtle dies we'll have a parade and give him a big funeral." One of the boys brightened up and said, "Dad, let's kill him."

V. *Make the most of the present.* Don't waste your energy worrying about the mistakes of yesterday or anticipating the problems of tomorrow. Today is all you possess. Use the present moment well and you will automatically prepare the way for a good tomorrow.

VI. *Cultivate a sense of humor.* There is a "time to weep and a time to laugh." We all need comic relief now and then. I feel sorry for the person who lives without humor because he takes himself much too seriously.

VII. *Cultivate an educated heart.* Make others happy. Do something for others three times a day. One of the best descriptions of Jesus is that "he went about doing good." No wonder the people loved him. If we don't have many friends, we do well to examine our attitudes toward others.

VIII. *Don't expect to please everyone.* We all make mistakes every day. That is why we need to pray, "Forgive us our debts as we forgive our debtors." It is good to strive toward perfection as those who "have not attained," but it is bad to expect to be perfect. God alone is perfect.

IX. *Cultivate a love for beauty.* "Whatsoever things are lovely, think on these things." A. J. Cronin wrote of a trip to Florence when he fell into conversation with an old gardener who told him, "I see my cherry trees in bud, and then in flower, and then in fruit, and then I believe in God."

X. *Give yourself to a cause bigger than you.* Live for something which will evoke your best possibilities. Lose yourself in an important task and you will find yourself.— Max R. Hickerson.

SUNDAY: JUNE EIGHTH

MORNING SERVICE

Topic: Set Free to Serve
SCRIPTURE: Gal. 5:13–6:10.

Freedom can never be separated from responsibility without endangering freedom. We are liberated for a purpose, and that purpose is to serve. This means that our freedom is not an unconditioned freedom but has several conditioning factors placed upon it in order to safeguard and maintain it.

I. *The law of love.* (See Gal. 5:13–15.) (a) Our freedom reminds us that the purpose of our liberation is to free us for service which we are called to do in a spirit of love: "by love serve one another" Paul reminds us of the greatest commandment of love in terms of which the entire law is fulfilled.

(b) How does the love commandment fulfill the entire law? Presumably by compressing the essential feature of all of the seven hundred plus laws of the Old Testament so that a person who could live the life of love required by this commandment would automatically find himself above reproach with regard to the spirit and intention of the other laws.

(c) One must be sure that his love for God is both mature and informed. The opposite of service through love is expressed in v. 16 in terms of a rather sophisticated cannibalism in which people "bite and devour" one another.

II. *The law of the Spirit.* (See Gal. 5:16–26.) (a) The spirit of God in which true freedom is found is opposed to both the flesh and the law. As such, walking in the Spirit assures that we will not err either in the direction of legalism or antinomianism. Paul catalogues a list both of the works of the flesh and of the fruit of the

Spirit to show how antithetical they are to each other. It is instructive that he speaks of "fruit" rather than "works" of the Spirit. This choice of words is fortunate because it conveys the nonlegalistic, spontaneous, God-centered approach to righteousness that Paul has urged throughout. One does not perform works; because of the spirit of God in him he produces fruit.

(b) The spirit of God is nonlegalistic, but it is not illegalistic. That is to say that the fruit of the Spirit is not in violation of the law since "against such there is no law."

(c) Since the Spirit is in opposition to the flesh, the negative counterpart to walking in the Spirit is crucifying the flesh. The spirit of God is active and productive in us only when "passions and desires" have been nailed to the cross.

III. *The law of maturity.* (See Gal. 6:1–7.) (a) Serving through love involves a helpful and gentle disposition toward those who become guilty of moral failure. The goal of such helpfulness and gentleness should be that of restoring the erring. One will find this attitude encouraged in himself if he will recall in humility that the same moral failure could have been his.

(b) The absence of such humility is strongly censored as self-deception, and the suggestion is made that the reason why people are sometimes judgmental rather than helpful toward the weak is to make themselves seem morally superior. Because of this Paul urges a level of spiritual maturity and achievement that will not make it necessary for the Christian to find someone morally inferior with whom to compare himself.

(c) Verses 2 and 5 provide an interesting study in contrasts. The former verse tells us we are to "bear one another's burdens"; the latter, that each man will have to "bear his own."

(1) How are the verses to be reconciled? Verse 5 is setting forth an ideal, what each person should envision and expect of himself. Verse 2 is reckoning with the realistic situation of our world in which many people are not that mature. Justice requires that each person bear his own load. Love in the face of injustice is willing to carry its own load and also that of a weaker brother. Humility is willing to accept help when it is needed.

(2) Although we tend to expect more of others than we do from ourselves, Christian maturity would require us to reverse that expectation. The Christian growth process would move us from a relationship of dependence to one of independence to the supreme level of interdependence, giving and taking as love and need require.

IV. *The law of the harvest.* (See Gal. 6:7–10.) One variety of self-deception has been mentioned in v. 3. Another is mentioned here: the belief that because one is free he can avoid the law of the harvest. One does reap what he sows. This is applied to both the good harvest of the Spirit and the bad harvest of the flesh. Just as it is a warning to the fleshly sowers, it is an assurance to the spiritual sowers. Because of the promise of reaping eternal life, this should encourage us to prolong the time of our sowing and to enlarge the scope of our sowing.—W. Clyde Tilley.

Illustrations

A CHILD IN CHURCH. While sitting in the church pew, I noticed one of the offering envelopes in the holder on the back of the seat in front of me had some pencil marks on it. I was curious. I took it out of the holder to examine it more closely. I saw a crudely drawn figure of a man with sharp zig-zag lines running from his head upward toward the sky. I wondered what was in the mind of the child who drew that picture, for it bore all the marks of a child's drawing. Was the child drawing a picture of what was heard that morning from the sermon? Was the speaker saying something about lightning? Or did the double zig-zag lines reaching upward indicate a stairway to God, similar to what Jacob saw in a dream? I am not concerned about reconstructing the child's thinking, but I want to pay my respect to the mother who brought her child to church that Sunday. She demonstrated an awareness that her child would be blessed by sharing worship with the family.—Paul W. Milhouse.

CHRISTLIKE AT HOME. One of the most difficult places in the world to be Christlike is in your own homes. There are reasons for this. First, the closeness of family living often brings out the worst in us as well as the best. Secondly, we occasionally feel a need of "letting our hair down." Where might this be done? We choose not to do it at work or in the marketplace or in the school. Usually we choose the home. And we take each other for granted in the home. That has a positive point and a negative. On the positive side, it's a good thing when your behavior, your disposition, and your dependability are such that others can rely on you and can "take you for granted." But it's a sad thing when this taken-for-grantedness disregards our feelings, our needs, our ideals, and our ambitions. Perhaps the home is one of the most difficult places to display Christlikeness, but there is no place in all of life that needs it more than does the family.—Jerry Hayner.

YOUTH'S WORLD. Instead of casting a critical eye at our young people, it would be better for adults to stop and think what kind of a world we have built for our young people to live in. It is a world so full of tension and strife that it is difficult enough for grownups, much less youth, to feel secure.—Billy Graham.

CHRISTIAN PARENTS. The best legacy that you as a parent can leave your children is the memory of a father and mother who genuinely loved God, loved each other, loved their children, and who had a positive outlook on life. If you are a happy, positive Christian parent, it is likely that your children will be happy, positive Christian children. You can count on it because your children are watching you. Whether you realize it or not, they are observing your every move, and they learn more from you than from all other teachers, pastors, and peers combined. For example, your youngsters learn about God and the Bible at church and Sunday school, but they look to you for the in-the-home examples of day-to-day Christian living. The attitude that you have toward spiritual matters will be mirrored in the attitudes of your children. If you serve roast principal, roast teacher, or roast priest at your dinner table each evening, your children will develop a disregard for their spiritual and academic masters.—*The Anglican Digest.*

Sermon Suggestions

THE LEADERSHIP OF A CHILD. Text: Isa. 11:6. (1) The days of childhood lead, form, and fix the future history and destiny. (2) The traits of childhood lead the way in all virtues of character. (3) The spirit of childhood leads in influence upon human society.—Arthur T. Pierson.

WAYS TO KNOW THE WILL OF GOD. Text: Rom. 12:2. (1) Seeking the dictates of conscience. (2) Seeking common sense. (3) Seeking the advice of a friend. (4) Seeking through reading the minds and wisdom of others. (5) Seeking the voice of the church. (6) Seeking inner light.—Leslie D. Weatherhead.

Worship Aids

CALL TO WORSHIP. "Both young men, and maidens; old men, and children: let them praise the name of the Lord: for his name alone is excellent; his glory is above the earth and heaven." Ps. 148:12–13.

INVOCATION. Teach us, good Lord, in our days of rest to put our worship and prayer first, and may we never let the services of the church be crowded out of our lives. Keep before us the vision of thy dear son Jesus Christ, who in his boyhood days worshiped with his family, and may that vision inspire us and all men to unite as members of the church universal in witness, in worship, and in love.

OFFERTORY SENTENCE. "As every man hath received the gift, even so minister the same one to another, as good stewards of the manifold grace of God." I Pet. 4:10.

OFFERTORY PRAYER. Awaken us to the claims of thy holy will, O God, and stir us with a passion for thy kingdom, that we may respond at this time with our gifts and also with our lives.

PRAYER. Our heavenly Father, today we offer hearty thanks for those who labor willingly to share the good news of Jesus Christ with our children. We are conscious not only of our own needs when we come to your house but also of the important work of sharing our faith with our children. As the generations come and go and as they walk across the stage of life, we accept our responsibility to teach by word and example what we have learned of faithfulness and responsibility.

We acknowledge that we have not always been faithful nor have we always acted responsibly toward those who need to know what motivates our lives and our concerns. Preaching love, we have too often turned aside from demonstrating that love in times of need. Affirming faith in Christ, we have sometimes declined to accept a personal challenge to impart that faith to children or to the world. Proclaiming an awareness that all we have and are has been given to us in trust for the common good, we have often been selfish and small when the need has been to be compassionate and outgoing.

Yet we have asked our teachers to announce the good news to our children. Show us the conflict between what we have said and what we have done. Help us not to forget that, by our own personal example of word and deed, we are the primary teachers of the values and the faith we truly hold. May our example be supporting evidence for the lessons our church school teachers impart, and may we be renewed in understanding of what you require of us: to do justice and to love kindness and to walk humbly with you.

So may we be faithful and supporting disciples of the man of Nazareth, whose life was a witness to compassionate love for all men: even Jesus Christ our triumphant Lord.—Madison L. Sheely.

EVENING SERVICE

Topic: Affirmations of Christian Parents (Children's Sunday)

TEXT: Luke 2:51.

I. We will attend the worship of the church regularly in order that we may be nurtured in our own Christian faith and that through our participation in worship we may be better prepared to lead our child by example and precept into a significant faith of his own.

II. We will study our Christian faith that we may learn more of its facts and principles so that as our child grows in body, mind, and spirit we may be able to answer his questions clearly, guide his thinking rightly, and nurture his soul lovingly.

III. We will worship daily in our home and will give thanks at meals and offer bedtime prayers even while our child is yet a baby. As he grows in years we will read to him such things as will help him grow mentally and spiritually in his understanding of God our Father and Jesus Christ our Lord, we will talk with him about these things, and we will teach him to pray. We realize that the first six years of his life will have the most influence on his character, his way of life, and his attitude toward life. We want them to be good years, full of Christian influence, leading him toward the day of his own decision to be a Christian and a member of the church of Jesus Christ.

IV. We will bring our child with us to church school and to church when he is old enough to share with others in learning and worship. We will do our part to cooperate and help in the church's program of education as it seeks to aid us in raising our child to the abundant, well-founded life of a mature Christian. We recognize that this is a joint effort but that the ultimate responsibility is ours for we are the parents, and to us God has specifically entrusted the life and well-being of our child.—Jack Van Ens.

SUNDAY: JUNE FIFTEENTH

MORNING SERVICE

Topic: Are You Satisfied with Your Church?

TEXT: Ps. 65:4.

The author of Ps. 65 says in enthusiastic terms that he was satisfied with the church of his day. Why was the psalmist satisfied and happy with the church of the sixth century B.C.?

I. *He knew that his church was one place where everybody was welcome.*

(a) Unlike many worshipers of his day, the psalmist acknowledged that God was the Lord of all of the earth, not just of the Jews. "To thee shall all flesh come," he said. All flesh, all peoples, all races, and all cultures were welcome in his church. The temple of God was a place where everybody was wanted, and the psalmist was happy and satisfied because that was true.

(b) One reason many Christians are dissatisfied with their church today is because their church is not really as inclusive as it should be. A church that is inclusive and friendly is made up of hospitable people who gladly welcome visitors and newcomers without regard to wealth, social status, race, or condition. The members recognize that their church is God's house and that whosoever will may come. Such a congregation inevitably is a growing congregation of happy, satisfied people, regardless of who is pastor or whatever the denomination.

II. *He knew it was a place where anything could be brought to the Lord.*

(a) Notice the gamut of issues the psalmist in vv. 1–3 says may be brought before God in his church: praise, vows or obligations, sins, transgressions, and all in public, corporate worship. The psalmist's church was a church where everyone knew that it was perfectly acceptable to bring anything and everything to the Lord.

(b) When Christians know that their church is a place where anything can be brought before the Lord, they know their church is a place of forgiveness, not judgment; that their fellow Christians care about them rather than blame them; and that their church is a hospital for the healing of sinners, not a sanctuary for saints. A church where people feel free to bring anything and everything before the Lord is the church of the Lord Jesus Christ, where cowards like Peter and doubters like Thomas and thieves like Zacchaeus know they are welcome.

III. *He knew it was a place where anybody could be made whole.* (a) "By dread deeds thou dost answer us with deliverance, O God of our salvation" (65:5), he wrote. He then went on to write eight more verses, the rest of this beautiful psalm, to catalog all that God had done to bless his people and make them whole. The psalmist was a satisfied man because he knew that his church was dedicated to God who can make anyone whole.

(b) Many people are dissatisfied with their church today because they feel the church no longer seems to recognize that its primary reason for being is to offer people wholeness of life or salvation from their sins.

(c) The church exists to bring men and women into a life-changing, life-redeeming, and life-enriching relationship with Jesus Christ. Whenever a person repents of his sins and accepts Jesus Christ as savior and lord, he becomes a whole person rather than a broken person, saved instead of lost, loving instead of loveless, and filled with new understanding and seeing the world with new eyes and full of new possibilities. People who have accepted Christ's call to discipleship become leaven who can change the lump of the world, salt to flavor the stew of society, and light to drive the darkness of sin out of every corner of the world.—Raymond W. Gibson, Jr.

Illustrations

OUT OF FOCUS. We seem to be obsessed by the notion that children are a race apart to be studied and analyzed like some curious species of beings from another planet; that youth is a strange colony from outer space that speaks another language, thinks other thoughts, worships other gods, and requires the most delicate negotiations before any contract can be established; that middle-age is some sort of problem requiring psychiatric help; and that the old are a unique but alarmingly numerous race of people who have to be coaxed into corners out of everybody's way.—David H. C. Read.

TWO HANDS.   During one of my children's sermons I asked, "Why do you love your daddy?" An eight year old said: "Because when I'm bad he spanks me with one hand. Then he hugs me with the other. And then he tells me he loves me."—Cecil B. Murphey.

Sermon Suggestions

THE THREE R'S OF CHRISTIAN HIGHER EDUCATION.   Text: John 20:31. (1) Responsibility. (2) Respect. (3) Reverence.—W. Burkette Raper.

THE MAN OF GOD.   Text: Ps. 1:1-3. (1) What the man of God is negatively. (2) What the man of God is positively. (3) What the man of God is consequently.—Stephen F. Olford.

Worship Aids

CALL TO WORSHIP.   "I will praise thee with my whole heart. I will worship toward thy holy temple, and praise thy name for thy lovingkindness." Ps. 138:1-2.

INVOCATION.   Almighty God, the giver and lord of life: we bless and praise thee for thy merciful keeping and gracious care, for all the gifts of thy providence and grace, and for all the blessings which manifest thy fatherhood. We thank thee for the faith which sustains us, the hopes which inspire us, and the light by which we daily walk. We thank thee for Jesus Christ, who by the life he lived, the temptations he conquered, the gospel he taught, and the cross he bore has brought us nigh to thee and closer to one another.

OFFERTORY SENTENCE.   "Of every man that giveth willingly with his heart ye shall take my offering [saith the Lord]." Exod. 25:2.

OFFERTORY PRAYER.   O Father of our Lord Jesus Christ, we dedicate these offerings to the fellowship of him, whom to know aright is life eternal.

PRAYER.   Our heavenly Father, long since have we been taught to name thee father. We pray that those of us who are earthly fathers may prove worthy of this high simile.

From thy divine wisdom may we gain understanding in providing for every need of those entrusted to us.

From thy holiness may we develop a righteousness that takes into account motive as well as deed, the pressure of circumstance as well as overt action; searches all night for the sheep that has strayed; waits, if need be, for an eternity with cords of drawing love.

And from thy forgiveness may we learn a compassion that accepts us while we are unacceptable; restores us while we are yet in our sins; puts the robe on our shoulder, sandals on our feet, and the ring on our finger.

So may we learn from thee both the cost and the joy of true fatherhood.—Hillyer H. Straton.

EVENING SERVICE

Topic: The Christ Whom We Proclaim
SCRIPTURE: Col. 1:19-23.
I. Christ is unconditional love. (a) Christ came to stir up people's cold hearts so that they might be aroused from their complacency, indifference, hedonism, and follow him. The Christian, who has experienced the unconditional love of God on the cross, has to be the vision of Christ in this world. Because we no longer live but Christ lives in us, we can cry out loudly and uncompromisingly the glad news of redemption, even if the world considers it

disturbing news. Christ came to disturb the consciences of people. The people who continue his mission must also continue to disturb.

(b) The Christian is one who brings the message of love uncompromisingly, not forcefully nor dogmatically but as a steady stream that finds its way around obstacles and into the cold hearts of people so that they may know the love of the Father. Because we have experienced being loved first, being loved in our estrangement and being taken as we are, we can turn around and do the same thing to every human being. That's how radical the unconditional love of Christ is.

II. Christ is unconditional freedom. Once we have surrendered our will to Christ and live within his unconditional love, then we are free.

(a) Freedom today usually means individualism and being free to come and go and do as I please. Ironically that freedom is our greatest evil. To live in that manner places my desires first, and whatever is left over can go to others. That way of life is causing guilt, defensiveness, loneliness, and fear.

(b) There is no way that we—if we are wrestling at all with our Christianity—can eat and waste the amounts that we do and not have some feelings of guilt. If we are in fact able to go blindly on our way, continuing to eat great amounts of beef and consuming more than our share of energy, completely insensitive to the millions that are starving, then we are people that the love of Christ has not touched.

(c) True freedom comes when we belong to the Christian community. When people are drawn to such a community and make a serious commitment to that body, they are drawn to a life of love and to the service of God and all humankind. Freedom is found in relationships that are open and loving, for it is in such a life that fear and loneliness does not dominate.

III. Christ is unconditional growth. Unconditional growth happens when we learn to love our enemies and to pray for those who persecute us. Unconditional growth happens only in community and when you see Jesus Christ in every person you meet. As we begin to expand ourselves in loving, so we grow in knowledge of ourselves.—Terry L. Henry.

SUNDAY: JUNE TWENTY-SECOND

MORNING SERVICE

Topic: The Responsibility of Hearing
SCRIPTURE: Matt. 13:3–9.

We commonly call this the parable of the sower, but as George Buttrick points out, it is more accurately described as the parable of the soils. It is the reaction of the soils, of the hearers, that makes the difference. This is the import of the parable.

I. The sower must possess the seed himself. (a) There is no point in our being concerned for a messed-up world characterized by crime, starvation, illicit sex, drug addiction, and the rest, if we ourselves are a part of the problem. We must first experience the truth of the gospel in our own lives before we can share it with others.

(b) A sower must be skillful. He must know something of ground composition and soil preparation. He must be aware of the laws of growth and patiently wait for results. All too often in our enthusiasm we are inclined to become overbearing. We tend to "jam religion down their throats" and turn the very people away we desire to win. Nor is it enough simply to have know-how and be attentive to our work. We need faith and trust. The farmer must be willing to spend his money long before he is sure of a return.

(c) Naturally the task of the sower cannot be overlooked. None of us can give eternal life nor can we make it grow and develop. That is God's prerogative. He alone gives the increase.

II. What the sower sows is equally significant, and that is the seed. "When he sowed, some seeds fell by the wayside."

(a) In explaining the parable to his disciples, Jesus left little doubt as to what he meant by "the seed." It is the word of God. (See I Pet. 1:23.)

(b) There are many today who are not sowing the seed of the living word. You can tell the kind of seed by the kind of fruit that is brought forth. Look around you. How much evidence is there in many of our churches today of transformed lives? Our pulpits are proclaiming politics and book reviews and social reform and pious platitudes. But can this bring change to the life that is blighted by sin?

III. Jesus pointed out that it was really the condition of the soil that determined the harvest of the grain.

(a) Some seed fell *by the wayside,* on the well-trod path that led through the fields. (1) Through constant usage the ground had become packed and hard. The seed had no chance to take root and grow. Soon the wind came and blew it away, or the birds swooped down and devoured it. There are those who have become callous to the message of the gospel. In failing to respond to God's claim upon their lives, their hearts have been hardened and their minds closed.

(2) Prejudice can blind people to things. Immoral behavior can keep them from an objective evaluation of their lives. Pride, fear of the unknown, and an unwillingness to change are all factors that harden the heart. The very pressures of everyday life have a tendency to crowd out any sense of the sacred. There is no one so blind as that individual who will not see.

(b) Other seed fell *on rocky ground.* (1) Immediately it began to grow because there was a thin layer of good soil. But just below the surface was a hard ledge of rock that kept the roots from digging deep. Soon the hot sun and blustering wind killed the new life.

(2) Our churches are full of superficial Christians. In a moment of emotion they take their stand, but over the long haul, when the going gets rough, they are no-where to be found. Gerald Kennedy says of them, "We ought never to allow the church to become a hiding place for people whose lives are cluttered up with rocks and who propose to do nothing about it."

(c) Other seed fell *upon thorny ground.* (1)

This is the best soil yet, but the farmer calls it "uncleansed." To the naked eye it looks rich and productive. The seed is sown with every good intention. Only when it begins to grow do we become aware of the impossibility of harvesting. There is no way of separating the thorns from the grain. In due course it too gets choked out by the uncontrolled weeds of the field.

(2) Jesus indicated at least three kinds of thorns to be aware of. There are the cares of the home, family life, bills and sickness, schooling, what have you. All of them are legitimate, yet because of misplaced priorities they often become enemies of the best. There is the deceitfulness of riches that chokes off the word. There is the lust for worldly things such as business success, pleasure, power, and acceptance. These too can keep us from putting God first. The thorn of compromise has ruined many a Christian life.

IV. Not all of the seed fell on poor soil or poorly prepared ground. Some of it fell *on good ground* "and brought forth fruit." In likening this kind of soil to the listener, Jesus says it is a person who hears the word and understands it and responds to it. Most of us hear, but it is important to understand and respond. How important it is for each of us to know our own hearts and our response to his gospel.—Fred H. Boehmer.

Illustrations

TWO GENERATIONS.   A father and son ministered to the same congregation but thirty years apart. The father returned for a service and preached to a sparse congregation. Afterward he commented to his son, "When I used to preach here, no one in the village was absent without a reason." "When I preach now," replied the son, "no one is ever present without a reason."—J. Ernest Somerville.

HERESY.   John Wesley said that there is no such thing as a solitary Christian. The faith must be shared in order to be kept. Christianity is a social religion. It becomes dwarfed and blighted when alone; it thrives in numbers. But true to our ruggedly individualistic self-centeredness, we have tried to practice the Christian faith as if it were a home correspondence course in self-improvement. The great heresy in American popular religion is the notion that religion is a private affair, a secret contract between the believer and God.—William H. Willimon.

Sermon Suggestions

LISTENING TO THE SERMON.   Text: Jas. 1:19. The sermon is not a talk about God; it is an opportunity for God to talk to us. The purpose of the sermon is to affect a meeting between us and God. (1) Listen for what God has to say to you individually while the pastor is preaching. (2) Think of the pastor as sitting in the pew beside you, himself listening to what God has to say. (3) Think of the sermon as part of worship and not apart from it. (4) Remember that you have to finish the sermon in your daily life.—Harry A. Aufiero.

FOUR-LETTER WORDS.   (1) *Look.* Look squarely at the nature of your problems. Keep looking for the right solutions. (2) *Work.* Nothing will so fortify you against stress as hard, constructive work. (3) *Give.* Give yourself to people. (4) *Love.* Love nourishes and restores you. (5) *Pray.* Prayer connects you with spiritual power and builds inner strength.—George Scharringhausen.

Worship Aids

CALL TO WORSHIP.   "I will lift up mine eyes unto the hills, from whence cometh my help. My help cometh from the Lord, which made heaven and earth." Ps. 121: 1–2.

INVOCATION.   Our heavenly Father, who by thy love hast made us, and through thy love hast kept us, and in thy love wouldst make us perfect: we humbly confess that we have not loved thee with all our heart and soul and mind and strength and that we have not loved one another as Christ hath loved us. Thy life is within our souls, but our selfishness has hindered thee. We have not lived by faith. We have resisted thy spirit. We have neglected thy inspirations. Forgive what we have been; help us to amend what we are, and in thy spirit direct what we shall be; that thou mayest come into the full glory of thy creation in us and in all men.

OFFERTORY SENTENCE.   "Go, and sell that thou hast, and give to the poor, and thou shalt have treasure in heaven: and come and follow me." Matt. 19:21.

OFFERTORY PRAYER.   Help us, dear Father, to be cheerful givers of our time, means, talents, and self to the master that he may use us in the upbuilding of his kingdom.

PRAYER.   O God, we are here to learn something! We are here to be taught! We are here in this worship experience to be educated in your ways and to understand your purposes for us and all our fellow human beings.

But we are also here to be conditioned for our job. We are here to be renewed. We are here to sharpen our awareness, to cleanse our motives, and to straighten out our values.

Help us to understand that this experience of worship means everything to us. This is not just a pious exercise. Neither is it a matter of our being moved by great sermons, songs, and anthems, although these aspects of worship should help us. Nor is it a matter of our rejoicing in our goodness as we think condemnation of those we do not like or understand. It is a matter of recognizing that you are God. We are here to call upon you. We are here to begin to develop the capacity to love and to care for each other and for all the people of the world.

Save us from a wrong concept of why we are here. Grant that we may strain our minds and hearts to find a meaningful confrontation with you, however painful and joyfully traumatic the experience may be.—Lyle V. Newman.

EVENING SERVICE

Topic: The Church as Pastor
TEXT: Acts 20:28.
Wherein is the church our pastor in the realm of theology?

I. It is our pastor because its call is to shepherd the pasture where the believer feeds. Not to protect the source of spiritual food is to betray a trust. The primary pasture is the word of God. But there are secondary pastures to be protected such as the reading habits of our people and the speakers and singing groups to which they are exposed.

II. It is our pastor because it insists that theology must be in touch with real life, not theoretical life. It must answer questions that spring from common contemporary experience as well as the past and as well as schoolroom theorizing. The New Testament's demonstration of concern for the living present is the towering example here.

III. It is our pastor because it insists that theology must speak to persons as well as to principle. Separated from the person dimension, it tends to either scholasticism or mysticism.

IV. It is our pastor because it insists that theology must nurture devotion as well as dogmatics. Thielicke described this as "prayed dogmatics" and says "a theological thought can breathe only in the atmosphere of dialogue with God."

V. It is our pastor because it insists that theology must strengthen faith and not become lost in speculative philosophy. Unlike Descartes who said, "I doubt in order to know," sound theology must say, "I believe in order to know."—Neil E. Hightower.

SUNDAY: JUNE TWENTY-NINTH

MORNING SERVICE

Topic: The Christian Patriot (Independence Sunday)
TEXT: Matt. 22:21.

I. A Christian patriot is one who perpetuates freedom. (a) Freedom is perpetuated by those who are willing to accept the role of prophet and pioneer, pilgrim and soldier. But our freedom is not a privilege granted by any state or any group in society. Freedom is a God-given human or natural right.

(b) In order for a free society to function well there must be certain qualities of character in its citizens including a sense of moral responsibility, concern for the freedom and rights of others, an informed and educated electorate, and respect for intelligence. These are the marks of the free person. A Christian patriot perpetuates that freedom.

(c) The Christian patriot renders to Caesar that which is Caesar's and to God that which is God's. In the process he perpetuates to the best of his ability and at the sacrifice of his life if necessary the way of freedom. Yet when freedom is buried in human society and is no longer recognized or practiced, then the society collapses as a free society. We have seen that happen across the years of history.

(d) It is the imperative responsibility of every citizen and indeed the essential responsibility of the Christian citizen to perpetuate freedom by maintaining those conditions which make possible the continuance of freedom. Remember always that "eternal vigilance is the price of human liberty."

(1) A responsible exercise of your rights and privileges as a free citizen in a free land is the only authentic kind of freedom.

(2) It is with irresponsibility that freedom disappears.

(3) It is with responsible freedom that life is fulfilled. No wonder the Christian patriot perpetuates freedom.

II. A Christian patriot puts loyalty to God first. (a) Jesus established in the text the obligations of the Christian citizen. He acknowledged his responsibility as a citizen of the government of his day even though virtually a slave. But he put above and beyond that the ultimate loyalty as being obedience to God and rendering to God that which belongs to him.

(b) A Christian patriot puts loyalty to God first. Such loyalty may indeed require a critical attitude toward his nation when that nation's actions do not promote freedom and peace for all persons. This is not a lack of patriotism. This is a depth of patriotism that enables us to march to the beat of a distant drummer who is beating for us God's insistence upon justice and righteousness and love.

III. The Christian patriot seeks to create a Christian community in nation and world under God. Jesus set the pattern for our priorities as citizens of a nation and Christians in the world.

(a) Priority No. 1 for the Christian patriot is the sovereignty of God. One cannot understand the teachings of Jesus until he has seen that Jesus believed in the ultimate sovereignty of God. Rome had tremendous power and ruled the world of his day. But for Jesus, God was still the ruler, the ultimate sovereign to whom the Caesars were accountable.

(b) Priority No. 2 for the Christian patriot is the sacredness of human personality. This priority follows close upon the first. When we establish as the ultimate loyalty of our life our obedience before God, then we must with Jesus move toward a recognition of the innate sacredness of every human person. Jesus said your life is important and is significant in the scheme of things because God has created you in his own image. God has given you the greatest of all divine gifts—human personality. Therefore I must respect and honor you in the name of God because you are his child. Through Christ I am called to love you in my heart and will only your good because you are of God.

(c) Priority No. 3 for Jesus is the obligation to take the good news of God-given freedom to all persons and use our human efforts to see that they are privileged to enjoy that freedom.

(1) In Jesus' day political freedom was denied to most people. It was given to a relatively few. So the apostle Paul commented often on the fact of his being a "free man" as a citizen of Rome. Jesus believed that all persons are made free by their creator. Their inalienable rights are not taken from them without violating God's purpose.

(2) We in our land are engaged on several fronts in the effort to provide civil rights for various minorities who have not in the past or do not in the present enjoy the full measure of freedom which is their God-given right and their constitutionally granted privileges.

(3) The qualities that make for freedom can alone maintain a land in which all citizens exercise freely all privileges that any citizen exercises. These are the qualities that create Christian community—a community under God where there are no man-made barriers of race or status or national origin.

(4) Patriotism at its best is love of country only when God's love is in our hearts and we make a constant effort to create and maintain these Christian virtues in our human society. Such freedom expresses itself in a respect for persons as persons. It requires that we cooperate with all persons of good will for the common welfare of the human race. It demands that we assure by whatever honorable means are available that the liberty we enjoy is shared by all persons of the world. Only then can we be confident that freedom in this "nation under God shall not perish from the earth."—Hoover Rupert.

Illustrations

CHURCH AND STATE.   To the extent that we Christians are identified first of all with our nation-state and only secondly with loyalty to the transcendent Lord who judges all nations, we have difficulty communicating our faith to persons who are critical of or who feel themselves oppressed by the action of our nation. They do not believe us. They see us as "culture-Christians." They reject our testimony to our Lord because our real Lord seems to them to be one institution of our nation, or anti-Communism, or keeping America great. In the biblical struggle with this transgression, it was called idolatry.—Paul Minear.

THEFT. Every gun that is made, every warship launched, every rocket fired signifies in the final sense a theft from those who hunger and are not fed, those who are cold and are not clothed. This world in arms is not spending money alone. It is spending the sweat of its laborers, the genius of its scientists, the hopes of its children.—Dwight D. Eisenhower.

Sermon Suggestions

PAUL'S PATTERN FOR LIVING. Text: Gal. 2:20. (1) Nothing was too high to be attempted. (2) Nothing was too hard to be endured. (3) Nothing was too good to be hoped for. (4) Nothing was too precious to be given away.—E. D. Jarvis.

FAITH AT ITS FINEST. Scripture: Matt. 8:5–13. (1) The centurion's faith stemmed from a trustworthy character. (2) The second element in the centurion's faith was humility. (3) The centurion was a man of disciplined action. (4) The centurion was speaking with the spirit of a soldier, a man under authority. And as a soldier who knew authority, he recognized the authority of Christ.—Ralph W. Sockman.

Worship Aids

CALL TO WORSHIP. "How beautiful upon the mountains are the feet of him that bringeth good tidings, that publisheth peace; that publisheth salvation; that saith unto Zion, thy God reigneth!" Isa. 52:7.

INVOCATION. Almighty God, who hast given us minds to know thee, hearts to love thee, and voices to show forth thy praise, we would not know thee if thou hadst not already found us. Help us to know thee with pure minds and to praise thee with a clear voice.

OFFERTORY SENTENCE. "What shall I render unto the Lord for all his benefits toward me? I will pay my vows unto the Lord now in the presence of all his people." Ps. 116:12–14.

OFFERTORY PRAYER. We thank thee, O God, for another anniversary of our nation's independence and pray that this rich gift may be an opportunity to serve one another in love.

PRAYER. Almighty God, author of our freedom and the source of our precious liberty, we worship thee with thankful hearts in our free land.

Yet we know as Christians that we can never be truly free while any of our brothers are enslaved. We pray therefore for courage and power from on high to destroy the walls that divide us. The "no man's land" that separates our world into free and slave threatens our very earthly existence. Hasten the day, O God, when all men will acknowledge thee. Tame our rebellious spirits. Purge the hatred from our hearts. The madness of war is a constant alternative before us. Give us the wisdom, the concern, and the love that will enable us to live in peace with ourselves and with our neighbors.

We love our native land. Long may freedom's holy light burn bright. Forgive us when in indifference or in cowardice we have allowed these freedoms to slip from us. Forgive us when any group of us has denied the same freedoms and opportunities to others because of race or class or color.

Now strengthen us, O God, in our own personal prayer lives. We see thy son, Jesus Christ, retiring to pray and returning with unbelievable strength; yet we try to live our days in our own strength. Petty problems become gigantic obstacles. Life gets out of focus. Teach us anew to pray, to worship, and to ponder the holy scriptures.

Especially strengthen, we pray thee, those individuals who mourn. May the loss of loved ones not embitter or discourage them. May they know the mysterious confidence that comes to those who turn to thee, the Lord of heaven and earth.—William D. White.

EVENING SERVICE

Topic: A Personal Declaration of Independence

TEXT: Matt. 5:21.

When we talk of national freedom we

may forget that freedom's responsibility is personal. So as we celebrate a national anniversary I invite others to join me in a personal declaration of independence.

I. I declare my independence from patterns of the past. Not from the past, for I am indebted to the past far beyond what can be repaid. And the past is never wholly past. But patterns out of the past, the ways our ancestors did things, need not be for us. To appreciate the past is not to mimic its details. "New occasions teach new duties."

II. I declare my independence from mob rule. Maybe the statement is too strong, but the pressure to conform is greater than we realize. I do not like crowd pressure in communities and am more concerned about the devastating crowd rule of our minds.

(a) Crowds do not climb the heights. Crowds are stirred by emotions while minds wait. Persons endowed with certain unalienable rights are not designed to be treated as a mass.

(b) We hear much talk about common sense, which implies a common level. Who will stand free to seek the guidance of uncommon sense? "Do good to those who hate you." "Turn the other cheek." "Love your enemies." Jesus Christ refused the level of common sense in favor of uncommon sense.

III. I would like to experience patriotism at its highest level. True patriotism is not limited to praise of secure boundaries, high standards of living, and gross national product. Patriotism in the land of the free lifts up people, all people, under God because we believe that each is of God. The patriot seeks liberty and justice for all and knows that ultimate security rests in security for all.

IV. I hope to be independent enough to be obedient to God's will, as nearly as I can know it. "Is there any word from the Lord?" This question asked of Jeremiah haunts me. I believe that God is the lord of all the earth and of all people and that he has bigger designs for us than we are willing to accept for ourselves. To proclaim good news to all the world includes all the world—America, India, Africa and schools, industry, government, labor, and economics. These too are parts of the whole.

V. The message of Jesus Christ issues primarily in person-God relationships and person-person relationships. This is the first commandment. The gospel grants no release from "love your neighbor" in the temple, the marketplace, or the halls of government. "He has anointed me to preach good news, to proclaim release to the captives . . . to set up at liberty those who are oppressed" (Luke 4:18). "Those" includes all. I do not like the noise of rioters, but I am frightened more by the silence of the churches commissioned to proclaim good news. Hence my constant struggle to be free.—Wesley P. Ford.

SUNDAY: JULY SIXTH

MORNING SERVICE

Topic: When Christians Are Rejected
SCRIPTURE: Luke 9:51–56.

That the Samaritans rejected these Jews, Jesus and his followers, is not surprising. It certainly was not a surprise to them. The new element here is to be found in the way Jesus responded to that hostility.

I. To be inhospitable was a sin, so when the messengers were turned away from the Samaritan village, James and John sought permission from Jesus to bid fire come down from heaven and consume these wretched people. It was not fair to be rejected simply because they were Jews. Permission was not granted. Instead Jesus rebuked them. This must have perplexed them. They were suggesting a course of action which had in their view a respectable precedent to recommend it.

(a) Jesus understood the intensity of his disciples' reaction to rejection. They had made an investment. They had a stake in the success of their master's mission. They had made sacrifices to become his disciples. It was not easy to be thwarted. They also knew that the Samaritans were rejecting them as well as Jesus. Self-interest as well as loyalty was involved in their request for permission to call down fire from heaven.

(b) A second cause for the vehemence of James and John's reaction here was that the religion of the Samaritans was in so many respects similar to their own. The history of the feud between the Samaritans and the Jews is one of going separate ways for reasons beyond their control. It was not a schism, such as takes place when a church splits into factions, but the consequences were similar to that of a schism.

(c) The first thing the Samaritan woman at the well said to Jesus was that Jews and Samaritans had no dealings with each other, and it wasn't long before she was reminding him that Jews and Samaritans disagreed as to where God should be worshiped. But the reaction of Jesus to this kind of rebuff was not to call down fire from heaven. Nor did he say that the Jews were wrong to worship at Jerusalem. What Jesus did was to put these questions in a larger context and speak of the time coming when true worshipers would worship the Father in spirit and in truth. Schism is wrong because it diverts attention from what really matters in the sight of God.

II. Jesus did not give James and John permission to punish the Samaritans who had rejected them. Instead he rebuked them, and then called their attention to some of the costs of discipleship, not the least of which is having to deal with conflicting loyalties and affections when faced with rejections more personal than rejection by Samaritans.

(a) Jesus knew, as many of his followers came to know, that rejection of the gospel and the demands it makes by members of one's family is something that some of his disciples in every generation have to face.

(b) Often the gospel is misunderstood, having been presented inadequately. Often what is really being rejected is not Christianity but a particular person or group of people with whom Christianity has been associated. Sometimes the gospel is misused, as in the case of the young person who is more interested, consciously or not, in rejecting his parents or his background than in concerning himself with the needs of others. Often the gospel is rejected by family members because it disturbs a familiar orientation. The convert wishes to stress his membership in a family far larger than the one with which he or she has been previously identified.

III. For all kinds of reasons often the rejection is justified by the circumstances or at least it is understandable. How is the Christian to deal with it?

(a) We should not give in to the temptation to resent rejection, as did James and John.

(b) We can fix our minds on the example of Jesus who, although clearly not allowing his family to distract him from his mission, paid more attention to behavior than to the details of religious observance, confident that dedication, loving-kindness, compassion, and forgiveness can bring all sorts and conditions of men and women to the only belief that matters.—Edwin S. S. Sunderland.

Illustrations

LIGHT COMING.   The fundamental joy of the Christian religion isn't in living a good life. I can imagine getting tired of that! The fundamental joy of it is in standing with God against some darkness or some void and watching the light come.—Paul Scherer.

NO MAN IS AN ISLAND.   You hold a block of metal in your hand. And it's solid. Yet within the metal there are molecules or atoms, all moving by laws of their own. Press a block of pure gold against a block of silver. When you separate them they seem unchanged. But a good physical chemist will show you that where they have been in contact invisible flecks of gold have wandered across the barrier of structure and buried themselves in the silver. And atoms of silver somehow in the structure of gold.

I think that when people are pressed

close they act the same way. Part of you enters them, and part of them enters you. Long after you forget the names and faces, they are still a part of you. Sometimes it is frightening to think that every person you have ever hated or feared or run away from is part of you. But so is every person you have ever learned from and every friend you ever knew.—Theodore White.

Sermon Suggestions

LIVING IN GOD'S CHARGE. Text: I Pet. 5:7 (NEB). (1) Living in God's charge means that God's providence is over us and around us always. (2) Living in God's charge declares that his grace, renewed day by day, will sustain us. (3) Living in God's charge means accepting his directions and doing his will. (4) Living in God's charge means that in the end we shall share in his victory.—Alan Walker.

TESTED, TRIED, AND PROVEN. Scripture: Job 1:6–12. (1) In the eyes of Satan, Job could be made a failure. (2) In the eyes of man, Job was a failure. (3) In the eyes of the Lord, Job was a perfect man.—J. Walter Hall, Jr.

Worship Aids

CALL TO WORSHIP. "Lift up your heads in the sanctuary, and bless the Lord. The Lord that made heaven and earth bless thee out of Zion." Ps. 134:2–3.

INVOCATION. Merciful God, forgive the halting nature of our discipleship. We confess that so little of thy love has reached others through us and that we have borne so lightly wrongs and sufferings that were not our own. We confess that we have cherished the things that divide us from others and that we have made it hard for them to live with us. And we confess that we have been thoughtless in our judgments, hasty in condemnation, and grudging in our forgiveness. Forgive us, we beseech thee.

OFFERTORY SENTENCE. "Verily, verily, I say unto you, he that believeth on me, the works that I do shall he do also; and greater works than these shall he do. And whatsoever ye shall ask in my name, that will I do, that the Father may be glorified in the Son." John 14:12–13.

OFFERTORY PRAYER. Our Father, we thank thee that thou art so generous to us. All that we have is a gift from thee. Help us to serve one another so that we may reflect thy spirit and goodness.

PRAYER. O thou, who art slow to anger and who art loving and patient beyond our ability to measure or to understand, make thyself very evident to us this morning.

We need to see our Father and our God so that we may find direction to our lives, motivation for our deeds, and forgiveness for our sins. There is so much for which we need forgiveness and so much we need to confess for the good of our souls.

We have misused our talents, we have prostituted our gifts, and we have made a mockery of our blessings. We waste our time on useless and even immoral activities; we waste our money on useless and even immoral commodities; we spend our bodies without replenishing them; we cannot seem to find the happy medium between our eagerness to burn the candle at both ends and our fear of burning it even at one end. We have done away with drudgery only to find that we are bored with time on our hands; we have turned jobs over to machines until we are jealous of the machines, not because they have replaced our jobs, but because they have replaced us! We have fought to gain leisure time, and now that we have more leisure hours than work hours, we do not know how to use them and find to our disgust that even the pleasures we worked for get old too soon. Help us to learn the stewardship of time, physical energy, and material abundance.

There are people and causes dear to us that need our prayers. We pray for our president who needs our support, but, most of all, thy guidance and a sense of dependence on thee. We thank thee for his abilities, his fine mind, and his energy. Temper his gifts with wisdom. Help him in his decisions, and help us to discover that all leadership works miracles with cooperation and does little with criticism and bitterness at its heels.

We thank thee for our boys and girls, for the freshness and enthusiasm of youth and for the promises and potential that they hold. They are so easily led, so impressionable; perhaps it is the fault of the adult world that so many go astray. We present a poor example. We tell them not to do the very things they see us do, and we demand that they do the things we refuse to do. We pray not only for the juvenile delinquent in our society, but also for the juvenile in our delinquent society.

Our Father, lay burdens upon our hearts today. Let us be burdened to provide our sons and daughters for the service of the King of kings. Let us be burdened for some particular lost man or woman or boy or girl. Let us be in mental and spiritual pain until that person sees the light of Christ. Discipline our compassion and channel our zeal that they may be spent for others and persuaded always by our love for thee.—David V. Pittenger.

EVENING SERVICE

Topic: The Measure of True Greatness
SCRIPTURE: Mark 9:33–37.

I. True greatness begins with humility. (a) It begins when we break through our huge pride, which would absorb all of our time and efforts with looking after ourselves, and turn our attention to how we can serve others. "For which is the greater," asked Jesus, "one who sits at table or one who serves?" "But I am among you as one who serves."

(b) Those who are greatest in the kingdom of God have the least knowledge of it and are least concerned about it. They have put aside all sense of place and prestige. They are too busy spending their time in humble service to others under God's guidance to worry about where they stand in the hierarchy of heaven.

II. True greatness involves credibility. It requires matching our deeds with our words.

(a) We can talk all we want to about our faith, but the only way that we will be able to communicate it is to live it. The words of Jesus have authority for our lives because he lived those words day by day, all the way to the cross.

(b) Greatness is not something we need to crow about. It is something which is evident in the life of every Christian who has learned to discipline his life so that his will is subordinate to God's will.

III. True greatness can be measured by responsibility. (a) We are told that as Jesus was talking about those who are truly great he picked up a child and said, "Whoever receives one such child in my name receives me; and whoever receives me, receives not me but him who sent me." Jesus used that child to represent the needy of the world, the hungry, the poor, the lonely, the sick, the weak, and the helpless, those who need our love and care and concern.

(b) True greatness depends on our ability to put love into action and to respond to the call of the needy even as God had responded to our lives in the midst of our helplessness and estrangement from him. —Stephen G. Bray.

SUNDAY: JULY THIRTEENTH

MORNING SERVICE

Topic: Defeated While Winning
SCRIPTURE: I Kings 19:1–9.

We call to memory Elijah's heroic stand on Mount Carmel when he stood alone against 450 prophets of Baal worship. After rallying the people of God, he retreated to a place of quietness with his servant when a messenger of Jezebel the queen sent word that "about the same time the next day she would have his head." Now congratulatory messages were probably coming from many quarters for a successful crusade in the capital city, but this message was most unsettling to Elijah, and it would be to us too. He stood against 450 men, but his courage failed him when he came to face Jezebel. He is not to be overly criticized for his actions because she was a powerfully vile and wicked person. Nevertheless he is seen thundering loudly on Mount Carmel, and the next thing one knows is that he gets what few belongings he has and with his trusting servant flees for the hills.

I. God will not always be in the excitable acts of life even though they are religious.

(a) Let us remember Elijah on Mount Carmel less than two months before this experience at Mount Horeb. When nature seemed to get violent in its oppression of man, the common interpretation of the ancients was that the gods were angry. It is safe to say that in the ancient world, and even including the Jews, natural catastrophies meant that the gods—or as in the case of the Jews, God—were speaking. This was precisely the technique and psychology Elijah had used on Mount Carmel. He had asked God to speak by fire and so did the prophets of Baal.

(b) Now Elijah is seen standing on the mountainside and waiting for the voice of God as he is told. The fire comes just as it had done on Carmel, but the scripture says that God was not in the fire. Whereas on Mount Carmel God spoke loudly through the fire, now on Mount Horeb it is not so.

(1) Not all religious experiences are alike and neither should there be a design to make them so. There does seem to be an effort on the part of many to make every service a service of intense emotional display, or they consider the service a failure. Suppose that Elijah had said to himself, "God was in the fire at Carmel, so he must be in the fire now." Then when he did not hear the voice from the flames and when the flames died out, Elijah would have folded his tent and gone away disappointed because there was no presence of the Lord. To his credit he stayed and waited for God to manifest himself in another way than through fire.

(2) Most people make the mistake Elijah didn't make. The multi-media has placed Christianity on a stage with some stars and many of our youth parading with signs and loud noises about how excitable Jesus can make you. Some of this looks like madness to me, madness in the sense that the approach is the same as the approach of youth on drugs. It is predicated on how excited you can get and how that one can measure the excitement from Jesus as giving a greater kick than drugs. One sign actually read, "You can get high on Jesus."

(3) The church had better be very careful in attempting to place our outreach on the basis of equating God with luxury, equating God with show business, equating God with getting turned on high or emotionally charged, or just equating God with any one expression or standard. Then we limit him. God can and does come to us through exciting events, he does come to us through notable people, he does speak in many ways, but he cannot be limited to one area and I think that the church should be careful lest it give the impression that Jesus is now very popular and it is the "in thing" to turn on to this excitement.

(c) God did not come to Elijah in the fire or the whirlwind or the earthquake. He came to him in a quiet small whisper of a voice.

II. There is always the distinct possibility of having a condition of mind and heart that is alien to God.

(a) God asked Elijah, "What are you doing here?" He was out of the will of God. He was actually detrimental to God's kingdom because he was derelict in his duty. He had left his post of service. God's people were back in the homeland in need of their leader, and he was not there.

(b) Jesus indicated that there were two ways to life, two views to life, and two attitudes to life. One was considered for God, and one was against God. I don't think that God is neutral in life. I don't think that he can be put in a category of limbo. In the events which hold our lives together like threads in clothing God is there.

(c) Some of you are not Christians. You have never accepted God's son as your personal lord and savior. Why are you yet in this frame of mind and heart? "What are you doing here, Elijah?" Some of you refuse to be committed to the church and you claim to be Christians. "What are you doing here, Elijah?" Some of you retire from active participation each year and say: "I've done my part. Let another do it." Was that your only and highest motivation for service? "What are you doing here, Elijah?" Some of you know that you are allowing others to support the church financially and you are not doing your part. "What are you doing here, Elijah?" There is the distinct possibility that one can be in a condition of mind and heart which is alien to God. Elijah was in such a condition.

III. The transformation of Elijah took place in a broadening of his mind and experience.

(a) He observed all that was really happening around him. Now this sounds strange. Had he not always done so? I doubt it. When he was on Mount Carmel he was so busy being the hit of the show that he missed the real act. God had acted in great and awesome power on Mount Carmel, but Elijah, by so soon forgetting it and running, really indicated that he had not seen it all along. Now he is alone and the crowds are not applauding and urging him on. He really took a look at himself, and he saw God better too. He studied the various events such as fire, wind, and rock slides.

(b) Maybe we need what Elijah needed. We don't always need the revival atmosphere of a Mount Carmel, although a lot of folks want that all the time. Elijah had it, and it didn't last two days. He needed to take a close look at the events of his life and see God in them. This was a mind-broadening experience for him.

(c) A beautiful part of the story comes next. God tells him that he needs to have the experience of some new friends. It is after this that he meets Elisha, and they become fast friends. We, like Elijah, can become transformed people if we will take a good look at ourselves and our attitudes about God and if we will try to form new friendships. With all her faults the church is still the finest place I know to make lasting friendships. There is a wonderful tie that binds us together in the church.

(d) This old story is filled with deep and penetrating truths. It is the study of a man in despair, but he came through. It is the study of a man who needed his theology straightened out. It is the study of all of us who believe that where the action and where the excitement abounds God is. Not always so! Most of us live in the cave and not on Mount Carmel.—Merle Allison Johnson.

Illustrations

MEMORIES.   Greek legend tells about a woman who came to the River Styx to be ferried across to the region of departed spirits. Charon, the kindly ferryman, reminded her that it was her privilege to drink of the waters of the river Lethe and thus forget the life she was leaving. Eagerly she said, "I will forget how I suffered." "And," added Charon, "know too that you will forget how you have rejoiced." The woman said, "I will forget my failures." The old ferryman added, "And also your victories." She continued, "I will forget how I have been hated." "And also how you have been loved," spoke Charon. Then she paused to consider the whole matter. The end of the story is that she left the water of Lethe untasted, preferring to retain the memory even of sorrow and failure rather than to give up the memory of life's loves and joys.

LIFESAVER.   The *Titanic* sank on April 15, 1912, and the hundreds of survivors had Guglielmo Marconi to thank for saving them. Because of Marconi's invention of the wireless, the *Titanic* was urgently sending messages. It certainly was not Marconi's fault that some ships did not hear the messages or respond as quickly as possible. When the *Titanic* survivors arrived in New York City and learned that Marconi was staying there, they marched en masse to his hotel, cheered him, and shouted, "We owe our lives to you." Marconi could have demurred that he did not have them in mind when he invented the wireless, but they still would have known that he had saved them and been grateful to him.—David W. Richardson.

Sermon Suggestions

FACING TODAY'S GIANTS.   Text: I Sam. 17. (1) David dared to be different. (See v. 26.) (2) David recognized the giant for what it was. (See vv. 34–35.) (3) David prepared himself to meet the giant. (See vv. 38–40.) (4) David relied on God to help him defeat the giant. (See v. 45.)—Brian L. Harbour.

THE BROKEN THINGS OF LIFE.   Text: Acts 27:44. (1) Among the broken things of life one would think first of broken time. (2) The words have comforting suggestion for those who are suffering from broken health. (3) I want to go a little deeper from a shattered body to a shattered faith. (4) I apply the words to broken character, to those whose character is sorely broken and who today are on the margins of despair.—George H. Morrison.

Worship Aids

CALL TO WORSHIP.   "Come unto me, all ye that labor and are heavy laden, and I will give you rest. Take my yoke upon you, and learn of me; for I am meek and lowly in heart; and ye shall find rest unto your souls." Matt. 11:28–29.

OFFERTORY SENTENCE.   "Let the beauty of the Lord our God be upon us: and establish thou the work of our hands upon us; yea, the work of our hands establish thou it." Ps. 90:17.

OFFERTORY PRAYER.   O heavenly Father, we pray that thy blessings, which are as countless as the stars, may be so used as to bring light and love to thy children everywhere.

PRAYER.   Our Father, hear us, each one, as we present ourselves to thee. Hear our prayer of thanksgiving. Out of thy bounty thou hast blessed us many fold. Lines have fallen to us in pleasant places. Providence has given to us the privileges of freedom, of love, of opportunity, and of material blessing.

Forgive us, our Father, for allowing our complaints to betray the adoration due thy name. Intensify our love and our adoration for thee, and may our hearts truly praise thy name.

We are thankful today also, our Father, for salvation. Truly thou hast come to men in a wonderful way through thy son, Jesus Christ. Make us better disciples of him who has loved us when we were most unlovable and unworthy. May our feet and our hands be ready to do thy will at thy bidding.

Our Father, may we not pray selfishly today. Throughout the world are the masses of enslaved, hungry, and unclothed people who will spend this day in fear and sorrow. Make us uneasy, O God, in the presence of these needs, and may we in compassion be their brothers and sisters in sympathy and love. Strengthen the hand of missionaries around the world who are laboring to liberate humanity from the curse of sin and disease.

In this hour of divine worship, help us, our Father, to worship thee as we ought. May we leave tomorrow untouched until we have touched thee today. Bless each one present in thy church, and to those absent give counsel and encouragement. Visit those who are sick and convey the warmth of thy presence.

And now, our Father, we commit our hearts and our minds unto thee for this hour. May the words of our mouth and the meditations of our hearts be acceptable in thy sight.—C. Neil Strait.

EVENING SERVICE

Topic: Living Out Your Ideals
TEXT: Phil. 3:8.

I. You need to have an objective. (a) Paul had an objective. He knew where he was going. He was out to finish his race, to do the work the Lord Jesus had entrusted to him, "to declare the good news of God's love."

(b) There is a difference between having ideals and having an objective. Ideals are general; an objective is specific. I'm talking about a cause, something bigger than you are that you can give yourself to, so that you can say with Paul, "I don't count my life worth anything . . . I've got an objective, and that's what's important:

doing the work the Lord Jesus entrusted to me, declaring the good news of God's love!"

II. You need accountability. (a) The success of any runner is determined in part by accountability to the coach, to the team, and to the fans. And so it is with our lives. Without accountability we are just not going to be able to live out those ideals of ours. Without accountability we are going to settle for mediocrity every time. Without accountability we may get off to a good start, but we will never finish the race with the kind of record we had hoped for.

(b) Paul had accountability. "I just want to finish . . . doing the work the Lord Jesus entrusted to me." Declaring the good news of God's love was more than an objective for Paul. It was a trust.

III. You need an enabler. (a) Paul never lost sight of the fact that although Jesus had entrusted him with a specific work, the work remained Jesus' work. Paul never lost sight of the fact that for the work to succeed Jesus had to be in charge.

(b) You will find one who will share the burden of that accountability with you. For not only does Jesus give us the desire to live out our ideals, not only does he give us the conscience, but he also gives us the strength.—Arthur McPhee.

SUNDAY: JULY TWENTIETH

MORNING SERVICE

Topic: Amazing Grace

SCRIPTURE: Matt. 20:1–17 (RSV).

There are two ways of stating in contemporary terms what Jesus is saying here.

I. Jesus is saying that your worth as a person is not measured by how much you earn or how well you perform. Your worth is affirmed by God, your maker and sustainer—"the landowner." It is out of his "generosity," his holy will for your good, that God guarantees your value as a person.

(a) Among popular psychologies today there is much concern that we have a sense of self-worth, that we believe ourselves to be valued by someone, not least by ourselves. Such a sense of self-worth, we are told, is essential to our well-being, our mental health, and our social success.

(b) What is the source of our self-worth? On what ground may we believe we are worth anything to anybody?

(1) Our society tends to rate us in terms of measurable achievements: income, social position, and public recognition. That leaves most of us out in the cold. Most of us are anonymous, average, and ordinary —just regular people. Even our families don't always act as if we are worth much. Consequently many of us limp around with wounded egos, hiding our self-doubt, secretly wondering whether we are worth anything to anybody. And society says, "If you don't measure up, you're nothing."

(2) Jesus says something entirely different. He says that God affirms your worth as a person simply on the basis of his creative caring love for you. This is almost beyond belief, but it's precisely what Jesus came to declare and to live out. Jesus says, "Don't be misled by what society says; your value doesn't depend on material worth or social achievements but on the gracious will of God your maker." Don't even be misled by what religion is likely to say; your worth is not measured by your piety or your "good deeds" but by the unmerited freely-given grace of God, your creator and your savior.

(c) There's a sense in which this parable may have special relevance to those who are coming only lately to recognition as persons: members of minority and ethnic groups, women in society and in the marketplace. At this late date in our history— "the eleventh hour?"—Jesus is saying, "It's high time that you all acknowledge that every human being—regardless of ethnic, sexual, or national character—is a person valued by the God who made us all and who wills the good of us all." We are all his children.

II. Jesus is saying in this parable that the life-affirming love of God is not something you can earn; it is his free gift to you, to be accepted by you.

(a) Don't be misled by the usual teaching of religion which says that if you are good and behave yourself God will like you. The radical truth is quite different. God cares about you; like a cosmic parent he loves you. He offers you his care and support out of sheer "generosity," that is, his unwavering will for your good. You have only to accept the gift which he offers you.

(b) This is what Paul stated so dramatically in the teaching which has come to be known as "justification by faith." It might more accurately be called "justification by grace through faith," after the manner of Ephesians rather than Romans. This teaching was radical when Paul first dared to affirm it, just as radical as when Jesus had taught it only a few years earlier, and just as radical today even after centuries of affirmation and reaffirmation. Religion always tends to slip back into a set of moral rules to be obeyed and a set of ritual practices to be followed in order to win God's favor. Paul, flying in the face of his own tradition but following what he had learned about Jesus, said, What God is declaring in Jesus Christ is that he offers us his redeeming love—redeeming because also suffering—as "a gift to be received by faith" (Rom. 3:24–25).

(c) Paul could say this because Jesus had said it before him. That's the point of this parable, as of others. Indeed Jesus acted it out: "The Son of man came to seek and to save the lost" (Luke 19:10). God takes and holds the initiative in coming to you where you are. He offers you his caring love by which you may be healed and his creative power by which you may realize your potential.

(d) There's a risk in this. Some may say, "If the gift is free, I'll accept it and use it as I please." But any honest person knows that's phoney. Those who really open themselves to the freely-given grace of God realize full well that he will remake and transform their lives. Free grace is not cheap grace. Paul ran headlong into this and offered a creative response: "You are not your own; you were bought with a price. So glorify God in your body." Or as he put it just a few paragraphs later: "You were bought with a price; do not become slaves of men." (I Cor. 6:19–20; 7:23).— Chester Pennington.

Illustrations

MORE THAN MAN. A man who was merely a man and said the sort of things Jesus said would not be a great moral teacher. He'd either be a lunatic—on a level with the man who says he's a poached egg—or else he'd be the devil of hell. You must make a choice. Either this man was and is the Son of God or else a madman or something worse.—C. S. Lewis.

RESOURCES. Dietrich Bonhoeffer, facing certain death in a Nazi concentration camp, recited all his anxieties and uncertainties in a personal letter from his prison cell. Doubts flooded over him. Then mustering the resources of a lifetime, rooted and grounded in a Pentecost faith, he concluded: "Who am I? They mock me, these lonely questions of mine. Whoever I am, thou knowest, O God, I am thine."

Sermon Suggestions

MORE BELIEF AND FEWER BELIEFS. Scripture: Acts 17:22–28. (1) Jesus never required belief in a set of theological propositions before he would admit a seeker into his fellowship. He would say simply, "Follow me." The experience with him was the important thing, not the creed one might develop because of him. (2) Orthodox belief is not the Christian goal. An experience of the love of God in Jesus Christ is. (3) Only when truth has its inward side does it work its intended power. (4) God who was made known in Jesus Christ is worthy of our total devotion. In him is that truth for which we can live and die. Our personal experience with him makes all other things secondary by comparison.—John H. Townsend.

JESUS IS COMING AGAIN. Text: Acts 1:-10–11. (1) That day will be a day of revelation. (2) That day will be a day of salvation to those who have Christ as lord and savior of their lives. (3) There is a tragic side of the coming of Christ again. It will be a day of judgment.—Frank Pollard.

Worship Aids

CALL TO WORSHIP.   "Let us search and try our ways, and turn again to the Lord. Let us lift up our heart with our hands unto God in the heavens." Lam. 3:40–41.

INVOCATION.   Almighty God, our heavenly Father, who reignest over all things in thy wisdom, power, and love: we adore thee for thy glory and majesty, and we praise thee for thy grace and truth to us in thy Son our Savior. Grant us the help of thy Holy Spirit, we beseech thee, that we may worship thee in spirit and in truth.

OFFERTORY SENTENCE.   "The end of the commandment is charity out of a pure heart." I Tim. 1:5.

OFFERTORY PRAYER.   Dear Lord, as we travel the highways of life give us a generous and sympathetic spirit for all people in all circumstances of life.

PRAYER.   Almighty and everlasting God, from you we have received the gift of life, the call to commitment, the joy of service, and the burden of brotherhood. In acknowledgment of these your gifts, we bow in adoration. We know that we are not worthy to be called your children, for we have too often followed the desires of our own hearts and patterned ourselves after the hero of the moment rather than after the Lord of all the ages.

Forgive us our sinfulness, purify us with a new vision of our risen Lord, and raise us to newness of life.

In acknowledging our love for you, may we also fulfill the necessity of loving our brother, as we remember how it is written: "He who says he loves God and hates his brother is a liar."

We pray for the fellowship that ought to exist in your church. Help us to seek the forgiveness of brothers to whom we have spoken harshly. Heal us of the divisions of

heart and community that cause your church to be an object of scorn and ridicule. May your love always be present in our dealings with any man who claims the name of Christ, even all your children.

In our midst, may your spirit dwell continually so that we might speak the truth in love, seek your will for ourselves, assist those less skilled in the knowledge of Christ, and be strengthened ourselves.

We pray out of companionship with our Lord Jesus Christ.—Harold C. Perdue.

EVENING SERVICE

Topic: Growing in Love and Beauty
TEXT: "Inasmuch as you grow in love, you will grow in beauty. For love is the beauty of the soul." St. Augustine.

I. Ugliness takes many forms, but of all repulsive things the worst is a grotesquely deformed personality. Dirty streets, unkempt buildings, or even war-torn living quarters can't compare in ugliness to the hate and wantonness that produced them.

(a) Augustine brought sensitive Christian perception to bear on our misshapen spirits when he equated growth in love with growth in beauty. And even for those whose personalities have been permanently twisted there is hope, just as there is for the physically deformed who have learned not to permit themselves the indulgence of self-pity.

(b) Love is hope when practiced on a daily basis. Is it harder to say love is God than God is love? And with a little more verbal gymnastics, one might paraphrase Rom. 1:16 to read, "Love is the power of God unto salvation," and still be within the spirit of the law.

II. Love is the transforming action of God. No matter how often I allow myself to become bitter, cynical, or hostile, God reaches out gently through his word or a Christian friend and calls me back to his way of love. And that is the path from love unto beauty.

(a) Each of us has his or her perceptions of beauty. For those who see, God's handiwork often takes first place. Who can help being awed by the flaming pinks and oranges against a deep-blue sunset? For the blind the "feel" of things becomes a sense of beauty.

(b) The truest of all beauty lies in relationships. And it is in this the Christian can perform his greatest service by transforming ugly spirits into a thing of beauty through love.—David E. Hostetler.

SUNDAY: JULY TWENTY-SEVENTH

MORNING SERVICE

Topic: Our Mission in Three Words
TEXT: Matt. 24:14.

I. The first word is the key to understanding the other two. The "evangel" or "evangelion" is the way the church speaks about its central statement of faith and purpose.

(a) "Evangel" is a noun and thus the subject of every Christian verb, the point of reference of every Christian observation, and the starting place of every Christian pilgrimage. It is the word which is shared with all persons who "have ears to hear" because "faith comes by hearing the word of God."

(b) In an age that is known for its complexity, confusion, and conflict, the evangel is a word of comfort and hope.

(1) At a time of growing social distance and personal indifference it is the word of God that calls us to the love of neighbor.

(2) The word is the witness we bear because of the witness borne by God to himself in his divine self-disclosure through Jesus Christ.

(3) That word is not an idealism but a realism, not a speculation on what ought to be but a declaration on what is.

(c) At a time when foundations shake and crumble, it is a word of certitude. God is, and God's power and grace are dependable. Best of all, that word or evangel is the gospel which means "good news." Its central note is a promise that God has accepted us as we are and that all of creation is forever judged in terms of that acceptance and is safe in his care.

II. The second word is "evangelical." (a) Here is one of those words that ought to very naturally identify with the language of the church. It is the adjective form of the word "evangel." Its use is intended to suggest not just what we believe but what kind of people we are and not only the content of our persuasion but also the quality of our spirit or soul as a people. To say that one is evangelical is to accept the early definition of Protestants as a people who are "reformed, evangelical, and universal."

(b) Just as important is something that it implies about us, namely, that we are a beautiful people, *Christophorous* or "Christ-bearing" people filled with the attributes of the Spirit: "love, joy, peace, patience, kindness, goodness, faithfulness, gentleness, self-control" (Gal. 5:22). The sometimes divisive disputing over differing personal and social expressions of Christian faith and over the integrity of scripture—narrowly or broadly defined—serve only to distort the nobler meanings of a word that otherwise can convey something of the majesty and magnificence of a people who are called into a royal priesthood.

(c) To be evangelical is to participate in the word and spirit of God and to be drawn by that commitment into the company of others who are of like mind and spirit in the church.

III. If "evangel" is what we believe and "evangelical" is what we are, "evangelism" is what we do about it.

(a) Such joy cannot be contained. The compelling need to let others share in the prize which is every Christian's gift knows no bounds. Such is the nature of apostolic witness—the nature of our task in witnessing—with no other objective than that and to one end, namely, that everyone will love and glorify God always.

(b) It has seemed unfortunate that Christian evangelism has had such direct linkage with our regard for membership cultivation. Distinctions have been tragically obscured. Relating one's experience of the truth in Christ does indeed have an appeal of its own and has dramatically penetrated resistance to that truth. But witnessing for the sake of membership growth may dilute the truth, may circumvent it, or in some cases manipulate it in the interest of certain other goals. This need not happen, but the fact that it could happen is enough reason to argue against a view of evangelism and membership cultivation as parallel considerations.

(c) Our need is to discover afresh that beyond the sheer joy of telling the story, the church looks for those conditions that bear upon the lives of men and women and which prevent their hearing the church's word or accepting its promise. Thus the need for numbers is not only in order that others may, like ourselves, enjoy and glorify God forever but also in order that sorrow and suffering and bondage may be relieved in order that the word may at last become mission and that apostolic witness may at last become prophetic ministry.—Edsel A. Ammons.

Illustrations

LEFT IN DARKNESS.   A man was night fishing for striped bass at the base of the Guntersville dam in the Tennessee Valley river system. He had hung a gasoline lantern with a reflector over the side of the boat to attract the river minnows and in turn the hungry bass. Halfway through the night, the lantern went out, and he was left in darkness. Then came a strange realization. Behind that massive dam were billions of tons of pressure—water power. The turbines were humming and the giant dynamos were generating literally millions of kilowatt hours of power. But there the man sat forty feet from all that power in darkness, unable to utilize it. That is a parable and a symbol for all of us today. Here is God's great reservoir—God with all his resources churning out power that can make us better persons, bigger persons, happier persons, full of love and light and joy and peace. Yet too often we sit in darkness because we have no vital connection with the source of power.—Wayne Dehoney.

LEARNING TO LOVE.   A young rabbinical student one day burst into the office of his wise professor. The old Hasidic rabbi looked up rather surprised and said, "Yes, what can I do for you?" Without hesitation the young scholar said, "Sir, I just want you to know how much I love you." A sternness fell over the face of the old scholar, giving him a look of tempered steel as he said, "It is impossible for you to love me." "But I do love you," protested the young man. The old rabbi patiently listened as the young man continued to assure him of his sincere love. When he was finished the old Hasidic rabbi said, "Young man, you will be able to love me only when you know what makes me cry."—Kenneth Merckx.

Sermon Suggestions

SPEAK ALL THE WORDS.   Text: Acts 5:20 (RSV). (1) Social justice. (2) Personal redemption. (3) Comfort. (4) Stewardship. (5) Outreach. (6) Judgment. (7) Mercy.—Charles L. Allen.

SOME LAWS OF SPIRITUAL WORK.   Scripture: John 4:32–38. (1) Spiritual work is refreshing to body and soul. (2) There are seasons in the spiritual sphere—sowing seasons and reaping seasons. (3) Spiritual work links the workers in unity. (4) Spiritual work has rich rewards.—John A. Broadus.

Worship Aids

CALL TO WORSHIP.   "Know therefore that the Lord thy God, he is God, the faithful God, which keepeth covenant and mercy with them that love him and keep his commandments to a thousand generations." Deut. 7:9.

INVOCATION.   Mysterious God of creation, we are forever awed by the wonder of life here and now, beyond and forever. The more we learn of nature and existence, the more we ponder the puzzle of your conceptions. Through science and technology we have conquered boundaries unimaginable to our father's father.

Yet every answer leaves unknown, though sharper in its reality, the inexpressible nature of your word. The more we discover of the discernible, the more we anticipate our need of the eternal.—Richard D. Bausman.

OFFERTORY SENTENCE.   "Give unto the Lord the glory due unto his name: bring an offering, and come before him." I Chron. 16:29.

OFFERTORY PRAYER.   Our Father, take us with all of our failures and develop us after thine own heart. Give us more of the mind of the master, more of his spirit of compassion, and more of his sacrificial and loving heart.

A VACATION PRAYER.   Our God and gracious Father, accept the thanks of our hearts for those blessings which seem to us to have come nearest to ourselves: the love and service of parents, the understanding of friends, the sympathy of brother and sister, the instruction of teachers, the inspiration of preaching and poetry, the stirring of books, the delight of beauty and of music, the glory of light, the refreshment of rest, the nourishing of food, the fragrance of flowers, the grandeur of mountain and the majesty of the sea, the song of the birds and of brooks, the "wonderful clear night of stars," the color of field and forest, and the strength of the day and the soothing of the night. We bless thee for work and laughter, for eagerness and ambition, for thought and memory, for hope and faith, for consolation and insight, for quietness of heart and courage of spirit, for opportunities of service and sympathy, for the trust and the confidence, the promise and the progress of youth, and for all thy great goodness, Lord, we praise thee.—Boyd Edwards.

EVENING SERVICE

Topic: Religion Without Righteousness
TEXT: Amos 5:24.

I. The first sign of religion without righteousness is living on the level of the trivial.

(a) Perhaps the most damaging image of the minister of our day is one of a typical clergyman who is busy oiling ecclesiastical machinery. We destroy the moral implications of our faith by occupying ourselves with trivial things while the world blazes around us and we are not even aware of it.

(b) Amos was one of the first great religious leaders to see this truth. He knew that religion always loses its moral tone when its practitioners become preoccupied with trivialities.

II. The second sign of religion without righteousness is failure to identify with the weak, the poor, and the dispossessed. The contemporary church seems to have discovered ways to minister to those who control society. But this does not mean that the church can relax in its effort to speak to persons who do not have power, to people who are in dire need, and to groups who struggle for the rights of the weak and who speak for the voiceless and stand for the downtrodden.

III. Religion loses its righteousness when it substitutes words for actions.

(a) Amos rolled up his sleeves and waded into the circumstances of his day to do what he could to facilitate the will of God in the lives of his people.

(b) Jesus was a master with words, and the common people heard him gladly. Then, as he rode the crest of popularity, he announced to his closest friends, "We're going to Jerusalem." They tried to dissuade him. But his only answer to the most persistent of the apostles of caution was, "Get thee behind me, Satan" (Matt. 16:23).—Larry Baker.

SUNDAY: AUGUST THIRD

MORNING SERVICE

Topic: Out of Alignment (The Transfiguration)

TEXT: Matt. 17:6–7 (RSV).

The disciples saw Jesus "transfigured" —changed. But they were changed too. They were never the same again. And it was a change for the better. It was a day of growth and of renewal for them. The consequences of that day keep marching on down through the centuries. They touch us and our land and this day and this hour. Christian public worship is a little clearing in time provided through faith and tradition for us to be participants in the transfiguration and to be changed and renewed ourselves. That is why these doors have been opened again this day. That is why the hymns are sung and the prayers offered and the scripture read and the sermon preached, and the stained glass windows reflect the sky and the air itself is filled with a doxology.

I. In the language of our day we might say that Peter and James and John were realigned on the mount of transfiguration.

(a) Worship is a time for realignment, to refuse to accept our cold or greedy or anxious or self-centered ways as natural and uncorrectable. We come here to be reminded of who we are and to be renewed to participate in the promise and pleasure God expressed in the transfiguration.

(b) If Jesus were to walk with us through one of our vast parking lots, is it not possible to hear him saying, "See those steel radial tires on this car? They will soon be no good at all; one side of the tread is almost worn down, while the other has miles of good left in it which will be wasted because something is out of balance."

II. What are similar signs that individuals or churches or nations are out of alignment?

(a) Amos offered a plumb line to Israel and minced no words about the unbalanced wear and tear he saw in that nation's life. (See Amos 2:6–7.)

(b) There are symptoms in every public crime and private vice, in every war and every want, that we too are out of plumb, out of balance. There are as well personal symptoms of our need for realignment— short tempers and paralyzing anxieties and greed, lowered energy and many physical ailments rooted in sickness of spirit.

(c) How do we get realigned? That requires a revelation, a measuring stick that is in perfect harmony with the universe, a plumb line set by God into the heart of his people, a Christ, a Lord and Savior. Despite all the human limitations of our services, still where "two or three gather in his Spirit," in his purpose, in his name, Christ is there. His plumb line comes to its silent centering against the tilt and tip of our days. The whole event of Christians gathering together for prayer and praise, for celebration of word and sacrament is a human-divine encounter designed for joyous and liberating realignment.

III. More than alignment keeps us returning in season and out to the plumb line of corporate worship, to the site and sense of the transfiguration.

(a) If you have stood and watched your car on the alignment machine, it is really anchored there. For the time being it is not going anywhere. And that is proper and essential for that moment. But it was not made to stay forever high and lifted up on that contraption. Human beings are not created to stay in perpetual formal worship.

(b) Jesus and the disciples came down from the mount of transfiguration. Jesus saw to that! There was work to be done. So too prayer and worship and attendance upon the inner life with God is not simply a matter of realignment. It includes that wonderful moment of our response when we employ our human freedom which marks us in God's image, when we engage the gear, get out of park or neutral and open the gate allowing the energy of the urgent and loving and creative God to flow through us with moving and thrusting vitality, out into the pain and beauty of the road ahead with its traffic and resting places, with its dangers and its work, and with its ending place with the almighty God of us all.—W. Browne Barr.

Illustrations

MOUNTAINTOP AND VALLEY. Raphael painted a magnificent picture of the transfiguration of Christ. The picture is divided into two parts. The upper part shows Christ and the disciples on the mountaintop. The face of Christ, a revelation of love and beauty and goodness of God, shines like the sun, and the disciples around him are obviously having one of those peak experiences when the meaning all comes through. The lower part is a picture of human need—the sick boy, the worried father, the mother on her knees in prayer. And you know that the sick boy will be healed, the worried father will find peace, and the mother's prayer will be answered. The energy found in the mountaintop experience of God will be used for the healing of the human family in the valley.—Winfield S. Haycock.

WHICH AM I? No one of us is wholly and completely one person. There is within each one of us a light touch of the saintly in our best moments but enough of that which is devilish to prevent a claim of sainthood. There is a bit of courage to be found within us, but it is generously tempered by a dash of plain cowardice here and there. There are gracious impulses of generosity in our shining hours, but there are frequent lapses into unattractive selfishness. There are times when we can love lavishly and feel the better for it, but there are times when we wrestle with the dark enemies of envy and jealousy. There are times when a greatness of spirit enables us to forgive a grievous wrong, but there are long stretches of time when we nurture the grievance and gather its bitter fruit with unholy delight. There are times when we stand tall and strong alongside a worthy principle or a commendable ideal, but there are other times when we slip so easily into the luring compromises of moral mediocrity. There are times when we behold with astonishment the emergence of the best self from within and we are satisfied, but there have been other hours we would forget if we but could when we are bound to say with honest confession, "I know I was at my worst then." —Charles L. Copenhaver.

Sermon Suggestions

ABOVE THE SHADOWS. Text: Ps. 112:7. (1) To outsoar the shadows of our night demands an indomitable will. (2) The ability to outsoar our night demands a courageous faith. (3) To outsoar the shadows of our night demands a partnership with God.—Fred B. Chenault.

AND ARE WE YET ALIVE? Text: Charles Wesley's hymn, "And are we yet alive?" (1) To the activity of God in his world? (2) To the needs of God's children about us? (3) To the purpose of the church? (4) To the timely treasures of the faith? (5) To the heritage that we have?—Gerald R. Duncan.

Worship Aids

CALL TO WORSHIP. "He that dwelleth in the secret place of the most High shall abide under the shadow of the Almighty. I will say of the Lord, He is my refuge and my fortress: my God; in him will I trust." Ps. 91:1-2.

INVOCATION. Eternal God, in whom we live and move and have our being, whose face is hidden from us by our sins and whose mercy we forget in the blindness of our hearts: cleanse us, we beseech thee, from all our offenses and deliver us from proud thoughts and vain desires, that with lowliness and meekness we may draw near to thee, confessing our faults, confiding in thy grace, and finding in thee our refuge and our strength.

OFFERTORY SENTENCE. "Seek ye first the kingdom of God, and his righteousness, and all these things shall be added unto you." Matt. 6:33.

OFFERTORY PRAYER. Almighty God, whose loving hand hath given us all that we possess: grant us grace that we may honor thee with our substance, and remembering the account which we must one day give, may be faithful stewards of thy bounty.

PRAYER. Our Father and our God, it is time to pray, and in the silence of the moment, we think to ourselves, What shall we say when we talk to thee? For truly thou dost know us better than we know ourslleves; thou dost know what we need even before we ask.

Thous knowest the mistakes and the wrong that we have done. Thou knowest that at times we have been selfish, stubborn, and difficult to live with.

Thou knowest the "couldn't-care-less" attitude we so often have for someone different and for the person who really needs us. Thou knowest the pretending we do with each other and the false images we so often project. Thou knowest when we are afraid and timid and when we feel insecure.

Thou knowest the struggles that confront us, the things we wrestle with, and the things that irritate and gnaw at us and cause us to be anything but confident and sure.

Thou knowest the hectic pace of living under which we exist—the things we run to, the things we run after, and the tensions that pull us apart and keep us from being whole.

O God, what should we say when we talk to thee? Truly thou dost know us better than we know ourselves. Lord, the very best thing we can do is simply to thank thee for knowing us, for knowing our feeble frame of mind, and for knowing our life, our world, and our circumstances. We thank thee that, even after thou hast known us so completely, thou dost still abide with us and seek to bring us hope and love and the guiding spirit we need.

Lord God, we believe in thee, and so we ask thy power to come among us. We believe in thy son, Jesus Christ, and so we ask that his message of love may be the key to our living. We believe in the Holy Spirit, and so we ask that he may comfort and direct us when we are sick, when we are lost, and when we are in need of thy tender care.—W. T. Bloy.

EVENING SERVICE

Topic: Praise the Lord!

SCRIPTURE: Ps. 150 (RSV).

I. *Praise the Lord anywhere!* The psalmist writes, "Praise the Lord in his sanctuary and praise the Lord in his mighty firmament."

(a) Praise God in his sanctuary set aside to worship one who is from everlasting to everlasting. Worship his holy name with "a thousand tongues to sing our great redeemer's praise." Praise him, aware of his majesty in contrast to your misery as you confess your sins, "I am not alive, I only exist; I do not love, I only pretend," and praise him as you feel the forgiveness of a faithful father, "Listen! Your life is good; pick it up and walk."

(b) Praise God as you give of your money, knowing you have freely received and you must freely give; as you offer more than the weight of wealth, giving the beauty of your being "just as I am, without one plea."

(c) Praise the Lord in his mighty firmament for his temple is not confined to pulpit, pews, and lighted cross. It extends from mountain peak to sea level, from streets to stadiums, from this side of the tracks to the other side of the tracks, in country and city.

II. *Praise the Lord anyhow!* The psalmist writes, "Praise him with trumpet sound, lute, harp, timbrel, dance, strings, pipe, sounding cymbals." Our feeling for God cannot be hemmed in by form or order, tradition or innovation, dogma or denomination. God is so great as to be praised anyhow in any way. Praise him with Bach and blues, with stately hymns and emotional spirituals, with organ and trumpet, drum, guitar, tambourines, and dance. "Dance, then, wherever you may be; I am the Lord of the dance, said he." Praise the Lord in spite of and nevertheless, even when your "hosanna has passed through great whirlwinds of doubt."

III. *Praise the Lord anybody!* The psalmist says, "Praise him, all peoples, all inhabitants of the world, both low and high, rich and poor together." Praise him young and old, male and female, long hair, short hair, and no hair. The Lord is mighty to be praised. He is the Lord of all hosts. He delivers Noah from flooding waters; he delivers slaves from Egypt; he calls fishermen to his side; he raises people from grave's dark death to life's bright light. Praise God, anybody, everybody—intellectual and illiterate, urban and rural, preacher and parishioner, saint and sinner. Praise the Lord, anybody, everybody —he is exceedingly great; his name is excellent in all the earth; he is the light of our salvation; he is our dwelling place in all generations.—Phillip H. Barnhart.

SUNDAY: AUGUST TENTH

MORNING SERVICE

Topic: Do You Cross Your Fingers?
TEXT: Matt. 9:28.
When two blind men followed Jesus pleading with him to restore their sight, the master responded to their plea by asking, "Do you believe that I am able to do this?" He might have added, "Or do you have your fingers crossed?" The blind men responded by affirming their belief Jesus could do what they asked. The account ends with the words, "And their eyes were opened."

I. It is a sobering truth that in all of our human ventures belief is essential to the creation of that in which we believe.

(a) Creative victories are won not when we retreat from challenge but when we accept challenge with faith and in scorn of the consequences. In one of the most thrilling passages in literature there is a description of Leonidas at Thermopylae, resolved to stand and die for his country's cause. But Leonidas wished to save two young men by sending them home with a message to Sparta. He was met by the answer, "We are not here to carry messages but to fight."

(b) We are not here to carry messages or to spend our energies on trivialities. We are here to answer the challenge of evil with dedication to the good because we believe in it. We are here to sustain and support the values that endure beyond time and tide. Involved as we are in moral struggle, we are here to lend our strength to the kingdom of God and to create that in which we believe.

II. It is suggestive to notice only that we believe in order to create, but also that we believe in order to know. Anselm of Canterbury, active during the last quarter of the eleventh century, wrote, "I believe in order to understand." He sounded a solid note, for understanding of anything awaits belief in it.

(a) If we persist in believing what isn't so we are likely to find it difficult to believe the truth. The Christian faith is by no means uncritical or irrational, but it still remains true that we believe in order to know and to understand. Jesus put the truth simply when he said, "He who wills to do . . . shall know." That is to say, knowledge of the truth awaits belief enough to experiment with it. "Faith is an experiment which ends in an experience," said Dean Inge. It is willingness to risk experiment in order to attain validating experience.

(b) Nobody ever discovers the redemptive power of the Christian faith apart from a willingness to experiment with it in the interests of belief. Either we believe enough to risk our ventures in obedience to the master or we never know the redemptive power of faith in him. Debate proves nothing, but an experiment which ends in an experience is decisive.

(c) Belief in Jesus Christ or belief in God is something more than an affirmation of fact. It is an affirmation of trust, of confidence. If I believe in my neighbor, I would vote for him in an election or I might recommend him for a responsible position. I might seek his advice and support in my own ventures. If I believe in Christ as a revelation of both the nature and the will of God, I willingly risk experiment in order to know the truth of what I believe.

(d) The blind men who came to Jesus seeking healing believed in the love and the healing power of the master before their experience validated their belief. "Do you believe that I am able to do this?" They did not cross their fingers. They responded, "We do believe," and "their eyes were opened."

III. When we push the matter further we discover that we believe in order to be what we ought to be.

(a) Without belief in God our ethical ideals are simply human inventions without the slightest divine sanction or authority. They are not imperatives. On the contrary, they are electives. We can take them or leave them, depending on our inclination in the matter. But if we believe in God revealed in the mind and spirit of Jesus, the ethical values implicit in the sermon on the mount are the essential demands the universe itself makes upon us. We are constrained to obedience.

(b) We know, if we believe in Christ, that there are no little denials of big principles. If God in Christ is sovereign, then big principles are eternal, and every denial is a big denial and a mighty tragedy. Salvation is in recognizing that when a man chooses a dishonest policy over a great principle he is indulging in a deadly sin which, if persevered in, will destroy him. When he chooses integrity of spirit and devotion to principle in spite of opposition and difficulty he is supported by the deepest reality in the universe, the living God.

IV. We need to believe in order that God may find us. Aware of their need and believing in the master, two blind men opened the door to God's power in Christ. Both love and power were there awaiting belief. "Do you believe that I am able to do this?" When we believe, God finds us with his power and his love.

(a) The essential and ultimate affirmation of the New Testament is that God is seeking us. He finds us in our believing. We do not find him. C. S. Lewis notes wisely that it could not be otherwise. "If Shakespeare and Hamlet could ever meet it must be Shakespeare's doing. Hamlet could initiate nothing." It is the creator who initiates relationships with his created. So it is God who is seeking us far more ardently than we ever seek him.

(b) God is seeking us whether we are aware of it or not. We may suppose we can dodge him, but we merely get away from one place where matters are bad to another place where matters are worse and with the same wistful eyes staring at us. We are not free from his seeking no matter how much we may wish to avoid him. Never is it true that we cannot manage to find him. Always it is true that we cannot manage to lose him.

(c) It is in believing in the love of God revealed in Christ that we come to know God has found us. In that knowledge is our salvation and our hope. "Do you believe that I am able to find you?" Or do you cross your fingers?—Harold Blake Walker.

Illustrations

PRAY FOR ME.   George Bernard Shaw, a Protestant and a nonconformist, had a remarkable friendship with a Roman Catholic abbess, Sister Laurentia of the Order of St. Benedict. At the end of one of many letters to her, Shaw wrote: "P. S. I don't mind being prayed for. When I play with my wireless set I realize that all the sounds of the world are in my room; for I catch them as I alter the wave length receiver— German, French, Italian, and unknown tongues. The ether is full of prayers too, and I suppose if I were God I could tune in to them all. Nobody can tell what influence these prayers have. If the ether is full of impulses of good will to me so much the better for me; it would be shockingly unscientific to doubt it. So let the sisters give me all the prayers they can spare; and don't forget me in yours."

KEEPING ON COURSE.   Early in the last century, in the days when the great fleets of sailing ships went out of New Bedford to scour the oceans of the world for whale oil, the most famous skipper of them all was Eleazar Hull. He had no formal navigational training of any kind. When asked how he guided his ship infallibly over the desert of waters, he would reply, "Well, I go up on deck, listen to the wind in the riggin', get the drift of the sea, and take a long look at the stars. Then I set my course." One day however the march of time caught up with this ancient mariner. The insurance company whose agents covered the vessels of Captain Hull's employers declared that they would no longer write a policy for any ship whose master did not meet certain formal standards of education in the science of navigation. Three of the company's top executives waited on Captain Hull and put their dilemma as tactfully as possible. To their amazement the old fellow responded enthusiastically. He had, it appeared, always wanted to know something about "science," and he was entirely willing to spend several months studying it. He did so. Then he returned to his ship, set out to sea, and was gone for two years. When the skipper's friends heard that he was putting into port again, they met him in an informal delegation at the docks. They inquired eagerly how it felt to navigate by the book after so many years of doing it the other way. "It was wonderful," Captain Hull responded. "Whenever I wanted to know my position, I'd go to my cabin, get out all the charts, work through the proper equations, and set a course with mathematical precision. Then I'd go up on deck, get the drift of the sea, listen to the wind in the riggin', and take a long look at the stars. And correct my computations for error."—William Muehl.

Sermon Suggestion

MY LORD AND MY GOD!   Text: II Pet. 1: 16. (1) At the transfiguration Jesus appeared for the first time as the Son of God in majesty and glory. (2) At the transfiguration Peter, James, and John encountered God in the form of a man they had known and loved. (3) At the transfiguration the disciples began to understand that radical faith in God means not a religious system but rather a face-to-face relationship.— James G. Munroe.

Worship Aids

CALL TO WORSHIP.   "Oh that men would praise the Lord for his goodness, and for his wonderful works to the children of men! For he satisfieth the longing soul, and filleth the hungry soul with goodness." Ps. 107:8–9.

INVOCATION.   O God, we thank you for leading us until this hour. Direct us in the days ahead through the difficult places of decision. When the call seems clouded and the road is in poor repair, grant the boldness to face the future in faith and to fortify ourselves in truth. Help us to be ready to recognize our own inadequacy and your sufficiency.—John M. Drescher.

OFFERTORY SENTENCE.   "Every good gift and every perfect gift is from above, and cometh down from the Father of lights." Jas. 1:17.

OFFERTORY PRAYER.   Dear Father, help us to be ever concerned to find thy way for our lives, and may we never be satisfied to give thee our second best in return for thy great gift of love.

PRAYER.   Infinite Father, in the stillness of this moment, let the hush of your presence fall upon us that we in adoration may become aware that we cannot renew ourselves but can only be renewed by you; that we cannot forgive ourselves but can only accept your forgiveness; that we cannot love one another as we ought but must allow you to love others through us.

Forgive us for coming to this service of worship as if it were only a lecture exercising our intellects alone. Transform us in the depths of our being. Forgive us although we have been unforgiving, love us although we have been unloving, and hear us although we have been unwilling to listen to the cries of our fellow men. We confess that we want the church to sing lullabies, even though the gospel calls us to be Christian revolutionaries. For our sins of omission and commission, we ask your forgiveness.

Our thanks rise like mists in the morning sun as we reflect on the gifts we have received. Truly the earth is the Lord's and the fulness thereof. From the mystery of your creativeness we have been given life with emotion and intellect, the capacity to experience, to love, and to learn. As the past stretches behind us to the void before creation, so the future looms ahead with endless possibilities as it is lived in the context of your will. For this fact we are eternally thankful.

O Lord, hear our prayer for growth. Lead us beyond the hypnotic call of the world that the end of life is success and pleasure to the awareness that we only find life when we lose life to Christ. Strengthen us as modern-day disciples of Jesus Christ that we not only will be loyal churchmen and women but also will live for Christ in the workaday world. We have come to this service with a variety of needs and problems, conflicts, and desires. Direct us into the pathway of Christian fulfillment where we receive answers that bring an unfolding of life's myriad possibilities.

In this period of prayer we not only pray for ourselves but also for our church, our nation, and our world. Through the mystery of intercession, heal those of our fellowship who lie this day in illness, those who struggle with disrupted family relationships, and those who face difficult and trying decisions. Use our concern and love as the vehicle to wholeness, restoring them through Christ.

So challenge each of us in this time of worship that we place Christ at the center of our lives, heeding his call to take up our cross and follow him.—Carroll Emerson Ward.

EVENING SERVICE

Topic: On the Meaning of Redemption
TEXT: Eph. 1:7.

Three words in the Bible will help us to understand the meaning of redemption.

I. One is the word *agaradzo*. It means to go down into the market where merchandise is to be found and to buy it there.

(a) We find this meaning in Rom. 7:11 that man was sold unto sin. He is in the junk pile of castaways, driven out of the garden and out of fellowship with God and sold unto sin. Jesus goes to that junk pile and buys him back.

(b) The Mosaic law provided for the redemption of both property and person if they had been sold. (See Lev. 25.) The property was to be redeemed by the payment of the proper and just price, and the person was to be redeemed by personal kinsmen who would pay the full mortgage and the full requirements.

(c) Now Jesus came into the world market of mankind to buy us back from the wickedness of sin and from Satan. He paid the full, adequate, and just price for it, even the price of his blood.

II. The second word is *exagardzo*, to buy out of the market—not to buy it and leave it there but to buy it and take it out. And so Jesus comes to buy and to fetch out of the market that which has been sold unto sin. (See I Cor. 6:20.) In I Pet. 1:18–19 it is said that we are redeemed or bought back not by gold and silver or by any of the other material things of the world but by the precious blood of Christ.

III. The third word, *lutroo*, means free or loose. This refers to a person who sold himself or was sold by somebody else into slavery. It is the picture of a friend who pays the debt and fine of a prisoner and sets him free.

(a) Bought and set free is the message of redemption. Jesus Christ looked down from heaven and saw men and women bound with the shackles of evil. He said, "God being my helper, I will smite that wicked thing some day and set the people free." And he did.

(b) We who are redeemed by the blood of Christ may rejoice in the liberty wherewith Christ hath set us free. The mothering source of all freedom is religious freedom, the freedom of the soul. When that freedom is lost all other freedoms go with it.—M. E. Dodd.

SUNDAY: AUGUST SEVENTEENTH

MORNING SERVICE

Topic: Refreshed Through You

TEXT: Philem. 1:7.

There are some people in whose company we always are at our best. They draw out of us qualities and characteristics which create good feelings on every hand. In these relationships there is great reward. Philemon was one in whose company other people were inspired to be at their best. That happens to be the compliment the apostle Paul paid to Philemon. In Philemon's company Paul and others felt themselves to be at their best. Philemon was a good and gracious man. To be one who inspires the best in others at least three things are involved.

I. The capacity to bless and refresh other lives begins not with oneself but with the source of all refreshment, the Lord Christ.

(a) I never have been comfortable with the designation, "a self-made man." When that is said about a person, I understand the meaning involved and am glad enough to give credit to that person for using his talents well. But at a deeper level I am convinced that there really is no such thing as a "self-made man." The real problem that attaches to this designation is the way a so-called self-made person begins to worship his creator—himself—considering himself to be the author of all that he is and is becoming.

(b) I doubt that being in the company of this type of person is very inspirational. The allegedly self-made man might impress us, but I cannot believe that he would refresh us. Not self-made individuals but Christ-centered individuals constitute the truly inspirational lives around us.

II. One also has a love for people, following upon that initial love for Christ.

(a) When Paul wrote to Philemon asking him to forgive a runaway slave, moreover a slave who had stolen something, he was counting on Philemon's understanding and upon his love. If we accept the premise that "the people are the enemy," as certain spokesmen claim, then forgiveness is unlikely and reconciliation remote and brotherhood an empty ideal. But where people are loved and given the benefit of the doubt, amazing things occur. Onesimus, a wrong-doing slave, could be received as a friend and brother by Philemon because Philemon cared for others.

(b) Dick Sheppard said of the church, "The church often failed because it loved the souls of people but not people themselves." Philemon had to love people to receive back a runaway slave; he had truly to care.

III. Our lives in Christ and our love for others may require us to do the unexpected thing.

(a) Paul asked a slave-owner to welcome his errant slave and then incredibly to abolish the slave-master relationship. Onesimus was to be received as an equal, "as a beloved brother." The magnitude of that act probably escapes us now, but if we had lived in the first century such behavior would be mind boggling. But that was what Paul asked of Philemon, with Paul also doing an unusual thing, promising to make good any indebtedness or loss of property which Philemon had suffered.

(b) Doing the unexpected thing repeatedly is the experience of people who take the New Testament seriously. That book abounds with surprising things such as forgiving others seventy times seven, doing good to those who hurt you, giving with no thought of reward, or going the second mile when you expected one to be enough. For Philemon the unexpected thing was embracing a former slave as a fellow-servant of Christ. For every Christian the unexpected requirement one day or the next will come.

(c) We never know what opportunity God will provide to enable us to do something which may bless and refresh lives other than our own. No day need be humdrum and no experience uneventful if we alert ourselves to what God may require. If we perceive Christians to be those who impart refreshment to the world, then we always will be ready to do the unexpected thing.—John H. Townsend.

Illustrations

ABOVE REWARD. A visitor to New York was impressed by the courtesy of a bus driver toward the passengers on his bus. After the crowd had thinned out, he spoke to him about it. "Well," the driver explained, "about five years ago I read in the newspaper about a man who was included in a will just because he was polite. 'What in the world?' I thought. 'It might happen to me.' So I started treating passengers like people. And it makes me feel so good that now I don't care if I never get a million dollars."—Robert J. McCracken.

IN GOD'S IMAGE. I am made from the dust, but it is in God's image that I am made. I am God's creature, one of millions living upon the earth, yet even the very hairs of my head are numbered.—Alan Paton.

Sermon Suggestions

LESSONS FROM THE VINEYARD. Scripture: Matt. 21:33–43. The shortcomings that were the undoing of the people in the parable are shortcomings to which we too are liable. (1) We cannot relate to God with smugness. (2) We cannot forget that our membership in the church of Christ is due to the generosity of God's grace. (3) We cannot presume that we are in control of God's kingdom. (4) We cannot put ourselves beyond the possibility of punishment. (5) We cannot regard ourselves as indispensable because, now as always, God can raise up others to take our place. —*Dimension.*

LIVING WATERS. Text: John 7:37–39. (1) The source of this spiritual flow. (2) The secret of this spiritual flow. (3) The sufficiency of this spiritual flow.—Stephen F. Olford.

Worship Aids

CALL TO WORSHIP. "Bless the Lord, O my soul: and all that is with me, bless his holy name." Ps. 103:1.

INVOCATION. O God our father, who dost dwell in the high and holy place, with him also that is of a humble and contrite heart: grant that, through this time of worship in thy presence, we may be made the more sure that our true home is with thee in the realm of spiritual things and that thou art ever with us in the midst of our common walk and daily duties so that the vision of the eternal may ever give meaning and beauty to this earthly and outward life.

OFFERTORY SENTENCE. "Thy prayers and thine alms are come up for a memorial before God." Acts 10:4.

OFFERTORY PRAYER. We pray thee, O God, to give us sight to see the Christ, the insight to chose him, the steadfastness to follow him, and the stewardship of loyalty represented in these gifts offered in his name.

PRAYER. Our Father, thou art greater than our greatest thought of thee and higher than our highest aspiration, yet into thy presence we may come with an honest and contrite heart, a genuine need, and a touch of wonder. For thou art God whose domain extends from the farthest star to the most unnoticed person. And thy mystery and simplicity are both too much for us to see.

Today with thy help we search for a religion with the ring of authority. And as we pay attention to our lives and with grace remold their meaning, show us the holy amidst the commonplace, the miraculous in the routine. Having looked at life with artistic eye, let us never again dismiss our lives with half-glances, cold stares, or the condescending eye unseeing.

This is thy creation: thy blue sky, thy clouds, thy rain, and thy falling leaves. The passing of the seasons is more than a process of weather; it is thy quarterly changing of the guard at the palace which houses summer and winter, fall and spring.

To live is to participate in drama. Yet we confess that we have not always played our part with grace. We have called things god which are not God. We have worshiped at the wrong altars and burned incense at the wrong shrines. We have not loved when we have been loved and not trusted each other when we have been entrusted with life by thee. We have refused to accept wholeheartedly the good intent of others in the mending of differences.

Father, through the shadows cast on life by the immature kind of pride, wilt thou show us that even our virtues can become thy problem? Wilt thou stiffen our convictions and at the same time make more gentle our compassion, lest, in our desire to uphold what is right, we do what is terribly wrong in trying to play thy part and in failing to serve thee?

Bring us today into the life of freedom. Deliver us from the stupidity of being wholly at the mercy of the thoughts of the neighbors. Remind us that the wisest men are the last to criticize and that the critic is bearing careless testimony of his ignorance of thee.

Wilt thou bless our children if we be parents; wilt thou bless our parents, for all of us are children? In our daily relationships, help us to construct, not to destroy, and to practice in our private families the way of life we wish for in the family of man.

And help us to bring in tomorrow by a steadfast loyalty to our principles today. For today is thy kingdom come and today may thy will be done.—Paul R. Davis.

EVENING SERVICE

Topic: The Upper Room Communicants
TEXT: Acts 2:42.

I. This was a praying church. At the Jordan River while Jesus prayed, the Spirit descended upon him; and in the upper room while the disciples prayed, the blessed Spirit descended upon them. Let's keep this to the forefront in our thinking: the Spirit comes upon praying people. That which he did in the past, he will do again.

II. This was a concerned church. In the upper room every known step they could take had been taken in obedience to the divine command. These inadequate men longed to be adequate so that the world might know he had sent them.

III. This was a contrite church. In the upper room people were plagued with their own spiritual infidelity.

(a) They had failed him; some had lied about him; some had doubted him; all had forsaken him. What a wailing wall that upper room must have been! Was there ever such a valley of Baca? Were the angels ever so busy storing tears—bitter, scalding, salty tears—into the bottle of memory as in those ten days?

(b) These folk were rending their hearts and not their garments. Their harps were on the willows. An old Christian said, "There are only two places for God's people—in the dust and in heaven." Only in one or the other are we safe. These men in quest of the Spirit were in the dust—blessed dust—better than gold dust if in our prostration we seek the power of the Lord and see his glory.

IV. This was a confessing church. In that upper room no one ran his theological inch tape over his neighbor. They were all with one accord. No lip shot out in criticism; no finger pointed at a supposed leakage that hindered the coming of the promised power. They waited on the Lord and renewed their strength.—Leonard Ravenhill.

SUNDAY: AUGUST TWENTY-FOURTH

MORNING SERVICE

Topic: Follow Me
SCRIPTURE: John 21:1–19.

In the mist of an early dawn we see Jesus and the disciples by the shore of Tiberias, the same shore where earlier he had called the disciples to "follow me" as they were mending their fishing nets. His gracious invitation, spoken with an imperative note, was more like a summons. And it had set them on an adventure of the most incredible events. There was the arrest, the trials, and the unspeakable tragedy of Calvary. Their sun seemed to set at midday.

I. We hear Peter announcing his *intention,* saying, "I'm going fishing." (a) It was not in the positive tone that those of us in the modern fraternity of fishermen would speak it. It was the expression of frustration and a lost sense of purpose. In this moment Peter lost sight of having been called by Christ to a great task.

(b) Christ had called him to wide horizons and high purpose, but he was ready to limit himself. We always settle for much less when we allow our intention to be in conflict with his will for us.

II. Peter's action reveals the power of *influence.* The record states that a half dozen of the other disciples followed his example and went along with him. In like manner what a powerful influence our example has in regard to what we do about the call of Christ. Our loved ones, our associates and friends—what is our influence on them when it comes to the things of God in our life?

III. "They went forth immediately" speaks of the *impulse* of their action. There was no consideration of other claims upon them. Their action seemed dictated by the impulse of the moment. Still today there are many who allow their lives to be determined by circumstances or caprice or chance. They have no master's plan for their lives.

IV. As we follow the sequence of events with Peter, we are not surprised to see that his intention, influence, and impulse led him to *ineffectiveness:* "they caught nothing."

(a) It was not because they didn't try hard enough. They had toiled all night. It was not because they did not know how to fish. Peter had been a commercial fisherman.

(b) We also have been busy. No one can blame our ineffectiveness, our empty nets, on a lack of effort. But our life nets are often so empty. There is always an emptiness when we live apart from Christ. "They caught nothing." How pathetically do those seven men in that nighttime fishing expedition show us our need of letting Christ direct our lives.

(c) As the gray dawn shimmered on their tired bodies, they were making their way to shore when they saw the fire of coals and a solitary figure. Our episode comes to its surprise ending when the disciples heed the voice of Christ and cast their net once more on the other side of the boat. It is then that we witness the impact of their following the command of Christ. What results—153 fish!

V. Then we have that beautiful "fishermen's picture" of Christ—the open fire of coals and freshly cooked fish for tired, hungry fishermen. This picture gives us our concluding thought in the gracious *invitation* of Jesus, "Come and dine."

(a) What refreshment and replenishment of soul Christ has for each of us! When we have toiled and our energy is spent, the results have been discouraging. He has said to us, "Come and dine." The food has been prepared. Our strength and spirit are renewed.

(b) A beautiful ending to our story—feasting and fellowship by the seaside, the exhilaration of Christ's presence and the knowledge of his resurrection. None of the disciples demurred or declined that invitation. But of course there is more, much more in our narrative. The invitation "come and dine" was for a moment. There are other words and invitations that are for eternity.

(c) Christ still walks our roads today. He may interrupt us in our busyness, in our toiling, and in our emptiness and speak to our heart his great and gracious invitation, "Follow me." And you will never have a better offer than that.—Henry Gariepy.

Illustrations

OPPORTUNITY.   Tomorrow can belong to Christ in ways almost inconceivable in today's chaos. You can help to make sure that it is dawn, not dusk, in the era of Christian hope. Yours is the opportunity of a sinner saved by grace to work and serve toward the building of a better world —a richer culture and a more stable social order.—Haskell Miller.

PARABLE.   When the prosperous man on a dark but star-lit night drives comfortably in his carriage and has the lanterns lighted, aye, then he is safe, he fears no difficulty, he carries his light with him, and it is not dark close around him; but precisely because he has the lanterns lighted and has a strong light close to him, precisely for this reason he cannot see the stars, for his lights obscure the stars, which the poor peasant driving without lights can see gloriously in the dark but starry night. So those deceived ones live in the temporal existence: either occupied with the necessities of life they are too busy to avail themselves of the view, or in their prosperity and good days they have, as it were, lanterns lighted, and close about them everything is so satisfactory, so pleasant, so comfortable—but the view is lacking, the prospect, the view of the stars.—Soren Kierkegaard.

Sermon Suggestions

WHEN CHRIST SEEMS TO BE LOST.   Text: John 12:21. (1) When hid from us by the dust of controversy. (2) When hid from us by the framework of creeds. (3) When hid from us by partial or perverted presentations. (4) When hid from us by the stir of Christian activities. (5) When hid from us by the personality of the preacher. (6) When hid from us by ritual and formality. —W. A. Gray.

KICKING AGAINST THE PRICKS.   Text: Acts 26:14. (1) Jesus Christ is inescapable. (2) He is indispensable. (3) He is indestructible.—S. Robert Weaver.

Worship Aids

CALL TO WORSHIP.   "Trust in [God] at all times; ye people, pour out your heart before him: God is a refuge for us." Ps. 62:8.

INVOCATION.   Our Father, we thank thee for thy word and for the eternal truths which guide us day by day. We thank thee most of all for the living word, Jesus Christ, and the sureness of his presence. Teach us how to turn unto thee so that thy thoughts may be our thoughts and thy ways our ways.

OFFERTORY SENTENCE.   "And whatsoever ye do in word and deed, do all in the name of the Lord Jesus, giving thanks to God and the Father by him." Col. 3:17.

OFFERTORY PRAYER.   We praise thee, O God, for thy countless blessings and pray that thou wilt accept these gifts in gratitude in Jesus' name.

PRAYER.   O God, our Father, bless those who are tired, those who are overworked, those who have no joy of leisure, especially women who have the never-ending tasks which home and children bring.

Bless those who have no hours of work, no time when they can say that their work is done; mothers who are ready in the light and in the dark to answer to a child's cry; doctors and all who tend the sick, who day and night are ready to answer the cry of pain and the call of need; ministers who at morning, at midday, and at evening must be ready to answer the call of those in trouble and distress.

Bless those who are ill, and very specially those who are never fully well; those who are always struggling against some weakness; those who are always working under some handicap; those who must always be careful what they do.

Bless those who are beyond healing; those for whom the skill of man can do nothing more; those who must await the end. Even at such a time grant them the serenity which is certain that nothing in life or in death, in time or in eternity, can separate them from thee.

Bless those whose trouble is not of the body but of the mind; those who are nervous and highly-strung; those who are forever worrying about life and its problems; those who are easily upset and who panic when things go wrong; those who cannot cope with life and for whom the demands of life are too much.

Bless those who are at variance with each other; husbands and wives who have drifted apart and who, even if they still live together, have somehow lost each other; sons and daughters who left home in anger or in discontent and who have never returned; those who are kin to each other and who have quarreled so often about things which do not matter. Give to all such grace to take the first step to be reconciled to each other again.

Bless those who have allowed themselves to become soured and embittered; those who feel that life has been unfair to them; that no one's life is as hard and no one's sorrow as sore as their is; those who have a grudge against life; those whose accent is querulous complaint and whose whole attitude to life is sullen or rebellious resentment.

O God our Father, nothing but thine infinite grace is sufficient for the infinite need of human life. Grant that all in need may this day find their need supplied in thee.—William Barclay.

EVENING SERVICE

Topic: Things Money Cannot Buy
SCRIPTURE: Acts 3:6–8.

The account of Peter and John encountering a beggar at the Gate Beautiful highlights several lessons that let us know that money is not everything.

I. Instead of a loaf, he received life: "Such as I have give I thee." (a) The apostles did not have the money to share that would enable the crippled man to buy a loaf of bread, but they did have a healing power for his body and soul which was worth more than all the money in the world. They had been in touch with Jesus, and he had imparted to them spiritual life. Now they were in a position to communicate all that he had shared with them.

(b) The soul of man is too big to be satisfied with anything less than God. A loaf of bread would take care of a physical hunger only, but he was given a new life which would satisfy the hunger of his heart at the deepest level.

II. Instead of a tip, he received a trip: "Rise up and walk. . . . And he . . . stood, and walked." If the apostles had given him a token of money, he would have remained in his helpless condition. Instead they shared the healing name of Jesus with him, and he started taking a trip under his own power. No amount of money can buy this type of therapy, but the riches of Jesus make such a change a reality.

III. Instead of mere existence, he became exultant: "He entered . . . the temple, walking, and leaping and praising God."

(a) If the apostles had slipped a handful of coins into his hand, he would have remained in the same pitiful plight. The monotony of being at the gate each day to get enough money to merely survive would have been his lot in life. However he had a radical change for the better. He was filled with joy that was beyond description and radiant with glory.

(b) Money can buy acquaintances, but there's not enough money in the world to buy a single friend. Money can buy facts, but money can't buy wisdom. Money can buy social acceptance, but money can't buy virtue. Money can buy a reputation, but money cannot buy character. Money can buy objects, but money can't buy objectives. We exist on the things that money can buy. We live on the things it can't.—Mendell Taylor.

SUNDAY: AUGUST THIRTY-FIRST

MORNING SERVICE

Topic: My Redeemer Liveth
TEXT: Job 19:25.

The text is Job's statement of unwavering hope and trust in God in the present and in the future.

I. How does God make himself known to Job? (a) God appears as insight, as inspiration, and as a kind of eureka experience. Moments before Job praises God as redeemer he is the picture of despair and self-hatred. (See vv. 17–19.)

(1) Here Job is joylessly lamenting his loneliness and the loss of all his friends and even his wife. He is in the deepest form of depression, not even thinking about God or anything beyond himself and his sad situation.

(2) God comes as insight. God interrupts Job despite his depression. God almost always interrupts; he is unseasonable. He comes in the middle of the winter of our lives as summer, and he comes in

the summer of our lives as winter. He seems always to be inconvenient.

(b) God is most available to us in the tenseness of life. We have our fragile moments when we are most strung out, most furious, and most hurt. But at those moments we have little openings to God, little points of transparency.

II. God came as whirlwind, stirring up, cleansing, tearing down, and building up.

(a) The image of God as a whirlwind is unique to Job. And the image carries with it tremendous images of violence and sudden death. But perhaps more vividly, a whirlwind carries a sense of coming-out-of-nowhere, of unpredictableness, of a furtive movement to and fro, and of our inability to defend ourselves from its path.

(b) In the whirlwind Job finally understood God quite apart from himself and his personal needs. He could no longer finagle God into a corner for his own purposes. Job had thought, as many of us do, of God as the one from whom all blessings flow, the great provider, the king who would care for his loyal subjects. And then when the blessings stopped flowing, Job began to wonder if there was a God.

(c) Slowly out of the whirlwind Job began to see God as separate from anything he needed, separate from anything that God could do for him.

(d) The moment we begin to see God as a God for others and not just for ourselves, we begin to understand the God of the whirlwind. The moment Job stopped thinking about himself and began to think about God, God spoke to him.

III. What does such trust in God do for us? What difference does faith make?

(a) It helps us learn how to face the unknown, no matter how that unknown manifests itself to us. If there is a way of summarizing in one phrase the central anxiety of this present age it is the phrase "fear of the unknown." And if there is one thing that Job was prepared to face after his ordeal, it was the unknown future.

(b) Job became certain that even though God was silent, even though God could not always be known personally, and even though God was unpredictable in human terms, despite all these apparent limitations, God existed, God was and is, and most important for Job and for us, God shall be in the future. Job began to see that the meaningfulness of life does not come by way of today's intellectual understanding only. It comes with the willingness to be, to grow, to suffer, to lose, and to die. —Craig Biddle III.

Illustrations

KITCHEN SAINT. During the seventeenth century there lived in a monastery in Europe a priest by the name of Nicolas Herman, better known in church history as Brother Lawrence. This man was a real saint in the way he could make all time count for God. He was the cook for the other monks—a job he didn't like, and who can blame him? But he managed to reach a level of quiet peace and sanctity that is amazing. "The time of business," he said, "with me does not differ from the time of prayer. In the noise and clatter of my kitchen, while several persons are at the same time calling for different things, I possess God in as great tranquility as if I were at the blessed sacrament."—Nolan B. Harmon.

ACCEPTANCE. To choose the world is not merely a pious admission that the world is acceptable because it comes from the hand of God. It is an acceptance of a task and vocation in the world, in history, and in my time, which is the present. To choose the world is to choose to do the work I am capable of doing in collaboration with my brother to make the world better, more free, more just, more livable, more human.—Thomas Merton.

Sermon Suggestions

ENNOBLING LABOR. Text: Jer. 24:1. (1) Labor is noble when regarded as the service of God. (2) Labor is noble as it becomes a social service. (3) Labor is noble as it becomes an education of our highest nature.—W. L. Watkinson.

A GREAT LIGHT. Text: John 8:12. (1) A guiding light. (2) A cheering and gladdening light. (3) A healing light. (4) A liberating light. (5) A purifying light. (6) A revealing light. (7) A penetrating and powerful light. (8) An illuminating light. (9) An available light. (10) An experienced light.—Derl G. Keefer.

Worship Aids

CALL TO WORSHIP. "We are laborers together with God: ye are God's husbandry, ye are God's building. Let every man take heed how he buildeth. For other foundation can no man lay than that is laid, which is Jesus Christ." I Cor. 3:9–11.

INVOCATION. O heavenly Father, who hast given us a true faith and a sure hope: help us to live as those who believe and trust in the communion of saints, the forgiveness of sins, and the resurrection to life everlasting; and strengthen this faith and hope in us all the days of our life.

OFFERTORY SENTENCE. "God is not unrighteous to forget your work and labor of love, which ye have showed toward his name, in that ye have ministered to the saints, and to minister." Heb. 6:10.

OFFERTORY PRAYER. Our Father, help us this day to remember that we do not live in our own strength but that thou art our help and that from thee cometh even these gifts which we consecrate in Christ's name.

PRAYER. We are thankful, Father, for bread and meat, for the shelter of houses and good clothing, and for daily work.

We stand before you as debtors. Your handiwork has created the earth on which we stand. All that we know of love and patience, of truth and questing mind, and of beauty in face and music has come because of our sojourn here on earth—all this because of your labor of love. Indeed we are grateful.

We are also debtors to our fellow man. His labor at the far ends of the earth comes to serve us—his books, his art, and his music; his work on the assembly line, in the mines under the earth, and in the air above the earth. All this comes to refresh and bless our lives.

There is a paycheck which comes each week for all this, but there is more. We are colaborers together in the ongoing of your creation. In each of us there is a creative power. This is a part of your work. Let us use it not for mammon's sake but for goodness and beauty, working always as your stewards and to the benefit of our fellow man.

We hope that this prayer can be offered in the spirit of the carpenter of Nazareth. —Kenneth Watson.

EVENING SERVICE

Topic: The Carpenter of Nazareth (Labor Sunday)

TEXT: Mark 6:3.

I. As a carpenter, Jesus taught us how to work honestly. The parable of the laborers in the vineyard (Matt. 20:1–16) and his instructions to his disciples to go and take the coin they would find in the fish's mouth to pay the tribute (Matt. 17:24–27) imply that he was an honest man who fulfilled his responsibilities.

II. As a carpenter, Jesus produced the highest quality of work. William Barclay says that the word for carpenter means craftsman. He suggests that in the first century a craftsman with the simplest tools could turn his hand to any job. Jesus was a craftsman.

III. As a carpenter, Jesus was involved with people. Jesus is still in the business of repairing broken lives. Holman Hunt's "The Shadow of Death" depicts Jesus in the carpenter's workshop at Nazareth. It is the close of day, and the last rays of the setting sun are streaming in through the open door. The young carpenter, who has been toiling at the bench, raises himself for a moment from his cramped, stooping position and stretches out his arms. Just then the dying sun catches his figure and casts his shadow on the wall behind him. Its form is the form of a cross. His work was for people.—Charles Allen Reed.

SUNDAY: SEPTEMBER SEVENTH

MORNING SERVICE

Topic: Teaching Morals to Children (Rally Day)

Text: Luke 2:52.

Teaching morals in a pluralistic society is a problem for parents, public school teachers, and Christian educators alike. An authoritarian or sectarian mentality tempts us in spite of our better judgment. Some teachers avoid stubborn moral ambiguities by saying certain things are always right and others absolutely wrong. Our teaching problem in the church arises from five principles to which Christians must pay serious respect.

I. Christian faith at its center is not a set of moral regulations spelled out like so many embellishments on the ten commandments.

(a) Our faith provokes in us profoundly moral concerns. We are given by God's grace a way, a Torah. But at our roots, we Christians know, instead of a restricting law, a liberating joy in the God we meet through Jesus.

(b) St. Paul went so far in his experience of legalistic religious interpretations as to say, "The law is dead." It is freedom in Christ that creates our loyalty to God, and it is our love of neighbor that seriously probes all questions of personal virtue and social justice.

II. The Bible is more of a storybook about God's way with us than it is a cookbook of rules for proper behavior. It is through our celebration of the story that Christians are made whole by God's grace rather than through the personal virtues we cook up from the rules.

III. Moral character is a quality of persons, not a function of machines. We do not aim at programing our children and youth for automatic reflexes that make them perform in flat "moral" patterns of routine respectability. Rather we want them to be loving, creative persons with an inner freedom showing through in a zest for life. That means taking the risk of less respectability and traditional piety for the sake of a richer sense of relationship with God and an inner commitment to the lively fabric of human community.

IV. We should hold to a pattern of integrity not for fear of punishment or of disapproval from others or of losing a reward but from an inner conviction that it is simply the good to which we are committed. "I couldn't live with myself if I did that," a mature person might say. Many adults never mature that far. They find morality in laws and in the disapproval of others. When they can do for their own advantage what is unjust or deceitful, without danger of punishment or disapproval, they will. They do not reflect seriously on what is simply right, just, or true —to put it another way, on God's hope for the human community.

V. Moral reasoning depends on an ability to recognize the difference between private desire and moral obligation, between personal wants and a more objective rightness or goodness that can lay claim on us.

(a) St. Paul exhibited that ability when he wrote that he could "will the good" but that he found himself doing evil because of his own selfish inclination.

(b) This says to the teacher or parent in each one of us that our aim for moral maturity in our own family and church life will include a strong sense of selfhood and responsible relations to others. Much broader and deeper than obedience, we call this character.

(c) Merely enforcing rules that one church or teacher proclaims as the law of God forecloses personal reflection and practice in moral decision-making. It leaves open the possibility of retarded moral development or of moral cynicism if the student later questions these particular "godly" rules. Promoting unthinking obedience is really the opposite of teaching morality.

(d) Yet participatory moral development does not allow good leaders to play a nonpartisan role on moral questions. We need parents, teachers, and advisors of character and passionate conviction about justice and generosity, what is right and what is good.

(e) Moral reflection that leads to active commitment is one of the most characteristically Christian and spiritually essential lessons that we can teach and learn.—Gaylord Noyce.

Illustrations

PERPETUAL REMINDER.   In the city of Venice there is a peculiar custom. Whenever a prisoner is going to be condemned to death, a tall and elderly individual dressed in a long black cloak walks majestically to the center of the courtroom, bows solemnly to the judges on the bench, and in a cavernous voice pronounces the words, "Remember the baker!" Then he bows again and stalks away.

Three hundred years ago in that city of Venice a baker was executed for a crime of which he was not guilty. After he was dead and his innocence was established, the judges who condemned him gave a sum of money to the city, the interest of which was to be devoted to the setting up and perpetual burning in the Palace of the Doges of a lamp known as the "Lamp of Expiation." And so to this day, before a criminal is condemned to death, that ghastly individual enters the court and warns the judges that human justice is liable to err and that the innocent are sometimes condemned in place of the guilty.—Abdel Ross Wentz.

THE PROW.   The panelled front of the pulpit was in the likeness of a ship's bluff bows, and the Holy Bible rested on a projecting piece of scroll work, fashioned after a ship's fiddle-headed beak. What could be more full of meaning, for the pulpit is ever this earth's foremost part; all the rest comes in the rear; the pulpit leads the world. From thence it is the storm of God's quick wrath is first described, and the bow must bear the earliest brunt. From thence it is the God of breezes fair or foul is first invoked for favorable winds.

Yes, the world's a ship on its passage out, and not a voyage complete; and the pulpit is its prow.—Herman Melville in *Moby Dick.*

Sermon Suggestions

THE TEACHER IN THE CONGREGATION. Text: Matt. 28:20. As you think of teachers in the congregation, what qualities are important? (1) Teachers must know and love the Bible. (2) Teachers must know and love those they teach. (3) Teachers should provide models of discipleship, because, as Jesus said, "Every one when he is fully taught will be like his teacher" (Luke 6: 40). Paul recognized the same truth when he wrote, "Be imitators of me, as I am of Christ" (I Cor. 11:1).—Paul M. Lederach.

WHEN VIRTUE BECOMES A VICE.   Text: Luke 18:11. Perhaps the chief problem of life is not how to handle our vices but how to handle our virtues. (1) Certainly this is true if our virtues lead us to a false estimation of our own worth. (2) The principle holds when through pride we are betrayed into self-sufficiency. (3) The higher ways of life can be our stumbling block if in pride our minds are closed to the needs of others.—Gene E. Bartlett.

Worship Aids

CALL TO WORSHIP.   "Blessed is the man that trusteth in the Lord, and whose hope the Lord is." Jer. 17:7.

INVOCATION.   O Lord Jesus Christ, who art the truth incarnate and the teacher of the faithful: let thy spirit overshadow us as we meditate on thy word and conform our thoughts to thy revelation that, learning of thee with honest hearts, we may be rooted and built up in thee, who livest and reignest with the Father and the Holy Spirit, ever one God, world without end.—William Bright.

OFFERTORY SENTENCE.   "Remember the words of the Lord Jesus, how he said, It is more blessed to give than to receive." Acts 20:35.

OFFERTORY PRAYER. O God, thou giver of all good gifts, in gratitude we bring our gifts on this day of joyous worship. Refine them, we pray thee, in the mint of thy divine purpose and use them to the end that thy kingdom may come and thy will be done on earth as it is in heaven.

PRAYER. God of our fathers and our God, we thank thee for the traditions of this church. Age upon age has passed away, but still stands this bulwark of spiritual strength, a lighthouse upon this sea of uncertainty, a high tower of strength o'erlooking daily traffic, and a beacon unto hurried footsteps, proclaiming to all bewildered passersby thy love for man. Wars have come, storms have passed over, battles have raged, and the rains descended and floods have come, but still stands this symbol of mercy.

We thank thee for all its errands of love, all its deeds of kindness, and all its acts of benevolence; for all the minds it has given peace, all the hearts it has lifted up, all the souls it has strengthened, all the pains it has given balm, all the wounds it has nursed, and all the hurts it has healed.

We thank thee for its baptisms, confirmations, and weddings; for its long history of welfare and charity; for its records of ministries to hungering hearts, seeking minds, and embittered souls.

And now we come to pledge our vows that this ministry continue; that the blind be given sight, that the sick be visited, that the captives be freed, that children be taught, that youth be given guidance, that adults be challenged, and that the aged be comforted.—Fred E. Luchs.

EVENING SERVICE

Topic: Something to Sing About
Text: I Cor. 14:15.

Congregational hymn-singing has a secure foothold in the church because early references in the New Testament are to such singing. (See Matt. 26:30). They didn't listen to the choir sing a text from the psalms nor did they watch while Peter or James sang a solo. They all joined in the psalm together.

I. We need to sing with spirit as a means of expressing our enthusiastic love for God and our commitment to serving him. Young people hum and sing their spirited songs all day long because it expresses yearnings that are in their hearts, and we don't have to encourage them to be enthusiastic about it.

(a) The Lord doesn't care if you have a singing voice. He doesn't care what your voice sounds like. He wants to hear you express your faith in him. Many of us do not have perfect speaking voices, but that doesn't stop us from speaking. Many of us don't know all the rules of English, but we still use the language. Many of us have poor voices, but we should still sing. God does not care how beautifully you sing, but he does care to hear you praise him.

(b) Martin Luther believed that music is the most noble gift of God, next to theology. "The greatest innovation that the Reformation brought was congregational participation in song. Already in 1523 Luther had brought out a hymnbook. Indeed the Reformation gained much of its impetus and its strength from the desire to give back not only the Bible but also the hymns to the people." (Roland Bainton.)

(c) It is our joyful duty and privilege to sing with spirit, and if we fail in it, we come under the judgment of Isaac Watts who wrote, "Let those refuse to sing who never knew our God."

II. Let us sing in mind also, as Paul suggests in our text. (a) We must sing not only with spirit but with our mind. To sing with spirit only would be simply an emotional experience. Some of the gospel tunes that we may have learned in Sunday school and sing at hymn-sings are very spirited songs, but many of them are offensive to the mind. They have a catchy tune, but the words often do not make sense or, if they do make sense, they are very poor Christian theology. We must not swallow theological falsehoods as musical pills. Mary Poppins sang, "A spoonful of sugar helps the medicine go down." We must be careful that a spoonful of catchy music doesn't help bad theology go down.

(b) The words that we sing must express the thoughts of our minds. The hymnbook should be an aid to our singing and not a crutch. We are not singing the author's faith but expressing our faith, and the sooner we can sing it as our faith the bet-ter. When we know the words and have made the hymn our own, we sing the hymns from memory with our minds.—C. Thomas Hilton.

SUNDAY: SEPTEMBER FOURTEENTH

MORNING SERVICE

Topic: The Hands of Jesus
TEXT: Luke 24:39.

The New Testament constitutes a picture book of Jesus' hands.

I. *The creating hands.* "All things were made by him; and without him was not anything made that was made" (John 1:3). Jesus "is the image of the invisible God, the firstborn of every creature. For by him were all things created . . . visible and invisible" (Col. 1:15–16). All the mountains, all the seas, all the stars, all the planets, and all the galaxies were made by him. His hands flung those galaxies into space, "whether they be thrones, or dominions, or principalities, or powers: all things were created by him, and for him" (Col. 1:16).

II. *The healing hands.* (a) Lepers were social outcasts. They were to call out "Unclean! Unclean!" to keep people away from them. Jesus walked up to a leper and put his hand on him. Can you imagine what that meant to the leper? Probably years had gone by since the leper had felt the touch of a human hand, and Jesus touched him. The leper was healed.

(b) Think of the man born blind. Jesus took a little dust from the earth, collected saliva, and put it in the dust. He made a little salve and with his hands put it on the man's eyes. The blind man was healed. The touch of the hand of the Lord Jesus Christ is a healing touch.

(c) The hands of Jesus can heal your heart, heal your mind, heal your soul, and heal your body, if he wills. Has he come into your heart to heal your hurt? The hurt between you and your wife? The hurt between you and your son? The hurt between you and your brother? The hurt between you and your neighbor? The hurt of poverty? The hurt of bad health? What-ever it is, let Jesus touch you. He loves you. He wants to help.

III. *The compassionate hands.* He said, "I have compassion on the multitude, because they continue with me now three days, and have nothing to eat" (See Matt. 15:32). Jesus has compassion on the hungry people of the world. He has compassion on you in your need, in your hurt, in your place of suffering.

IV. *The hands of blessing.* "Verily I say unto you, Whosoever shall not receive the kingdom of God as a little child, he shall not enter therein. And he took up the little children and he blessed them." (Mark 10: 15–16.)

(a) You may have gray hair or you may have a bald head, but in God's sight you are as a little child. Jesus wants to take you in his arms and love you and bless you and change you and make you a new person. He wants to make your home a new place and give you hope and purpose and meaning in life, if you will let him.

(b) You have to open the door. You have to become as a little child. You can't come to Jesus with your shoulders reared back and with a lot of pride. You have to surrender that pride and say: "Lord, I'm a sinner. You died for me on the cross, and I'm coming to that cross. I want your blessing. I want forgiveness for my sins." Have you done that?

V. *The suffering hands.* He suffered when the soldiers drove nails through his hands. When they hung Jesus between heaven and earth, the terrible jolt tore his hands. After his resurrection the disciples could see the nail scars in his hands and the place where he had been pierced. The wounds were such that Thomas could have put his own finger into the holes. Jesus will wear those scars for eternity, and all that time we'll be saying, "Thank you, Lord."

VI. *The outstretched hands.* He is stretching out his hands to you and saying: "I love you, and I died for you. Come, let me be all that you need in your soul, in your heart, in your mind." He came not just to save you from sin and to save you for eternity; he came to save you right now, to walk with you now.—Billy Graham.

Illustrations

WHAT IS A CHRISTIAN?   A Christian is anyone who is consciously a follower of Christ, who looks to Christ as his pattern and guide and sincerely tries to live the Christ-life—the life of self-surrender and purity and love, the life that aims not to be ministered unto but to minister in the midst of a selfish and sensual world.—Durant Drake.

CHRIST THE LORD.   Jesus in the simplicity and manliness of his life; in his dedication, his utter surrender at whatever cost to himself, to the will of God and to his way with the world; in her perceptiveness of the nature of man, his insight into weakness as well as his strength; in his incomparable concern for the lost; in his daring challenge to the self-righteous; in his fearless acceptance of death—this Jesus, declares St. Paul, is Christ and Lord, both the representative of God and the master of men and all created things.—Theodore P. Ferris.

Sermon Suggestions

MEN AS CHRIST KNEW THEM.   Text: John 2:25. (1) To know men is to know their hearts and not merely their manness. (2) To know men is to know their temptations and not simply their sins. (3) To know men is to know their struggles and desires as well as their achievements. (4) To know men is to know their worth and not just their defects.—John Kelman.

OBLIGATED CHRISTIANS.   Text: Mark 16:15. (1) To claim to have Christian faith and not share it with those who do not makes this claim false. (2) To profess salvation without helping others to salvation is a false profession. (3) To claim to know Christ and not to share him with others means this claim is invalid. (4) To claim to follow Christ and not be involved in leading others to follow him is an empty claim. —John M. Drescher.

Worship Aids

CALL TO WORSHIP.   "Ye shall know truth, and the truth shall make you free. God is a Spirit: and they that worship him must worship him in spirit and in truth." John 8:32; 4:24.

INVOCATION.   O God, whose name is great, whose goodness is inexhaustible, who art worshiped and served by all the hosts of heaven: touch our hearts, search out our consciences, and cast out of us every evil thought and base desire; all envy, wrath, and remembrance of injuries; and every motion of flesh and spirit that is contrary to the holy will.

OFFERTORY SENTENCE.   "Unto whomsoever much is given, of him shall be much required: and to whom men have committed much, of him they will ask the more." Luke 12:48.

OFFERTORY PRAYER.   Cleanse and accept these our gifts, O God, and may they be used according to thy will to redeem, restore, and renew the ministries within thy kingdom.

PRAYER.   Our gracious heavenly Father, we pause humbly before thee in prayer. Thou hast never failed to meet our daily needs. In gratefulness we turn to thee this morning for thy goodness toward us which is shown in so many ways. In daytime the sun gives us light without failing, and at night we behold the beauty of the moon and the stars.

We come before thee, O Lord, to be reminded that thy truth needs to be brought before all the nations, but before this can happen, it needs to find a place within every individual believer.

Thou hast promised us that, where "two or three are gathered together in thy name," thou wilt make thy presence felt in their hearts. May we experience thy presence in this sanctuary. Let us not depart from this place without feeling deep in our hearts that thou hast spoken to us. Give us also the right directives through thy word.

We also come before thee with a prayer to meet our varied needs. We would not ask thee for them for selfish reasons, but let every need met by thee make us stronger in our faith. Once strengthened in faith, give us the desire to apply it for the advancement of thy kingdom in our midst.

And now, our gracious heavenly Father, look with thy compassion upon the sick and heal them, if it be thy will. Bring comfort to the sorrowing where human words fail. Sustain the weak with thy mighty hand where there is no other help available.—John P. Dany.

EVENING SERVICE

Topic: How God Can Renew Your Life
TEXT: Ps. 23:1–3 (NEB).
I. *God renews our lives through his spirit and through the living Christ within us and beside us.* As we realize his presence and his power we know that the kingdom of God on earth or anywhere else is not up to us. Of course we are not to become quietists in the passive, unproductive sense. We are not to fold our hands and acquiesce in evil. But when we "let go and let God," we relax without giving up the struggle.

II. *God renews our lives as we follow the good shepherd, even the Lord Jesus, and lose our stresses and cares and anxieties in helping others.* Our world needs all the healing forces which can be brought to it if it is to be restored to soundness. Basque shepherds say that even sheep search to find acceptance. After being well fed they rest. But one by one each sheep gets up and goes to the shepherd to have some burr removed from its fleece, to hear a word of approval or acceptance, or to receive an affectionate pat. So it is with human beings.

III. *God restores our strength and renews our life by restoring our confidence in life, that is, in God.* A sensitive Christian leader observed: "This is a time of fear, confusion, cynicism, even despair, a time of dissonance in music, abstractionism in art, confusion in education, a time of victims instead of heroes in fiction, of chaos in politics." So many try to live without God. The Bible pictures a dark world, but the great souls portrayed in that world were never wholly knocked out; cast down, yes, but never defeated. Let the living Lord of love renew your confidence in yourself, in others, in life, and in God.—David A. MacLennan.

SUNDAY: SEPTEMBER TWENTY-FIRST

MORNING SERVICE

Topic: When Life Is Falling Apart, What Then?
SCRIPTURE: Jer. 20:7–13; Matt. 16:21–27; Rom. 12:1–8.
Today's lessons provide clues about some steps we can take when life is falling apart. These passages bear a family resemblance. Each selection in itself is impressive. Together they reinforce each other and sparkle like expensive jewels on a velvet background.
I. The first clue can help stabilize us in an era of uncertainty. Have you ever tried to help someone and discovered that your help was unwanted or inappropriate? Perhaps you create more problems than solutions. Or have friends waited and expected you to stumble? Could it be that you have watched expectantly for a friend to fall?

(a) Jeremiah's confession may have grown out of his encounter with Pashhur, the priest and chief officer of the temple. Alternately drawn and then driven by a sense of divine compulsion, Jeremiah challenges the nation for its disobedience to God. His reward? Pashhur beats the prophet and has him placed overnight in stocks for "inappropriate" behavior. Following a night of physical and psychic pain, for he is locked up within himself, he bitterly laments. He is the laughingstock of the community. The man is lonely. His life seems to be falling apart. The foundations of his universe are shaking.

(b) Jeremiah wrestles with why he has been born. His promise of violence and destruction to the nation has not happened. He wants to save face with friends and to continue prophesying. Jeremiah promises himself that he will remain quiet about God's activity in his own experience and in historical events. He soon discovers that the word of the Lord feels like a ball of fire locked in his bones. Throughout the weeping prophet's struggles with doubt, he remembers that God is stronger than the opposition.

II. When life is falling apart, Jesus' example and hard words cut deep. Self-denial as the route to discipleship is an important clue.

(a) Usually we look for an easier way. Are we willing to settle for the meretricious glitter of the simulated? The pearl of great price will not be found marked down at a bargain outlet. The lesson from the gospel affirms that when life is falling apart then our best hope is an exclusive commitment to Jesus Christ as Lord.

(b) Any other choice ultimately leads to regrets. A person, an organization, or a country living with innumerable regrets is a pathetic sight. Energies dissipated. Skills untrained. Talents underdeveloped. Resources wasted. Society cannot collect dividends from uninvested lives. No amount of money can buy life or love or redeem wasted days and broken lives.

III. The one we worship is best understood in Jesus Christ. The apostle Paul knows that fragmentation rather than wholeness results whenever doctrine is segregated from ethics. Theology unrelated to practice makes both poorer. When life is falling apart, expressing Christlike action in every relationship is basic. One of the greatest powers in the world is the power to choose between alternatives.

(a) When life is falling apart, we need to look at ourselves and others in a fresh way. For instance, the United States has six per-

cent of the world's population and consumes about fifty percent of the non-renewable resources utilized. Is there any wonder that developing nations dislike America? Merely because we have the ability to do something is not sufficient cause to do it. What effect may my action in an organization or a nation have upon others?

(b) The earth's resources belong to all the people, not merely to the rich or to the strong. We did not create the world's resources; they are a gift. They were here before we were born; they will be here after we have died. Paul reminds the Christians in Rome that as members of the body of Christ they have a variety of gifts to be used for the purpose for which they have been given

(c) The community of faith is responsible for the proper functioning of the church's ministry of reconciliation. All ministry is a function of membership in the body of Christ, that is, bringing together the broken pieces of human life. When foundations are shaking and life is falling apart, we are to offer our life to God as a living sacrifice. We put ourselves under obligation to serve God in the new age as though the kingdom of God has already arrived. Then we discover ways to use the available resources for the benefit of the world and in gratitude to the giver of every good and perfect gift.—William H. Likins.

Illustrations

INSCRIPTION.   Over the triple doorways of the Cathedral of Milan inscriptions span the length of the great arches. Over one is carved a wreath of roses with the words, "All that which pleases is but for a moment." Over another is sculptured a cross with the legend, "All that which troubles us is but for a moment." But over the great central entrance is the inscription, "That only is important which is eternal."

FACING THE STORM.   John Buchan told of walking in the Scottish highlands one late autumn day as the snow began to fall.

He noticed that the sheep began to come up out of the hollows onto the bare hillsides. Later he met the shepherd and remarked to him how foolish the sheep were to leave the protection of the hollows to come up into the face of the storm. But the shepherd told him that the sheep knew the snow would drift in the hollows. If they stayed there they would founder and die. Their only safety was on the open hillside facing the storm.—John Robert McFarland.

Sermon Suggestions

A GREAT PRAYER.   Scripture: Ps. 51 (LB). (1) A great plea. (See v. 1.) (2) A great person. (See v. 1.) (3) A great pollution. (See vv. 1–2.) (4) A great prisoner. (See v. 3, 11.) (5) A great pardon. (See v. 7, 15.) (6) A great purity. (See v. 2.) (7) A great praise and proclamation. (See v. 13, 15.) (8) A great promise. (See v. 17.) (9) A great peace. (See v. 8, 12.)—*The Preacher's Magazine.*

MORNING PRAYER.   Scripture: Ps. 5:1–12. (1) A prayerful invocation. (See vv. 1–3.) (2) A prayerful contemplation. (See vv. 4–7.) (3) A prayerful supplication. (See vv. 8–12.)—Stephen F. Olford.

Worship Aids

CALL TO WORSHIP.   "The Lord is great in Zion; and he is high above all the people. Exalt the Lord our God, and worship at his holy hill; for the Lord our God is holy." Ps. 99:2, 9.

INVOCATION.   Father God, we come to this place to ask for a new vision of your presence and a resurrected spirit of life within history and beyond history. We come as humble pilgrims, none of us possessing all faith and knowledge but all of us seeking your truth as it lives in our midst. Be with us now, we pray, that we may be aware of you in a special way and, being thus aware, that as we live in the world we may be aflame with your joy.—Richard D. Bausman.

OFFERTORY SENTENCE.   "Every man according as he purposeth in his heart, so let him give; not grudgingly, or of necessity: for God loveth a cheerful giver." II Cor. 9:7.

OFFERTORY PRAYER.   Our Father, help us to trust thee more fully and to accept our responsibility toward thy work and thy children who are our brethren in Christ.

PRAYER.   Creator God, who art beyond space, broader than earth's horizons, deeper than the ocean, we approach thy holy place desiring to comprehend with our little minds the vastness of thy being. We are blessed in the adventure of divine orderliness. Thy laws are visible among the courses of the stars. Day and night, heat and cold, seasons of planting, growing, and reaping speak of the balance of all thy creation. With thee we declare, "It is good!"

Thou architect of the universe, we see thy hand in the majesty of mountains, amid blue lakes, and in golden fields. We acknowledge thy image in humankind. The work and progress in the expressions of man only constitute his daily assistance to thee in thy unending creativity. Thou art in the man with the hoe and spade and beside those at the wheel, the bench, and the desk. Thou art in souls and minds where brush and pen tell of thy glory. Viewing this artistry, we see it is indeed good!

To thee, maker of heaven and earth, we give thanks for spiritual communication through thy son Jesus Christ. For the instruments of prayer and worship where spirit with spirit meet in holy fellowship we are grateful. Upon the radar of thy love we are found. Here we receive goodly direction. May all races of humankind experience a spiritual blending, the re-creation of self, and the adornment of the robes of righteousness and peace. We praise thee in all thy works!—Harold A. Schulz.

EVENING SERVICE

Topic: Fundamentals of the Faith
TEXT: Eph. 2:19.
    I. There must be a vital faith in the liv-

ing Christ on the part of the members of every church. This should be far more important than denominational memberships or differences of opinion. Paul said, "Ye serve the Lord Christ" (See Col. 3:24.)

(a) When I went to seminary, we had a motto: "Woe is unto me, if I preach not the gospel!" (See I Cor. 9:16.) That should be the motto not only for every clergyman and every priest in the church, but it should also be the same for every member of the church—to preach the gospel, the good news of Jesus Christ, so that no longer will men and women live with a feeling of loneliness or despair but with confidence in the knowledge that God is their Father and his love is revealed through this same Jesus Christ.

(b) The early Christians were not well-educated men and women. There were some like Luke the physician, but in the main they were what we would call run-of-the-mill, ordinary people. But they had a great faith. They believed his promises, and they went forward, confident that as long as he was with them nothing could stand against them.

(c) The odds arrayed against this little Christian body of believers were simply fantastic! All the power, the prestige, the rulers with their armies—and yet Christianity marched forward across the known world as a conquering force. Their church was built upon the foundation of a belief in the living Christ, the savior and redeemer.

II. The early church, this little, growing Christian group, had a strong corporate sense.

(a) It is true that there were not many well-educated or wealthy people, but they had a great feeling of being one together when they came to worship in the homes, in the catacombs of Rome, wherever they were able to meet. They had this sense of warm fellowship which attracted others.

(b) People said, "Look how these Christians love one another!"—and they did not say it to be sarcastic or cynical. They were amazed at the way these people were concerned for one another. They really cared for each other, and wherever you find a church with this concern, this fellowship, this warmth, and this desire to break through all of these different barriers and be one together, then nothing can really stand against such a church.

III. Racial and class barriers were down. They did not look at a person's color. They did not ask to which group he belonged in society. As long as he believed in the Lord Jesus Christ, he was welcome. They were as one.

IV. The church was filled with an evangelical zeal to win souls for Christ. I believe that this is the great enterprise of the Christian church.—Terence J. Finlay.

SUNDAY: SEPTEMBER TWENTY-EIGHTH

MORNING SERVICE

Topic: What Must I Do to Be Lost?
TEXT: Luke 15:4, 8.

I. Like a sheep, you can wander off. (a) One does not get lost in one big jump nor overnight. We can get lost little by little, inch by inch. So it is with a sheep. A sheep can see no more than six feet ahead. It cannot see a green pasture on the other hill, but just what it sees six feet away. He wanders off six feet by six feet by six feet. We do the same: "One time won't matter," "A little won't hurt," "A little stealing," or "A little pregnancy."

(1) A boy made an experiment with a frog. When he put the frog into boiling water, the frog jumped right out. Who wouldn't? Then he put the frog into water of room temperature. Gradually he increased the heat until the frog was boiled to death.

(2) The young man was strapped to an electric chair. When he was asked if he had anything to say before the current was turned on, he said: "This all started when I stole a nickel from my mother's purse. Then I started taking things at school and the drug store. I joined a couple kids and began breaking in. When we robbed a bank, I shot a cop. It all started with a nickel."

(b) To keep saved, we need to keep close to the good shepherd. Get no farther than six feet away! Stay close to his precious bleeding side. Live like him. Go with him everywhere. Talk with him daily in private devotions. Never get out of Jesus' sight. Walk in his steps.

II. Like a coin, you can drop off. (a) Like a coin, you can be lost if you don't know where you are. A fourteen-year-old boy was put into a "home" because he continually ran away. When he was at home for a year, he was asked how he managed to stay. He replied, "If I just knew where I was, I would run away."

(b) Like a coin, you can be lost if you are in the wrong place. A lost key or pair of glasses is lost because it has been misplaced. It is not where it ought to be. We get lost when we are not in the right place at the right time. Elijah was lost in despair out in a wilderness, and God asked, "What are you doing here, Elijah?" On a Sunday morning are you in the right place if you are not in God's house?

(c) Like a coin, you can be lost if you are out of circulation.

(1) A coin out of circulation does itself and nobody else any good by being alone, isolated, and ignored. What happens when a Christian stops praying, stops worshiping, and stops going to church activities? The longer he is out of circulation in the church's fellowship, the farther he gets away from God.

(2) To stay saved we must keep active in the church, bound together in supportive and saving fellowship. A school teacher planned to take her fifth grade class to see the sights of Manhattan, but she made no plans to take helpers to keep the children from getting lost or hurt as they walked on the busy streets of New York. One mother was scared to let her son go under these conditions, but since her son insisted, she yielded. When he returned, she asked him how the teacher managed to handle the group of thirty across the streets. "Did she give you lots of instructions?" "No." "Did she say anything?" "All she said was, 'Hold onto the rope.'"

(3) To keep saved we must continually renew our faith and rededicate ourselves to Christ. As we once gave him our love and loyalty, we need to do it again each time we sing the "offertory." At a revival a wealthy man was asked to give his testimony. He told about his first job when for a day's work he received a half dollar. That night he went to his church's revival. When the offering was received, he wondered if he should put in all he earned, his half dollar. The witness continued, "The reason God has blessed me with wealth is that I gave him all that I had." When he sat down, an old whitehaired lady in the next pew tapped him on his shoulder and said in a loud whisper, "I dare you to do it again."—John R. Brokhoff.

Illustrations

CHRIST'S PRESENCE.   Leslie D. Weatherhead told of a dream in which he stood in Christ's presence and was invited to have any question answered. "Believe it or not," he writes, "in the glory of his presence it seemed utterly unnecessary and meaningless to ask him anything. There was such an overwhelming feeling of supreme joy that questions no longer needed to be answered. It was sufficient to know there was an answer. I knew that all was well."

UNDERSTANDING THE ATONEMENT.   Two soldiers were stationed on the front lines in Europe during World War II. Although they looked alike, their backgrounds were vastly different. The first man had been quite successful in life. He had been able to save enough money to be thinking of starting a business of his own after the war. His companion had been in and out of prison for much of his life. His future was bleak. Suddenly in the trench where they were sitting a shell exploded, mortally wounding the first soldier. As he was dying, he said, "You take my name and make a new life for yourself."—Norman R. Meservey.

Sermon Suggestions

HOW GOD REVEALS HIMSELF.   Text: Isa. 40:5. (1) God reveals himself in his marvelous creation. "The heavens declare the glory of God; and the firmament showeth his handiwork" (Ps. 19:1). (2) God reveals himself through people. Through Moses we glimpse God's law, Amos showed us his justice, Hosea his love, and Micah his ethical standards. (3) God's supreme revelation of himself is in Christ. "He that hath seen me hath seen the Father." (4) One other way God reveals himself. I have no name or explanation for it. We may call it the "still, small voice" or the impress of his spirit on us.—Charles L. Allen.

HOW SINFUL IS SIN?   Text: Luke 15:17–19. (1) It is sinful because it violates the laws of life. (2) It is sinful enough to severely hurt the sinner. (3) Sin is sinful because of what it does to God.—Jerry Hayner.

Worship Aids

CALL TO WORSHIP.   "O come, let us sing unto the Lord: let us make a joyful noise to the rock of our salvation. Let us come before his presence with thanksgiving, and make a joyful noise unto him with psalms." Ps. 95:1–2.

INVOCATION.   Lord God Almighty, holy and eternal Father, who dwellest in the high and lofty place, with him also that is of a humble and contrite spirit: we come before thee, beseeching thee to cleanse us by the grace of thy Holy Spirit, that we may give praise to thee, now and forever.

OFFERTORY SENTENCE.   Every man hath his proper gift of God, one after this manner, and another after that." I Cor. 7:7.

OFFERTORY PRAYER.   O God, help us so to practice by our gifts and our lives the divine principle of goodwill that in our homes, our communities, and among all the nations of the earth men may enjoy the boon of peace.

PRAYER.   Almighty Father, giver of all grace, the refuge of all who flee to thee, the helper of those in need, and the one sure resource in times of trouble: hear us now, we pray, as we approach thee through worship and adoration.

Forgive us wherein we have held onto half-truths, smugly congratulating ourselves that we are not as other men. Forgive us for closing out insight with the attitude that we have arrived already at the truth. Forgive us wherein we have accepted the cliches that are bandied about as defenses for our consciences.

Open our minds to the call of love that we may measure our attitudes and responses by this standard. Forbid that we should shunt aside concern for others as a pretense for minding our own business. Help us to avoid the arrogant spirit that causes us to feel self-made. Enable us through prayer and worship to reassess the reasons we like to give why we have succeeded and others have failed. May we have the empathy to feel what it means to be black-skinned, to be unable to pay the rent, to be unemployed without hope of a job, to be caught in the squeeze of our automated industrial age without developed skills, or helplessly sent to fight a people who have done us no harm. Almighty God, whose essence is love, draw back the curtains behind which we in a false security congratulate ourselves that we may try the spirits again to see whether or not we have any right to feel acceptable in thy sight.

And now, our Father, we lift up our concerns for family life, fraught as it is with problems of child care, the creeping infirmity of advancing age, the greater responsibilities that rest upon the shoulders of maturing youth, the sorrows that attend parting, and the joys of making new homes. Uphold with thy comforting spirit all of those who have survived beyond the life spans of their nearest and dearest. Light up the heart of the lonely with a continued involvement and concern that they may apply themselves unto wisdom until the dayspring breaks and the shadows flee away.—James R. Duncan.

EVENING SERVICE

Topic: The Prodigal Son: Three Questions

SCRIPTURE: Luke 15:11–24.

I. Where is judgment in this story? It

seems like just a sentimental story of a father forgiving a son, and of course he does. There is no holiness of God, no otherness of God, no judgment, no righteousness, and no cross. Or is there? Not only is there the punishment of the far country, but the cross, the price that is paid for sin, is found in the hands of the one who told the parable. A price must be paid for going home. In Jesus Christ the price has been paid.

II. If his money hadn't run out, would he still be there? (a) What if, instead of running out of money, he had made money in a far country? What if he had invested in equities five years ago and then changed to C. D.'s three years ago and now, perhaps, who knows, got back into equity holdings just recently? If he had done well, would he still be there?

(b) There is no answer to this question.

There is only another question. Would you? Does it take bankruptcy? Does it take illness or fear of death? Does it take depression or war? If his money had held out, would he still be there? Would you?

III. Why did Jesus tell the story of the prodigal son? I believe he told it to tell the Christians of the Middle East and the Christians of your town and my town that we are free. We can choose. We can live in a far country. And I think he told it to tell us that Thomas Wolfe is wrong and Jesus Christ is right: "You *can* go home again." And I think he told the parable of the prodigal son to say to you and to me: "What is your far country? Is it success, is it escape, is it fear, or is it loneliness?" He told us the parable to say to you and to me: "You can come home. Come home."— James H. Daughdrill, Jr.

SUNDAY: OCTOBER FIFTH

MORNING SERVICE

Topic: The True Vine (World Communion Sunday)

SCRIPTURE: Isa. 5:1–7; John 15:1–11.

When Jesus says, "I am the true vine," he is declaring that the purpose of God entrusted to Israel is in fact being fulfilled in him. He is the true Israel. All the prophecies in the Old Testament about Israel's being a special people to carry out God's purposes in the world are claimed by Christ to be fulfilled in him.

I. Jesus' interest does not lie in defending that claim. He assumes the acceptance of it by his disciples. What he wants to bring home to his listeners is who they are in relation to him. If he is the vine, then who are they? (See John 15:5.) His emphasis is upon how his disciples relate to the "true vine."

II. When Jesus says, "I am the vine, you are the branches," he is defining a most intimate relationship of us to him. Branches are a vital part of a vine. They receive sustenance from the vine trunk and, if broken off, die. They have no real existence apart from their vital connection to the vine.

(a) Jesus says that the same is true of his followers. Apart from a life in vital relationship to him, we can do nothing. Our whole life comes from the flow of power from him to us. For a Christian life to be vital it must be organically related to Christ.

(b) Because he is referring to a personal relationship as he speaks of a vine and its branches, he uses the word "abide." Those who would be his disciples must abide in him and let him abide in them. The difference between vines and persons is that a vine shoot has no choice but to be a part of a vine, but a person can be attached to Christ only by will. Our relation to Christ must be as vital as a branch to a vine. This can only be maintained by a commitment to faith that is constantly sustained.

II. To abide in Christ we must put our faith and trust in him. We need to recognize that what we are asked to do is not simply to commit ourselves to a creed or dogma about Christ but to this person. In him shall we find the source of our values, purpose, and direction.

(a) Our relationship to Christ is very much like a love-relation. Jesus says, "Abide in my love." When we commit ourselves to Christ we center our lives exclusively upon him and no other. Here is the one to whom I can give myself completely with no thought of anyone else taking that place. I am committed body and soul.

(b) Some translators render Jesus' word "remain" instead of "abide." In this case Jesus tells his disciples, "Remain in me." The relationship that is begun must be continued.

(1) John Henry Newman said that "faith is a habit of the soul." Faith is keeping alive our relationship to Christ—the habit of living in perpetual reference to him.

(2) Jesus says we do this by letting his words and commandments abide or remain in us. Our relationship to Christ is not a nebulous mystical experience but a vital confrontation with his words. When we remain in Christ we dwell upon his words.

(3) Jesus says that when his words really dwell in our heart, then our prayers will be answered. Indeed that is how they find their answers. Letting Jesus' words take hold of our lives, we shall be able to lay hold of their promises.

III. The whole purpose of his coming is for God's true people to bear fruit. That was the obvious purpose of a vine in Jesus' day. It was the obvious desire of God in claiming a people of his own to be his vineyard. It was because Israel, God's vineyard, had not borne fruit that it was necessary for Christ the true vine to come.

(a) The purpose of our abiding in Christ and he in us is to bear much fruit. Our abiding in Christ is not just a matter of having a "little Jesus in our hearts." It is a matter of so letting Christ's love capture you that you must express that same love toward others. It is looking so hard at Jesus that you can remember his likeness in every hurting person whom you encounter.

(b) We cannot abide in Christ if we cannot abide those needy ones of his who are our brothers and sisters in Christ. Christ has come as a vine seeking branches bearing fruit. We cannot abide in his love if we do not let love be expressed through us into loving care for others.

(c) Jesus entices us into fruitfulness by picturing it as a life of joy. (See John 15: 11.) Abiding with Christ, we share his joy. It is as we live fruitful lives of love to God and to one another that we shall know the joy that cannot be taken from us.—Colbert S. Cartwright.

Illustrations

CLOUD OF WITNESSES.   Noting the small congregation emerging from mass one Sunday morning, a cynic approached the church's priest and said: "Not many at church this morning, Father. Not very many at all." The old priest remained poised as he replied: "You are wrong, my son. There were thousands at church this morning. Thousands and thousands and tens of thousands."—Roy Bassett.

MINISTRY OF RECONCILIATION.   All night long, November 14, 1940, German planes bombed England's industrial heart, Coventry. Not spared was her fourteenth-century inner-city cathedral. Only its stone walls, tower, and stone floor remained. As the old wooden roof burned, three things were released. First, the massive wooden beams fell to the floor and smoldered for days. Some people wired two charred beams together as a cross and scratched "Father, forgive"—words which were to become the prayer and pledge of Coventry's new ministry.

Second, released by the fire-bombing were large, hand-forged nails which for over 500 years had held the beams in place. Three of these bound into a "cross of nails" became another symbol of Coventry Cathedral's reconciling mission in the world.

Released too was a spirit of reconciliation, a determination to show God's forgiving love in a mangled world—first toward Germans and then toward all people in the family of humankind. Today Coventry still sponsors an English-German student work-exchange program. In student housing at the cathedral are youth from all over the world, sharing in the unity of Coventry's mission, living out the reconciling meaning of forgiveness.—Katherine Miller Meacham in *These Days.*

Sermon Suggestion

HOW CAN I FIND GOD?   Text: Job 23:3. (1) God comes to us in our ordinary, everyday life. It may be in the line of duty. (2) Many a person has found God in his work. (3) Many a person has found God in social situations where he has been seeking to render service. (4) There are those who find him through beauty. (5) There are those who find him through music. (6) There are those who find God through suffering. (7) There is a mighty host who find God through Christ.—Robert J. McCracken.

Worship Aids

CALL TO WORSHIP.   "The cup of blessing which we bless, is it not the communion of the blood of Christ? The bread which we break, is it not the communion of the body of Christ? For we being many are one bread, and one body: for we are all partakers of that one bread." I Cor. 10: 16–17.

INVOCATION.   God of all life, we have come here today alone as persons, together in families, all joined in the community of Christian faith. Though we seek your face in the world of life we ask your blessing in these moments of withdrawal. Take us not from the world, but prepare us for life in the world. Let us not imagine special privilege for ourselves, but let us encourage common opportunity for all. Give us not love for ourselves alone, but make us instruments of your love in the midst of every human place.—Richard D. Bausman.

OFFERTORY SENTENCE.   "He that hath a bountiful eye shall be blessed; for he giveth of his bread to the poor." Prov. 22:9

OFFERTORY PRAYER.   O thou who art the Father of all, may we live as the children and brothers of all whom thou hast made to dwell upon the face of the earth that thy kindness may be born in our hearts.

PRAYER.   O thou great Spirit who didst brood over the chaos and make out of it an orderly universe, we come to thee that thou mayest make order and harmony out of our chaotic lives. With us all things are temporary and passing; with thee is eternity. Give us a glimpse of things eternal that we may know how our lives fit the everlasting pattern of thy kingdom.

We thank thee, O Lord, for this World Communion Sunday. Today as on no other day we feel the kinship deeper than blood brotherhood that binds us to all others in the world who call upon the name of Christ. It is marvelous to us that that little fellowship of the upper room is now a great body of millions in every land under the sun. Let the bread and the cup offered throughout the world this day be received as from his own pierced hands, and in receiving these symbols into our bodies grant that we may truly receive him into our souls.

We pray, O God, for thy poor, blind, and suffering world. We thank thee for what peace there is, and for the great fear of war that is in all human hearts. To that fear add, we pray thee, a willingness to pay the price of wholehearted devotion and obedience to thee which alone can buy lasting peace. And quicken the church that she may speak so as to be understood and heeded by all the peoples of earth.

Begin with us, O Father. Our gifts are not great, but we offer them willingly to thee. Our gifts are as alike and as different as we, but receive them, O God, as thou didst receive the gift of Jesus—for the salvation of mankind and the coming of thy kingdom. Hear us, O Lord, for we pray in his holy name.—Nathanael M. Guptill.

EVENING SERVICE

Topic: Keepers of the Faith
TEXT: II Tim. 4:7.
God's people are protecting, preserv-

ing, and promoting the gospel, or as Paul would say, "You are the keepers of the faith." How are Christians to go about this matter of preserving and passing on the faith?

I. A Christian must have a faith that is worth keeping. (a) Much of what passes today for Christian faith is mere intellectual assent. Multitudes of people give lip service to their creed and readily agree that a deep and abiding faith is good to have. They quickly add that this kind of faith has not been theirs to experience. A mother or grandmother was so religious that surely she had enough to pass on to her children. This kind of faith has been drawn so far downstream that it is diluted beyond recognition. A faith that is worth keeping must come from the source.

(b) Christian faith is like a mountain stream. Rain from heaven falls and filters through trees, ground vegetation, roots, and soil. This pure and cool water collects in a mountain spring and then runs off in a brook. Soon the little stream of pure water is joined by other streams and becomes a creek. The larger stream passes through towns where it collects impurities. Many miles downstream the creek has grown into a river and is unfit for human use until it is filtered and treated. The only way to get pure water is to climb the mountain to the spring.

II. Keepers of the faith have found a faith that will keep them. If one is always slipping and falling and doing embarrassing or degrading things, it may be his faith is not sufficient to keep him. James says, "Unto him who is able to keep you from falling," and a faith which does not do that is not a faith worth keeping. One should not have to carry his faith. His faith should carry him. Faith will not stop temptation, but it will stop you from yielding. Faith will not hold back trouble, but it will get you through it. This kind of faith is not drawn from polluted waters downstream but is freely given him who climbs the mountain and returns to the source.

III. Keepers of the faith have a faith worth passing on. Much of what our culture produces is used a few times and then discarded like a threadbare garment. A man should build his faith like the architect builds a cathedral. Some have lasted a thousand years. We sing about the faith of our fathers. If some of today's children sing about the faith of their fathers and mothers, it will be a sad and short tune. But not so with God's true keepers of the faith. He tries, proves, tests, and exercises his faith until all flaws are detected and corrected. Jesus said, "This comes only by prayer and fasting."

IV. The keeper of the faith knows that anything worth preserving for the future must be built today. He is willing to sacrifice, to work, and to become involved in the life of his church. This is what the apostle meant when he said, "I have kept the faith." He kept it because he had a faith worth keeping. It had kept him for many years, and with all of his being he believed it must be passed on.—Willis E. Dewberry.

SUNDAY: OCTOBER TWELFTH

MORNING SERVICE

Topic: The Beautiful Life

TEXT: John 12:32.

Where does one look for the beauty that transfigures life? When you ask that question about people like Jesus, the answer is obvious.

I. They found it in people. (a) Think about the teaching of Jesus and the form in which most of it is presented. Jesus taught in parables, little stories about people. All kinds of people figure in those stories. What does that tell you about Jesus? It tells you that he found in all sorts of people something of abiding value, something worth caring for, and something ultimately worth dying for. You cannot read the gospels and miss that. It is there on every page.

(b) The lesson that has to teach us is inescapable. If you are in search of beauty, the place to start looking for it is in people. Don't get me wrong. Beauty is not all you'll find in people. There's a good deal in the make-up of the human race that is anything but lovely. And the worst of which some human beings are capable is unspeakable. But that is not the last word about people. What is truly astonishing about them is the goodness of which they are capable, the love, the sacrifice, the uncomplaining kindness, the forgiveness, the generosity, even the nobility that they exhibit every day. If you don't know how to make a start in living a beautiful life, begin by looking for the goodness in the lives of the people around you. You'll be astonished how much there is.

II. If the first place to look for beauty is in people, the second place to look for it is in nature. That may seem so obvious as hardly to require saying.

(a) It is only relatively recently in history that people have realized how beautiful the natural world is. The ancients, by and large, seem to have been unmoved by the beauty of the created world.

(b) There are only two really great literatures that were created before the time of Christ, the Hebrew scriptures and after them the writings of the Greeks. Have you ever observed that neither one of these for the most part so much as notices that the world is a beautiful place to live in, to say nothing of responding to the beauty that is all around us?

(c) It is not until you come to Jesus that this discovery is made again. He speaks quite naturally of sun and rain, of birds that fly in the heavens and nest in the branches of the trees, of lilies of the field, so lovely in themselves that one can only say of them that "Solomon in all his glory was not arrayed like one of these." Jesus saw the world as God's world, so his eyes were open to behold its beauty.

III. The third place to look is within yourself. (a) Somewhere in each human heart God has placed a spark of the divine. And no matter how long it may have been neglected and no matter how deeply it may have been buried, it can never be entirely extinguished. It is there, and if you look for it you will find it.

(b) You will find it in your own capacity to love, to forgive, and to bring happiness into other people's lives. You can be sure of that. Because there is not a person in the world who hasn't somewhere in him the seed at least of this most precious of God's gifts.

(c) These are things that you can do something about. The first thing you can do is to thank God for all his goodness. And the second thing you can do is to express that thanks in terms of acts of kindness to other people. There are always opportunities for kindness.

(d) God extends to all people everywhere an invitation to the life of beauty. All we are asked to do is to accept and live. —Charles H. Buck, Jr.

Illustrations

OBSCURE HEROES.   Not a day passes over the earth but men and women of no note do great deeds, speak great words, and suffer noble sorrows. Of these obscure heroes, philosophers, and martyrs, the greater part will never be known till that hour when many that are great shall be small and the small great.—Charles Reade in *The Cloister and the Hearth*.

OFF CENTER.   A dean at Princeton University said one of his boys found a record of a Beethoven sonata, bored a hole about a half inch off center, and played the record from that hole. It was the same record, but the music sounded like the cackling of a thousand Walt Disney witches. And a life a half inch off being God-centered won't make music, just noise.— Frank Pollard.

Sermon Suggestions

GUIDELINES FOR CHRISTIANS.   Text: I Cor. 12:31. (1) It is better to be guided by our admirations than our disgusts. (2) It is better to give life than to take it. (3) It is better to forgive than to treasure grievances. (4) It is better to pray than to criticize. (5) It is better to trust than to doubt. (6) It is better to stand alone in doing what is right than being with a million doing wrong.—John M. Drescher.

WHO ARE YOU?   Text: I Cor. 3:4. (1) The man the world thinks you are. (2) The man your friends think you are. (3) The man you think yourself to be. (4) The man God knows you to be.—James Stalker.

Worship Aids

CALL TO WORSHIP.   "Delight thyself also in the Lord; and he shall give thee the desires of thine heart. Commit thy way unto the Lord; trust also in him; and he shall bring it to pass." Ps. 37:4–5.

INVOCATION.   Grant, O Lord our God, we beseech thee, that now and every time we come before thee in worship and in prayer we may be vividly aware of thy presence, become conscious of thy power and a sense of thy protection, and finally know in our hearts and minds and souls the wonder and the grace of thy peace.

OFFERTORY SENTENCE.   "Thou crownest the year with thy goodness . . . Samuel took a stone, and set it between Mizpeh and Shen, saying, Hitherto hath the Lord helped us." Ps. 65:11; I Sam. 7:12.

OFFERTORY PRAYER.   Dear Lord and Savior of us all, may we become obedient to thy will both in the dedication of our tithes and of our talents.

PRAYER.   Eternal God, who dwellest in the high and lofty place, yet also in him who is of an humble and a contrite heart, be to us this hour a living presence. Be like the sun which, though it is far away, is with us in its warmth and light; like the air which though it encompasses the planet, yet is about us and within us with its vital ministries.

We come to thee because we desire liberated lives. Free us from inner tyrannies that imprison us. Deliver us from our fears. Haunted by dread and enfeebled by timidity, we make our own souls jails and our own anxieties jailers. Grant us fresh faith and new courage. Send us out with restored confidence in ourselves, our fellow men, and thee.

Free us from our doubts and disheartenments. This universe and our lives within it are mysterious beyond our comprehension. Let not the mystery frighten or dismay us. Quicken in us confidence that, even when we do not know the explanation, there is an explanation. Drive out our fearful doubts with a fresh faith. May we rejoice in the truth we can see and live by that we do know.

Free us from our sins. We have often defeated thy purpose in our lives, have wronged our own souls, and have hurt our fellows. We could have been transparent to thy shining, so that through us this world would have been a fairer place and the faces of our friends more radiant. Grant us that this day our consciences may deal honestly with us and that we may deal honestly with them. Send us out chastened, penitent, and forgiven.

O God, free us from the imprisonment of our griefs. Let not sorrow master us. Give us altitude and strength of character that we may rise above life's hardships and be victors over them. Spirit of the master, who didst make better use of thy cross than of any other instrument life shaped for thy hand, give us thy faith and courage, that with the very hardships which beset us we too may help to save the world.—Harry Emerson Fosdick.

EVENING SERVICE

Topic: The Ministry of the Laity (Laity Sunday)

TEXT: Matt. 5:13.

I. Jesus was not directing these words to a group of persons in a theological school who had dedicated themselves to the full-time ministry of the church as clerics or pastors. Among those who heard Jesus that day doubtless many did devote their lives afterward wholly to spreading the good news of Christ—his life and teachings, his death and resurrection, and his living presence among his followers. But most of those to whom he addressed himself continued to be fishermen, tax collectors, soldiers, carpenters, or shepherds. And they, as well as Peter and Andrew, James and John, added daily to the church "such as should be saved" (Acts 2:47).

II. The function of the church to be the salt of the earth could only be fulfilled then and now by the laity. And lay men and women must be "laity" in the biblical sense—"the people of God in the world."

(a) In common speech a layman in any walk of life is one who is an unauthorized amateur. In the church he stands over against the clergy, the "professional, full-time Christians." He is "only a layman"—a part-time Christian even though he may spend a good deal of time and money doing "church work."

(b) This concept of the laity is a far cry from the biblical meaning of the word *laos*, which in the Old and New Testaments is a key word meaning "the people," all the people of God as distinguished from the peoples of other loyalties among whom they lived.

III. The church today is failing to accomplish its primary task of penetrating and transforming the world. "Ye are the salt of the earth"—not a small segment of it. "God so loved the world"—not just a part of it.

(a) The first covenant about which the Bible speaks is not the covenant with Abraham and Israel or the church but the covenant with Noah and the whole living creation. The last promise we have from God is not the promise of a renewed church but of a new heaven and a new earth. Yet so often has the church neglected its responsibility for the world.

(b) The church does not exist for itself but for those outside it. The church owes a service to those who do not belong to it —a service which nothing can replace and which it alone can render.—Carl J. Sanders.

SUNDAY: OCTOBER NINETEENTH

MORNING SERVICE

Topic: Humanity's Most Baffling Problem

TEXT: Rom. 8:19 (MOFFATT).

Humanity's most baffling problem is man. He is the greatest barrier to the moral and spiritual progress of the race. Man is always standing in his own light. He builds his economic and social utopias only to see them collapse because of the weakness and sin of the human stuff out of which they are fashioned. Let us see if we can determine the reason for his repeated failures.

I. When we examine the constitution of man, we find in him a basic dualism—body and spirit.

(a) His bodily part is linked to the earth and earthly things. Physically he is part of the animal kingdom. Physiologists tell us that in his bones and muscles, his blood system and nerve structure, and in respect to most of the organs of his body he is definitely linked to the lower forms of life. The materials of which his body is composed are all found in the crust of this planet and are subject to the laws of chemical action. When he dies, these elements will return to the dust from which they came. Man cannot disown his proved physical kinship to the earth and to all the other creatures that live on it.

(b) When we turn to his spiritual nature, we find that he stands altogether apart from the rest of creation by virtue of qualities which he shares with none other save his fellow men. These spiritual qualities link him to God. In man's development we witness the emergence of self-consciousness, moral-consciousness, and God-consciousness. Even between the lowest type of man that exists on the earth and the highest animal, there is a vast gulf. Most remarkable of all, man even at his very lowest possesses innate powers that, as experience has shown, can be developed into the full life of the spirit.

(c) Man's body is one with the material universe in which he makes his home, but his spirit is akin to the eternal creative spirit and bears the likeness of God. Looking up at the starry heavens, man can truly say: "O God, I think thy thoughts after thee," for he finds in his own mind a counterpart of the creator's. Creation itself is a mirror in which he sees reflected his own face.

(d) Since there is in man this duality of body and spirit, man has grown into Godlikeness only as he has learned to discipline and master the flesh. The animal and the spiritual are at war in man. As man progressively struggles against the dictates of the physical, he grows in moral and spiritual stature. No longer does he need to be a slave to biological laws, for he learns to govern himself by the laws of the spirit. The man who is spiritually immature feels that material things are all-important. He surrounds himself with them. He becomes their prisoner. The spiritual element in man's constitution must conquer the material. The soul must triumph over the body or man is undone.

II. Our text is one of the toweringly great texts of the New Testament, for it reveals the depth and breadth of the apostle's understanding. What he is telling us is that the final purpose of creation is the triumph of the Godlike in man. Paul daringly suggests that the entire universe, animate and inanimate, waits with eager longing for something that is anticipated, as spectators strain forward at the ropes to catch the first glimpse of an approaching triumphal procession.

(a) "Even the creation waits with eager longing," says the apostle. Those words "with eager longing" are an attempt to translate a remarkable Greek expression. Literally this means "to await with uplifted face." Here is the whole earth and all the creatures that inhabit it, including mankind, standing with uplifted, eager face, waiting, watching "for the sons of God to be revealed," for man to rise out of the beast into divine sonship and cry to the heavens, "Father, we stand ready to do thy bidding." Then man can live with his fellow men in peace, for he shall see in all men of every race and clime the features of a brother and a child of God.

(b) "The whole creation groaneth and travaileth together in pain until now." The apostle likens creation to a woman in childbirth, and the travail is but a prelude to a new life. "So," says Paul, "new life can come to a world in travail if it will but respond to the message of Christ's gospel."

(c) The whole creation through the centuries has been sighing and groaning, "waiting for God's sons to be revealed." Read the brutal and tragic record of man's inhumanity to man. Intertribal wars, interracial wars, and international wars have been the rule with brief intervals of uneasy peace. Within nations too there has been terrible strife—class against class, race against race, and creed against creed. Even the dumb creatures have suffered along with man. The very earth itself has been scarred and gashed by the fury of man's evil passions. And what of today? What of the present moment?

III. No scientist has yet devised a formula to show us how to live together. And science never can devise such a formula.

(a) We already possess it in the religion of Jesus Christ with its twofold revelation.

(1) An overwhelming assurance that God is in truth our heavenly Father.

(2) An equally overwhelming assurance that in Christ every man is our brother.

(b) This program can save the world, and there is none other that can. When shall we Christians really believe in the truth of the Christianity we profess? When shall we live as though we believed it? When shall we forsake the role of spectators and instead enter into the battle to play a part worthy of followers of Christ?

(c) When has an American statesman stood up before the representatives of other nations and affirmed that justice and freedom and truth may be suppressed for decades but that they are positively bound to win out in the end, for "the eternal years of God" are theirs? When have they declared that the Christian program of the fatherhood of God and the brotherhood of man offers humanity its last, best, and only real hope? So basic is this twofold Christian program that it will commend itself to many people whose religion is other than that of Christianity. There are intimations of these two great truths in many other religions, but they come to their full fruition in the teaching of our Lord.

(d) Having inquired about the faithfulness of our American statesmen, let us ask ourselves how much time, thought, and concern do we give to see that this golden ideal for which the whole creation longs may come to a final consummation. Our American missionaries are profoundly influencing the moral fabric of lands and peoples. I feel confident that they are making a larger contribution to the future welfare of America and to the advancement of Christ's kingdom in the world than are all our governmental representatives.—John Sutherland Bonnell.

Illustrations

WHAT DO WE SEE? Raymond Brown reminds us that "Jesus' first words in the fourth gospel are a question that he addresses to every one who would follow him, 'What are you looking for?' " Well, what are we looking for? What are our goals, our values, and our dreams? Where do we see ourselves a year from now or five years from now or twenty years? What do we hope to accomplish, to contribute, and to stand for?—T. Guthrie Speers, Jr.

SAVING THE CHURCH. Centuries ago the pope of Rome had a dream. In his dream he saw his great cathedral swaying in the wind, threatening to fall into ruins. So sure was he that it would become a wreck that he burst into tears. Then he saw a little man run toward the swaying cathedral and prop it up with his hand, and it stood firm. The next day a man wearing a peasant's garb came to see him. The pope recognized in his visitor the man he had seen in his dream. "What are you going to do?" asked the pope. "I am going on a great adventure" was the answer. "What is that adventure?" the pope questioned. "I am going to save the church" was the reply. "How are you going to save it?" the pope next asked. "By obeying Jesus Christ" came the assured answer. The name of that man was Francis of Assisi.—Clovis G. Chappell.

Sermon Suggestions

INTO THE HARVEST TOGETHER. Text John 4:35. The challenges which we face in these days show us why we must go together into the harvest. (1) The task is great. (2) The need is deep. (3) The competition is strong. (4) The time is short.—Cecil B. Knight.

ON WANTING TO GET AHEAD. Text: Ps. 106:12. Men drive to get ahead. Christ can redeem our striving by keeping God in our lives where he belongs. Some deeply important things happen in us when Christ touches our ambition. (1) We are kept humble by seeing all that we owe. (2) In the striving of a day like ours Christ gives something deeper to fight for. (3) Because of Christ we know that the greatest of success is not in our having but in our loving. —Gene E. Bartlett.

Worship Aids

CALL TO WORSHIP. "The kingdoms of this world are become the kingdom of our Lord, and of his Christ; and he shall reign for ever and ever." Rev. 11:15.

INVOCATION. Almighty God, fountain of all good, kindle in us insight and aspiration, that this hour of prayer may be a moment of time lived in eternity. Open our ears that we may hear. Soften our hearts that we may receive thy truth. Reveal thyself to us here that we may learn to find thee everywhere.

OFFERTORY SENTENCE. "Therefore, as ye abound in every thing, in faith, and utterance, and knowledge, and in all diligence, and in your love to us, see that ye abound in this grace also." II Cor. 8:7.

OFFERTORY PRAYER. Dear God, help us to become unobstructed channels that thy love may flow through us to others and our gifts may be used for the proclamation to all men of thy saving goodness.

LITANY. Almighty God, we come in prayer because you have opened the way to us through your loving mercy. You have called us your children and have welcomed us into your heart even when we have rebelled against your leading. You have made us and we are yours, bound together as the family of faith within the endless circle of your love.

Our Father in heaven, draw us close to you and to our brother.

O God of righteousness and truth, we seek to honor you by our obedience. Forgive us when we speak your name but do not live in harmony with your purpose. Have mercy upon us when we wear our piety to be seen by men but do not submit the depths of our hearts to your rule.

Our Father, let your name be hallowed by our commitment to the way Christ has shown us.

Eternal God, help us to know the joy of your kingdom. Amid the rise and fall of the empires of men, help us to catch a vision of that kingdom which endures age after age. We would seek to do your will and thus enter into that new order of peace and love and hope. Forgive us for placing our trust in things, and restore our confidence in all that truly abides.

Our Father, let your kingdom come on earth as it is in heaven as we do your will and pray for your coming reign in the hearts of all men.

O God, we give thanks for the provision you have made that our daily needs may be met. You have given us food and have created a world of rich resources. We confess our dependence upon you for life itself; yet we also rejoice that you have made us partners in your work of creation. As we enjoy and use these gifts, help us to care about all your people. Help us to give bread to others, especially that bread of life which nourishes the soul.

Our Father, give us each day our daily bread and help us to be faithful stewards of all your gifts.

Our loving Father, we are thankful for your mercy which marks your dealings with us. We have hope because we believe in your forgiveness, and we can walk each day in the assurance of newness of life. Help us to confess our sins, to be honest with you and with our brother, to seek your mercy, and to know your healing which cancels out guilt and fear. Make us loving and forgiving in relationships with one another that we may fully experience the wonder of your grace.

Our Father, forgive us our sins as we forgive one another in the spirit of Christ.

O God, strengthen us in mind and will to resist the temptations and to endure the trials of this age. Help us to make the right choices as we are confronted with the hard decisions of the day. Give us faith to see even in the hour of testing that your love never changes and that the victory of your purpose is certain. Deliver us from bondage to fear and futility; give us power to find the victory through persistent faith.

Our Father, give us strength for the hour of temptation as we trust in Jesus Christ. For yours is the kingdom unfailing, the power unfaltering, and the glory unending, now and forever.—James L. Merrell.

EVENING SERVICE

Topic: Reasons for Loving God

SCRIPTURE: Ps. 18.

Ps. 18 pictures for us the love relationship between God and his followers. The psalm begins with an affirmation of love—"Lord, how I love you" (v. 1). Every spiritual adventure begins with a deep and committed love. Nate Saint spoke of his commitment in these terms: "Discipline, devotion, decision."

I. There are the *reasons* for this love: "You have done such tremendous things for me" (v. 1). "All I need to do is cry to him—oh, praise the Lord—and I am saved from all my enemies!" (v. 3)

II. There are the *resources* of this love spoken of in v. 2: "The Lord is my fort where I can enter and be safe; no one can follow me in and slay me. He is a rugged mountain where I hide; he is my Savior, a rock where none can reach me, and a tower of safety. He is my shield. He is like the strong horn of a mighty fighting bull." These figures of speech describe the strength and security of love of which the psalmist speaks.

III. There is the *reachability* of this love. In v. 6: "In my distress I screamed to the Lord for his help. And he heard me from heaven; my cry reached his ears." In v. 16: "He reached down from heaven and took me and drew me out of my great trials. He rescued me from deep waters." Here is love from man to God and from God to man.—C. Neil Strait.

SUNDAY: OCTOBER TWENTY-SIXTH

MORNING SERVICE

Topic: What a Protestant Believes (Reformation Sunday)

SCRIPTURE: Gal. 2:11–21.

I. The sole head of the church is Jesus Christ and not an infallible vicar. No one individual is the head of the church or has been given power to be. Christ is its head. The relationship to Christ does not depend upon our relationship to the church, but our relationship to the church depends upon our relationship to Christ.

II. The will of Christ for the church and its members is revealed in the Bible. *Sola scriptura*—scripture alone! The sufficiency of the scriptures is the rule of faith and practice for all Christians. In Luther's day the Bible was written in Latin and chained to the pulpit. Only the priest could interpret it. To translate it into any other language was to perform a surreptitious act which was heresy and punishable by death. That's why John Wycliffe, a Bible translator, was burned. Like Luther, Wycliffe wanted the Bible to be read by clergy and laity alike. It was God's word to all. Through the power of the spirit of God we understand it. We seek guidance and we receive it. This gave birth to religious freedom—each man or woman alone with the Bible. No doubt this is what has given birth to so many Christian sects, but it is basic to the Reformation teaching.

III. Justification by faith. Man is not saved by his good works. Good works must follow, but man is saved by his faith in God. He cannot be saved by taking trips, paying money, or saying prayers but, as Luther wrote in the margin of his Bible, by grace alone. *Sola fide!*

IV. Every soul can have immediate access to God. He needs no priest, no saints, and no images as a mediator for him. Each is his own priest. He confesses his own sins to God, and God forgives without benefit of an intermediary. We are also priests to each other, said Luther. We hear each other out. We listen to each other's heart cry. We are brother to each other in Christ, and in this sense we are priests to each other.

V. Strangely enough, he said the church is essential. The community of believers and its fellowship, ordinances, shared experiences, and convictions are indispensible. For Luther this was not doctrine but simply practical experience that we must be Christian in his church.

VI. There should be no double standards between laity and clergy. In Luther's day holy saints were supposed to be above lay people. Luther brushed this aside. All stand equal before the judgment of God. All are to obey the whole law of Christ. All are called to be saints.

VII. All honorable vocations are callings and are sacred. How we forget that in our status-seeking society where we put some people on pedestals and put others down. Luther contended that a dairy maid might sweep the floor to the glory of God as much as a priest who handled the elements at the sacrament of the Lord's Supper. It is a part of God's plan for living. Whatever we do, if it is honorable, is good. I remember my mother telling me as a child, "Son, whatever job you get, if it is an honorable job and it honors God, it is as good a job as anybody has." But we judge each other as man judges and not as God judges. As such we stand condemned.

VIII. The equality of man. Nothing gave impetus to religious liberty and political aspiration more than this teaching from Luther. Luther would not look up to any man, however rich, powerful, or important he might be. But neither did he look down upon any man. All are equal in the sight of God. In his treatise on Christian freedom he said that the Christian is the freest man of all, and yet he is the servant of all. So we live, not to be victimized by other people, because we are as important as they. But we sense also that anyone else is as important as we.

IX. Luther gave us congregational singing. His musical heart rang with melodies, and the reform churches were soon singing them too. When Charles Wesley wrote his 6000 hymns, he was solidly within the Protestant tradition.—Thomas A. Whiting.

Sermon Suggestions

TRIUMPHANT SAINTS.   When you look at the figures of the apostles as they are most commonly represented to us in the stained glass and statuary of our churches, they usually have one thing in common: they are triumphant. Their robes are full and clean, and their heads are held high and often surrounded by a circle of light to set them off from the crowd. They appear to be as unlike you and me as anybody could possibly be, and there is not the slightest chance that we would be mistaken for them. We are separated from them by time and place, but also we are separated from them by attitude. They, after all, are saints and we think of ourselves as ordinary people. Whereas they triumphed, we are more likely to pray for the power to cope. As they are remembered for what they did, we often prefer anonymity in the face of both challenge and difficulty. When we see them only in that way, it is a commonplace for us to assume that the age of greatness is past and by every stretch of the imagination beyond us. That is both unfortunate and untrue.—John P. Miller.

CORPORATE WORSHIP.   The word "worship" means "worth-ship." We come to God to see again his worth in Christ, to see our worth as his children, and to see the worth of our fellow worshipers. It's something we just can't do alone. We sing together. We lift our voices in praise; we feel our fellowship of sin; we confess our guilt. We have an atmosphere of forgiveness because we all need it. We feel a fellowship that sustains our faith. Evelyn Underhill said, "In the long run we come closer to God in common worship than in closet worship."—Ralph W. Sockman.

Sermon Suggestions

WHAT MAKES A GREAT CHURCH?   Text: Eph. 3:21. (1) Great faith. (2) Great commitment. (3) Great love. (4) Great joy. (5) Great hope. (6) Great vision. (7) Great willingness to serve.

PROFANING GOD'S NAME.   Text: Exod. 20:7. (1) We profane God's name by our language. (2) We take God's name in vain by not taking him seriously. (3) We take God's name in vain by refusing his fellowship and his help.—Charles L. Allen.

Worship Aids

CALL TO WORSHIP.   "O love the Lord, all ye his saints: for the Lord preserveth the faithful. Be of good courage, and he shall strengthen your heart, all ye that hope in the Lord." Ps. 31:23–24.

INVOCATION.   Eternal and ever-blessed God, grant this day light to the minds that hunger for the truth and peace to the hearts which yearn for rest. Grant strength to those who have hard tasks to do and power to those who have sore temptations to face. Grant unto us within this place to find the secret of thy presence and to go forth from it in the strength of the Lord.

OFFERTORY SENTENCE.   "It is God who is at work within you, giving you the will and the power to achieve his purpose." Phil. 2:13 (PHILLIPS).

OFFERTORY PRAYER.   O Lord Jesus Christ, who hast taught us that to whomsoever much is given, of him shall much be required: grant that we, whose lot is cast in this Christian heritage, may strive more earnestly by our prayers and tithes, by sympathy and study to hasten the coming of thy kingdom among all peoples of the earth, that as we have entered into the labors of others, so others may enter into ours, to thy honor and glory.

PRAYER.   Give us, O Lord, a church that will be more courageous than cautious; a church that will not merely "comfort the afflicted but afflict the comfortable"; a church that will not only love the world but will also judge the world; a church that will not only pursue peace but will also demand justice; a church that will not merely seek to be served but will also serve; a church that will not be content to pray "Our Father" and deny in practice our oneness in Christ; a church that will not remain silent when men are calling for a voice; a church that will not pass by on the other side when wounded humanity is waiting to be healed; a church that will not "pray for tasks equal to her powers, but for powers equal to her tasks"; a church that will choose the hard right against the easy wrong; a church that not only calls us to worship but also sends us out to witness; a church that will follow Christ even when the way points to a cross.—R. E. Gosse.

EVENING SERVICE

Topic: Christian Unity
SCRIPTURE: Eph. 4:3–6.
I. Christian unity arises from the unity of our God. Here in these verses the word "one" occurs seven times: one body, one Spirit, one hope, one Lord, one faith, one baptism, one God and Father of us all. Notice how the unity of our Christian experiences arises out of the unity of God.

(a) There is one body because there is one Spirit. And there is only one body because there is only one Spirit indwelling and animating the body.

(b) There is one hope, one faith, and one baptism because there is only one Lord Jesus, who is the object of all three.

(c) There is only one family because there is only "one God and Father of us all, who is above all and through all and in all." So the one Father creates the one family; the one Lord Jesus creates the one faith, hope, and baptism; and the one Holy Spirit creates the one body. There can only be one Christian family, there can only be one Christian faith, hope, and baptism, and there can only be one body because there is only one God.

II. You can no more multiply churches than you can multiply God. Is there only one God? Then there is only one church. The unity of the church is as indestructible as the unity of God himself. It is no more possible to split the church than it is to split the Godhead.

(a) We need to draw a distinction between the church's unity as an invisible reality in the mind and the sight of God, on the one hand, and the churches' disunity as a visible appearance, on the other, contradicting the invisible reality. We are one. God says so. And yet outwardly and visibly we belong to different churches, churches which sometimes work in competition with one another.

(b) Paul recognizes this, and in the very passage in which the unity of the church is so emphatically asserted, the possibility of disunity is also acknowledged. (See v. 3.) How can the apostle Paul urge us to maintain something that he says cannot be destroyed? I suggest it has only one possible explanation, and that is that to maintain this unity means to maintain it visibly. It means to maintain it "by the bond of peace," that is, by living in peace with one another. It means that we are to demonstrate to the world that the unity we say exists indestructibly is not the rather sick joke it sounds but is a true and glorious reality.—John R. W. Stott.

SUNDAY: NOVEMBER SECOND

MORNING SERVICE

Topic: Called to Be Saints
SCRIPTURE: I Pet. 1:13–16; 2:4–5, 9–10; John 17:13–19.
All who have believed on Christ to the saving of their souls God calls saints. He expects them to be dedicated to him and faithful in his service. When they are faithful to their trust, the Lord can rely on them to carry out his purposes.

I. *The call to holiness.* (See I Pet. 1:13–16.)
(a) To counteract the tendencies to do wrong, Peter urged believers to live soberly and hopefully, looking to the return of our savior. He challenged them to

nourish in their hearts a steadfast hope, one that is defiant of changing circumstances.

(b) Because God is holy, his children are exhorted to be holy also. He has a perfect right to demand that his children be characterized by holiness. It is good to know that we can depend on God to provide the necessary strength for us to live in a manner which pleases him.

II. *The call to priesthood.* (See I Pet. 2:4–5, 9–10.) (a) All of us whom Christ has saved are priests and are permitted and enabled to share in the continuing work of the Lord by offering ourselves in loving obedience to him and in loving service to our fellowmen for him.

(b) The birth from above qualifies one for the royal priesthood. Whatever of dignity, privilege, responsibility, and power there may be in royal priesthood, we must remember that it belongs to all believers in Christ and not merely some of them.

(c) The functions of the royal priesthood may be summarized in three words —sacrifice, intercession, and benediction. As members of the priesthood we come into God's presence, bringing our gratitude, praises, and worship interceding with him and others. God is seeking worshipers, workers, and witnesses who through enabling grace will live, speak, and act in such a manner as to be a blessing to others.

III. *The call to prayer.* (See John 17:13–19.) (a) A large portion of the earthly life of Christ was given to prayer and meditation. In the Lord's Prayer (John 17) Christ did not ask the Father to deliver the disciples from temptation, suffering, and sorrow but that they might be preserved while passing through these experiences.

(b) Neither did Christ pray for the satisfaction and honor of the disciples but for their sanctification. He prayed that they might be set apart to do the specific work of representing him effectively. God's truth constituted the means through which they were to be sanctified. His representatives needed special cleansing grace to make them vessels fit for the use of the master.—H. C. Chiles.

Illustrations

FACING TEMPTATION.   When faced with temptation, ask yourself this question: What would Jesus do if he had to make the decision instead of me? We might not like the answer; we might not feel big enough for what he wants us to do or not to do; but if we follow his will, he will give us the power.—*The Anglican Digest.*

WHERE WE WORSHIP.   Yes, I know all the excuses. I know that one can worship the creator in a grove of trees or by a running brook or in one's own house as well as in a church. But I also know, as a matter of cold fact, that the average person does not thus worship.—Theodore Roosevelt.

Sermon Suggestions

DO ALL THINGS WORK TOGETHER FOR GOOD? Text: Rom. 8:28. (1) This passage does not promise that everything will work out well. Rather it recognizes that evil and suffering are a normal part of life. (2) "In everything, God works for good." That word "everything" means what it says. Not only is God at work in those pleasant hours when life is a song. God is also at work during those experiences which are difficult to bear. (3) It is impossible to overestimate the importance of a serene faith in God during any experience of suffering or tragedy. To those who love God, who accept suffering and bear it with spiritual courage, suffering becomes one of the most remarkable means of attaining spiritual maturity there is. (4) We can trust God in these sufferings of ours. Not that they will be less painful. Evil they are and evil they remain. Even God in his overruling providence cannot make them good. But we can cling to God's own promise that he will work with us and will be able to succeed insofar as we respond to his love disclosed to us in Jesus Christ.—Robert J. Arnott.

THE NEW WINE FROM HEAVEN.   Text: Acts 2:13. The Christian, being drunk on the heavenly wine, has the excitement, the senses changed, and the emotions stirred in a spiritual way as compared to the person who drinks of the natural, earthly wine. (1) The Christian will walk differently. (2) The Christian will talk differently. (3) The Christian will see differently. (4) The Christian will hear differently.—W. L. Menzo.

Worship Aids

CALL TO WORSHIP. "Now in Christ Jesus ye who sometimes were far off are made nigh by the blood of Christ. For he is of our peace, who hath made both one, and hath broken down the middle wall of partition between us. Now therefore ye are no more strangers and foreigners, but fellow citizens with the saints and of the household of God." Eph. 2:13–14, 19.

INVOCATION. Almighty God, who of thy great mercy hast gathered us into thy visible church: grant that we may not swerve from the purity of thy worship but may so honor thee both in spirit and in outward form that thy name may be glorified in us and that our fellowship may be with all thy saints in earth and in heaven.

OFFERTORY SENTENCE. "I will freely sacrifice unto thee: I will praise thy name, O Lord; for it is good." Ps. 54:6.

OFFERTORY PRAYER. God of all good, who hath rewarded our labors, we acknowledge thankfully thy favor and do now dedicate a share of our material gains to the even more satisfying ministries of the spirit.

PRAYER. O God of love, who has called us to walk and to work with you, give us courage to think clearly about the meaning of life. Give us vision to accept responsibilities that relate to the problems of people and nations.

Help us to match the day's demands with abilities made strong by our opportunities. Deepen our concern for all people everywhere. Grant us the determination to do all within our abilities to bring about a united, peaceful, and transformed world.

Direct us in developing and serving through new forms of ministry in our changing world. So may the day soon come that persons in every walk of life will recognize their God-given opportunities and responsibilities within their own daily relationships.—Gene N. Branson.

EVENING SERVICE

Topic: The Impossible Dream
SCRIPTURE: Dan. 2:19–23.

I. *Man is helpless without God.* This dream or nightmare so disturbed Nebuchadnezzar that he knew it must have some special significance. He used it to put his wise men to the test. Obviously they failed to reveal the dream to him or the interpretation (vv. 1–13).

II. *God's power is available through prayer.* Daniel requested the privilege of interpretation. He shared with his companions the impossible situation. They prayed. God revealed the dream and its interpretation to Daniel (v. 19). An exquisite hymn of praise is vv. 20–23.

III. *God controls world governments.* Daniel's interpretation of the dream extends from v. 31 to v. 45. Most conservative scholars suggest that the four kingdoms referred to are the Babylonian, the Medo-Persian, the Greek, and the Roman. The main point is that "the powers that be are ordained of God" (Rom. 13:1). No nation including our own could exist apart from the permissive will of God.

IV. *God's kingdom is everlasting.* The image which symbolized the kingdoms of this world was destroyed by a stone cut out without hands (vv. 34–35). This is an obvious reference to the miraculous nature of the kingdom of God. Verse 44 declares that in the days of the kings represented by the feet of iron and clay the God of heaven shall set up a kingdom. It shall never be destroyed. It shall consume all other kingdoms. In the days of the Roman Empire, God revealed himself in Christ, who was born in the flesh and under the rule of the Roman government. He set up his kingdom. Though it still coexists in the midst of earthly governments, it is destined to outlast all of them. The ultimate victory belongs to Jesus Christ.—Scott L. Tatum.

SUNDAY: NOVEMBER NINTH

MORNING SERVICE

Topic: Your Money and Your Life (Stewardship Day)

TEXT: II Cor. 9:8.

How shall we define Christian stewardship? Some years ago the United Stewardship Council joined in the following statement: "Christian stewardship is the practice of systematic and proportionate giving of time, abilities, and material possessions, based on the conviction that these are a trust from God to be used in his service for the benefit of all mankind in grateful acknowledgement of Christ's redeeming love." Such a definition enables us to see the implications for our lives in the words Paul wrote to the Corinthian Christians about their obligation to care for the needs of others. He appealed for their generous response in meeting those needs.

I. God has given us *life*. All of life is involved in stewardship. Human life is the first and greatest of God's gifts and simply to be alive is to carry great responsibilities. Life is a sacred trust, an endowment of the heavenly Father. He depends on us and holds us accountable to use our lives to help accomplish his purposes.

II. God has given us *time*. We cannot say how much time any life will have to use as stewards, but whatever time we have is a gift from God. And we must use it with wisdom and faithfulness in every activity of every day. We are called of God to use our time in doing our share in the fulfillment of God's plan and purpose for his world.

III. God has given us *health*. For some of us that is not much of a gift. Our physical or emotional health leaves a great deal to be desired. Yet for most of us he gave superior minds to be used in discovering what God's plan and purpose for our lives really are. Our bodies were given us by God for our occupancy through which we can accomplish the work of God. Therefore we must treat our bodies with respect and take care of them, not to harm or abuse them. The body is "the temple of God."

IV. God has given us *talents*. We were born with potential talents that are unique. The question we must ask ourselves is what we are doing with what we have been given in talents and capacity. To use our talent wisely is to develop others. To fail to use them is to lose them.

V. God has given us *relationships*. Our friendship and love for each other are gifts of God. I would be lost without the human relationships which enrich my life. My parents provided for me because of their love; they helped me learn and grow as a part of a family in loving relationship. In my work my fellow workers are important to me through their Christian behavior and their supportive caring. In the church I participate with others in worship and fellowship, in service and study, and these meaningful relationships enrich my life beyond my deserving.

VI. God has given us the *gospel*. Here is the good news that God has come to us in Jesus Christ to assure us of his love, his care, and his power to bring strength into our daily living. He has made us partners in the Christian life. That partnership is three-fold in its exercise.

(a) I receive the gospel, experiencing the good news for my own life through my response of faith to God's grace.

(b) I share the gospel by doing my share to bring God's word to my world that others may have the same chance I have had to believe in God and to share life that is eternal.

(c) I must reflect the gospel through the way I live. The manner in which I accept my responsibilities as a Christian steward influences others with whom I am in relationship. I need to appreciate the fact that, whoever I am, I can be responsible either for the gospel acceptance by others or its rejection because of what they find in me or don't find in me of Christ.

VII. God has given us *property*. "I brought nothing into this world, and it is certain I will take nothing out of the world when I pass from it." Everything I have—my legally owned property, my bank account, my insurance policies, my business, and my stock—all my real property has come to me through God's grace. Only the calloused or indifferent would fail to sense the need to give something in return.

(a) I am required not only to acquire what property may come into my possession with honesty and integrity but also to use it as a trustee who administers that property.

(b) I am required to give of that money to serve the work of God wherever I have a chance to contribute. So I must give regularly and with some system in proportion to the gifts I have been given. If I really love God, then I will gladly dedicate a portion of my income and property to God's service to help meet the needs of my fellows. I give because God has given me. Because God loves, I live. How can I live fully unless I use my money to express my loving gratitude for God's gifts?—Hoover Rupert.

Illustrations

SLENDER WIRES. How strange that a widow with only a "handful of meal" should be "commanded" to offer hospitality! It is once again "the impossible" which is set before us. It would have been a dull commonplace to have fed the prophet from the overflowing larder of the rich man's palace. But to work from an almost empty cupboard! That is the surprising way of the Lord. He delights to hang great weights on apparently slender wires, to have great events turn on seeming trifles, and to make poverty the minister of "the indescribable riches of Christ." The poor widow sacrificed her "handful of meal" and received an unfailing supply.—John Henry Jowett.

ETERNAL CONSEQUENCES. A dying man who was not a Christian said to the pastor who visited him, "If I give all my money to the church, will it help in eternity?" With an eye to the church's budget deficit, the pastor responded, "Well, it wouldn't hurt to try." Jesus would say that what we do with our money now will help in eternity.

It won't buy salvation, but the way we use our money, the proportion we give to the church, and the investments we make will have eternal consequences. You invest your money in the work of God, and when all your money is gone, those investments will still be paying their dividends.—Brian L. Harbour.

Sermon Suggestions

CHARACTERISTICS OF FRIENDSHIPS. Text: Jas. 2:23. (1) Friends trust and love one another. (2) Friends have frank and familiar intercourse with one another. (3) Friends delight to meet each other's wishes. (4) Friends give gifts to each other. (5) Friends stand up for each other.—Alexander Maclaren.

WHERE YOUR TREASURE IS. Text: Luke 12:34. (1) The evaluation of anything depends upon the quality of our characters. (2) What a person treasures depends upon the things upon which he sets his affections. (3) The treasures that enrich our lives depend upon the ends to which we devote our talents.—Fred B. Chenault.

Worship Aids

CALL TO WORSHIP. "I will bless the Lord at all times: his praise shall continually be in my mouth. O magnify the Lord with me, and let us exalt his name together." Ps. 34:1, 3.

INVOCATION. Eternal God, who committest unto us the swift and solemn trust of life, since we know not what a day may bring forth but only that the hour for serving thee is always present, may we wake to the instant claims of thy holy will, not waiting for tomorrow but yielding today. Consecrate with thy presence the way our feet may go, and the humblest work will shine and the roughest places be made plain.—James Martineau.

OFFERTORY SENTENCE. "Upon the first day of the week let every one of you lay by him in store, as God hath prospered him." I Cor. 16:2.

OFFERTORY PRAYER. Our Father, may we who have seen thy providential hand in all the experiences of our lives seek to possess such greatness of mind and spirit that we shall be enabled to offer these gifts with an unselfish joyfulness.

LITANY. O God, we thank you for assigning us the significant role of stewards in your kingdom.

Help us to be good stewards of all you have placed in our care.

We thank you for a daily allotment of time without which we could do nothing.

Help us to use all our hours in ways that are in line with your will.

We thank you for the ability to do and to learn to do literally millions of marvelous tasks.

Help us to develop and use our varied skills in accord with the counsels of Christ.

We thank you for money and for all to which it serves as a key.

Grant that all our earning and spending, all our investing and giving, may be acceptable in your sight.

We thank you for all the resources with which the world has been supplied.

Grant that we may so use the soil, the air, the water—all of nature's bounty—that future generations may not be robbed by our irresponsibility.

We thank you for the gifts of freedom and influence.

Help us to use whatever freedom and influence we have for worthy objectives and purposes.

We thank you for healthy bodies and sound minds.

Grant that we may shun all habits and practices that unnecessarily reduce our physical or mental well-being.

We thank you for the priceless privilege of children.

May we never betray so great a trust.

We thank you for the glorious gospel of Christ.

Help us to live according to the light Jesus has given us, and guide us in sharing this light with others.—William C. Sanford.

EVENING SERVICE

Topic: Entrusted with Talents

TEXT: Matt. 25:24–25 (RSV).

It is the man of marginal ability, the man without any ambition, who gets rebuked. Instead of being grateful for the chance, what did the man do? He retreated into the protective shell of his inferiority complex. He could have handled the $1,000, but he allowed himself to be defeated by his fear of defeat. Probably he said something like this to himself: "What can I do? What's the use of my competing with those who easily leave me far behind? What's the use of my trying to collect my little interest on the thousand when somebody else knows how to double it? There are others better suited for the job. Let them do it."

I. Such an attitude fails to recognize that the work of the world, the majority of it, the brunt of it, is shouldered by men and women of modest ability. We need the geniuses, but we need the men and women of common ability too. The architect may design his skyscraper, but without the bricklayer and the plumber and the electrician it will never come to life. The princes of the pulpit may preach their sermons and the theologians may write their monographs, but without the faithful Sunday school teachers, without the deacons, without the saints who flesh out their Christianity seven days a week, without the parents who are concerned about their children's spiritual welfare, the church would go nowhere.

II. The greatest performances are seldom solos. Think of what Edison owed to his assistants. Think of what Lincoln owed to his mother. Think of those who have prepared you for your greatest achievements and who assisted you in them. And think of those whose work had gone before. Greatness is not a solo effort. Greatness always stands upon the shoulders of common, ordinary persons like you and me.

III. The greatest men and women are not always the most gifted. Often God comes into the life of a man or a woman of very ordinary ability and uses that person mightily. Think of Moses or Peter or Paul before God came along. Don't you bury that chance when it comes. Don't take a chance on failing God and failing the rest of us because you're afraid of personal failure and embarrassment.

IV. God expects us to use the gifts he has entrusted to us, no matter how few or many. He is not really a hard taskmaster as the one-talent man imagined. He asks only that we use the abilities and opportunities he has entrusted to us for his glory and for the edification of his body. The gifts of course are not meant for personal gain but for the edification and the ministry of the church. But to bury them is just as irresponsible as to squander them.—Arthur McPhee.

SUNDAY: NOVEMBER SIXTEENTH

MORNING SERVICE

Topic: The Authority of the Bible (Bible Sunday)

TEXT: II Tim. 3:10–17.

I. The supreme authority of the Bible is limited to matters of faith and practice, matters of right belief and right living. While many of us cannot with integrity affirm its authority in matters such as science and other fields, we can affirm its supreme and final authority in matters of faith and practice regarding the nature of God and the nature of man and the nature of their relationship, and the life God calls us to live and the meaning of that life and the meaning of our death. As Paul wrote to Timothy, "All scripture is inspired by God and is useful in teaching the faith and training in right living." In matters of faith in practice the Bible is the supreme authority for the Christian. Everything, including our individual spiritual experiences, must be tested over against the word of God in scripture.

II. The authority of the Bible is found primarily in its being the written word of God with a capital W rather than its being the words of God with a small w. Just as I am using words as a vehicle, a channel, a bridge of communication today, so the Bible is God's word, God's bridge of communication with humankind. What is authoritative for us is not the printed words on the page but the message of God, the word of God which comes to us in and through these words. For the Christian community the Bible is the word of God as no other word written by human beings. It is the supreme word of God.

III. The authority of the Bible as a whole supercedes the authority of any single part. The Reformers made a great deal of the principle that scripture should interpret scripture and by that they meant that that was a consistent witness, a consistent word shining through scripture as a whole, and it is this consistent witness of the whole which claims our first allegiance and controls our response to any part of it.

IV. The authority of the Bible is focused in its revelation of God in Jesus Christ. Here is the clearest expression. Here in Christ the very incarnation of this consistent word shines through the entire sweep of scripture. He is the incarnate word of God, he is our Lord, our final ultimate authority. Luther speaks of the Bible as the manger in which Christ lies. Its primary purpose is to witness to him, and therefore its focus, its center of authority, is found in that witness to Jesus Christ.

V. The authority of the Bible is something you must discover. I cannot convince you of it. I certainly cannot prove it in rational or objective fashion. I can only witness to it in my own life as millions of other Christians have in theirs. For those who have discovered it and experienced it and received in it and have submitted to it, its authority is overwhelming.

(a) Kenneth Foreman suggested that discovering the authority of the Bible is something like discovering the greatness of the music of Bach. Suppose you didn't believe it. I could remind you that most of the world has considered Bach a master in the field. I could rent a hall and employ a person to make a speech to you every seventh day telling you what a great musician Bach was, but that still wouldn't convince you. But study Bach yourself, listen to his music, be open to its majesty, let those soul-shaking harmonies possess you, and then you will know. And once you've discovered it, nothing can shake you from what you know to be true.

(b) You say the Bible doesn't speak to

you. It's a dead book sitting on the shelf. Perhaps you have never really seriously read it. Perhaps you have never read it as an active participant in it rather than a detached spectator. Perhaps you have never been open to its message. You have never really listened to its music or wrestled with it.

(c) If you really want to discover the truth and authority of the Bible, you must study it prayerfully, read it carefully, listen to it, be open to it, create the context in which God can speak his word to you through its pages, and then somehow the same Holy Spirit under whose inspiration it was written will convince you of its authority, its liberating power, and its glorious truth.—Douglas W. Oldenburg.

Illustrations

TRANSLATION.   The Bible is intended to be its own interpreter and, like the religion which it proclaims, is ordinarily easily understood by the plainest and most unlettered of men. Christian scholars have translated it, retranslated it, and then translated it again. There seems to me only one thing left to be done with it, and that is to give us a literal and faithful and understandable translation of it in practice. —William Booth.

STANDARD AND RULE.   God's Word alone is and should remain the only standard and rule to which the writings of no man should be regarded equal, but to it everything should be subordinated.— Martin Luther.

Sermon Suggestions

CHRISTIANITY? SO WHAT?   Scripture: I Cor. 15:3–10. (1) Just suppose no one really cared whether moral standards were maintained or not. What would happen to our nation? (2) Just suppose no one really cared whether individual liberties were preserved or not. What would happen to the freedom we so enjoy? (3) Just suppose no one cared whether the gospel of Christ was taught or not. Would there be any hope for this world?—Glenn E. Hanneman.

POWER AT WORK.   Text: Eph. 3:20 (RSV). (1) Consider how this power of the spirit can work within us to reveal new insights. (2) Consider how this power works within us to renew our energies. (3) Consider further how this power of the spirit can work within us to give "a peace that passeth understanding."—Ralph W. Sockman.

Worship Aids

CALL TO WORSHIP.   "Thy word is a lamp unto my feet, and a light unto my path. I have sworn, and I will perform it, that I will keep my righteous judgments. Quicken me, O Lord, according unto thy word." Ps. 119:105–107.

INVOCATION.   O Lord God, who hast left unto us thy holy word to be a lamp unto our feet and a light unto our path: give unto us all thy Holy Spirit, we humbly pray thee, that out of the same word we may learn what is thy blessed will and frame our lives in all holy obedience to the same, to thine honor and glory and the increase of our faith.

OFFERTORY SENTENCE.   "Offer the sacrifices of righteousness, and put your trust in the Lord." Ps. 4:5.

OFFERTORY PRAYER.   Our Father, help us who claim to be Christians to bring forth fruit consistent with our profession of faith. May these tithes and offerings be so used that others may hear the glad story of thy redeeming love.

PRAYER.   Eternal God, in whom there is no beginning or end, no daylight or darkness, and who is the same yesterday, today, and forever individually and corporately we stand in constant need of your renewing presence and forgiving love. We are like travelers through a desert, and you, O God, are a welcomed oasis. Spiritually we are dry and parched and need the living water that only you can give. Let us drink deeply of your well of righteousness.

Fill us, O Lord, with power and purpose so that we can continue to be travelers for good in your world.

Lord God, we confess that we have not always traveled on your behalf. Shamefully we admit that we have taken many journeys on our own behalf and haven't even bothered to consult you, but the law of diminishing returns always sets in and we find ourselves used up, depressed, and feeling flat.

Spirit of the living God, come into our lives with love that we may journey forth as reconcilers and that we may go to our neighbors in their need and give them a cup of cold water in your name.

God of the ages, come into our lives with joy that we too may be able to share the good news of your eternal life with those who are cringing in fear at the threat of death.

Father of our Lord Jesus Christ, come into our lonely lives and fill us with your peace that passes all understanding, and when we are filled with peace, send us out to be peacemakers in a world where brother is pitted against brother. May each of us be girded with Christlike power, and may we use this power purposefully to witness to your kingdom which we have experienced here this morning.—George L. Earnshaw.

EVENING SERVICE

Topic: A Biblical Approach to Christian Education

TEXT: John 20:31.

The Bible is the unique book of our Christian faith. Here, as nowhere else, we are put in touch with the God we worship, the Christ we serve, the source of power for our lives. It is the basis for our knowledge of God and of God's intention toward us and for us. Here we find the way of liberation from human bondage and the life that is appropriate to those made in the image of God. As Christians we are a people of a book and that book is the Bible. It is essential that our Christian education be biblically centered. Every Christian needs to know this book above all other books. We need to keep vitally in touch with the sourcebook of our faith.

I. We must maintain a balance between dealing with the words of the Bible and dealing with the word of the Bible, who is Christ Jesus. There are the many words of the Bible, and there is Jesus of whom the scriptures say he is God's word incarnate —enfleshed. Should our attention center primarily upon every word of the Bible as being the revelation of God or primarily upon Jesus as being the revelation of God? Too often we opt for one or the other, thus breaking the tension and losing the balance. But to do so is to end up with something less than what the Bible offers us.

II. We must maintain a balance between the study of the content of the Bible and the living out of Christian faith in daily living. There is the need to know what the Bible says. There is the need to put one's biblical faith into practice. Where should our emphasis be in our church school? We tend to opt for one or the other, losing our balance and cutting the tension between things that need to be held together.

III. We must maintain a balance between finding out what the meaning of a biblical passage had for its own day and time and what it means for us today. It is imperative that we study a Bible passage thoroughly until we can really grasp what it meant to those for whom it was written. Equally important is the searching out of how that passage applies to you and me and our world in the present time. Where should our emphasis be? We are tempted to tip the balance to one side or the other. —Colbert S. Cartwright.

SUNDAY: NOVEMBER TWENTY-THIRD

MORNING SERVICE

Topic: What We Can Do About Our Hungry World (Thanksgiving Sunday)
SCRIPTURE: Isa. 58:6–12.

There is something about the Thanksgiving season that makes us feel a little uncomfortable. We begin to recall just how much we have in comparison to the rest of the world. Most of us have never seen a hungry person or seen starving children. We do not even like to think or talk about it. I don't like to talk about it. I could be discussing a much more pleasant subject, except that God is calling us to care about needs of his children on this planet.

I. How would God have us see the need?
(a) He might say to count the number of times you breathe in thirty seconds. Most of us would breathe about ten times. He might say that is the number of people who died of starvation during that half minute. During the hour we are together 1,200 will have died of starvation or malnutrition. One billion people are mentally or physically retarded because of a poor diet. One half of the human race exists in conditions of chronic poverty that keep them underfed and uncertain about their next meal.

(b) Hunger is the human family's most devastating foe. It is also the conquerable foe. We possess the technical knowledge and the economic resources to overcome hunger within twenty years. Does the well-fed world have the will to engage in this battle? Will Christian people make the long-term commitment to win this decisive battle?

II. Once we see the need and sense that the problem is not overwhelming, we are strengthened in our efforts when we understand that response to hunger is deeply and profoundly Biblical. (See I John 3: 17–18.)

(a) Notice what God's word means by love. Love means action to help hurting people. If our religion closes our hearts to the hungry of the world, then we are casting our vote for Karl Marx's devastating conclusion that "religion is the opiate of the people."

(b) Scripture reveals a generous and gracious creator who planned a world that would adequately nourish its inhabitants, but creation has been disrupted. The Genesis picture tells the story. Adam and Eve are in a beautiful, abundant garden, but they desire more than they have been given. Their greed makes them vulnerable to the serpent's tempting appeal to reach beyond their limits for the forbidden fruit so they will no longer need God.

(c) Scripture reveals that God is doing everything short of taking away our freedom to lead us to a future when there is enough for all.

(d) That new creation has its beginning in Jesus Christ. The only miracle reported in all four gospels is the feeding of the multitude. God wants to get our attention to help us see this picture. Hungry people. Human need. The disciples appear confused. Then someone begins to share. Perhaps there are others. We do know that human sharing in Christ's hands met the needs. That is our picture of hope.

(e) From Genesis to Revelation the Bible talks about God's concern for food for all his children. To neglect this area is to be guilty of apostasy. We can face the need. We can realize that concern and action is profoundly biblical.

III. We can challenge widely held myths that undercut effective response to hunger.

(a) The first myth holds that hungry people are getting what they deserve since we all have basically the same opportunities in life. This attitude ignores the fact that most of the world's hungry are in underdeveloped nations that have for centuries been dominated or ruled by colonial powers. Two hundred years ago we broke the yoke of colonial oppression. Many countries have been unable to do so until very recent times.

(b) A second myth is the idea that the problem is so serious that nothing can be done. The image of a lifeboat is frequently used. The people of the western affluent nations are likened to people installed in lifeboats. The people of the poor nations are like people swimming in the sea, all clamoring for a place in the lifeboats. The situation is so desperate that the only alternative is to start banging the hands of those who try to grab on. If one doesn't keep fighting them off, we will all sink. We need to understand that we are in the same boat called planet Earth. Our situation is more like a great ocean liner in which a few first-class passengers are wasting food that could be shared with the increasingly restless third-class passengers.

(c) A third idea that we call into question is that as Americans we are already doing enough or too much. Most of our foreign aid goes for military assistance. Our total foreign aid represents one-fifth of one percent of our gross national product. We are the wealthiest nation in the world, yet we dropped to fifteenth place on the list of seventeen major donor nations engaged in donor assistance to the third-world nations.

IV. There are several positive steps we can begin to take immediately. (a) We can simplify our own life-styles. The average American generally eats each day 900 more calories than needed and twice the protein the body can use. Simpler diets are sounder diets. We can consume less.

(b) We can use our influence to let our leaders in Congress and the White House know we care about the hungry of the world. We can write letters and talk to people.

(c) We can decide that as a congregation one of our priorities for years to come will be concern for the hungry.

(d) We can have hope. Our temptation is to give up in despair. We can have hope and gratitude for a Lord whose creation is still adequate if we work with him.—Joe A. Harding.

Illustrations

LARGE COMMA. One of the sons of Karl Barth was asked to preach at a church during the Sister Corita Kent carnival years. As he walked to the pulpit to deliver his sermon, he saw a large day-glo banner proclaiming, "God Is Other People." Taking out his felt pen, he walked over and inserted a large comma after "Other." Then, considering his sermon to have been delivered, he left.—Nicholas E. Hodson in A. D.

TIMES FOR BLESSING. When shall I "bless the Lord"? When he blesseth thee? When the goods of this world abound? When thou hast great abundance of corn, oil, and wine, of gold and silver, of servants and cattle; when this mortal health remaineth unwounded and sound; when all that are born to thee grow up, nothing is withdrawn by immature death, happiness wholly reigneth in thy house, and all things overflow around thee; then shalt thou bless the Lord? No, but "at all times."—St. Augustine.

Sermon Suggestion

THE GRACE OF APPRECIATION. Text: Mark 14:8. (1) One must distinguish true appreciation both from flattery and praise. Flattery is veiled insult, and praise may be condescension in disguise. (2) This gift of appreciation is always the mark of a noble, generous nature, just as the constant habit of depreciating is the sign of littleness. (3) One turns to the story of the master and sees how gloriously Christ appreciated. That was why life blossomed in his company. (4) Love is the secret of appreciation. Love is not really blind; it has the most generous of eyes.—George H. Morrison.

Worship Aids

CALL TO WORSHIP. "O come, let us sing unto the Lord: let us make a joyful noise to the rock of our salvation. Let us come before his presence with thanksgiving, and make a joyful noise unto him with psalms." Ps. 95:1–2.

INVOCATION. O God our Father, giver of all good things, we are grateful for the Thanksgiving season of the year when we come with gratitude for bountiful harvests filling granary and bin. Give us such a spirit of thankfulness that every day and every season and all thy continuing gifts may be occasions for thanksgiving and all the year be blessed with an ever-continuing gratitude. As thy mercies are new every morning, so may our praise rise to thee each day and hour.

OFFERTORY SENTENCE. "Give, and it shall be given unto you; good measure, pressed down, and shaken together, and running over." Luke 6:38.

OFFERTORY PRAYER. O thou source of all light, open our blind eyes to see the beauty of the world as thy gift, and grant us the will and wisdom to do our part in bringing thy light into dark places.

PRAYER. O Lord our heavenly Father, from whom cometh every good and perfect gift and under whose loving care we abide always, we bow before thee as a fellowship of kindred minds to thank thee now, our God, with heart and hands and voices.

We praise thee that thou hast surrounded us with thine infinite goodness, that thou hast continually poured forth thy benefits age after age, and that of thy faithfulness there is no end.

For the beauty of the earth and the bounty it produces for our physical need, for the order and constancy of nature which brings us day and night, summer and winter, seedtime and harvest, and for all gifts of thy mercy, we are thankful.

For the power of love that binds us together as families and inspires us to establish our homes, to clothe our children, and to provide food for their growth, and for the resources of mind and strength that enable us to do this, we give thee hearty thanks.

For our work that calls forth the noblest within us, for our country founded on thy precepts of liberty and justice, for our schools that lift us above the plane of ignorance, and for the countless organizations whose purposes are for the welfare and happiness of mankind, we express our profound thanks.

Above all, O God, we praise thee for thy son Jesus Christ who lives within our hearts; for thy Holy Spirit who renews, comforts, and inspires our souls; for thy word that reveals truth to our minds; and for thy church whose prophets, saints, martyrs, and ministers have helped us remain steadfast in our faith. For all these channels through which our spiritual needs are met, we raise our voices in humble thanks.

Let the memory of thy goodness fill our hearts with joy and gratitude, and may our lives be an acceptable expression of our thankfulness now and in all the days to come.—Donald A. Wenstrom.

EVENING SERVICE

Topic: The Grace of the Lord Jesus Christ

SCRIPTURE: John 1:1–5, 14, 16.

I. The grace of the Lord Jesus Christ means the attractiveness of Christ, for grace is attractiveness. It is beauty. It has a magnetic comeliness. The very thing that is true of his life. From the time of his birth; from the entrance into his ministry; from the way people came about him because he taught as no one had taught before, teaching with authority, the authority of himself; because of his life and of his testimony of self-authenticating witness to the men and women, young and old, who are around him, there is a grace about that, a beauty, a magnetic comeliness. As he moves into Jerusalem on Palm Sunday and as he moves toward the cross with an awareness of the inevitability of that quality of grace, we find that we follow him wherever we can and that he leads us into greater truth of his word.

II. Grace is seen as forgiveness, and that's where the cross comes in. An understanding that the cross of Jesus Christ is the evidence of the grace of God. Karl Barth said, "The mercy, nevertheless, with which God steps out from the mystery of his majesty and holiness and turns to address man, that is in Jesus Christ, that is in his cross." And Christ said, "And I, if I be lifted up, will draw all men unto myself." We respond that there really is nothing that we can do. Nothing in our hands we bring; simply to his cross we cling. That's a response to grace, an understanding that we are the recipients of the unmerited favor of the grace of the Lord Jesus Christ. That's the amazing grace about which we sing and to which we hold. That grace costs, the cost of a cross. There is no such thing as cheap grace, for grace is not just attractiveness; grace is forgiveness.

III. Grace is power. (a) We think of grace sometimes being the opposite of power, but there is an irresistible grace of God in Jesus Christ. The vulnerability of the God revealed in the cross of Christ has the power of love about it. And the resurrection is God's seal placed upon that sacrifice, and the attractiveness and forgiveness become for us the beginning of a new age of the grace seen as power as we move toward the end time with an awareness that we move in an age which is ruled over by the grace of our Lord Jesus Christ.

(b) The grace of the Lord Jesus Christ is an affirmation not only of his effectiveness and of his forgiveness but also of his power over all the ages. Christ, I am Christ. And let that name suffice you. Aye, for me too he greatly hath sufficed. Lo, with no winning words would I entice you. I have no honor and no friend but Christ, so through life, death, through sorrow and through sinning, he shall suffice me for he hath sufficed. Christ is the end for Christ is the beginning. Christ, the beginning, for the end is Christ.—J. Randolph Taylor.

SUNDAY: NOVEMBER THIRTIETH

MORNING SERVICE

Topic: God with Us (Advent)
TEXT: Matt. 1:23

I. If Jesus is "God with us," then we must obey him. When we love someone to whom we owe obedience, it is easy to be obedient. When we love God, it is easy to be obedient to his word and to follow his commandments. And we love God because he first loved us. When there is an absence of love for God, there is an absence of obedience to his laws. Christmastime is an ideal time to take inventory of our love for God. How much do we love him? Are we obedient to him and his word?

II. If Jesus is "God with us," then we must trust him. It is gratifying to know that there is someone in whom we can put our complete trust. We must have faith in the character of God, knowing that when we commit our life, our family, and our future to him, he will provide what is best for us. Oftentimes circumstances will deceive us and will discourage our having complete trust in God. Still, we have the assurance that he is with us; and when God is with us, there is no risk involved in putting our trust in him. Since we have the assurance that he is with us, we must trust him.

III. If Jesus is "God with us," then we must strive to be like him. What a great accomplishment it would be if we would be like Christ in all of our actions, our conversations, our attitudes, and the decisions we make! We would save ourselves needless worry and anxiety. We would not be offensive to anyone. Our decisions and our actions would always bring glory to the son of God. There is encouragement in knowing that God is ever-present to help us become more like his son, Emmanuel. God honors the desires of our heart to be Christlike. He provides Spirit-motivation to help us reach this goal. He provides the grace to patiently and faithfully pursue the goal of Christlikeness.

IV. If Jesus is "God with us," then we must worship him. The presence of God inspires worship. However, it is our duty to worship him on those occasions when we might not sense his presence as keenly as we do at other times. When we think of God's goodness and mercy to us, we want to worship and adore him. We want to express gratitude to our heavenly Father who gave us his only begotten son and to our Lord for his willingness to become our savior.

V. If Jesus is "God with us," then we must love him. Those in whose heart the love of God dwells are wonderful people. It is an enjoyable experience to be around people who love God. Their dedication causes others to want to love him. And when we love God, we will also love everyone else—without exception! God requires all of our love. If we love him, there will be no room in our hearts for loving the things of the world. When we love God, we will keep his commandments. (See II John 1:6.)—O. W. Polen.

Illustrations

INCARNATION.   God could, had he pleased, have been incarnate in a man of iron nerves, the stoic sort who lets no sigh escape him. Of his great humility he chose to be incarnate in a man of delicate sensibilities who wept at the grave of Lazarus and sweated blood in Gethsemane. Otherwise we should have missed the great lesson that it is by his will alone that a man is good or bad and feelings are not in themselves of any importance. We should also have missed the all-important help of knowing that he has faced all that the weakest of us face, has shared not only the strength of our nature but every weakness of it but sin. If he had been incarnate in a man of immense natural courage, that would have been for many of us almost the same as his not being incarnate at all.—C. S. Lewis.

HAPPIEST BOOK.   Confessedly the New Testament is a grave and even a stern book, never shirking ugly facts but facing them with honesty and frankness. Yet could we read it for the first time, what would strike us most in it would surely be that this is the happiest book in the whole world. It thrills with joy; its message is a gospel, a shout of good news; it is the breaking through of midday sunshine on a morning that had been bleak and gray. So Christ himself certainly meant it to be. Indeed one could trace Christ's progress through the country by the happiness that he had left behind. Where he had passed, sorrows were healed and diseases cured, shadows lifted from strained minds, and souls restored to health and strength and cleanness. The early Christians were the happiest of people, and they caught the infection of that happiness from their master."—Arthur John Gossip.

Sermon Suggestions

LIVING IN HOPE.   Text: I Pet. 1:3. (1) Christian hope is sourced in the resurrection of Jesus Christ. (2) Christian hope is sensitive to God's will and seeks to live obediently to his truth. (3) Christian hope is sustained by trust. (4) Christian hope is strengthened by prayer.—Walter L. Dosch.

BEHOLD YOUR GOD.   Text: Col. 2:9. Five facts point decisively to the overwhelming conclusion: "In him dwelleth all the fulness of the Godhead bodily." (1) The first cardinal fact is the claim Jesus made for himself. (2) The second decisive fact concerns his sinlessness. (3) The third decisive fact is this: Jesus does for men what only God could do. (4) The fourth decisive fact is the universality of Jesus. (5) The most decisive of all is the divine self-verification of Christ in conscience.—James S. Stewart.

Worship Aids

CALL TO WORSHIP.   "Whatsoever things are true, whatsoever things are honest, whatsoever things are just, whatsoever things are pure, whatsoever things are lovely, whatsoever things are of good report; if there be any virtue, and if there be any praise, think on these things." Phil. 4:8.

INVOCATION.   Almighty God, who in thy providence hath made all ages a preparation for the kingdom of thy son: we beseech thee to make ready our hearts for the brightness of thy glory and the fulness of thy blessing.

OFFERTORY SENTENCE.   "Prepare ye the way of the Lord, make straight in the desert a highway for our God." Isa. 40:3.

OFFERTORY PRAYER.   Open our eyes that we may see thy goodness, O Father; our hearts that we may be grateful for thy mercies; our lips that we may show forth thy praise; and our hands that we may give these offerings according to thy wish and desire.

PRAYER. O God, who art worthy of a nobler praise than our lips can utter and of a greater love than we can give or understand, receive us as we draw near to thee in simple faith and childlike confidence. To believe in thee is to find meaning in life. To experience thy forgiveness is to find healing and peace. To meditate on thy purpose and power is to know the secret of hope. To trust and love thee is to face life and death unafraid. We thank thee for thy gifts to us: our families, our friendships, the books that instruct us, the music that inspires us, for the church, the scriptures, the sacraments, above all for Jesus Christ, thy son our savior.—Robert J. McCracken.

EVENING SERVICE

Topic: Are You Ready for Christmas?
TEXT: Isa. 40:3.
I. Are you ready for Christmas? There are presents still to be bought, cards to be addressed and mailed, a tree to be purchased, decorating to be done, and a hundred other things that must be done before the big day arrives. We may get all of that done and be ready for the festivities and family time and nevertheless miss the central message of this season, the celebration of the advent of the Christ. Are we ready to celebrate again the birth of the prince of peace and lord of lords?
II. Bethlehem had looked for the messiah for centuries, but they were not ready

for his coming. Neither was the innkeeper, nor the shepherds, nor Herod. For years the nation Israel had read, prophesied, and predicted that the messiah was soon to come, yet when he came they did not recognize him.
III. The world was not ready then nor am I sure that it is today. We are ready for a manger scene and even talk about a sweet baby, but are we ready for Christ who confronts us with a challenge to a higher level of being and living? We will not automatically experience the real depth of Christmas. We cannot turn a knob or change a dial and have instantaneously the spirit of Christmas.
IV. The spirit of Christmas is partially the giving and receiving of presents, the festivities and decorations, sending and getting greeting cards, going home again and renewing family ties, and preparing and enjoying festive meals, but the Christmas spirit is primarily an awareness and response to the great miracle of God coming into the world uniquely in Jesus Christ. It is a sense of wonder at the greatness of God's love and redemption; it is a feeling of acceptance and belonging to the creator of life; it is an awareness of our deep need of the message of the angels of joy, peace, and redemption.
V. Let us now prepare again for the celebration of the birth of the Christ by our worship, prayers, attitude, activities, decisions, and daily living. Let us commit anew our lives in this Christmas season to Jesus Christ and to his way of love and sacrificial living. Are you ready for Christmas? If not, there is still time to prepare your life personally for the impact of his living presence.—William P. Tuck.

SUNDAY: DECEMBER SEVENTH

MORNING SERVICE

Topic: The Sounds of the Season (Advent)
TEXT: Heb. 1:1-2.
I. The first sound of the season of Advent is the sound of music to which we are introduced as children.

(a) If your personal pilgrimage through Advent parallels my own, then music plays a principal role in your celebration of this season. The music of Advent lifts the heart and inspires the imagination. What creates a stronger spirit of adoration, wonder, and praise than the powerful grandeur of Handel's *Messiah* sung by a competent choir accompanied by a great organ and an accomplished orchestra?

(b) Music has a message all its own, and the message of the music of Advent directs our thoughts to the one eternal God who loved the world so much that he sent his own son to be our savior and lord.

II. The second sound of the season of Advent is the sound of voices. (a) In the store you hear the exchange between salespeople and customers, in homes you hear the question, "What do you want for Christmas?" and on the radio you hear the urging of advertisers, the hucksters of our materialistic age.

(b) The voices heard in the church during Advent are often those of children and young people preparing for the annual Christmas pageant, mingled with the voices of their teachers and parents urging them to perfection of performance.

(c) Other voices speak from scripture, "the cradle in which Christ lies," as Luther put it. We hear the ancient prophets speak in Isa. 9:2–6 and Mic. 5:2. We hear the laughter of Elizabeth and the uncontainable joy of Mary in Luke 1:46.

(d) From the past, men and women of faith point to the God of steadfast love who does not forget his people but prepares them for the fulness of time when the savior will be born into the world.

(e) Mingled with the memory of the first Advent are the hopes for the second Advent. We hear the promises of Jesus of Nazareth. (See Matt. 24:37–42.) His voice we must heed. "Maranatha"—even so come, Lord Jesus.

III. The third sound of the season of Advent is the sound of temptation.

(a) This is a time when we are tempted to eat too much, when we practice financial irresponsibility ostensibly for the sake of love, and when many consume too much alcohol. Instead of Advent being a period in which to prepare room in our hearts for the messiah of God, it degenerates into weeks of self-indulgence when daily schedules permit no room for Jesus, his word or spirit.

(b) What can we do, you and I, to hold at bay the siren sounds of the season? How can we keep from spending more money

on each other than we should? How can we prevent office party merry-making from slipping into sexual indulgence? How do we limit the list of those to whom we send season's greetings?

(c) Only intentional living can overcome pre-Christmas pressures. Decisions must be made weeks before as to what part of the budget will be spent for toys, what part for clothes, and so forth, lest last-minute emotionalism destroy peace of mind. What parties we will attend and what we will do at them might need examination. Will there be some division of labor, or will it all fall on mom? Will entertaining be a joy or a chore? What values rise to the surface in this holy season? (See Matt. 6: 25–33.)

IV. The fourth sound of the Advent season is that of silence. (a) Advent should be for listening. Our stormy, hectic, battered souls need quiet, peace, and healing which can only come when the body and the mind are at rest. (See Ps. 46:10; Isa. 30: 15.) "Where meek souls will receive him still, the dear Christ enters in."

(b) Advent is a season for being silent so that we may hear what God has to say to us. He is a personal God, and the Bible pictures him as one who listens to his people and hears them. (See Exod. 6:2–5; Luke 1:13.) God is a God who listens. We, his covenant people, are to listen. Read once more the ancient record of the birth of Jesus in Bethlehem of Judea. Ponder in the silence of your own soul the significance of this event. Behold, the savior of the world! Give to him your heart in gratitude and offer to him your prayers and praise.

(c) One more reason remains for silence as a sound to be observed during Advent. It is that we may hear the cries of the oppressed of our generation. Can we hear the hurt of battered women and children, the victims of war and crime, poverty, and cruelty? Are our ears tuned to the whispers of the lonely, the aged, the alienated, the stranger, the failure? And out beyond our national borders are many millions who do not know this savior nor have they heard of a gracious God. Do we listen to their need in these days of celebration?

(See Luke 4:18–19.)—Robert J. Hoeksema.

Illustrations

CAPACITY FOR JOY.   In "The Wapshot Scandal" by John Cheever a group of carolers is moving through the snow, singing the songs of Christmas. The singers are invited into the parson's home to warm up with hot chocolate. They continue to sing around the piano. As they sing "Joy to the World," the wife of the local plumber is deeply moved. The author explains: "That song was Mrs. Coulter's favorite, and it made her weep. The events in Bethlehem seemed to be not a revelation but an affirmation of what she had always known in her bones to be the surprising abundance of life. It was for this house, this company, this stormy night that he had lived and died. And how wonderful it was, she thought, that the world had been blessed with a savior! How wonderful it was that she should have a capacity for joy!"

BROTHERS IN CHRIST.   During World War II, I was the pilot of a heavy bomber on a certain mission to Genoa to destroy submarine installations. We were shot down and captured. Four of our crew survived, and for several days we were kept in a little provisional jail that was actually a stable for horses. One day, as we heard marching feet outside, the gate was thrown open. A German lieutenant came in and ordered us into the courtyard. There we saw a group of armed German soldiers in formation and behind them a truck. The four of us were ordered into the truck. Four guards, one for each of us, got in. The truck soon began its journey toward Germany from Italy. Just the week before, as my plane had crashed, I discovered the reality of God in my own life and in the world. As I sat there suddenly I was overwhelmed with homesickness. I realized that quite possibly I would never see my family or home again. In one instant I began to sing. I sang for quite a while, and then the other three surviving members of my crew, with the same feelings, joined in.

None of us could carry a tune, and we made what must have assuredly been one of the worst quartets ever formed. Yet we sang with a deep feeling coming from our hearts because of the unknown fate ahead. At one moment we began to sing the Christmas carols, "O, little town of Bethlehem," "Hark! the herald angels sing," "Silent night, holy night, all is calm and all is bright." As we were singing this hymn, suddenly we heard a beautiful baritone voice. I looked up into the eyes of one of the German guards. When we had finished, we began again. And you know what happened? By the time we had finished singing the second time, we were eight men, joined together in praising God for the moment when Jesus was born in Bethlehem. The guns were placed on the floor, and for the rest of that trip we shared and we laughed as we traveled together. One moment we were enemies who would have killed one another at the slightest mistake in the midst of a war. The next, when we suddenly realized that we all knew Jesus, we were brothers in Christ. The war came to an end for us in the back of that truck. The guards delivered us to the prison, no longer at the point of a gun but with an embrace and an expression of their desire that soon we would return home to our nation and to our loved ones.
—Jule Spach.

Sermon Suggestions

THE SAVIOR OF SINNERS.   Text: I Tim. 1:15. (1) The revelation of the savior. (2) The redemption in the savior. (3) The recommendation to the savior.—Stephen F. Olford.

GUARD YOUR THOUGHT LIFE.   Text: Phil. 4:8. (1) Concentrate on the truth as opposed to falsehood. (2) Concentrate on the serious as opposed to the frivolous. (3) Concentrate on the right as opposed to the convenient. (4) Concentrate on the clean as opposed to the dirty. (5) Concentrate on the loving as opposed to the discordant. (6) Concentrate on the positive as opposed to the negative.—Brian L. Harbour.

Worship Aids

CALL TO WORSHIP. "Arise, shine; for thy light is come, and the glory of the Lord is risen upon thee. Life up thine eyes round about and see." Isa. 60:1, 4.

INVOCATION. Our Father, help us during this special season to remember the many ways thou hast pointed out to us the coming of our Lord Jesus Christ. May we be ever mindful that thou wilt not let us sit in darkness, but if we are receptive we will see the light of thy many signs in the prophets, in the lives of our neighbors, and in the eyes of our family.

OFFERTORY SENTENCE. "To do good and to communicate forget not: for with such sacrifices God is well pleased." Heb. 13:16.

OFFERTORY PRAYER. O God, who didst give to us the gift of thy son, stir us with such love toward thee that we may gladly share whatever thou hast entrusted to us for the relief of the world's sorrow and the coming of thy kingdom.

PRAYER. We thank thee, O Father, for "love divine, all loves excelling, joy of heaven, to earth come down"—for this love that becomes real to us through the lives of others: the tender care of a mother, the support of a father, the fidelity of a mate, the encouragement of friends; for the promise of life that Christ's coming affirms for all men everywhere; for the life of this congregation in which our lives are intimately set in worship, study, and service.

O God, who didst cause thy light to shine out of darkness in the face of Jesus Christ, illumine our lives to reveal to us our inconsistencies, our motives that are less than Christian, and our hypocrisies that deceive. In this same light may we experience that fire that refines so that the name of Christian may not be betrayed in us. In these moments of worship may the creative power of thy word create in us a stronger faith and a deathless hope. May we come in such an attitude of openness of mind and heart that we may receive the fullness of thy grace and truth coming to us in thy advent in Christ. Strengthen us to do our part to make Christ known, loved, and served in our homes, community, and world.

Our prayers are offered in the strong name of him who is our peace, even Jesus Christ our Lord.—John Thompson.

EVENING SERVICE

Topic: Welcoming the Christ Child
TEXT: Rev. 3:20.

An old legend, told with many variations, pictures the Christ Child seeking admission to Christian homes on Christmas Eve. How shall we welcome him—in what manner, with what desires, in what attitude of mind and spirit?

I. Shouldn't we welcome him penitently? It's the only proper feeling in his presence because, no matter how free of gross sin we know ourselves to be, something about Jesus makes us aware of greater goodness yet to be attained.

II. How can we welcome Christ fittingly as long as ill will rankles in us toward those who have offended us? You say, "That's hard to do!" It can be done only by keeping steadily in mind that greater than any debt owed to us is the debt God in Christ pardoned in us.

III. A renewed determination to live generously toward others is part of an appropriate welcome for the Christ Child.

IV. It is always good to welcome Christ with a fresh recognition that in him the presence and power of God are wonderfully revealed. "His name shall be called 'Emmanuel' which means 'God with us' " is the heart of the Christmas message.

V. No welcome of Christ is complete unless we determine to let the faith which bears his name pervade our whole life. To celebrate Christ's coming and then live the rest of the year as if he had never come and to let the Christmas light shine upon us a little while and then put it aside as we pack away the Christmas lights when the season is over is to miss the great wealth of Christian faith and experience.—J. Francis F. Peak.

SUNDAY: DECEMBER FOURTEENTH

MORNING SERVICE

Topic: The Incarnation of Christ (Advent)

Text: John 1:14.

I. The incarnation declares a truth about Jesus Christ. (a) In v. 1 John identifies the word, the logos, with God. He says that the word was *theos.* Then in v. 14 John identifies the word, the logos, with man. He says that the word became *sarx.* He does not mean that God simply took on a human body. The word for body in the Greek is *soma,* but John does not use that word. Instead he uses the word *sarx,* flesh, which includes man's body, mind, soul, and moral nature. *Sarx* includes everything that makes man man. It means that God became one of us.

(b) The incarnation means that in Jesus Christ humanity and divinity, man in all his finiteness and God in all his infinitude, *theos* and *sarx,* came together as one. The New Testament writers always asserted this truth about the person of Christ (he was fully God and fully man) in relationship with his work.

(1) John says that the word became flesh. Why? So that those who believed in him could have the power to become the sons of God. (See v. 12.)

(2) Paul told the Corinthians that God was in Christ. (See II Cor. 5:19.) Why? So that he could explain further that Christ was reconciling them to the father.

(3) Paul wrote, "When the fullness of time came, God sent forth his son, born of a woman" (Gal. 4:4). Why? So that he could immediately add, "In order that he might redeem those who were under the law."

(c) The incarnation of Christ (his person) is always closely related with the atonement of Christ (his work). Jesus' incarnation insures his ability to save. If he was less than God or different from man, he would not be able to save us. But because he was both man and God he is able with one hand to gather all humanity under his care and with the other to usher us into the presence of God.

II. The incarnation declares a truth about God. (a) John says that the word of God *egeneto* flesh. What does this Greek word mean?

(1) Some say that it means "the word became flesh." But that implies a change from one state to another. And it is clear that even after the event described in v. 14 the word was still the word.

(2) Others say that it means "the word was born as flesh." But in the previous verse another verb is used for "to be born," and it is unlikely that John would use two different words in successive verses to mean the same thing.

(3) The best translation seems to be "the word came on to the human scene." "In Jesus God came all the way downstairs." God himself became a part of the human scene. He came to where we are.

(b) There is an abyss between man and God caused by our sin. Because of our sin we have been separated from God. But the glorious good news is that God does not wait for us to approach him, he does not wait until we are worthy of him, and he does not wait for us to take the initiative, but instead while we were yet sinners, indifferent and unconcerned, God took the initiative in coming to where we are.

(c) John says that the word dwelled among us. The verb translated "dwelled" literally means "tabernacled among us" and calls to mind the Old Testament context out of which the idea came.

(1) Adam and Eve were in perfect fellowship with God and were able to communicate with him as he walked in the garden in the cool of the day. But when they were ejected from the garden they no longer had a place where they could get in touch with him. And God seemed to be distant.

(2) Moses found a place where he could talk with God, the holy mountain, and every time he needed to clarify God's plan

and purpose he would go back to the mountain.

(3) Then one day God instructed man to build a tabernacle, a tent, out of wood and skin which would symbolize his presence in the midst of the Israelite camp where they could get in touch with him.

(4) This was later replaced by the temple with its holy of holies, and once a year the high priest would enter the presence of God to communicate with him.

(d) John says that God has pitched his tent right here in our midst in Jesus Christ. The God who created all things has come to us and has given us a place where we can get in touch with him. And for all men of all ages who want to know God and experience fellowship with him, Jesus Christ has become the way.

III. The incarnation is important because of what it says about man.

(a) Psychologists say that we are faced by a "crisis of insignificance" today. Not "Who am I?" but "Am I worth anything?" is the question that plagues us. We have been dehumanized by the mechanistic nature of our computer age. Our lives have been disrupted by national and international affairs over which we apparently have no control. We have been depressed by our age of the superstar where one's worth apparently is measured by the brilliance of his athletic ability or the beauty of her body. And looking at ourselves we realize we are neither brilliant nor beautiful. We have been deceived by false images. We strive to fit these images, but when we do we do not shake the haunting question of our worth.

(b) There is nothing disgraceful about being human for God himself became a man. When God was incarnated into human flesh, when he became one of us, he lifted up humanity, sanctified it, put his stamp of approval on it, and said, "Being a human is something special."

(c) He not only died for us but also lived with us. Because he came in Christ and through him reconciled us to himself, we are no longer nobody's nobody. We are God's somebody. When you look at yourself in the mirror you are looking at somebody. You are a son of God. You are a child of the king. You are a joint heir with Christ. You are somebody.—Brian L. Harbour.

Illustrations

LIVING EXPECTANTLY. In Sargent's mural of the Old Testament prophets the early figures are portrayed in varied postures, mostly with heads downcast, Hosea with face shrouded in a white mantle. But at the end three figures stand erect and alert, eyes fastened upon the future, faces illumined by a great light from beyond. With the prophets it was the expected messiah who drew their gaze forward and set them aglow with expectancy. Theirs is the invariable posture of the true Christian life its whole course through. The eyes of faith are eagerly expectant toward the future. The best is yet to be. God intends for us all such good things as pass men's anticipation.—Henry P. Van Dusen.

CROWDED INNS. If Mary and Joseph were turned away, it was not that there was any ill will against them but simply because the innkeeper was so harried with other people that he had no patience to look at any more. These travelers from Nazareth had come late, the inn was crowded, they could not get in, and that is all there was to it. Just so casually, through the drift of circumstance and not through any particularly hostile will, may Jesus be excluded from the inn of our hearts. We have merely filled all the space we have with other guests. We do not mean to be irreligious, but our thoughts and feelings are so occupied with other matters that religion cannot find a place. We too are like the inn where the first come are the first served. In this world, with its noisy and demanding clamor, the crowd of common thoughts and common interests has poured in upon us and taken possession of our time and our attention, and when Christ comes, with his infinite gift for the enrichment of our souls, there is no room for him in the inn.—Walter Russell Bowie.

Sermon Suggestions

THE SPIRIT OF CHRISTMAS. Text: John 1:14. (1) Christmas is the spirit of wonder.

(2) Christmas is the spirit of receiving. (3) Christmas is the spirit of giving.—James A. Lollis.

GOD INCARNATE. Text: Matt. 1:23. (1) The one who had drawn near to man. (2) The one who had taken upon himself our nature. (3) The one who was not ashamed to call us brethren. (4) The one who had identified himself with our suffering, our weakness, our sorrow, and our death.—John Sutherland Bonnell.

Worship Aids

CALL TO WORSHIP. "Lo, the star, which they saw in the east, went before them, till it came and stood over where the young child was. When they saw the star, they rejoiced with exceeding great joy." Matt. 2:9–10.

INVOCATION. Dear Christ, who art the light of the world, shine, we pray thee, so that all who walk in darkness and dwell in the land of the shadow of death may have the light of life. May thy word at this season be for us a lamp unto our feet and a lamp unto our path.

OFFERTORY SENTENCE. "Seeing ye have purified your souls in obeying the truth through the Spirit unto unfeigned love of the brethren, see that ye love one another with a pure heart fervently." I Pet. 1:22.

OFFERTORY PRAYER. May we find it to be a joyful experience, O Lord, to offer these gifts in the name of Jesus. Grant unto us the wisdom of the men of old who found a token in a star, worshiped the child as a newborn king, and made offerings at his feet.

PRAYER. O thou who in the worst of times proclaimed the best of hopes and sent the Christ child in the fulness of time, make receptive our hearts to receive this little one who changed the face of history. Make clean our lips and wash white our hearts. Let scripture tell the story. Let music take us again through the paths of time. When we cannot grasp the fact, help our imaginations to lay hold of the story and make it live.

Help us to remember that many followers of this Bethlehem babe will find it difficult to worship him. They are hungry through no fault of their own. While we worship in comfort and warmth, their bodies are cold. Maybe their hearts are bitter. Maybe they have lost the capacity to love. The world has been cruel. They have never felt our handclasp. God, are they bitter because of us? Do they hate their fellowmen because of us? Help us so to transform our love into deeds that they may know that this is thy world.

Incite us to act now. Let not this season of seasons pass without our giving ourselves to missions of mercy, errands of love, and works of charity. Let not the day mock us. Help us to lay hold of the goodwill generated by this birth. Let it soften the wrath of those who misunderstand their fellowmen and those who hate their brothers. Help us to rejoice with exceeding great joy as we bring in thankfulness our gifts to the Christ, believing that, despite all the Herods, Christ's message shall yet be written on every lintel and sung at every hearth.—Fred E. Luchs.

EVENING SERVICE

Topic: What Does Christmas Mean?
TEXT: Gal. 4:4–5.

I. Christmas means that *God is interested.* Paul said, "God sent forth his Son."

(a) God is not a far-off, impersonal, indifferent power, insensible to and unmoved by man's problems. He is personal and responsive, involved and loving. The psalmist wrote, "Like as a father pitieth his children, so the Lord pitieth them that fear him." We need this sense of security which comes from knowing that God is interested in us.

(b) This is the gospel: God is interested. When the time was right, he intervened on man's behalf. "God sent forth his Son." The message of Christmas, the import of the baby in the Bethlehem manger, is that God is interested.

II. Christmas means that *God is acting.* "God sent forth his Son . . . to redeem them that were under the law."

(a) Sending his Son was not only a show of God's interest. God acted on our behalf. He acted to free us from the bondage and frustration of attempting to keep God's laws by our own efforts. Precise and consistent obedience to the divine will is beyond our natural ability. Our imperfections can never satisfy the perfect God. We are forever defeated and always under condemnation when law-keeping is the basis of our would-be relationship with God.

(b) God acted to redeem us. It is comforting to say, "The Lord is my shepherd." But it is more deeply satisfying to hear Jesus say, "The good shepherd giveth his life for the sheep." Not only God with us but God acting on our behalf. This is what Christmas means. The angel announced to Joseph: "Thou shalt call his name Jesus, for he shall save his people from their sins." The Christ child, whose birth we celebrate at Christmas, was God's action. For, as Paul wrote, "God was in Christ, reconciling the world unto himself."

III. Christmas means that *God is completing.* Our verse states, "God sent forth his Son, made of a woman, made under the law, to redeem them that were under the law, that we might receive the adoption of sons." He acted to redeem us because he wants to bring his relationship with us to completion: he wants to make us his children. As Paul goes on to say: "God hath sent forth the Spirit of his Son into your hearts, crying, Abba, Father. Wherefore thou art no more a servant, but a son; and if a son, then an heir of God through Christ."—Bramwell Tripp.

SUNDAY: DECEMBER TWENTY-FIRST

MORNING SERVICE

Topic: The Cradle and the Throne (Advent)

TEXTS: Luke 2:7; Rev. 1:14–15.

Those two texts mark the beginning and the end of the story that the New Testament has to tell about Jesus. At first sight you would not recognize them as belonging to the same story. A little child whose cradle was a manger because the eastern inn could find no room for his mother at her critical hour and this mystical picture of one who has power written on brow and feet and lips—what possible similarity is there between the two portrayals?

I. The first picture conveys the romance of Christmas. (a) Through all the centuries since, the imagination of mankind has played about the cradle in the manger and the shepherds in the nearby fields. Art has pictured the scene, and legend and music have found their themes in it. But we must never forget that the romance of Christmas springs from a very deep source. There is nothing romantic about a baby being born in a stable. In the world of today children are being born every day in just as incongruous surroundings.

(b) The romance of Christmas is the association between the highest and the humblest. Apart from what men have come to believe about Jesus, Bethlehem is a commonplace.

II. The second picture seems completely divorced from this world. (a) The mystic figure standing amid the golden candlesticks seems remote and unearthly. What possible relationship can it have with the Jesus about whom the gospels tell us? But may we not be entirely wrong in thinking along those lines? Is there not a human background in the mystic figure of the book of Revelation?

(b) Does not the hair as white as snow express the feeling that Jesus is ageless—the same feeling that John must have had when the first words of his story were about the beginning of creation? Are not the feet of fine brass symbols of the tireless errands of love that Jesus took in response to human need, while the eyes like a flame of fire are pictured memories of a look, sometimes tender, sometimes with the fire of righteous anger in them against spiritual pride and oppression?

III. What message have these two extremes for us—the lowly beginning and the exalted climax?

(a) When we are thinking of the human

life of Jesus, of the way in which he came into the world, and of the unfolding incidents of his youth and later ministry, we only see them partially and imperfectly unless there is in our minds a sense of the divine background to it. These facts do not form merely a little isolated romance of beauty. They spring from the love and purpose of God, and they have a message which is as true today as when the stars looked down on the fields of Bethlehem.

(b) When we have before our minds pictures of Christ enthroned in heaven—the far-off savior and judge of men—we are set upon false tracks of thought at once unless all the time we hold onto the connection between those pictures and the Jesus of the gospels.

(c) The images may be different, but Christ does not change. He is the same whether earth or heaven is the stage. The connection between the two is unbroken and unbreakable. It is not one part of the story which can form a saving faith but the whole, beginning at Bethlehem and reaching its climax in his exaltation to the right hand of God.

(d) The whole spirit and inspiration of faith depends upon the connection between his cradle and his throne, so that we neither lose Christ among the clouds nor amid the centuries but find in him one who is the same yesterday and today and forever.—Sidney Berry.

Illustrations

FORGIVE. The day before Christmas was hectic. Father was worried with bundles and burdens. Mother's nerves reached the breaking point more than once. The little girl seemed to be in the way wherever she went. Finally she was hustled up to bed. As she knelt to pray, the feverish excitement so mixed her up that she said, "Forgive us our Christmases, as we forgive those who Christmas against us."

ESSENCE. What is the thought of Christmas? Giving. What is the hope of Christmas? Living. What is the joy of Christmas? Loving. No silver or gold is needed for giving if the heart is filled with

Christmas love, for the hope of the world is kindly living, learned from the joy of God above.—Laura Hooker.

Sermon Suggestions

CHRISTMAS PARADOXES. Text: Luke 1: 30–31. (1) On the first Christmas day the greatest person on earth was the smallest. (2) On the first Christmas day the richest person on the earth was the poorest. (3) On the first Christmas day the most eloquent person on the earth was speechless. (4) On the first Christmas day the weakest person on the earth was the strongest.

CHRISTMAS GREETINGS. Text: Luke 2: 10. (1) May your Christmas be joyous through Christ. (2) May your loneliness give way to fellowship. (3) May your insecurity be superseded by confidence. (4) May your despair be replaced with hope. (5) May your darkness be turned into radiant light.—Carl J. Sanders.

Worship Aids

CALL TO WORSHIP. "Behold, I bring you good tidings of great joy, which shall be to all people. For unto you is born this day in the city of David a Savior, which is Christ the Lord. Glory to God in the highest, and on earth peace, good will toward men." Luke 2:10–11, 14.

INVOCATION. Hushed be our hearts, O God, by the mystery and the wonder of the birth of the Christ Child. Make us truly wise with the wisdom of a little child that once again the highest truth may be born afresh in our hearts. Let not our souls be busy inns that have no room for thy son, but this day throw wide the doors of our lives to welcome our holy guest.

OFFERTORY SENTENCE. "When they were come into the house, they saw the young child with Mary his mother, and fell down, and worshiped him. And they presented unto him gifts; gold, and frankincense, and myrrh." Matt. 2:11.

OFFERTORY PRAYER. Our Lord Jesus Christ, whose birthday has become a season of benevolence and giving, bless these our gifts which we offer in thankfulness for thyself, God's unspeakably precious gift.

PRAYER. Almighty God, our heavenly Father, who hast given us in the midst of the bleakness of winter the gladness of thy coming in Jesus Christ, we are gathered here to praise thy name. Wilt thou so prepare us in spirit, wilt thou so clarify our minds and stir our hearts that we may be fully alert and awake and sensitive to the wonder of this season. We thank thee for the glory that has been revealed, and we ask that thou wilt open our eyes so we may see it.

We thank thee for the spirit that has been let loose among men, creating goodwill and understanding and harmony for a season. May we so lay hold upon the secret of thy spirit and may we be so claimed of thy Holy Spirit that the goodwill and the harmony and the happiness of this time of year may become the very spirit of our lives always.

We pray this day for those who are not able to be with us but whose hearts and minds are joined with us in this time of praise and worship. Bless those who are sick. Enlarge their horizons. Give to them vistas that lie beyond their distress—even of thy glory and thy peace. Wilt thou be with those who are enmeshed in the complications of this, our life. Wilt thou grant to them thy guidance and thy counsel; and as they grope in the darkness, may their hand touch thy hand and find thy leading which lights their way to peace.

Wilt thou bless our families and our homes in this sacred time that the glorious meanings of this season may once again live in our hearts. At the very center of all of our busy activities may there be a glorious peace where we adore the holy child of Bethlehem and once again commit ourselves in loyalty to him whose coming brings us our life.

Now bless us in this time of worship and in all that we do in this Christmas season; and always may we give honor to Christ whose coming has given thy gladness to the world.—Lowell M. Atkinson.

EVENING SERVICE

Topic: Three Voices from the East
SCRIPTURE: Matt. 2:1–12.

I. I am Caspar, a priest of Zoroaster, and now forever a servant of the most high God. I left the hills and plains, the steppes and deserts of Samarkand and came to Jerusalem because a strange star had arisen in the zodiac of the fish. I had always wandered far from the beaten tracks of men. From youth I had not been satisfied with the legends of my people.

One day there came to the town of Samarkand a Jew, wandering through the earth after the fashion of his people. This Isaac of Damascus told me of the God whose name is Jehovah, who desires of men the sacrifices of a broken and contrite heart.

"But," I said, "how can I know this God? For too long I have worshiped ideas and fantoms of the mind. I must have a God I can see and touch, a God who in turn is touched by my weaknesses and understands the foibles of mortal clay. I am done with distant gods who dwell in the sheen of blinding and unapproachable light."

Then Isaac told me of the promised messiah, of the one who would be called Immanuel, of the day when Jehovah was to step out of his far away heaven and talk as a man with the sons of men. I came to know the promises of the prophets Isaiah and Micah. And so it was that, when one day a wondrous light appeared in the Jewish zodiac, I resolved to leave my home and my altar and to journey to the land of the Jew to see if perchance the messiah had been born.

I struck south through Seleicia, followed the Euphrates through Mesopotamia, pushed west through Syria to Damascus, and came at length to Jerusalem. I wrestled with the Shamal, the dust-laden wind from the north that chokes and strangles, battled the southwest monsoon, was drenched by many a rain, blistered by hellish suns—but still I followed after the star. And at last I found the tiny town of Bethlehem and threw my tired body before the holiest picture of God that any man could see—a baby, sweet and innocent, lying in a manger. Before him I poured the gold of my chalice and to him I gave my life; for a man can do no other when at last he finds the God who loves well enough to wear human flesh.

It was God who gave me the sign in the east, who led me to Jerusalem, who spoke to me from the scriptures, who directed me to Bethlehem, and who brought me home in safety. Where hearts are eager to find the king, there are always signs which lead at last to his presence chamber. The method of guidance may be mysterious, but the fact is certain.

II. I am Melchior of Aparnea. I dwelt hard by the Caspian gates, a son of a royal house, and a fanatical devotee of the hardest cult of Zoroaster. There came to my father's house word that a rebel priest in Samarkand, one Caspar, had listened to the fables of a renegade Jew who believed there was but one true God who would one day reveal himself by becoming man. I resolved to silence this Caspar's tongue with my own knife, and under an oath I left the region of the great oak forests, the tiger, the red and fallow deer. I traveled to Samarkand only to find that Caspar had fled west to Jerusalem in search of a new Jewish king. Resolved to revenge his insult of our noble religion, I pursued him to the very court of Herod where I found him one night inquiring of this petty monarch where the Christ was to be born.

Gleefully I thought my quarry as good as dead and ordered the servants to purchase some myrrh in the bazaar so that I might embalm the rebel magi's corpse after the manner of our faith. As I listened within the shadows of the colonnades, I heard things that quenched my fury. This Herod was only great by virtue of his great wickedness. Now in his old age, without love or loyalty, he was trapped by the fears born of his misdeeds. He trembled for his throne when he heard the story of Caspar.

Suddenly I saw myself thirty years hence mirrored in Herod. My hand fell from my scimitar as God closed in upon my conscience. I saw myself reflected in the bloated eyes of Herod the Great. I saw in this cringing, calculating, crafty monarch the end product of an evil conscience—full of fears and shrinking from the good news that a king who would reveal the fulness of God's love had been born.

I joined Caspar as he journeyed to Bethlehem to find this wonderful child. And when I found him, my sin fell from me. I felt as though I had swallowed sunshine! For the first time in years I felt clean and well inside. The myrrh, which I bought to embalm the corpse of Caspar, I left as a gift for the infant king.

III. I am Balthasar of Gur. The gods gave me money, intellect, and a ready wit. The one bought me women, the other knowledge, and the third kept me from prison. I respected neither God nor man. My whim was my will. Of all human flesh I loved only Caspar of Samarkand, the teacher of my youth.

Soon women became dull and sensual pleasures jaded. Sport became insane. I turned to my books again, but neither the philosophy of the Shahnama, the satire of Firdousi, nor the morals of Sadi brought satisfaction. In desperation I set out for Samarkand to find Caspar only to discover that he had gone to Jerusalem to find a newborn king. I set out after him and at last found him in the city of Jerusalem at the court of a jackal named Herod.

Then he told me a baby had been born who was to reveal the true God. All the wisdom of the ages was to come to fruition and meaning as at last men were to see the very nature of God clothed in real flesh and blood. I was enthralled beyond all telling.

I surrendered my cockiness and foppishness that day, and left my frankincense at his cradle. But I have come to warn you, and I am the last that shall come to help you find the star. Many on Main Street cannot find the star of wonder because they know the facts of the story too well. Theirs is the deadness of familiarity. Help them find the star by making Christ real and fresh and vital in your own life. Go to Main Street! Live out your faith with its people! Then, but not until then, will you find the star! Christmas is not a philosophy to be contemplated; it is a reality to be experienced!—John F. Crouthamel, Jr.

SUNDAY: DECEMBER TWENTY-EIGHTH

MORNING SERVICE

Topic: **Coping with Change (Watch Night)**

TEXT: Mark 2:22.

Change is upon us even as it has always been upon us. We had better learn how to cope with it or else it will capture us.

I. Though in the midst of change, let not change overpower us. The new is not always the best, even as the old is not always the best. It is necessary to hold onto that which is good even while one is caught up in the process of welcoming the new.

II. The positive force of change steadily operates within us. It is in our very nature to change, even though we may paradoxically resist change itself. Shakespeare understood this fact and wrote, "Presume not that I am the thing I was." You may contend that you remain the same, and you may be right in part but only in part.

(a) Our interests change. Our tastes change. Our loyalties change. In many important ways, I am the same person I was twenty years ago. But since then I have lived more, experienced more, wept and laughed more, suffered and enjoyed more. I have had a longer time to observe and take notes on life. I have turned from this interest to develop that interest. I have concluded that what I once thought was terribly important is not as important as I had first thought. I may not claim to be a better nor a wiser person, but it would be inaccurate to judge me as exactly the same man.

(b) Hold on to hope. Without hope, life would turn cold and meaningless. Will you see the very fact that I am a person of hope means that I am a person who has some confidence in the possibilities of change? Zangwell was right when he saw this: "Take from me the hope that I can change the future and you will make me mad." The words belong together: hope, change, and future.

III. Change is not only a part of our nature; it is also necessary to survival.

Surely we must know that we cannot survive in a nuclear age with a tribal morality. We cannot dare to maintain a racially prejudiced world in a world of mass media, jet transportation, and the emergence of developing nations. It is no longer rational to believe that the world can be fenced off into a ghetto here and a ghetto there. That time is past. Change is necessary for human survival.

IV. Change should be seen as a challenge that serves to stimulate us and invigorate our lives. It keeps life from becoming dull and drab, flat and stale. Ellen Glasgow commented, "The only difference between a rut and a grave is their dimensions." Do we not say to one another from time to time, "I think I need a change!"

(a) We do need a change of pace and perspective, environment and atmosphere. Why? Because in change there is challenge and stimulation. We turn for a book that expresses a provocative point of view, summoning readers to change this or that. It is challenging. We attend a play where the playwright rubs our minds with exciting new ideas, and we leave eager to rethink our thoughts and share them with others. We are up against an old familiar problem, and the usual answers are not working as well as they once did. We are called to change approaches, and this is a challenge to mind and spirit. The fossil fuels may run out on us, and we'll have to change our ways. What a challenge to our creative ingenuity.

(b) Change can mean the release of new vitality, the excitement of a new possibility, and the creating of a tension within the mind that produces new and wonderful results. Change is challenge. It challenges decline and decay. It keeps us alive.

V. We can remain stabilized and retain security even in the midst of a "future-shock" kind of change in the knowledge that in the midst of change some things there are that do not change. Underneath all the changing circumstances of life, birth and death, good fortune and ill, the health of youth and the infirmities of age, the hours of laughter and the times of sorrow—"underneath are the everlasting arms of God."—Charles L. Copenhaver.

Illustrations

NEW WOOD.   An admirer asked Longfellow how he sustained his high level of vigor and productivity. Answering, he turned to an apple tree standing in full view, its blossoms beautiful and fragrant. "That apple tree is very old," said Longfellow, "but I never saw prettier blossoms upon it. I've noticed that the tree grows a little new wood each year, and out of the new wood those blossoms come. Like the apple tree I try to grow a little new wood every year, out of which my heart blossoms."

A NEW YEAR'S CREED.   I will talk health instead of sickness.

I will talk prosperity instead of failure.

I will carry good news instead of bad news.

I will tell the cheerful tale instead of the sad tale.

I will mention my blessings instead of my burdens.

I will speak of the sunshine of yesterday and tomorrow instead of the clouds of today.

I will encourage instead of criticize.

I will be a friend to everyone.—*The Wesley Courier.*

Sermon Suggestions

ON PILGRIMAGE.   Text: Heb. 11:8–9. (1) Pilgrimage is the inexorable law of life. (2) Pilgrimage is the central temper of our faith. (3) Pilgrimage is—all along and at the end—God's summons and God's invitation.—Henry P. Van Dusen.

GAINING A FRESH GRIP ON LIFE.   Text: John 20:28. (1) People who have gained a fresh grip on life usually begin by looking beyond the tiny circumference of their own lives. (2) After a person begins to live beyond himself, he may step up to the next level of conversion which is actively to participate in the life of a Christian community—the church. (3) People who leap beyond themselves and who link arms with Christians in worship still feel something is missing. The process of conversion never stops. Christ must become more than a figure rising from the ashes of history whom we adore. He must become a friend to whom we can talk, a guide who shows us a better way, and a refuge upon whom we can cast our cares. (4) There is still a deeper level of conversion a Christian can experience. It is to take Christ as savior. (5) When Christ becomes lord, he is the commanding center of life.—Jack R. Van Ens.

Worship Aids

CALL TO WORSHIP.   "O Zion, that bringeth good tidings, get thee up into the high mountain; O Jerusalem, that bringeth good tidings, lift up thy voice with strength; lift it up, be not afraid; say onto the cities of Judah, Behold your God!" Isa. 40:9.

INVOCATION.   As we begin another day, most gracious Father, make us to know that we never drift out of thy love and care. Faces may change and conditions may alter, but thou art never so near to us as when we need thee most.

OFFERTORY SENTENCE.   "Walk in love, as Christ also hath loved us, and hath given himself for us as an offering and sacrifice to God." Eph. 5:2.

OFFERTORY PRAYER.   Our Father, we bow in humble gratitude that as a new year dawns we may call on thee to guide, strengthen, bless, and forgive, and that through these gifts we may share thy love with all who call upon us and thee.

PRAYER.   O God, who art from everlasting to everlasting, we thank thee for the things that last in this world of change. We seem to spend so much of our energy struggling for things that are here today and gone tomorrow. Teach us to build on the rock that endures.

We thank thee for our families, for, after the last dish has been dried and the youngest child graduated, we still have an indissoluble bond one with another. Forgive us for being so busy buying shoes for the children that we fail to make their acquaintance. Help us to create families that will outlast homes.

We thank thee for friendships that transcend time and distance. Preserve us from being so ambitious for things that we miss people. Deliver us from the poverty of having everything but friends. Teach us the joy of entertaining angels unawares.

We thank thee for the church, outlasting empire after empire. We thrill to join forces herein with thee and with one another, knowing thy work is to be carried on here and thy will to be done after we have gone to be with thee.

We thank thee for eternal life, thy promise that all our worthy struggles are not in vain, that our friendships will not be cut off, that we shall all be together in thy house of many rooms as Christ hath promised us.—Harry W. Adams.

EVENING SERVICE

Topic: After Christmas Lift-Up
TEXT: Luke 2:20.

I. A lot of people have a let-down after Christmas. Maybe it's because Christmas has given us such a lift-up. There's something magical about the Christmas season, sometimes even to the point of being artificial. Our attitudes and ways usually change for the better at Christmas. We like what we see and wish we could keep it. We hate to see it end.

II. We are no different than those who experienced that first Christmas. Jesus was born. The star shone in the east. The wise men arrived. The shepherds came. The most unique event in history had occurred. The wonder and the majesty of God's incarnation had happened, but those witnessed all that could not remain in Bethlehem forever. Like the shepherds, we must return to work, to school, to the customary, to the normal.

III. The road back from significant events is not always an easy one. It is much easier to go forward with eager anticipation and excitement than to look backward at some important happening. Eventually that for which we wait comes. When we reach the peak, we must go down the other side of the mountain. The shepherds returned; so do we.

(a) The shepherds on their way back took with them some of the joy of their experience. What more can we do, we who are returning from Christmas, we who are on our way back to our various fields and pastures of endeavor? We have witnessed Christmas. We have experienced its excitement and joy.

(b) On our way back from Christmas we can glorify and praise God for all we have heard and seen, for all we have experienced this Christmas—children's sparkling and excited eyes, giving and receiving from family and friends, the attitude of peace and goodwill even if it's momentary, the warmth and love we've shared, the music and songs. The words of Christmas from the ancient gospel writers renew within us the fact that God has come and is in the world, that the Christmas story is one of God's love for us and all people.

(c) What could be more appropriate on our way back from Christmas than to glorify and praise God for all we have seen, felt, and heard in the holiday season?—Paul A. Layton.

SECTION X. Ideas and Suggestions for Pulpit and Parish

A CARING COMMUNITY. To emphasize the church as a caring community the Reformed Church in Bronxville, New York, has named a ministry committee. Each committee member establishes a genuine and personal relationship with an elderly church member who lives alone or is unable to attend worship services. The committee maintains a "transport-escort" service for persons needing rides to church, sponsors a hospital supply closet of useful equipment that is loaned to those in temporary need of such things as a hospital bed or a wheel chair, distributes cassette tapes of recorded church services to home-bound and hospitalized members, and makes available a comprehensive file of nursing homes, health-related facilities, and retirement homes.

DIRECT MAIL OUTREACH. Members of the Parkway Cumberland Presbyterian Church in Nashville, Tennessee, contact new residents, newlyweds, new parents, and the hospitalized by mailed letters of welcome, congratulations, comfort, and invitation which are followed by phone calls and personal visits. Church members serve as contact and resource people in variously designated areas in the community.

WE CHOOSE TO CARE. The motto of the Church of the Nazarene in Arvada, Colorado, is "We choose to care." Choosing to become involved and concerned with each other's needs and problems and those living nearby, members distribute in calling and ministering a pamphlet entitled "We Choose to Care" which contains a message that in part reads: "As a church we have made some choices. We choose to be a church that cares when sorrow comes, when sickness comes, and when loneliness comes.

"We choose to care by offering friendship, by reaching out in love, and by being concerned.

"We choose to meet the needs of our neighbors by seeking to discover their need and by seeking to find ways to do something about it.

"We choose to offer an acceptable love to you in your deepest need and to accept you in Christian love just as you are.

"In a world which competes for the minds of your children, we choose to care by giving them a solid foundation upon which to build.

"In a society which tends to undermine the values of the home, we choose to care by strengthening those values.

"In a world which has lost its sense of direction, we choose to care by pointing to the one who said, 'I am the way.'

"In a society where truth is a changing thing, we choose to care by pointing to the changeless one who said, 'I am the truth.'

"When the eternal questions of meaningful existence—Why am I here? What is life all about? and Where am I going?—are often ignored, we choose to care by pointing to the one who said, 'I am the life.' "—*The Preacher's Magazine.*

FRIENDSHIP VISITATION. On two successive Sundays in April the First Presbyterian Church in Alliance, Ohio, schedules an interfamily visitation. Believing that a strong church is one where members know and care for one another, the church solicits one hundred participants who each visit a home listed on a letter containing instructions. On the second Sunday each person visited on the first Sunday is urged to call upon another church family. If all goes well, as many as two hundred homes are visited.

SING-A-PHONE. Members of the Chapel Class in the Centenary United Methodist Church in Lynchburg, Virginia, on Sunday mornings dial the numbers of shut-in and hospitalized parishioners and sing a gospel hymn.

ROUND TWO. The Dublin Community Church (UCC) in Dublin, Ohio, has formed a group called Round Two for widows and widowers who meet once a month to discuss topics such as the effects of the death on the window or widower's children, self-identity, remarriage, and problems peculiar to grief experiences.

HELPING HANDS. Less fortunate families in the community are assisted by "Helping Hands," a ministry of the deacons in the First United Presbyterian Church in Alliance, Ohio. After quietly checking to determine that a real need exists, the church distributes at Christmas and throughout the year food and other necessities directly to families or in cooperation with agencies such as the Salvation Army. An effort is made to provide a personal touch in this ministry, and when requested family counseling is made available.

MISSION FESTIVAL. Members of the Westchester Christian Church in Los Angeles, California, received a valuable education in overseas work during a mission festival featuring a West African Christian speaker, a meal whose menu suggested foods eaten by overseas Christians, and visual displays.

ADOPT A MISSIONARY. Members of the First Baptist Church in Lancaster, South Carolina, have been invited to adopt a missionary whose birthday is the same as that of the church member and to whom the member will occasionally write and send a birthday gift and about whose field of service and work he will come to know.

BIRTHDAY FELLOWSHIP. The Taylor Avenue Church of the Nazarene in Racine, Wisconsin, schedules each month a "Just for Fellowship" period following a Sunday evening service when people having birthdays and anniversaries during the month may share an informal celebration.

SATURDAY SCHOOL. Sunday school on Saturday? That's the way it is at the New Shiloh Baptist Church in Baltimore, Maryland, where a declining Sunday school attendance and the inevitable limitations of time for an adequate study program following the worship hour suggested that a new approach was needed. So the Sunday school concept with its emphasis on Bible study was moved to Saturday mornings with Bible study according to age groups held from 10 to 11:30, followed by group activities, and a four hundred percent increase in attendance and a significant addition among teenage participants.

HYMN CHOICES. Morning worship was altered at the St. John's United Church in Oakville, Ontario, to make possible a Hymn Hit Parade Sunday. Members listed their ten favorites, and the ten most popular were sung. Top hits: "Abide with Me" and "Amazing Grace."

SERMON OUTLINE. An outline of Sunday's sermon is included in the newsletter of the Cumberland Presbyterian Church in Fayetteville, Tennessee, so that members may give personal preparation and thought to the message prior to the service and may better follow and remember the sermon during and following its delivery.

THE MINISTRY CENTER.   The Central United Protestant Church in Richland, Washington, has a ministry center where lay volunteers gather for fellowship and service. The center's work includes telephone answering, envelope addressing, record keeping, newsletter and bulletin preparation, and telephone witnessing. The center's hours, which range from ninety minutes to full afternoons, are scheduled differently each weekday for the convenience of parishioners who might otherwise have conflicting work times.

TO EQUIP THE SAINTS.   In an effort to enlarge outreach and to increase membership the First Baptist Church in Los Angeles, California, held a series of training programs specifically designed to "equip the saints" in an understanding of the Christian faith, to provide a biblical and doctrinal foundation needed for a confident witness, to interpret the various ministries of the local church, and to train people how effectively to "gossip the gospel."

SPIRITUAL GIFTS.   The Diocesan Committee on Lay Ministry of the Episcopal Diocese of Alabama held a two-day Spiritual Gifts Workshop at which the twenty-five spiritual gifts mentioned in the New Testament were discussed and participants sought to identify and to find ways of exercising the particular gifts God has given them.

BLESSING OF ANIMALS.   A parade and blessing of the pet animals of parishioners is held annually at the St. Mary's-in-the-Hills Episcopal Church in Lake Orion, Michigan. The hymn sung in this revival of an ancient Christian practice is, appropriately, "All things bright and beautiful, all creatures great and small."—*The Living Church.*

COLOSSAL WORK DAY.   On a Saturday in spring members of the First Baptist Church in Seattle, Washington, come together for a general clean-up and fix-up of the church property. Espousing the idea that many hands lighten the work, the participants attack the jobs to be done with paint brushes and yard tools during what they call the Colossal Work Day.

RICE BAGS.   During Lent members of the United Methodist Church in Springfield, Virginia, put money in small rice bags that remind them of the way Indian families give a small part of their daily portions of rice to the church. The rice bags are taken to church on Palm Sunday and Easter. A typical project benefited by the rice bag collection: wells in India.

SUGGESTIONS FOR GIVING.   One pastor writes: "At the beginning of the Lenten season we ask families to keep track of their expenditures for food and to give ten percent of what is spent to the Easter offering. The offering tripled the first year and has remained high during all the years we've done it."

Another congregation challenged its members to sign a pledge to give up a meal weekly throughout the year and give the money saved every month for the relief of hunger and suffering around the world. It was calculated that if every one of the 642 members did this, by the end of the year they would be able to contribute $25,038 for this cause.

A concerned Christian suggests: "At every meal, when you set the table for your family, set a place for one of the world's hungry. Put a box at that place and into it put the cost in actual nickles, dimes, and dollars of feeding one extra person at that meal. Accumulate the money meal by meal, and at the end of the month take it to your church to help the starving and suffering persons of the world. If we are willing to include the hungry in every meal we serve, however simple or lavish, we could make a difference."—*Presbyterian Survey.*

LENTEN CROSSES.   Members of the Lynnwood Reformed Church in Schenectady, New York, celebrate Lent by making and sharing crosses. In the weeks prior to Lent each member is invited to make a cross of any material and attached to a cord for wearing around the neck. On the first Sunday in Lent the crosses are placed over the arms of an eight-foot, birch-log cross, and members select crosses to wear during the worship service, returning the crosses so that others may wear them on successive Lenten Sundays. On Easter worshipers wear the crosses home but give them to the first persons to notice and admire them after explaining Christ's sacrifice.—*The Church Herald.*

TEN GREAT SUNDAYS. Why suffer from after-Easter blahs? To sustain the Lent and Easter momentum the the First United Methodist Church in Royal Oak, Michigan, keeps the Easter glow alive and growing by scheduling "Ten Great Sundays After Easter." Worship centers in biblical drama, youth participation, Mother's Day, Father's Day, Grandparents' Day, Heritage Sunday, Memorial Sunday, Great Church Music Sunday, Student Recognition Day, etc. A brochure listing each Sunday's emphasis, sermon title, descriptive material about the service, and additional activities planned for the Sunday is sent to all church families.

DREAM SUNDAY. On the Sunday following Easter, often called Low Sunday, the members of the Pasadena Community Church in St. Petersburg, Florida, were asked to submit program ideas and recommendations for broadening the scope of the life and service of the church. Many suggestions offered on "Dream Sunday" were immediately incorporated into the church program. Others became blueprints for church planning.

BROWN BAG SERMONETTES. During worship services of the First Congregational Church in Colorado Springs, Colorado, children aged three to eleven are invited to the front and Jerry M. Jordan, pastor, removes from a brown bag such items as a pair of work gloves, a turkey wishbone, or hot cross buns, each a clue to the sermonette for the children.

BIBLICAL DRAMATIZATIONS. From time to time John W. Eyster, pastor of the First Congregational Church in Emerald Grove, Wisconsin, substitutes the Sunday morning sermon with a dramatic portrayal of a biblical personality. Dressed in an authentic costume and having researched the life and times of the Bible character, he speaks in the role of a disciple, for instance, and then responds to questions from the congregation in a manner consistent with what is known about the individual's activities and beliefs.

CLOWNS FOR CHRIST. To spread the gospel and to make others happy by making them laugh is the purpose of an unusual group of young people and adults in the First United Methodist Church in Hurst, Texas, called "Clowns for Christ." Coached initially by a professional clown, who showed them the possibilities of this kind of ministry, the performers have shared their Christian witness at nursing homes, hospitals, school carnivals, church meetings, and even birthday parties.—*The Texas Methodist.*

PUPPET PREACHER. Mr. Rabbit, a soft, furry puppet much loved by the children of the First Congregational Church in Ithaca, New York, resides weekdays in the cupboard of Pastor Duane Cossart and during Sunday worship services engages in conversations with the pastor. Mr. Rabbit, a wise old man who has the total respect of the children, is the dean of the puppet family that also includes such Bible-teaching members as Silly Sally, a sometimes serious young woman; the Professor, a caricature of some church members who teach at Cornell University; Harvey, a self-centered teenager; and Alfred the Frog, who is alert to environmental concerns.—*A.D.*

LAW DAY SERVICE. An annual ecumenical worship service marks Law Day at the Episcopal Church of the Advent in Birmingham, Alabama. The midday service, held on a weekday, emphasizes the Judeo-Christian concepts of law and justice that are fundamental to our nation's legal system. Attorneys, judges, court officials, law office staffs, and members of their families are invited to attend.

BACKYARD VESPERS. During the summer months the St. Mark Cumberland Presbyterian Church in Oklahoma City, Oklahoma, holds a series of vespers for worship and fellowship of members and their neighbors in the backyards of parishioners' homes.

REQUESTED SERMONS. Pew cards in the Irvington Presbyterian Church in Indianapolis, Indiana, give worshipers an opportunity to suggest sermon topics for the month of July. Typical requests include "When God Forgets," "Do the Good Die Young?," "The Authority of the Bible," and "Christian Marriage." Topics not used in the sermon series are often used in church school discussions, Wednesday evening dinners, and other church activities.

MIDWEEK WORSHIP. Thursday night worship services are held during the summer months in the First Baptist Church in Seattle, Washington, primarily for the benefit of parishioners who are away on weekends.

FALL ROUNDUP. The Sunday school of the Eastland Road United Methodist Church in Atlanta, Georgia, gave a new twist to the traditional Rally Day activities by observing a fall roundup, inviting members to wear western attire, and urging everyone to return to the "ranch" for the fall and winter months. To emphasize the theme a horse was tethered on the church lawn.

WORSHIP SANS LAITY. Turning from the customary Laity Sunday service, one church held worship without greeters at the door, unlighted candles, undistributed bulletins, an empty choir loft, an offering uncollected, and a dedication of workers with youth with no one to be blessed. During the message, given by a lay worker, an appeal was made for the laity to become involved in the work of the church. Promptly acolytes lite the candles, choir members took their places, ushers passed out bulletins and prepared to receive the collection, youth workers went forward for

the dedication ceremony, greeters stood at the doors to meet the people following the service, and everyone was reminded in an unforgettable way of the importance of laity to the church.—*Michigan Christian Advocate.*

"CAN-DO" RALLY. In September and in anticipation of a new church year, the United Methodist Church in Zebulon, Georgia, holds a "Can-Do" Rally at which members attend group meetings to discuss and write down what are considered to be the particular needs of the church. Then the groups are brought together for discussions on the ways these needs can best to met.

FAMINE VIGIL. Young people of the Rockaway United Methodist Church in Boonton, New Jersey, sponsored a thirty-hour "famine" to emphasize the problem of world hunger. During a nonbreakfast hour, an unlunch period, and a foodless supper information on the need for nourishing food by many people throughout the world was circulated. Donations of money in lieu of food were contributed to relief agencies.

COMMUNION ATTIRE. Members of the Cumberland Presbyterian Church in Sacramento, Kentucky, dress as representatives of all areas of the church's missionary endeavor at the World Communion Sunday service.

THE ROCK. A rock from the spot where Jesus is said to have given the sermon on the mount has been placed on the communion table of the First United Methodist Church in Houston, Texas. Selected by Charles L. Allen, pastor of the church, and removed by permission of the government of Israel, the rock, which weighs more than one hundred pounds and which Jesus may have seen or sat upon, symbolizes the teaching and preaching of our Lord.

BREADS. The message of World Communion Sunday is interpreted at the First Baptist in Seattle where laity representing differing national and ethnic backgrounds serve breads common to various regions of the world.

ADVENT WREATH.   A wreath of hay and thorns reminds worshipers at the First United Church of Christ in Carlisle, Pennsylvania, not only of Christ's birth but also of his death.—*A.D.*

CHEER IN BOXES.   Volunteers in the Broadmoor Baptist Church in Jackson, Mississippi, baked more than 10,000 Christmas cookies which the church young people put in boxes and delivered personally to patients in local hospitals and residents of area nursing homes. Each box contained two dozen cookies, a spiritual booklet, and a Christmas greeting.

A CHRISMON TREE.   Does your church have a chrismon tree? A chrismon is a monogram of Christ, a symbol of Jesus or of the Christian church. In addition to crosses, crowns, stars, and Greek letters are several hundred signs used throughout Christian history. Nearly twenty years ago the Lutheran Church of the Ascension, 295 Main Street, Danville, Virginia 24541, started the chrismon tree idea by making and hanging monograms on a fir tree during Advent. The Danville church office distributes four books on making chrismons titled *The Basic Series, The Christian Year, The Advanced Series,* and *Chrismons for Every Day.*

AN ACT OF LOVE.   To give special meaning to your Christmas observances plan to do something for someone as an act of love. If possible, make the act a secret one so that you cannot be thanked and nobody can do something in return. It should not be geared to an exchange of gifts but directed to a plan of loving action for which you get no return whatever. Write your act on a piece of paper. Fold the paper and put it in the special box containing the notes of Christian actions by others in the parish. On Christmas Eve the box will be presented at the altar, and later the box will be unlocked and the papers reverently burned without being read.—*The Anglican Digest.*

SECTION XI. A Little Treasury of Illustrations

THREE QUESTIONS. A young lady was soaking up sunshine on the beach when a little boy approached and asked, "Do you believe in God?" The young lady nodded considerably surprised. "And do you always go to church on Sunday?" "Yes, I do," replied the young lady, getting more interested. "And read the Bible?" "Every day." The little boy was noticeably relieved. "Well, then, will you please hold my quarter while I go swimming?"

IS THERE A FUTURE? The English novelist and scientist, C. P. Snow, was asked what he regarded as the main difference between the world in which he grew up and the world that we all share now. Without hesitation he said, "The absence of a future." But there is a future, and the one single message that the community of believers brings to humanity is that because there is a visible presence, a human community that expresses the evidence of becoming fully human, there is a future. And because the head of this body is Jesus Christ, that future is also only in him.—Samuel T. Kamaleson.

PLACING BLAME. In an economy move the city fathers of an Arizona town sought to remove the number of stops each trash collection truck would have to make by providing larger barrels to be shared by two families. They were immediately confronted with great resistance from the householders. Some wise person solved the problem by arranging for three or more families to share each barrel. The resistance had risen, so it appears, because if only two households used each barrel you would know that if you hadn't made the contribution that aroused interest, your neighbor had. With three or more contributing to the trash can, that certainty was removed and you could never be sure who was responsible.—Dean E. Dalrymple.

HALF-WAY CONVERSION. E. Stanley Jones told about a Hindu convert who joined their church. Since it was a very small congregation, they weren't able to afford the services of a custodian, so every member was expected to take his or her turn. Jones asked the convert one day when he was going to volunteer to take his turn, and the convert replied, "Brother Stanley, I am converted, but I am not converted that far."—Gary L. Reif.

MOURNING FOR LIFE. In the opening lines of Anton Chekov's play *The Sea Gull*, Boris the schoolmaster asks Marsha, "Why do you always wear black?" And she replies, "Because I'm in mourning for my life." As the play continues, one realizes that the reason for her mourning is not only that her love for Constantin is not returned but that her whole life is filled with despair and meaninglessness which she thinks might be alleviated if Constantin would love her but which never happens because in the end he kills himself.—William H. Tiemann.

WEIGHT OF THE WORLD.   One of New York City's most celebrated highlights is Rockefeller Center. Located between Fifth Avenue and the Avenue of the Americas, this prominent site occupies over twelve acres of ground and includes more than fifteen modern, twentieth-century buildings. Rockefeller Center is famous also for its glittering bronze statue of the Greek god Atlas carrying the globe of the world on his mighty shoulders. He is bending forward, as if straining against the tremendous weight. Yet directly across the street from this straining statue is an interesting paradox. Facing Atlas is St. Patrick's Cathedral. And inside the door of the cathedral can be seen another statue of another person supporting the world. It is a statue of the Christ Child. Gracefully seated near the center aisle, Jesus is serenely holding the globe of the world in the palm of his hand.—George F. Riley.

BLESSING.   In the spring of 1931, when the communists were rolling over Spain and burning churches, hospitals, and convents, an old Spanish priest of 86 years of age was led out before the firing squad. His hands were tied. As his last earthly wish, he begged that they untie his hands that he be able to bless them as his parting gesture. One of the guards, thinking that he was being made a fool of, seized an ax and hacked off not only the ropes but the priest's hands as well. The old priest then lifted his mangled arms, in writhing pain, over the executioners' heads and moved the bleeding stumps of his arms in a blessing over them saying: "I forgive you. It is my final wish that God too will forgive you and bless you."—George F. Riley.

THREE WISHES.   I asked a student what three things he most wished. He said, "Give me books, health, and quiet, and I care for nothing more." I asked a miser, and he cried, "Money, money, money!" I asked a pauper, and he faintly said, "Bread, bread, bread!" I asked a drunkard, and he called loudly for strong drink.

I asked the multitude around me, and they lifted up a confused cry in which I heard the words: "Wealth! Fame! Pleasure!" I asked a poor man, who had long borne the character of an experienced Christian. He replied that all his wishes might be met in Christ. He spoke seriously, and I asked him to explain. He said, "I greatly desire three things: first, that I be found in Christ; second, that I may be like Christ; third, that I may be with Christ."

A FATHER'S LAMENT.   I was visiting a terminal patient in the hospital, and he began talking of his life. He told me how hard he had worked and how he had held two jobs to provide well for his family. But because he was working so long and so hard, he never really had time to spend with them. He put his children through good schools and did everything that is considered ideal in our society. But he told me: "If I could go home once more, I would go fishing with my son. He always wanted to, but I never had time." The patient did get the chance to go home again briefly. When he came back to the hospital, just a few days before he died, he had a pure, beautiful look on his face. He told me: "I went fishing with my son. It was the best day in my whole life." That was the last thing he ever talked about.—Elisabeth Kübler-Ross.

HEART OF GOD.   "God has put his heart on paper." So said William Booth in 1894. He was describing the scriptures as the record of God's revelation of himself in terms of human experience. Without the Bible our ideas of God would certainly be nebulous and without doubt erroneous. But in its pages God has shown his heart, and in the life of Jesus that heart took human form.—Frederick L. Coutts.

GREATEST DANGER.   *The Saturday Review* reported that in the Great Apes House of the New York Zoo, between the gorilla and orangutan displays, is an exhibit titled "The Most Dangerous Animal in the World." The exhibit consists simply of a mirror. Under the mirror into which you look there appears the following message:

"You are looking at the most dangerous animal in the world. It alone of all the animals that ever lived can exterminate (and has) entire species of animals. Now it has achieved the power to wipe out all life on earth including its own."

ESSENCE.   We mostly spend our lives conjugating three verbs: to want, to have, and to do—craving, clutching, and fussing—forgetting that being, not wanting, having, and doing, is the essence of the spiritual life.—Evelyn Underhill.

THE GLORY OF GOD.   John Muir stood with an acquaintance at one of the great viewpoints of the Yosemite Valley and, filled with wonder and devotion, wept. His companion, more stolid than most, could not understand the feeling and was so thoughtless as to say so. "Moff," said Muir, with the Scottish dialect into which he often lapsed, "can ye see unmoved the glory of the Almighty?" "Oh, it's very fine," was the reply, "but I do not wear my heart on my sleeve." "Ah, my dear mon," said Muir, "in the face of such a scene it's no time to be thinkin' o' where you wear your heart."—Robert Underwood Johnson.

THE LAST PAGE.   When Ralph Smith was a little boy he liked to read mysteries. He particularly enjoyed reading the adventures of an undercover agent named Sam something or other.

One night, long after bedtime, Ralph had his flashlight in bed, reading under the covers about his favorite undercover agent. Agent Sam had just been captured by the bad guys. They tied him up, wrapped chains around him with heavy weights attached, and threw him into the sea. As Sam was sinking deeper and deeper into the dark, cold ocean, Ralph's mother came into his room, pulled the cover back, grabbed the book, and said, "Go to sleep!"

Now Ralph was a pretty good boy. He wanted to mind his mother, but he could never sleep with Sam in that condition. So he got up, got the book, and went to the bathroom. He turned to the last page and read about Sam's being given a medal by the President, and the crowd was cheering for him. So he knew that somehow Sam had gotten out of the ocean and was all right.

It is the same for us. When you and I choose to be on the Lord's side, we know how it's going to turn out. So, no matter what we're going through at the moment, we can get a peek at history's last page and read: "There shall be no more death, nor sorrow . . . neither shall there be any more tears."—Frank Pollard.

THE KEY.   Two boys left their home town to venture into the world. First, they requested of a hermit a philosophy for their lives. On being questioned, one boy said the people at home were self-centered, greedy, and cynical. The other thought those at home were good, kind, sincere, and full of love. To each the hermit replied, "The people out in the world will be exactly the same!" Each person is the key to how he or she will find other persons on the Christian pilgrimage.—William W. McDermet III.

SOMEONE WHO CARES.   R. Mabel Francis tells of a Japanese woman whose heart was yearning for someone on whom to lean. She said: "I went to the temple and drew lots to see if I could not get some comfort. I opened the little package which fell to me and inside it said: 'There is no help for you. Lean on your own shadow and go on.' I was more desperate than ever. I looked at the great sun by day and the moon by night and felt there should be someone somewhere who would care for one so needy as I." Then as a Christian told her of our heavenly Father she burst out with a joyful shout while tears of relief rolled down her face. "I thought there ought to be such a God," she cried. "Oh, I have found him at last!"—Nevin Webster.

VITAL NERVE.   When Saul Bellow accepted the Nobel Prize for literature, the speech he made reflected the longing for his understanding of the meaning of life which he also expressed in his novels. He said, "Out of the struggle at the center has come an immense, painful, longing for a broader, more flexible, fuller, more coherent, more comprehensive account of what human beings are, who we are, and what this life is for." With this, he touched a vital nerve. What is this life for? That is the question that will not go away. It taunts us when occasionally we are called to hold on to life heroically or when some shattering tragedy invades our experience and shoots into our veins the numbing serum of defeat.—Joel H. Nederhood.

MOVING FORWARD. God did not guarantee security to his people as they hesitated on the edge of that grim and barren wilderness, but as long as they moved forward in trustful and obedient faith they found in God an unfailing source of security.—Leonard Griffith.

UNHEARD MUSIC. Luigi Tarisio was found one morning with scarcely a comfort in his home but with 246 exquisite fiddles, which he had been collecting all his life, crammed into an attic. The best fiddles were in the bottom drawer of an old rickety bureau. In his devotion to the violin he had robbed the world of music all the time he treasured them. Others before him had done the same so that when the greatest Stradivarius violin was first played, it had had 147 musicless years.—Gary L. Reif.

THANKING GOD. Corrie ten Boon suffered horrible hurts under her Nazi captors because she protected persecuted Jews. Under the eyes of the Nazis, she built a hiding place for them. Arrested and in solitary confinement, she prayed for her jailers. In her lonely cell, forbidden to speak, she thanked God for the bit of heavenly blue light that filtered through the tiny high window. Stripped naked in the concentration camp, she sustained her sister Betsie, reminding her that Jesus was stripped naked at Calvary. A Nazi matron beat a prisoner, and Corrie prayed for the matron. Jammed in prison, she thanked God for the crowding, for there were now more with whom to share the message of

her Lord. But she hesitated when her sister thanked God for the fleas. That was just too much!—Albert J. Kissling.

UNDERSTANDING. Moving fences, climbing walls, and breaking down barriers is what Christianity is all about, and yet so few of us in the church seem to understand. Perhaps that is why Liston Pope of Yale Divinity School said to his class one day, "If everyone in the world became a Christian tomorrow, the world would not be much worse than it is now."—Harold P. Lewis.

INASMUCH. John Hightower was a member of a church that had a real problem. A young man of about twenty loved to come to church and sit on the front row. But he was twisted in mind and body. His face was so drawn and contorted that the saliva constantly ran from one corner of his mouth, and he made strange grunting sounds that sometimes were disconcerting. Not only that but he twisted around a lot and that was distracting to everyone. Things got so bad the problem was discussed at a board meeting. What should be done? Should they tell the young man he could no longer come? Should they ask his parents to keep him home? Should they tell the ushers to refuse to let him in? The question was so sticky that they did what all good boards do—they tabled the matter. Hightower was also the chairman of the board of a great corporation in that city and one of the most beloved and respected men in town. He hadn't spoken during the board meeting, and the following Sunday morning the people were astonished to see him as he led the feebleminded boy down to his place on the front pew. Hightower sat beside him and placed his arm about him. All through the service he tenderly cared for him and even managed to keep him fairly quiet. He did this every Sunday for two years until the boy went to live with God.—Harold P. Lewis.

PROOF OF FAITHFULNESS. My own experience convinces me that the people who most effectively give proof of faithfulness to God and love for their fellows do it simply and quietly. They're the teachers who struggle week after week with a class of squirming kids in order to implant some seeds of faith; men and women who give their time to lead youth groups; people who willingly accept the burden of caring for bedridden parents or relatives; pastors who shun the race for honors or public acclaim and devote their lives to humble congregations. This is what James calls "pure religion and undefiled." Of such is the kingdom of heaven.—Albert P. Stauderman in *The Lutheran.*

MOUNTAIN VIEW.   An old man, high up in the mountain, sat in the sun looking down on the little valley where he lived. He was asked: "What brings you way up here? This is a tough climb." "Well, son," he replied, "it's like this. All my troubles and heartaches are down in that little valley, and when I'm down there they seem awful big. But up here they seem pretty small, especially when I see what a little bit of these big mountains my little valley is." —W. Wallace Fridy.

SMOLDERING   DISOBEDIENCE.   When Norman Vincent Peale was a boy, he bought a cigar to prove his manhood. Walking down the street, puffing the cigar, feeling both hard-boiled and a little sickish, he met his preacher father. Hoping to divert his father's attention, he put his hand with the cigar in it behind his back and pointed to a circus poster with the other hand, asking to go to the circus. His father replied, "Norman, never make a petition and at the same time hold a smoldering disobedience behind your back."— James E. Carter.

AROUND THE HORN.   Years ago when men went to sea in wooden ships, experienced sailors were an imperative to navigate hazardous waters. So when a young man looking for a seaman's job went to a hiring hall in London, he was asked if he had ever been around the horn. Shipping companies and sea captains wanted experienced men who had made at least one and preferably two trips in the

rough seas around Cape Horn. The would-be sailor admitted he had never made that voyage. The hiring agent took him to a back room. In the middle of the floor lay a steer's horn. The agent instructed the job seeker to walk slowly around the horn. The young man did as instructed. "Now you qualify," said the agent. "You can have a job!"—Edgar Cooper.

CONFESSION.   Henri Nouwen tells of a Lutheran bishop who in World War II was held in a German concentration camp. An SS officer tried by torture to force a confession from him. Though the pain of the torture was deliberately increased, it could not break the bishop's silence. The infuriated officer, hammering his victim with harder and harder blows, finally exploded. "But don't you know," he shrieked, "that I can kill you?" Leveling his eyes at his bullying master, the bishop said slowly, "Yes, I know—do what you want—but I have already died."

In an instant, as though paralyzed, the officer could not raise his arm. It was as if his power over the bishop had been suddenly taken from him. Why? Because his presupposition was—a perfectly normal one—that the bishop's life was the most precious thing he had and he would therefore hold onto it by confessing to a lie. What was the point of further violence when torture had been turned into a piece of futility?—Paul S. Rees.

OVERCOMING.   In her novel *Great Son,* Edna Ferber tells the story of Pansy Deleath and her mother. They moved to Alaska in 1898 when the Gold Rush was making a madhouse of that sparsely settled land. Those were desperate days for Pansy and her mother. Their hopes for wealth were shattered and their meager savings insufficient to provide food and shelter in that situation of almost unbelievable extremity. As fate would have it, Pansy's mother became desperately ill. During the long weeks of hardship which followed, they fought for survival. There came the day when Mrs. Deleath was ready to give up, but Pansy with a brilliant combination of psychology and common sense said: "Mama, after this we can stand anything. It's kind of wonderful to know that from now on—you never have to be afraid again."—Harold P. Lewis.

PRISONER. As soon as you begin to take yourself seriously and imagine that your virtues are important because they are yours, you become the prisoner of your own vanity and even your best works will blind and deceive you. Then, in order to defend yourself, you will begin to see sins and faults everywhere in the actions of other men.—Thomas Merton.

BEAUTIFUL FACE. What is the most beautiful sight ever to delight your eyes? For me it is not the rounded and pink cheek of a sleeping babe, lovely as that is; nor the saucy independence and irresistible appeal of a beautiful girl in her teens; nor the exuberant and self-confident energy of a strong, handsome young man; nor the tender sight of a young mother nursing her first-born. The loveliest sight I ever see is the face of an old man or woman, beautifully wrinkled, gloriously seamed and chiseled by time, with lines that tell of strenuous days, hardship, a combination of both defeat and victory. Such a face as is illumined with a light from within has wondrous attraction for me. There is kindness and wisdom and patience in it. There is strength and endurance and stern conviction in it. There is love and loyalty and faith in it. There is the capacity for wonder, for delight, for surprise, for fresh visions of truth and beauty.—Richard C. Raines.

GREETINGS. The Russian, Popov, is supposed to have left Russia for Poland and sent back a postcard reading, "Greetings from free Warsaw." Traveling on to Czechoslovakia, he sent one reading, "Greetings from free Prague." Stopping next in Hungary, he wrote, "Greetings from free Budapest." Eventually a card came from him in Vienna. It read, "Greetings from free Popov."

SINKING. A pious New England farmer one day broke through the surface of what we call in this part of the world a "quaking" bog. His leg went down into the quicksand. The more he struggled, the deeper he sank, even though he tried time after time to extricate first one foot and then the other. Finally his frantic cries attracted rescuers. As he was being pulled out of the quicksand, one of his helpers heard him mutter these words: "All right, Lord, I needed the exercise, but you could at least have given me something to hold on to."—Edward C. Dahl.

THE SONG THEY SANG. The Norwegian poet Bjornson was asked what incident in his life had given him the most pleasure. He replied that on one occasion, after he had aroused the displeasure of the Norwegian Parliament, some members marched in protest and broke the windows of his home. Afterward the protestors marched down the street singing the Norwegian national anthem. Bjornson laughed, for he was the author of the anthem. They had smashed his windows, but they were singing his song.—Naomi Ruth Hunke.

THE STAR THROWER. Loren Eiseley in *The Unexpected Universe* describes a walk along the beaches of Costabel littered with the debris of life, where "death walks hugely and in many forms." Eiseley watched the sea rejecting its offspring. Various life forms would fight their way through the surf only to be cast back upon the shore. Among these were starfish with their arms thrust up stiffly in gestures meant to ward off the stifling sand and mud. As Eiseley walked along, he saw a man bent over one of these starfish, and he was saying to himself, "It's still alive," and with a quick yet gentle movement he picked up the star and flung it far out into the sea. "It may live," he said, "if the off-shore pull is strong enough."

Eiseley walked on and then looked back. He thought to himself: "For a moment in the changing light the sower appeared magnified, as though casting larger stars on some greater sea. He had, at any rate, the posture of a god." But Eiseley, even with this observation, "walked away from the star thrower in the hardened indifference of maturity." He considered himself an observer and a scientist. The star thrower was mad.

Later Eiseley returned to the beach, reflecting upon his experience. He wrote about what happened: "Silently I sought and picked up a still-living star, spinning it far out into the waves. I spoke once briefly. 'I understand,' I said. 'Call me another thrower.' Only then I allowed myself to think, he is not alone any longer. After us there will be others."

What we do here, upon this beach of life, may seem pale and small, compared with the immensity of everything about us. But as Eiseley said: "We must cast slowly, deliberately, and well. The task was not to be assumed lightly, for it was men as well as starfish that we sought to save." Each of us must be a hurler of stars. Each of us must extend that effort and that energy to keep alive the things in which we believe. —John H. Townsend.

ABOUNDING MYSTERIES. Adolph Harnack said to his students at the end of a difficult philosophical discussion: "Gentlemen, as we seem to have solved this problem, I see at least three new ones opening before us, more difficult than this. In probing the mysteries of the universe and of life, we are like children wading on the shore. The further we walk out, the more we become aware of the depth of the sea. Let us be humble."

STRUGGLE. In *The Crucible*, Arthur Miller emobdies the struggle between good and evil in the person of John Proctor. Caught up in the witchcraft trials of Salem, Massachusetts, John, a simple farmer, is drawn into the vortex of evil that raged during that particular period of colonial history. Having admitted adultery with a young woman befriended by his wife, John in his guilt is tempted to lie by accusing others of witchcraft in order to save his own life. The last scene of the play is in a prison cell. John awaits the morning sun and death at the end of a hangman's rope. If he will confess, his life will be spared—but at what cost? John struggles for his own integrity in the face of the forces of evil that are overwhelming. He wavers, burdened by guilt. He signs the confession but refuses to hand it over to his tormentors. In a final burst of integrity that transcends the instinct to preserve his life, John tears up the confession and says: "Now I do think I see some goodness in John Proctor. Not enough to weave a banner with, but white enough to keep it from such dogs." To his weeping wife he counsels: "Give them no tear. Tears pleasure them. Show honor now, show a stony heart and sink them with it." To those who plead with Elizabeth to have her husband confess, she replies: "He has his goodness now. God forbid I take it from him."—Harold R. Fray, Jr.

KALEIDOSCOPE. During the civil and religious strife of the Reformation in England, Protestant Roundheads stormed into cathedrals, destroying religious symbols. In Winchester Cathedral they wrecked a huge stained-glass window which majestically dominated the long cathedral. On the cold stone floor lay fragments of the beautiful colored glass. The shattered pieces, which once had shaped a Rembrandt-like scene, could not be restored to form the original picture. What could be done? Board up the window? Throw out the glass? With love and care, the people picked up the pieces. Long before the time of abstract art, they leaded the broken glass together with hope and returned it to the round window. Today, 300 years later, the same sun shines through the same beautiful colors of fine stained glass, a kaleidoscope of pieces, rearranged in a different and even more meaningful way.—Katherine Miller Meacham.

FAILING FORWARD. When Arthur Gordon was a beginning journalist, he interviewwd Thomas Watson and asked him for the secret of his legendary career in bringing IBM to where it was as the leader in the computer industry. Watson replied simply, "I have learned how to fail forward!"

This involved accepting the fact that we humans are imperfect and choosing to learn from failure rather than letting it crush us into despair and bitterness. He told of an early childhood experience in

New England where a neighboring farmer went out one morning and found his plum tree had been blown down the night before. When asked what he was going to do, he answered tersely, "I'm going to pick the fruit and burn the rest." This made an indelible impression on the young lad and became a working model to him of how to handle failure.—John R. Claypool.

IDENTITY.   Martin Buber recounted a dream in which he stood before the judgment seat awaiting a verdict on his life. Thunderous words issued forth: "Martin Buber, I ask you not, 'Why were you not Moses?' I ask you only 'Why were you not Martin Buber?' "—William D. Webber.

SPIRITUAL TRAINING.   When a football coach wants to build a good team, he does not send it out on the field to play with soft pillows. He puts it to work against rough opponents, a bucking frame, a tackling dummy, and he puts it through exercises that are strenuous. God does the same thing with us to give us the strengths of steadfastness and patience in our character. He marches us at times against tough opponents, against temptation, against public opinion, against discouragement. —Louis H. Evans.

A LAYMAN'S ACHIEVEMENT.   In Canterbury, England, I found a copy of *The Ruined Abbeys of Great Britain* by Ralph Adams Cram, an authority on the Middle Ages. While discussing such abbeys as Glastonbury, Lindisfare, and Whitby, he mentions that these were all abbeys of the order of St. Benedict. Cram believes that in the rule of St. Benedict you have a detailed and definite statement of the essentials of the gospel. St. Benedict was a layman, born about 480 A.D. and died about 543. His monastic religious order was established about 529.

In 1316 a very careful study was made of the evangelistic results that had accrued to the movement called the Benedictines. The study revealed almost the unbelievable. In 800 years from the order of St. Benedict came 24 popes, 200 cardinals, 700 archbishops, 15,000 bishops, 15,000 abbots of distinction, and more than 40,-000 men and women who were known as saints. What a tremendous evangelistic endeavor.—Carl J. Sanders.

FENCE STRADDLER.   A timid minister, who often straddled the fence, was told by one member of his congregation to preach the "old-fashioned gospel" and was instructed by another to be "broadminded." The result was evident next time he preached: "Unless you repent, in a measure, and are converted, so to speak, you are, I am sorry to say, in danger of hell-fire and damnation, to a certain extent."— James N. Griffith.

REMEMBER THE WIG.   In Chambers' *Book of Days*, a nineteenth-century almanac, the story is recounted of a barber who was so successful at his trade that he was able to return to his hometown and indulge his religious inclinations by becoming pastor of a small chapel. When a member of his parish needed a wig, the parishioner came to the barber turned minister and asked if he would make a wig. The minister obliged his parishioner, but when the wig was delivered, not only was it twice as expensive as it should have been, but worse, it was of very poor quality. Thereafter, whenever "anything particularly profitable" escaped the lips of the preacher, the parishioner would observe to himself, "Excellent, but, oh, the wig."— Norman R. DePuy.

PROBLEM.   The real problem of Christianity is not atheism or skepticism but the nonwitnessing Christian trying to smuggle his own soul into heaven.—James S. Stewart.

MORE BEYOND.   For centuries the motto of Portugal was a Latin phrase meaning "Nothing more beyond." Only that part of the world which clustered around the Mediterranean Sea was known by man. They believed that if one sailed past Portugal out into the ocean he would fall off the edge of the world into endless space. Located at the extreme end of the world, Portugal considered itself the last word and thus proudly displayed the phrase "Nothing more beyond." Then there came the shattering news that a whole new world had been discovered on the far side of the ocean. The decision makers were forced to decide what they should now do with their beloved motto. They decided to strike out the negative. Now their motto read "More beyond." Rather than the end of the world, they now considered themselves the gateway to all the promise and glory which the newly discovered Americas offered. In a striking parallel Christ struck the negative from the meaning of death. The motto of the church is "More beyond."—Warren A. Nyberg.

ADMISSION. A woman with a grudge wrote a number of crank letters to Muriel Lester's school in England. The superintendent of the school guessed her identity and asked her to give up the libelous habit. At first the woman vowed innocence, but when the letters were produced she broke down, dropped her head, wept many salt tears, and remarked, "Oh, Miss, I am as good a woman as God ever made, only I cannot live up to it!"

THE LIVING PRESENCE. Through nineteen centuries Christians have shared in an experience which they have felt they could best describe as being with a Presence which they have associated with the historic Jesus seen in the pages of the New Testament and with the eternal God. Of their honesty in reporting that enduring and repeated experience there can be no doubt. Nor can there be doubt that through that experience they themselves have been transformed. Through it they have been lifted out of moral defeat and impotence into victory and from despair to triumphant hope. Through it they have found power to go through suffering, disappointment and the loss of loved ones, of health, and of worldly goods, and to face physical death, not only unafraid but also with quiet confidence and joy. Through it strength has come to them to battle, single-handed or with a small company of kindred spirits, against enthroned wrong and age-long evils, and yet to do so in humility, without vindictiveness, and in love.—Kenneth Scott Latourette.

TWO INVITATIONS. While visiting America, Henry Drummond received two invitations to dinner at the same time. One was from Oliver Wendell Holmes to meet Henry Wadsworth Longfellow, and the other was from Dwight L. Moody to meet Ira D. Sankey. Drummond loved the poems and the books of Holmes and Longfellow, but he believed that he knew where truer poetry was to be found. To his mind it lay in that story of the good shepherd and his lost sheep which Elizabeth Clephane and Sankey and Moody had made real to him in the song "The Ninety and Nine." Drummond accepted Moody's invitation.—C. Elsie Harrison.

REVERENT UNDERSTANDING. I well recall the day when I stepped for the first time within the Church of St. Croce in Florence. It is my favorite church in Italy. Perhaps this is because its architecture is of that pure gothic type of which one sees so little in Italy. One wearies of the heavy baroque of the Roman churches. Or it may be because of the lovely chancel windows whose glass is reminiscent of Chartres or Bourges. It is a treasure-house of art and sculpture. In its crypts and chapels lie some of the greatest men of Italy.

As you enter, a dim but beautiful light rests upon all that half-hidden, mysterious wealth of sacred beauty with which you are surrounded. You stand still for a moment, hushed by the solemn splendor. Then slowly you advance along the sculptured pavement, stopping now and again to examine some exquisite carving, some wonderful bit of sculpture, until at last you arrive at the transepts. There on the walls are the famous frescoes of Giotto illustrating different episodes in the life of St. Francis. They are half obliterated, and one hopes no hand will seek to restore them.

All around one is a beauty which appeals powerfully to the imagination. But that beauty reveals itself only to the inquiring mind. One needs one's Ruskin to understand the meaning of these delicate sculptures on the pavements, many of them so effaced that one can barely trace the beautiful lines and figures. One needs patience and much reverent curiosity if one is to make out the delicate carvings on the pavement or trace in their relation to each other the different figures of the frescoes.

No hurried tourist understands St. Croce. But the reverent mind, after once it has caught the beauty and the appeal of that glorious interior, delights to spend long hours and even days within these walls, moving with curious, intent, and inquiring interest from spot to spot, finding always something to delight, to fascinate, to inspire.

Such, I believe, was the mood of the psalmist. To dwell in the house of the Lord, to behold the beauty of the Lord, to inquire in his temple—this cannot mean that he wanted to live within the walls of a building all the days of his life. It can mean only that he found life, existence, experience, when once it had been permeated with the life of God, so incomparably rich, so inexhaustibly beautiful, that he asked nothing more for himself than that he should make fresh, constant discoveries of its richness and its significance. Precisely, that is, as the lover of St. Croce inquiries in that temple, so the psalmist declares that the "one thing," the one controlling and dominant desire of his life, is to discover for himself with grave and reverent curiosity the meaning and the beauty of a world, a life, an experience that is permeated with the life of God.—Raymond Calkins.

IMPLORING ARMS.　The sculptor Auguste Rodin in one of his masterpieces, "The Centauress," depicts in its lower part, near the base, the feet of a beast that is being sucked down by the mud. The upper part of this same being is not a beast but a manlike figure struggling to be free from the mud. He stretches imploring arms heavenward as if reaching for the helping hand of God.—Herbert E. Hudgins.

WINNING WHAT WE WANT.　There is nothing quite so pathetic as the devious methods we use to win what we want from others. To flatter them in exchange for attention. To nag them with our needs, imaginary or real. To force them to be submissive in the hope that then they will like us. To praise others for the sole reason that it will be to our advantage. To conform to any fashion unless someone would think us out of step. To trim every decision and deed in the sight of prevailing prejudice in order to remain in the fellowship. What a terrible need for love such subterfuges imply and what futility there is in each one.—Samuel H. Miller.

GENIUS AND DEMON.　Charles H. Spurgeon related an experience he had when he visited the library of Trinity College. His attention was arrested by a statue of Lord Byron. The librarian said to him, "Stand here, sir." He did as he was directed, and as he looked at the statue, he said: "What a fine intellectual countenance! What a grand genius he was!" Then the librarian suggested that he take a look from the other side of the statue. As he did, he said: "Oh! what a demon. There stands the man who could defy God!" Then the librarian explained that the sculptor had designed the statue to show the two characters—the almost superhuman qualities—that Byron possessed and "yet the enormous mass of sin that was in his soul." The human heart carries and perhaps "will always carry, its cruelty and its springtime in his heart."—Charles F. Jacobs.

THINKING AND ACTING.　It is perilous to separate thinking rightly from acting rightly. He is already half false who speculates on the truth and does not do it. Truth is given, not to be contemplated, but to be done. Life is an action, not a thought. The penalty paid by him who speculates on the truth is that by degrees the very truth he holds becomes a falsehood.—Frederick W. Robertson.

SPARK OF ETERNITY.　Peer Holm in *The Great Hunger* was a great engineer, world famous, companion of kings and rulers of men. His feats of skill were dramatic—

bridges across impassable rivers—railroads over deserts—tunnels through great mountains and under streams—dams in dangerous mountain passes. Favored above most men in wealth and honors, he went his successful way.

Then came reversal, failure, poverty. He finds himself, when the toboggan stopped, back at the little village where he had started. Health broken, life ruined, he ekes out a meagre living for his wife and little girl by tilling a plot of ground and working part-time in the village blacksmith shop. He, Peer Holm, the great engineer, helper in a village blacksmith shop!

Peer Holm had a neighbor, a crotchety old man, who had a fierce dog. He warned him that the dog was dangerous, but the neighbor only growled, "Hold your jaw, you cursed pauper."

One day as he goes home he hears a shriek, runs and finds the dog at the throat of his little girl, tears the dog off and lifts the bleeding body of his little Asta and carries her into the house. "A doctor is often a good refuge in trouble, but though he may sew up a ragged tear in a child's throat ever so neatly, it doesn't necessarily follow that it will help much." This was his way of announcing to a friend that she was killed.

The sheriff shot the dog. The villagers wanted to drive the man out, a dn when the sowing time came they would not sell him any grain. His fields were ploughed but bare. No seed could he beg, borrow, or buy. The boys hooted at him on the road.

Peer Holm could not sleep for thinking about this treatment of his neighbor. One early morning he rose and, going to his shed, took his last half bushel of barley and climbing the fence sowed it in his neighbor's bare field.

You cannot conceal a thing like that. The harvest time tells its story. As the spring went on his deed was revealed because part of his own field lay bare and the neighbor's field was green.

They asked him why he did it, and Peer Holm replied: "The spark of eternity was once more aglow in me, and said, 'Let there be light.' Therefore went I out and sowed the corn in my enemy's field that God might exist."

DIET.   The African missionary went on an expedition with an old native. They stopped for lunch. It did not take the missionary long to eat his. But the old man ate slowly. The American chafed at the delay. "Have patience," said the native. "Don't you see I am eating my wife?" That remark sounded ominous. The old man explained: "My wife fixed this lunch for me. She spent her time and her strength on it. Part of her love and her life went into it. Do you want me to gulp it down with no thought of her?"—John M. Versteeg.

WHAT GOD CAN DO.   In 1872 Dwight L. Moody attended a meeting conducted by Henry Varley in a hay mow in Dublin. He heard the speaker say quietly, "The world has yet to see what God can do with and for and through and in a man who is fully and wholly consecrated to him."

Back in London the next Sunday, as he thrilled to the preaching of Charles H. Spurgeon, the words of Varley repeated themselves in his mind, "The world has yet to see . . . with and for and through and in a man!"

Moody pondered: "Varley meant any man! Varley didn't say he had to be educated, or brilliant, or anything else—just a man! Well, by the Holy Spirit in me, I'll be one of those men."

REVERIE OF A DOWNTOWN CHURCH.   I am a downtown church. Some people rather pity me, for they think I am destined to grow weak and die. They do not know me, or they would know better.

I have an honorable history. I was here more than a century ago, and I will still be here a century hence. Long after neighborhoods have changed, good neighborhoods have deteriorated, strong neighborhood churches have become weak neighborhood churches, I will continue to be strong.

For I am in the heart of a city, and my ministry is not to a section of the town, but to the entire city, for I reach out in every direction. My ministry touches every neighborhood, and it extends to all classes.

I am not provincial in my outlook. In me the rich and poor mingle in the fellowship of worship; through me the poor are ennobled and enriched, and the rich are made generous and gentle.

I live to serve. I exist for others. This may be the reason why I continue to keep my strength through the years. It is sometimes said that I am not so convenient to attend. But whoever said that religion is to be a thing of convenience?

I leave my future to you, for my place in the city depends upon your loyalty. I believe that I can count on you.

ADVICE.   A centipede, suffering from arthritis, went to the wise old owl for advice. The owl thought for a long time and then replied: "Centipede, you have one hundred legs swollen with arthritis. My advice is that you change yourself into a stork. With only two legs you would cut your pain 98 percent. Then by using your wings to stay off your legs you wouldn't have any trouble at all." The centipede was delighted with the suggestion and asked the wise old owl how he could change into a stork. The owl quickly replied: "Oh, I wouldn't know about the details. I offer only general policy."—William P. Gray.

DAY OF JUDGMENT.   The preacher was describing the Day of Judgment. "Lightning will crackle," he said, "thunder will boom, rivers will overflow, flames will shoot down from the heavens, the earth will quake violently, and darkness will fall over the world." Whereupon a small boy in the front pew turned to his father and asked, "Do you think they'll let school out early?"—*The Baptist Record.*

THE STORY OF A PRINCE.   In a distant kingdom beyond the seas lived a prince who was anxious to prove his worth by some brave deed. There came a report that in another kingdom a wild beast was ravaging the land and killing the inhabitants. The prince determined to go and slay the beast. Accompanied by a band of faithful followers, he set out for the other kingdom. As they journeyed they often slept out under the stars.

One night they were sleeping at the foot of a mountain when an earthquake caused a landslide. As a mass of rock and earth came down the mountain it buried in death some of the prince's companions. The prince was rescued the next morning by an old shepherd, and he was taken to the shepherd's hut. He was nursed back to health, but the accident left him a cripple. When the day's work was done the shepherd used to go to the village and take to the children toys he had made. With his simple gifts he brought smiles to children's faces, and older people of cynical and sour dispositions were happy when they saw him. Sometimes the crippled prince went with the shepherd to the village, but he would always say on his return, "What a simple thing to do!" The shepherd died, and the prince felt he must carry on for a time lest the children should be too disappointed. He found so many things to do for people that he was too happy in his service to leave.

When he died the old king, his father, brought his body back home. He ordered buried with him the sword which had come down through the family for the reigning prince and issued this proclamation: "The royal sword will be buried with my son because no one will come after him so worthy of it. He set out to slay a monster and make a great name for himself. He ended life by serving the simple folk in little village far away. Life changed his plans but he carried on!"—Ivan Lee Holt.

MIRACLE OF LOVE.   Do you remember the great trial scene in Sir Walter Scott's *Waverly* in which the Highland chieftain, Fergus Mac-Ivor, is condemned to death for the crime of treason against his sovereign, King George? It is after the judge has put on "the fatal cap of judgment," that Evan Maccombich, one of Fergus's retainers, rises up in the court and asks to be heard. When given permission he addresses the judge: "I was on'y gangin' to say, my lord . . . that if your excellent Honor and the honorable court would let

Vich Ian Vohr gae free just this once, and let him gae back to France, and no' trouble King George's government again, on'y six of the very best of his clan will be willing to be justified in his stead; and if ye'll just let me age doon to Glennaquoich, I'll fetch them up to ye mysel', to head or hang, and ye may begin wi' me the very first man."

There was a ripple of laughter through the court at this quixotic suggestion. Whereupon the clansman turned to the spectators, and he said: "If the Saxon gentlemen are laughing because a poor man such as me thinks my life, or the life of six of my degree, is worth that of Vich Ian Vohr, it's like enough they may be right; but if they laugh because they think I would not keep my word and come back to redeem him, I can tell them they ken neither the heart of a Hielandman nor the honor of a gentleman."

Here was a humble clansman whose love for his chief moved him to look into the face of death without a tremor. This is the miracle of love.—John Haynes Holmes.

SOURCE OF STRENGTH.   It is an ironic fact that in this nuclear age, when the horizon of human knowledge and human experience has passed far beyond any that any age has ever known, that we turn back in this time to the oldest source of wisdom and strength—to the words of the prophets and the saints who tell us that faith is more powerful than doubt, that hope is more potent than despair, and that only through the love that is sometimes called charity can we conquer those forces within ourselves and throughout the world that threaten the very existence of mankind.— John F. Kennedy.

DECALOGUE FOR WORLD CITIZENSHIP.

I. Blessed are the nations that exalt righteousness.

II. Blessed is that emerging unity of nations who despise war in all its forms and who strive for noble pathways of understanding.

III. Blessed are those who seek liberty in all the earth, yet always in the framework of responsibility.

IV. Blessed are the people of earth who rejoice in modesty, humility, and graciousness.

V. Blessed are the citizenry of many lands who elevate true processes of education, erasing all cesspools of crime, ignorance, and poverty.

VI. Blessed are all members of the new humanity who keep sacred the temple of their body, sprun harmful drugs, and banish pollution.

VII. Blessed are the growing army of the compassionate who scorn cheap opulence and multiply care, love, and helpful ministries.

VIII. Blessed are those nations who grow taller when on bended knee; they will be exalted.

IX. Blessed is the fellowship of people who share concerned brotherhood of heart, mind, and means, color lines long forgotten.

X. Blessed are democracies of earth who cultivate the dignity of labor, the universality of earning one's own living, and contented citizenship.—Austin W. Guild.

DAWN IN THE PYRENEES.   Hilaire Belloc was not only a philosopher and a well-known writer but also an experienced mountaineer. On one occasion he invited a friend quite unfamiliar with mountain-craft to go with him on a walking tour over the Pyrenees into Spain. On the journey they were unexpectedly compelled to spend a night near the summit of a lofty peak. Belloc recorded that they lay down on a narrow ledge and, covering themselves with their meager garments, waited for the day. Toward morning a storm arose and the fierce wail of the wind aroused his inexperienced fellow traveler from a troubled sleep. In a frenzy of fear he shook Belloc into wakefulness and cried, "I think it is the end of the world." "Oh, no," replied the veteran Belloc, shouting above the fury of the wind, "this is how the dawn comes in the Pyrenees." —Theodore Cuyler Speers.

ON THE NATURE OF GOD.   God is un-wearied patience, a meekness that cannot

be provoked; he is a never-ending merci-
fulness; he is unmixed goodness, impar-
tial, universal love; his delight is in the
communication of himself, his own happiness to everything according to its capacity. He does everything that is good, righteous, and lovely. He is the good from
which nothing but good comes, and re-
sisteth all evil only with goodness.—William Law.

WITNESSING COMMUNITY.   The church
is not an institution parallel to that of the
state or the nation. It is rather a witnessing
community. It is the community that
speaks for the kingdom and not only by
words but also by a life-style where we
dare to practice a love for which the world
is not yet ready.—Krister Stendahl.

SCHOOL OF SUFFERING.   Those who
heard Jenny Lind, the sweet singer of
Stockholm, told of the wonderful quality
of her voice and the charm of the songs
she sang. Yet few knew that she owed as
much to the school of suffering and of sorrow as to the academy where her powers
were developed. Her childhood was full of
sadness. She was an orphan. The woman
with whom she lived used to lock her in
the room each day while she went out to
work. The only means of whiling away the
long hours was for the child to sit by the
window and sing to herself.

One day a passerby, who happened to
be a music master in the city, heard the
voice of the unseen singer. He detected in
it possibilities. He called a friend to his
side, and together they listened to the
wonderful voice within. Getting in touch
with the child's guardian, they subsequently made arrangements for the almost
friendless girl to be given a chance. There
were many difficulties to be overcome, but
step by step she mounted the ladder of
fame. She captured London, Paris,
Vienna, Berlin, and New York. Some say
there never was such a voice, thrilling like
the thrush, pure as the notes of the lark.
But those who knew her best realized how
the sorrows of her childhood gave a richness and depth to her songs that otherwise
were unattainable.—J. W. G. Ward.

REALIZATION.   Self-respect cannot be
hunted. It cannot be purchased. It is never
for sale. It comes to us when we are alone,
in quiet moments and in quiet places, and
when we suddenly realize that knowing
the good, we have done it; knowing the
beautiful, we have served it; knowing the
truth, we have spoken it.—Whitney Gris-
wold.

WHY I COME TO COMMUNION.   I come
not because I am worthy, not for any righteousness of my own, for I have grievously
sinned and fallen short of what by God's
help I might have been.

I come not because there is any magic in
partaking of the symbols of Christ's body
and blood.

I come not from a sense of duty that is
unacquainted with deep appreciation for
this blessed means of grace, the highest
privilege in Christian worship.

I come because Christ bids me come. It
is his table, and he extends the invitation.

I come because it is a memorial to him:
as oft as it is done in remembrance of him.
Here is vivid portrayal of the redeeming
sacrifice of the Christ of Calvary. His
matchless life, his vicarious sufferings, and
his faithfulness even unto death are
brought to mind, and I bow humbly before him and worship.

I come because in contemplation of the
Father and his Son, our savior, I am
moved to thanksgiving for so great salvation.

I come because in this encounter with
the savior I am made to feel the wrongness
of my sins—base desires, unchristian motives, hurtful attitudes, vain ambition, and
the things I have done which I ought not
have done and the things I have failed to
do which God expected me to to do. I
acknowledge my utter unworthiness and
walk again the painful but necessary path
of repentance.

I come because forgiveness is an insepa-
rable part of true repentance. I arise with
the assurance of pardon, rejoicing in the
opportunity of a new beginning.

I come because I arise from the Lord's
table with new strength, new courage, new
poise, and new power to face the demands

which life will lay upon me.—Robert L. Jenks.

RESPONSIBILITY AND FREEDOM. We find it momentous that Lincoln used the word "responsibility" nearly as often as he used the word "freedom."—Carl Sandburg.

NOT FOR OURS ONLY. Young Henry Holland, a son of an Anglican country parson, was born in 1875. Like some men born in clergymen's families, he was not as attached to the church as his father might have wished, and when he was in the early twenties he went to Edinburgh to study medicine. He said later that he decided to "go into medicine to get out of the church." When he got to Edinburgh he was surprised to find quite a number of students who were preparing to be medical missionaries. He also found that some of the most brilliant doctors on the faculty were active Christians and taking part in the activities of the University Christian Medical Association. All this made him think, although he didn't say anything about it and didn't change his course.

He had seen day after day over the mantelpiece in the common room a cryptic motto: "Not for ours only." Finally he got up the courage to ask one of the students what it meant, and the student pointed out that it was the completion of I John 2:2. In a way which we cannot understand and certainly cannot explain, a flash of light illuminated the mind and spirit of that young, potential doctor. It changed the course of his life. He became a doctor, as he had planned, but for a different reason and with a different purpose. He was a medical missionary and was sent to the border country between Afghanistan and Pakistan and to a town called Quetta. There was no hospital, no doctor, nothing in the way of medical light or service.

He responded to the light. He went and was there for fifty-six years, the builder of a hospital, the great eye surgeon of India. In those fifty-six years it is estimated that he gave sight to 100,000 persons. An American doctor who went to see him, as a great many did, said when he came home: "I was not prepared to grasp at once the stimulating, striking character of this dynamic and expert eye surgeon. But in a few moments his simple and compassionate nature, radiating from his inner warmth, embraced me, and I knew that here was a very good and great man." He had become a son of light.—Theodore P. Ferris.

SEQUENCE. There is no shuffling or chance in the moral world. Impulses lead to choice, choices become habits, habits harden speedily into character, and character determines destiny.—Charles R. Brown.

TWO VOICES. Underneath all the arches of Bible history, throughout the whole grand temple of scripture, these two voices ever echo: Man is ruined! Man is redeemed!—C. D. Foss.

JOYFUL BOOK. The New Testament is the most joyful book in the world.

It opens with joy over the birth of Jesus, and it ends with a superb picture of a multitude which no man could number, singing Hallelujah Choruses. No matter where you open it, amid forunate or discouraging circumstances, you always hear the note of joy.

Even when a company of friends gather at a farewell supper before their Leader is crucified, he says to them, "These things have I spoken unto you, that my joy may be in you, and that your joy may be made full."

Even when their best Friend has gone, the mourners take "their food with gladness and singleness of heart, praising God." If they are flogged for their faith, the disciples depart from the council rejoicing that they are "counted worthy to suffer dishonor for the name."

When an apostle is put in jail overnight he passes the time singing, and if you listen to him in his Roman prison, you will hear him dictating, "Rejoice in the Lord always: again I will say, Rejoice." There is enough tragedy in the New Testament to make it the saddest book in the world, but instead it is the most joyful.—Harry Emerson Fosdick.

TWO FACES.   A legend tells us that a powerful king commanded legions of soldiers and with them conquered vast domains. He was wise, brave, and feared by all, but no one loved him. Each year he grew more severe and also more lonely. His face reflected his greedy soul. There were deep lines about his cruel mouth and deep furrows on his forehead.

In one of the cities of his kingdom lived a beautiful girl. He wanted her for his queen and decided to speak to her of his love. Dressing in his finest robes and placing a crown on his head, he looked into the mirror to see what kind of picture he would make for the beautiful girl. He saw only that which brought fear to his own heart—a cruel, hard face which looked even worse when he tried to smile.

Quickly he called for his court magician. "Make me a mask of the thinnest wax so that it will follow every line of my features, but paint it with your magic paints so that it will make me look kind, pleasant, and true. Fasten it to my face so that I shall never have to take it off. Make it handsome and attractive. Use your greatest skill, and I will pay you any price you ask."

The magician replied: "This I can do on one condition. You must keep your own face in the same lines which I paint, or the mask will be ruined. One angry frown and the mask will be ruined forever, nor can I replace it."

"I will do anything you ask," said the king, "to win the admiration and love of the girl. Tell me how to keep the mask from cracking."

"You must think kindly thoughts, and to do this you must perform kindly deeds. You must make your subjects happy. You must replace anger with understanding and love. Build schools for your subjects instead of forts, hospitals instead of battleships. Be gracious and courteous, and above all you must be honest with all men."

So the wonderful mask was made, and no one would have guessed that it was not the true face of the king. So handsome was it that the beautiful girl became the queen of the realm. Months passed, and though the mask was often in danger of ruin, the king fought hard with himself to keep it intact. The subjects wondered at the miraculous change which had been wrought and attributed it to his lovely wife who, they said, had made him like herself.

Since gentleness and thoughfulness had entered the life of this man, honesty and goodness were his also, and soon he regretted having deceived his beautiful wife with the magic mask. At last he could bear it no longer and summoned the magician. "Remove this false face of mine!" he cried. "Take it away. This mask is not my true self."

"If I take it away," said the magician, "I can never make another, and you must wear your own face as long as you live."

"Better so," said the king, "than to deceive one whose love and trust I have won dishonorably. Better that I should be despised by everyone. Take it off, I say, take it off!"

As the magician took off the mask, the king with fear and trembling sought his reflection in the mirror. His eyes brightened and his lips curved into a radiant smile, for the ugly lines were gone, the frown had disappeared, and his face was the exact likeness of the mask he had worn. His face had come to reflect the attitude of his heart. He had become a living witness to the proverb, "As a man thinketh in his heart, so is he."—Homer J. R. Elford.

REQUIREMENT IN PRAYER.   To pray is so necessary and so hard. It is hard not because it requires intellect and knowledge or a big vocabulary or special technique but because it requires of us humility. And that comes from a profound sense of one's brokenness and one's need. Not the need that causes us to cry, "Get me out of this trouble, quick!" But the need one feels every day of one's life—even though one does not acknowledge it—to be related to something more alive than one's self, something older and something not yet born that will endure through time.—Lillian Smith.

IDEALS AND PLANS.   Apathy can be overcome only with enthusiasm, and enthusiasm can be aroused only by two things. One is the ideal that takes the imagination by storm. The other is a definite and intelligible plan for carrying the ideal into practice.—Arnold J. Toynbee.

GLORY AND GRACE.   Justice William O. Douglas recalled how at the age of seven or eight his mother told him how wonderful his father had been. They had moved from a little town in Washington to Portland for an operation which proved to be fatal. Before the operation his father had said: "If I die, it will be glory. If I live, it will be grace." These words were beyond the understanding of a small boy, but years later they came back with meaning to interpret a great crisis in his own life. To die is glory. To live is grace. They could only mean that beneath the changes of this present life, beneath our toil and love, beneath our laughter and tears, is the great foundation of the unchanging goodness of God. And if life carries us into open sunlit fields, this is God's grace that overflows the cup of life. And if the pathway turns toward the valley, even this is appointed in a divine wisdom for a glory not yet seen. —Harold E. Nicely.

THE HEART'S CAPACITY.   William Allen White in his autobiography wrote of a boyhood friend and playmate, Temple Friend, who was kidnaped by the Indians when about one year of age. Temple's grandfather was an itinerant missionary to the Indians. He persisted in his faith that his grandson was alive.

Coming to an Indian village, he made it a practice to line up all the boys near the age of his grandson. Whispering quietly in the ear of each boy so as not to startle him, he repeated the name of his grandson, "Temple, Temple." Time went by and his faith seemed hopeless.

About eight years later he came to an Indian village remotely situated from his usual circuit. There were about a dozen boys eight to ten years of age. Gathering them together as he had done many times before, he once more whispered in the ear of each boy the name of his grandson Temple. At the middle of the line one boy's face lighted up suddenly, and he responded, "Me, Temple!"

No explanation can be satisfactorily given as to how, across the intervening years since his kidnaping at such an early age, this boy retained the memory of a name long unheard. But the story reveals both the capacity of a heart to remember a heritage and the persistent search love makes for its own.—William F. Keucher.

AN ASTRONAUT'S WITNESS.   I felt very close to God, right from the very beginning of the flight. Just after insertion in earth orbit I could look out my window of the command module and see the moon clearly framed right in the middle of the window, and I knew we were on our way and that God was going to be with us. It was just a feeling that I had at that time. As our flight progressed, we had several small problems but always the direction was clear that we were going to continue the mission successfully. And those moments that I spent on the lunar surface were the most thrilling moments of my life. And again it was not because I was physically on the moon but because I was closer to God than I had ever been before and that I felt his presence.—James Irwin.

A MORNING RESOLVE.   I will try this day to live a simple, sincere, and serene life, repelling promptly every thought of discontent, anxiety, discouragement, impurity, self-seeking; cultivating cheerfulness, magnanimity, charity, and the habit of holy silence; exercising economy in expenditure, generosity in giving, carefulness in conversation, diligence in appointed service, fidelity in every trust, and a childlike faith in God. In particular I will try to be faithful in those habits of prayer, work, study, physical exercise, eating, and sleep which I believe the Holy Spirit has shown me to be right.

And as I cannot in my own strength do this, nor even with a hope of success attempt it, I look to thee, O Lord, my Father, in Jesus Christ, my Savior, and ask for the gift of the Holy Spirit.—Forward Movement.

CHRIST'S POOR BOOKKEEPER. Some years ago there was a missionary, an Englishman, stationed in India who never could keep his accounts and finances in order. He was many times chided and rebuked by the home board but always in vain. He simply could not keep his books straight. So the home board relieved him of his position and sent a man in his place who was a good bookkeeper. The missionary who was dismissed, instead of going home to England, went off on his own account in a new section of India where no missionary had ever gone before.

Many years passed and the mission station where this good man but poor bookkeeper had once lived reached out into adjoining fields and sent missionaries into the section where this man had gone unaided and alone. One missionary began to tell the people the story of Jesus, how he was the poor man's friend, how he loved little children, and how he healed the sick, and to his surprise the people seemed to understand at once. Their faces were aglow, and one of them said: "Sahib, we know this man of whom you tell us. He has been living here for years." The missionary then discovered that the man who had been dismissed by the home board because of his poor bookkeeping had come into that section and lived among the people, visiting them in their sickness, ministering to them in their times of need, and incarnating the very spirit of Christ. Perhaps this particular missionary was not even up to the average in ability, but in fidelity he was a star of the first magnitude. —Edgar DeWitt Jones.

STRENGTHENED BY PRAYER.   Henry M. Stanely was a strong man. As a reporter he was sent to Africa to find the missionary David Livingstone. In his diary he wrote: "On my expeditions prayer made me stronger than my nonpraying companions. It did not blind my eyes, nor close my ears, nor dull my mind, but on the contrary it gave me confidence. It did more. It gave me joy and pride in my work and lifted me hopefully over 1500 miles of forest track, eager to face the day's perils and fatigue. By prayer the road sought for has

become visible and the dangers immediately lessened, not once or twice or thrice but repeatedly, until the cold unbelieving heart was greatly impressed."

INVOLVEMENT.   A businessman, whose parents and wife were sincerely and actively involved in the worship and projects of their church, never had become involved himself. His philosophy was: "If I lead an honest, decent, and useful life, that is all that is required."

One night he had a vivid dream in which he died and knocked at the door of heaven. St. Peter answered and asked his name. He gave it and waited. At last St. Peter said, "I'm sorry, but your name isn't here."

Excitedly he asked: "Is my wife's name there? It should be. She never missed a worship service unless she was ill. She was active in all the church organizations. I never complained when dinner was late because she came in from church work just before I arrived. I gave her all the money she asked for the church and never begrudged it. She was good enough for the both of us."

With a sad smile, St. Peter said, "Yes, she was good enough for both of you."

He awakened with his pulses throbbing madly. Recalling the dream and thinking it through, he said: "I never looked at it that way. I must get personally involved."— John N. Link in *The Northern Light.*

UNASSAILABLE CASTLE.   On a certain hilltop in Europe there stands an ancient castle which emerged from the feudal wars unscathed and impregnable. But if you examine this age-old structure carefully, you will find evidences in the masonry that it was not always impervious to attack. More than once in earlier times its walls were breached, but always its defender turned defeat into future advantage, building more massively the bit that had crumbled, pushing out flanking towers, investing the bulwarks with cunningly devised slopes and angles, until at last, defying the full force of the invader, it stood unassailable. —Carl Hopkins Elmore.

THE RIGHT WORDS.   A few months after moving to a small town a woman complained to a neighbor about the poor service at the local drug store. She hoped the new acquaintance would repeat her complaint to the owner.

Next time she went to the drug store, the druggist greeted her with a big smile and told her how happy he was to see her again. He said he hoped she liked their town and to please let him know if there was anything he could do to help her and her husband get settled. He then filled her order promptly and efficiently.

Later the woman reported the miraculous change to her friend. "I suppose you told the druggist how poor I thought the service was?" she asked.

"Well, no," the woman said. "In fact—and I hope you don't mind—I told him you were amazed at the way he had built up this small town drug store and that you thought it was one of the best run drug stores you'd ever seen."

CONVICTION OF SIN.   It is often said nowadays that the church is losing her power because she no longer talks enough about sin. It seems to me on the contrary that the word has been over-used. The lavish application of it in our meditations to all our faults is a sure way to morbidity and a common way to religious mania. Conviction of sin is a healthy state of mind, not a dark emotion in which all sense of moral proportion is lost. When we use the term "sin" to magnify all the little frailties that have nothing remotely resembling wickedness behind them, we make ourselves censorious in trifles, forget our charity, and lose that understanding humor which God gave us to make us tolerable to one another and to ourselves.—T.E. Jessop.

NO CHOICE.   Several years ago John Coventry Smith told the story of a conversation between Howard Lowry, president of Wooster College, and Dr. Sarvepalli Radhakrishnan, the Hindu philosopher. Lowry remarked that he was sometimes embarrassed by the Christian claim of the uniqueness of Jesus Christ, which is at the heart of evangelistic preaching. To say to India, "Jesus Christ is the light of the world"—isn't that arrogance? Is not that a subtle form of exalting ourselves, as if to say, "We only have the light." Dr. Radhakrishnan paused and replied: "Yes, but the Christian has no choice. This is what your scriptures say. You cannot say less. You are saved from arrogance when you say it in the spirit of Jesus Christ."—Samuel H. Moffett.

DIRECTION.   Marriage consists not of two persons looking into each other's eyes but of two persons standing shoulder to shoulder, both looking in the same direction.—Antoine de Saint-Exupery.

THE CHRISTMAS GUEST.   Kenneth I. Brown tells of an American botanist searching in Colombia, South America, for a rare plant specimen to add to his botanical museum. A native Carib guide named Pedro is engaged to assist with the search, and as a guide he begins by leading the way into the Colombian wilderness. At nightfall on Christmas Eve the botanist and Pedro arrive at an isolated Indian village named Cispatia, inland on the Mulatto River. Pedro, before their arrival, indicated that no white man has visited Cispatia for twenty years. The botanist thus expects an unusual reception but in no way is prepared for the overwhelming respect, reverence, and even worship that is accorded him the moment he sets foot in the village. Language being a problem, the botanist can only behave graciously and responsively to the exaggerated attention he receives.

After a lavish meal is served him—from the hands of the tribal chieftan—a partially paralyzed young muchacha seeks him out. As the other villagers watch intently the girl walks awkwardly toward the American, drops her staff, and stumbles and falls into his arms. A moment later she leaps from him into the shadows, and the villagers suddenly raise their voices in haunting, unmusical, but somehow joyous refrains.

The next morning, Christmas Day, the American is wakened by the same strange chanting, only to discover himself surrounded by gifts and trinkets brought by the natives. Perplexed, upset, and anxious to depart, the botanist finds Pedro and gives the order to leave. Before he can go, however, the chieftain makes a request of him, translated by Pedro. "Bless," he is asked, "bless the people." Bewildered, unused to religious expressions of any kind, the American obliges by repeating over them a scripture verse remembered from childhood, and then swiftly he and his guide make their exit.

"Pedro, what did it all mean?" he asks after they are beyond the village. "You know," Pedro replies. "I don't know," the American says. "Tell tell me."

Slowly, reverently Pedro answers, "Christ come." Stunned by the thought, the American, who had taken the villagers' homage as the white man's due, hears Pedro explain: "Old miss'nary tell— Christ come. He come day 'fore Christmas; come up river at shade-time in dugout with hombre. He stay at Cispatia. They know at Cispatia." And then in the hush of the jungle, the distant canting of the villagers ceasing, Pedro leans forward to ask, "It is true, no es verdad, you are, you are —he?"—John H. Townsend.

SOMEBODY CARED.   One season a class of young people in the church where I served decided that on Christmas morning they would take bags of popcorn, candy, and fruit to each of the children in the wards of one of our county hospitals. They found that most of the children already had received some gift, but as they went down the wards they discovered one lad who had nothing to show that anyone had visited him. His face shone as they gave him the colored bag of dainties. Most of the other children began devouring their fruit at once, but as the young people came back through the ward they saw that this little fellow had placed his fruit and candy out on the pillow, in plain sight, without having eaten any of it.

"Why don't you eat it, son?" asked the teacher of the group as she came up to the bed.

"Nope," said the boy, with a quiver in his voice, "I'm going to keep it out there so all the kids can see that somebody did care about me when it was Christmas."— Albert W. Beaven.

COUNTING FOR SOMETHING.   It is no unworthy thing to wish to count for something and to do a great work in the world; but we shall count in the final audit not by the measure of our capacity, our business, our energy, but of the tenacity and vitality of our faith and our love.—Richard Roberts.

THE DECISIVE POWER.   No situation remains the same when prayer is made about it. There are influences of many kinds, good and evil, operating in every cause and in every soul, and each of these has power as an element in the battle between good and evil, but the decisive and essential factor in each case is the loving power of God called forth, or rather made way for, by the intercessions and prayers of Christian folk. For a time things may seem to go on much as before, but the decisive power has entered in, and even mountains must move. Prayer always creates a new situation.—George Stewart.

INDEX OF CONTRIBUTORS

SERMON TITLE INDEX

(Children's stories and sermons are identified cs; sermon suggestions ss)

SCRIPTURAL INDEX

INDEX OF PRAYERS

INDEX OF MATERIALS USEFUL AS CHILDREN'S STORIES AND SERMONS, NOT INCLUDED IN SECTION VIII

INDEX OF MATERIALS USEFUL FOR SMALL GROUPS

INDEX OF SPECIAL DAYS AND SEASONS

TOPICAL INDEX

278